Dear Kath, Love Ron
Letters 1937 to 1946

Dear Kath, Love Ron

Letters 1937 to 1946

With best wishes to Pam,
from Mike Spathaky.
Enjoy!

edited by
Mike Spathaky

The Book Guild Ltd

First published in Great Britain in 2019 by
The Book Guild Ltd
9 Priory Business Park
Wistow Road, Kibworth
Leicestershire, LE8 0RX
Freephone: 0800 999 2982
www.bookguild.co.uk
Email: info@bookguild.co.uk
Twitter: @bookguild

Typeset in 12pt Minion Pro

Printed and bound by CPI Group (UK) Ltd, Croydon, CR0 4YY

ISBN 978 1912881 642

British Library Cataloguing in Publication Data.
A catalogue record for this book is available from the British Library.

MIX
Paper from
responsible sources
FSC
www.fsc.org
FSC® C013604

In memory of
Kath Spathaky (1918-2017)
and
Ron Spathaky (1914-2013).

Ron and Kath Spathaky, September 1939

Contents

Introduction

"Dear Kath, Love Ron" consists of the letters my father wrote to my mother from 1937 to 1946, mostly while he was serving in the British Army. There are also just three letters from Mum to Dad, a handful from other people, some transcripts of conversations with them both and a memoir that Mum wrote in her seventies. I have included some of Dad's poems where they relate to the contents of the letters.

Dad – Ron Spathaky – served in England, Tunisia, Italy, France, Belgium, Egypt and Palestine during and after World War II. The letters do not describe any battlefield exploits. As a member of the Army Educational Corps, Dad never came near to the front line. A major interest of the letters lies in what they reveal of his relationship with Mum during the extended periods of separation that his army life imposed. Their relationship was at times loving, caring and passionate, but sometimes despairing, tempestuous and stressful almost to breaking point.

Mum – Kath Spathaky, née Cree – kept the letters in a cardboard box for about seventy years. My brother, sister and I discovered them when she moved to a nursing home at the age of 95. Most were in their original folded state, many in their envelopes, and they were more or less in chronological order. Mum agreed that I should take them and look after them.

She had clearly kept the letters in date order at one time, but I think that as she got older she became less careful about keeping them that way. A degree of detective work was needed to get them back into order. After sorting, I started photographing the collection using a fairly ordinary digital camera. There are over 325 letters and other documents such as postcards and telegrams. The total number of digital images was nearly a thousand.

I then started on the transcription. My aim has been to create a text that is as close to the originals as possible. The handwriting was normally fairly easy to read and there are very few cases of doubt about the actual words.

There are many references to people, places and events, however, that will appear abstruse to many readers, partly due to the passage of time and the fact that the letters were never intended to be read by anyone other than their recipients, and partly because the language of Mum and Dad's political culture was that of a distinct minority of the period. Sometimes the letters are deliberately cryptic to avoid the attentions of the military censors.

I have therefore attempted to clarify all references that might be unintelligible. Dad makes numerous references to books he has read or wishes to read, people who were mutual friends or in public life at the time and places he visited or where he was stationed. I have tried to trace full references for all of these. The results of these researches are given in footnotes.

Occasionally Dad's words are not clear or he omits or misspells words. I have corrected trivial errors. Where the interpretation might be critical, I have given my interpretation in square brackets [like this]. Readers should be aware of Dad's rather archaic or pedantic use of 'I should' where almost everyone today would write 'I would'. It can be confusing. Readers may notice one or two other idiosyncrasies.

As I went along, I wrote short commentaries between the letters to keep the reader abreast of the time-frame and general context. Throughout the book my words are in italics, while plain type signifies direct quotation of words which are Dad's, Mum's or, occasionally, those of other writers.

It took me sixteen months to transcribe the letters and create a first draft of this book. I managed to keep more or less to a schedule of typing one letter every day, working from the photographic images and referring only occasionally to the original paper documents.

The reader should expect the letters to be imbued with the language of dialectical materialism, the ideology of Marxism–Leninism. It is clear that Mum and Dad shared their commitment to that ideology and would understand the nuances of meaning which only that shared commitment would convey. So when Dad writes on 7th June 1942 that he has been sunbathing and adds that it "has not contributed to the cause very much" I know he means that his sunbathing has not advanced the Communist Revolution.

I admire my parents for their steadfastness in adhering to their communist ideals through the period of these letters. It has become clear to me that communism in the 1920s and '30s was a relevant response to the gross inequalities and repression that the working classes of Britain and other countries suffered through the operation of the capitalist system. Furthermore, the Communist Party of Great Britain was the only party in the country that consistently throughout the 1930s opposed and warned about the rise of fascism at home and abroad. Communism was the prevailing orthodoxy of political discussion in our family throughout my childhood until I was a teenager, when Mum and Dad left the Party.

All discussion in the family was influenced by political considerations. The influence on me has been lifelong, so that supporting the equality of women, rejecting discrimination of all kinds, fighting for the rights of workers against the oppressive actions of employers and championing human rights have generally been sine qua nons of my life. For Mum's and Dad's influences I am truly grateful.

I have tried to avoid making value judgements about the contents of the letters. To nitpick what Dad and Mum wrote at this distance of time or to edit out any passages would not be fair to their memories and would surely introduce a subjective bias. I feel too close to my parents to do that. Let the letters stand as they are; let Mum and Dad be revealed, as surely they are in this collection, by their own words.

Some of my relations and other people who knew my parents may be shocked by some of the events revealed in these letters. Mum and Dad were not saints, and we should not expect them to be, nor portray them as such. I am unrepentant in publishing these letters in full as they stand. Of course, they are incomplete but they are what we have and are as close to the truth, the whole truth and nothing but the truth as we can get, untainted at least by any censorship by me.

I love them both.

Mike Spathaky
May 2019

Chapter 1

Growing Up

Dad was born in Cardiff in 1914 as Ronald Victor Spathaky. His father, Albert Victor Spathaky, had been born there too, the son of a Greek seaman, Antonio Spathakis, who had settled in the docks area of the city in the 1870s and married an Englishwoman, Emma Tucker. She had been born in a workhouse across the Bristol Channel in Somerset. Antonio signed his surname as Spathaky in the marriage register. After fathering three girls and three boys he died of a heart attack at the age of 40. Albert was the youngest child, just a year old when his father died. Soon afterwards, Albert's mother Emma married another Greek seaman, Gerasimo Angulatta.

In 1913 Albert – Grandad Spathaky to me – married Clara Retchford, who was originally from Redditch, Worcestershire. Ron, my father and their only child, was born in November 1914, and they gave him a fairly conventional Anglican upbringing.

In 2011, when Dad was 96 and almost blind, I asked him about his childhood and he agreed that I should write down what he said. I had done some research in public archives and so asked him about some of the names I had come up with.

When I told him that I had found that Albert's step-father was called Gerasimo, he replied:

I have heard the name Gerasimo many times.

Dad would have been seven years old when Gerasimo, his step-grandfather died. He had previously told me about visiting an old lady whom he called

Granny Pack; I belatedly realised that this was Emma. Although she had married Gerasimo Angulatta as her second husband when Albert was aged two, Granny Spathaky would have been the name used for her by the family, including Albert's five older siblings and their children, since they would have known her when Spathaky was her surname.

I had a cousin Leonard who lived near the fields down by Llandaff Road… I had an Aunt Rosa who lived at the bottom of Cathedral Road. Her surname was Economides.

I knew from my family history research that Rosa was one of Albert's two sisters. Leonard Howells was her son from her first marriage. She had remarried after Leonard's father had died. Grandad's other sister Maria married Vivian Thomas and Daphne was one of their two daughters.

Daphne was a very familiar name. I remember the part of Cardiff she lived in – somewhere on the eastern side; also Uncle Vivian.

What Dad never told me was that he himself was a page boy at the age of ten at Daphne's wedding to George Harper. Dad continued:

I lived at Plasturton Gardens, in Cardiff, a street with a little park in the middle – a small park with a park-keeper who called in occasionally. I went to school in Talbot Street; Canton School was an elementary school, I think.

Modern aerial photographs show Plasturton Gardens as a well-heeled looking, tree-lined street with substantial, stone-built, villa-type, three-storey houses – and a small park in the middle.

Albert followed the profession of cinema manager until his retirement, and we think it was through their work that he met his wife Clara Retchford, my Grandma Spathaky, as she was an accomplished pianist and played for the silent films.

Decades later Dad told his granddaughter, another Emma, that he used to stand by the piano when his mother was playing in the cinema for the silent films. He also had to wobble a large sheet of metal when the sound of thunder was required.

The family moved to Cromer on the North Norfolk coast for a short while. Dad continued his recollections:

I have a sensation that I was quite small when we moved to Cromer. I remember it was quite cold so we must have been there in winter as well as summer. I went to a primary school. My dad was manager of the cinema in the town. I used to go to see the films quite often.

We lodged with some people called Blogg, who were famous as coxes of the lifeboat. Quite often they were called out to ships in distress; he went out in his oilskins.

It was a terraced house. I remember walking around the town, getting to know it and the big parish church. I remember walking along the promenade in pretty cold weather.

Henry Blogg was indeed a famous lifeboatman – the most decorated one in Britain.

There was a road that struck out eastward *[from Cardiff]* towards Newport. I used to cycle out that way, also on towards Monmouth. There used to be fairly wide stretches of rough country to the east of Cardiff where the suburbs gave way to open farmland. All my cycling was on my own – I don't remember any friends. I went to Cardiff High School – they tried to teach me Welsh, with little success.

This means that the family moved back to Cardiff after their stay in Norfolk.

We left Cardiff in 1926 and went to Swansea. We lived on the Gower Peninsula. I can't remember how long. I was very fond of the Gower, a delightful part of the Welsh coast. I remember a friend called John Gill, a bookish boy who introduced me to detective stories.[1]

---

1   But see footnote on page 5.

Some years ago Mum told my brother Dave that there was some scandal involving infidelity by Grandad Spathaky. Apparently it was because of the scandal that they moved from Cardiff and it was also probably why Dad was an only child. Dad continued:

From Swansea I think we went to High Wycombe. We lived in a built-up but pleasant area right in the very centre of High Wycombe, a place that made furniture. I have a clear memory of the little workshops where they made the furniture by tapping dells *[=dowels]* into holes in the furniture to hold it together.

I kept pigeons on the roof of the cinema. I had a loft of half a dozen of them. We lived in a flat which was part of the cinema premises.

I went to High Wycombe Grammar School. I can remember walking quite a walk away from the town centre up a steep hill every morning to the school which was at the top of the hill. I walked with a neighbour who used to buy a special kind of toffee, Walters' Palm Toffee.

I think it was a boys' school. I was almost twelve, I think. I played rugby and cut my knee badly on a nail on someone's boot. The Headmaster, Mr Arneson, brought me home to our flat in his car. I studied French, Latin and the usual range of subjects in a grammar school. I was there a year at the most.

Advertisements in the Buckinghamshire Herald described Albert V Spathaky in April 1924 as the manager of the Palace Cinema in High Wycombe and "late Manager, Capitol Super Cinema, Cardiff".[2]

On 11th April 1925 the Herald carried an advertisement for the Palace Cinema where Lillian Gish was starring in The White Sister:

By F. MARION CRAWFORD. PALACE AUGMENTED ORCHESTRA and Effects, Grand Organ, under the personal direction of Leonard Jennings and Albert V. Spathaky. Vocalist in Gounod's Ave Maria, Miss MARGARET COLLINS. TO-NIGHT & SATURDAY, APRIL 11th. (Closed GOOD FRIDAY).[3]

---

2   The Buckinghamshire Herald, 12th April 1924.
3   Ibid., 11th April 1925.

Dad was only nine years old in April 1924 so his chronology seems a bit confused. Dad said he was about twelve when they moved to Sheffield but I think he was fourteen.

Certainly his father was in Sheffield by January 1929, for in that month he was convicted of several offences against the safety laws for cinemas. Part of his defence was that he had only been in the job for a short time.[4]

Nether Edge Grammar School was the school I went to, on the edge of the built-up area of Sheffield. I walked up a hill to the school from our house in Nether Edge.

We used to cross the road every day to a separate building for the school dinner. Puddings were detested by all the boys in the school. We were adept at getting rid of them behind the panels of the wall.

I played rugby not soccer at Nether Edge. I played scrum half. We played against Aberdare.

It seems unlikely that a school in Sheffield would play against Aberdare 200 miles away and, as Aberdare is only 25 miles from Cardiff, I guess that Dad is confused with playing rugby at Cardiff High School or at Swansea. Confusion about the chronology of the family's moves may be because Grandad might have moved to a new job some time before Grandma and Dad followed.

I remember very clearly a rather bookish lad who was a great reader. His name was John Gill.[5] He had read a lot of Edgar Wallace. I remember reading Wallace's *Bones of the River*.[6]

I also played cricket. I took up boxing some time about then and was also good at athletics – I won the Victor Ludorum at the annual sports day. I was Captain of my House but not Head Boy. I did Latin, English and French in the Sixth Form.

4   Sheffield Daily Independent, 8th January 1929, p4.
5   A sign of Dad's occasional confusion is that he also mentioned John Gill as a friend in Swansea (page 3) as well as in Sheffield. The latter is the more likely.
6   *Bones of the River* by Edgar Wallace, pub. Newnes, London, 1923

I have Dad's Nether Edge sports medals. They include the Senior High Jump, 100 Yards and Cross Country in 1930, the Tug of War in 1930 and 1931, a runner-up medal for Heavyweight Boxing in 1931 and the Senior Long Jump medal for three years running, 1930 to 1932.

I remember our home at Nether Edge very clearly – a detached home with a longish garden. I was quite sweet on a girl who lived nearly opposite. But I didn't ask her out.

My parents moved away to Warrington. I moved into digs with a schoolmate. It was not a very happy time because I didn't get on with the schoolmate.

I cycled to Paris one year. All I remember is having a very cheap road atlas. I drew a straight line on it from Warrington to Paris and followed it as closely as possible.

I remember Dad telling me this when I was quite young and showing me the actual pocket atlas with the line drawn with a pencil and ruler.

I stayed in a sort of youth hostel in Paris. I went on the Ile de la Cité, the island in the Seine, and went round the cathedral of Notre Dame. I remember the imposing towers of the cathedral… The hostel was in the rue Mouffetard in the student quarter. It was a house where a famous French scientist called Joule lived.[7]

I met an interesting young woman living in the hostel and doing a degree course. She was nicknamed l'Impératrice by the other residents.

---

7   In fact, James Prescott Joule, despite his French-sounding surname, was English, although he may have stayed in Paris at some time. Maybe Dad was referring to Lavoisier, who worked in the same area of physics and lived in Paris.

"Did you have long conversations into the night with her?" I asked.

Yes, my French was a bit rickety at that time. I met a male student who was very well off, I think. He dropped some kind of jewel into the river. He was showing me round Paris. We dredged the mud around where we sat but didn't find the ring. He took us up to the Panthéon – me and one or two English people, that is.

I must have been about 15 or 16, I think. I crossed from Newhaven to Dieppe… From Warrington it took about a week to get to Paris. I was in Paris about two weeks and a week cycling back. I was already in the Sixth Form and went back to my final year at School.

Dad was a year younger than his classmates at school so it would have been 1931 when he made this trip, when he was only 16.

The following year I went to the University of Sheffield and moved into University digs.

I remember the very crowded lecture course for the new students. I got drawn into anti-fascist demonstrations. I was already a fairly committed communist through the influence of Jacob Miller, an older boy at my school.[8] Our friendship continued at university.

So, Dad was only 17 when he went to University in 1932, his eighteenth birthday being in November. Dad's course at Sheffield University included a return to Paris for a term spent at the Sorbonne. A few years before he died I asked if I could select a few of his books to keep, and one I chose was Sweet's Anglo-Saxon Reader.[9] *He had written on the flyleaf, "R. V. Spathaky, Sheffield University, 3rd Year Arts, 1934", and then "Brighton Intermediate School 1936". He continued:*

---

8   A fellow pupil at Nether Edge GS but two years older, Jacob Miller was influential in recruiting Ron to communism. His parents were Russian subjects from Lithuania who settled in Sheffield, where Jacob was born. Jacob was Secretary of the Sheffield Anti-War Movement. He graduated (Hons. Economics) from Sheffield University in 1934. (*The Spy Who Came in From the Co-op* by David Burke, pub. Boydell, 2008.)

9   *An Anglo-Saxon Reader in prose and verse* by H Sweet, pub. Oxford, 1879

Sheffield University Union Representative Council 1935-36.
Dad is in the front row, fourth from the left.

I was a member of a communist cell at the university. I became President of the Student's Union in my final year, which became an automatic sabbatical year, so afterwards I stayed another year to complete my studies. I knew an older student called Sykes who was also a communist. He was later a lecturer in French at Leicester University.[10]

Graham Stevenson has described the left-wing activism at Sheffield University at that time:

[Tom Driver's] remarkable ability and intelligence saw him study English and Literature at Sheffield University, where he became the editor of 'Arrows', the university magazine. In 1933, he joined the Communist Party and participated in sales of the Daily Worker in Sheffield, outside the steel and engineering factories, and in the University...

---

10 Leslie Sykes, born Sheffield 1912, grad. Sheffield 1933, Professor of French, Leicester University 1947 to 1978, Deputy Vice-Chancellor, died 2001.

Tom Driver was Chair of the Sheffield University Socialist Club from 1933-35. Along with Norman Dodsworth, Tom was the thinker of the Group and, under their leadership, the Communist Party had leading positions in almost every student society, even the Christian Society!

The Communist Student Group was often called upon to lead demonstrations of the unemployed, so as to stand in for and prevent the arrest of NUWM[11] leaders. The University Socialist Society, largely led by Communists, staged a demonstration on May Day 1935. This was the first time that students in Sheffield other than Communists had ever identified themselves with working class struggles.[12]

In 2009 Dad remembered Norman Dodsworth[13] as a "charismatic leader of students". He didn't mention Tom Driver to me but must have known him and probably worked closely with him. Like Dad, Tom Driver later became a French teacher. By coincidence I remember Tom Driver being president of my trade union, the NATFHE[14], in the 1970s when I was working in community education. I didn't know of his background or his connection to Dad at that time.[15]

In March 1935 Dad had an article entitled 'Anti-War', published in the periodical New University.[16]

On Tuesday 25th June 1935, the Sheffield Independent reported: "the award of B.A. Hons. degree, II-2, to Ronald V. Spathaky in the School of Modern Languages and Literature." In the year after graduating, Dad added a teaching qualification to his degree. In a letter dated 7th June 1942 he refers to having worked in London as a clerk.[17]

---

11   National Unemployed Workers' Movement
12   Driver, Tom, in Graham Stevenson's website 'Compendium of Communist Biography', extracted 4th Dec 2016
13   Probably the same Norman Dodsworth who was a Head Teacher in 1965.
14   National Association of Teachers in Further and Higher Education.
15   Wikipedia, Tom Driver
16   *New University,* New Series 6:11
17   See page 147.

I didn't link up with the university communists for some time after I left.

In 1936 he obtained a full-time teaching post at the Brighton Intermediate School in Sussex. I don't know why he chose to move to Brighton. I know of no previous connection he had to the town. Perhaps it was simply a job that came up.

* * *

Unlike Dad, Mum was born into a politically active working-class family. Her parents, Sid and Annie Cree, were from families long-established in the Chesterfield area. Sid was a master fitter and turner. After marrying in Chesterfield parish church the couple settled in Sheffield, where Mum was born two days before Christmas in 1918. Her brother Gordon was then nearly four years old.

The area of North-East Derbyshire and South Yorkshire was a crucible of working-class consciousness and the Cree family were heirs to the culture which it engendered.[18] Mum's great-uncle, Joseph Cree (1850-1919), also a fitter and turner, had been sacked by the industrialist Charles Markham, a so-called 'benevolent paternalist,' for being a member of a trade union.

Mum's father, Sid Cree, was a shop steward at a Sheffield steel-works, but these were the years of the Great Depression and he was often out of work. Some of the people Mum remembers from those days were: Bill Ward and his family, Kath Duncan and George Fletcher. Mum wrote this memoir at my suggestion in September 1989:

When I was born, just five weeks after the *[1918]* armistice, it must have been a trying time for my mother. Aunt Gertie, her next eldest sister, who lived with us at 21 Brathay Road in Sheffield is reported to have complained of wet clothes always being dried round the kitchen fire. However, my father, unlike so many young men, was at home,

---

18   See *The Making of the English Working Class* by E P Thompson, pub. Gollancz 1963 and Penguin 1968

live and well. He had spent the war as a skilled fitter and turner at the steel works. (Was it Vickers or Firth's?) Later there was to be a period of unemployment but I only remember him working in a garage at Rotherham, managed by a cousin of my mother's. He used to walk to and from the local station, Brightside, and I would sometimes go to meet him on my scooter after Mum had seen him in the distance. She said he had a very distinctive walk which she could recognise "a mile off".

There was open ground opposite where we lived and about a quarter of a mile away the "pit hills" which were the result (I think) of some open-cast mining which had gone on during the war – a wonderful playground for my brother Gordon (nearly four years older than me) and his friends. I don't remember venturing far, except on one occasion. The boys had built a rough raft to sail on a pool of water – only about ten feet across. I begged a turn on it and promptly fell in! I think I had been sent to tell them dinner was ready. I expect there were recriminations but I can't remember a great uproar.

My earliest memory is of waiting by the desk[19] while Mum searched for my birth certificate. It was to be my first day at school. She sent Gordon and Jack Ward on ahead while she searched. She must have found it because I did eventually start school. I recall waiting in a queue one Monday morning and noticing that other little girls were wearing their Sunday dresses to "wear them out".

Mum and Dad were recruited into the Communist Party in the early twenties by our neighbour Bill Ward, also a steel worker and father of Jack, Eric and Alan. Later they were able to claim to be foundation members and I, much later, jokingly, to be a "birthright Communist" just as some Quakers claim to be birthright Quakers.

We had no garden but a wide asphalt area at the back which made a good rounders pitch. There were two other houses besides us and the Wards. One family had four children and they were very quiet and withdrawn. The father may have been unemployed – certainly they were poorer and we all had to be kind, especially to the one who I think now was mentally retarded. The fourth family were the Acreds

---

19   It is actually a bureau, and I have it still – Ed.

and they only had one girl. Edna who had dancing and elocution lessons. One hot summer day she taught us all to do the Charleston.

When I was about six or seven we moved to number 23, which had a front garden and a little more privacy but the back yard was smaller so we still went back to play in the bigger yard.

All these houses had running water – a cold tap over a large stone sink – but no bathroom or indoor sanitation. Outside was a WC shared with one or more other families. When I was about nine or ten I was sent to the local slipper baths occasionally. It was probably a tedious job heating the water and filling and emptying the zinc baths we all used.

By then my mother had been elected to the Sheffield Board of Guardians who operated the Poor Law relief and she was often busy at committees and with other "duties," so she would sometimes bring a packed lunch to us at school. Normally we walked home for a mid-day meal; I wonder how many miles we walked each week

I can remember her election campaigns in Attercliff*[e]* and singing in the street, "Vote, vote, vote for Annie Cree."[20] One of the perks of the job was Christmas Day in the Workhouse! I was dismayed at the sight of hundreds of miserable looking people sat at long wooden tables, husbands and wives separated. I expect we had a good meal but I don't really remember.

Children's parties were fairly rare events but I can remember one when my mother went to buy the cakes and pastries from George Fletcher's shop, where she had a discount.[21] I was well aware that most mums did their own baking, and this buying was not so good. Mum could have done it but she didn't have the time.

Then she was elected to the Executive Committee of the Communist Party, partly to increase the number of women on it. She had to go to

---

20   "True some party members were able to gain the respect of the electorate at a municipal level. Between 1928 and 1933, communists such as… George Fletcher, Annie Cree (Sheffield)… were elected on to district councils, boards of guardians and education authorities." *Class Against Class: The Communist Party in Britain Between the Wars* by Matthew Worley, pub. Tauris 2002, pp181-2.

21   George Fletcher was a prominent member of the Communist Party in Sheffield. Stories of his bakery fill a whole chapter in *Free but Not so Easy* by Bas Barker and Lynda Straker (pub.1989, Derbyshire County Council). He has been described as "one of the best loved labour movement leaders in the city" (*Compendium of Communist Biography* by Graham Stevenson, www.grahamstevenson.me.uk).

London for weekends where she stayed in hotels and visited theatres, and this must have widened her horizons enormously.

She was in part responsible for my father getting a job in R.O.P. (Russian Oil Products). At first he worked at Castleford and came home only at weekends but he had a car! I can remember two or three different models. We used to go out to the Peak District on Sundays and in 1929 we went on a holiday, in a fairly large model, to Southport. We also took Auntie Kitty and Uncle Bob (Windle) to Bridlington for their holidays.

We had gone rambling in Derbyshire with the Co-op Ramblers since I was in a push-chair and I have memories of trudging down to the tram fairly early on Sunday mornings to cross the City to Fulwood terminus or to catch a train to Grindleford. I can remember the fuss over the mass trespass over Kinder Scout[22] although we were not on it.

My father was also active in the Trades Union movement and the National Council of Labour Colleges, some of whose books remained in our bookcase for many years. Gordon once took a part in a production of "The Ragged-Trousered Philanthropists" at the AEU[23] Institute near the Wicker. It was held in a large room upstairs and I can still visualise the elaborate wallpaper. I could not understand the play very well. In fact much of what was said and done around me was puzzling. I recall my mother explaining to me the plot of a Jack London novel which I was reading.

The class struggle was simple – workers against capitalists, but the middle classes seemed to receive most hatred, the petit bourgeoisie who preyed on both sides. I recall the '26 General Strike and rushing home to say the trams were running again, but they were being manned by "blacklegs" so I was told.

I was happy to be sent off to my grandmother's house at 118 Derby Road, Chesterfield, whenever Mum had a conference to go to. I would be put on a bus at Pond Street, Sheffield, and met by Auntie Ada at Sheffield Road, Chesterfield.

---

22   Led by communist Benny Rothman on 24th April 1932 to highlight the prohibition on access to areas of open country. The leaders were jailed.
23   Amalgamated Engineering Union

Ada was the one who made most fuss of me. She and Kitty were the only ones still living at home with Grandma Mellor. Kitty was engaged to Bob Windle whom she married around 1930 but Ada did not marry until 1942. It puzzles me where they all slept when my grandfather was alive, as there were five girls and a boy to find beds for. He died the week Mum was twenty-one. It isn't surprising she married at twenty-three, although she continued to help financially whenever she could.

There was great excitement one weekend I was at Derby Road. A lorry crashed into the front lobby. There was a lot of noise and loads of rubble but no-one was hurt. I had this exciting tale to tell when I returned to Sheffield on Sunday evening. Private phones were unheard of then so Mum just had to worry and fuss.

I also had two weeks at 118 when Mum went to look after Auntie Aggie when the twins were born. I had some school work to do including a composition on Queen Matilda. I mixed up the Rivers Rhine and Rhone and the piece of paper as evidence was around for many years. When the twins were about one month old Max had to go into hospital. The nurse put a hot water bottle too near him which burnt his leg. There was much fuss and discussion over this.

We also kept in touch with my father's relatives, visiting at Christmas and holiday times. The cousins Dorothy, Irene and Edgar were fairly near to us in age but we did not meet often enough to be really close.[24] Dorothy and Irene met more frequently and became good friends. I do remember one Christmas at Calow when the snow was very deep. Gordon and Edgar made terrific toboggan runs.

Uncle Edgar lost a leg in the first World War for which he was given a pension – about three pounds a week I think – and he was also able to work at his trade as a printer. This meant they were somewhat better off, not that he didn't deserve it – he had considerable pain in many ways. They lived at first in Chatsworth Road *[Chesterfield]* but then were able to buy a modest terraced house in Hasland and later a

24 Cousins on Mum's father's side: the Crees

bungalow in Queen Mary Road. They were also able to help Dorothy when she married in 1939.

They had such things as a gramophone and records and a camera and two weeks holiday every year, all luxuries to us. Auntie Dora was however very kind and generous, particularly to Irene. She also virtually adopted a girl called Annie Hardy as a friend and companion for Dorothy. Annie was with them most of the time, just going home to sleep. But could Auntie Dora talk!

Auntie Edie was married to a miner, Will Hayes, and they had a very hard time. First they lived in Arkwright Town, a very grim mining village. Then they moved to a country cottage with a large garden where they kept chickens. Later they moved to the new model mining village of Duckmanton. Here there was a bathroom with an outside door where the miners could bath before going indoors. Pit-head baths came much later!

Later still, when Irene was at the High School, they moved to a fish and chip shop at Whittington Moor. Edgar helped his mother but it was hard work. However they were eventually able to buy themselves a terraced house on Whittington Road.

With hindsight I realise that all the Cree family – my Dad, Uncle Edgar and Auntie Edie, had very gentle temperaments. I can't remember seeing any of them angry, unlike the Mellor sisters who could be very forthright, although they could also be very loyal and helpful to each other.

I attended Owler Lane Elementary School until I was ten and a half. It had large playgrounds at a slightly higher level; an area which was cultivated by the pupils (under supervision) but no playing fields.

I had been "teacher's pet" during my last two years at Owler Lane. My teacher, Miss German, must have learned of my parents' political activities, and she offered to take me to some missionary society meeting. I was not very impressed. She took me back to the door of my home so I invited her in – only to find my parents still out and Gordon and Jack Ward playing cards. However she was a good teacher and it was probably due to her that I passed the scholarship at ten plus.

The 'scholarship' was usually taken by Class VI when they were eleven plus, but Class V were allowed to enter for practice. Usually a few passed – there were four of us in 1929.

I went to the Central School for Girls, then in Leopold Street in the centre of Sheffield. No-one from our area was going there at that time so it was a lonely journey for me on bus or tram and then a walk across the City. Once a week we went to play hockey on fields way out towards the outer suburbs, where eventually a new school was built.

My mother did her best to prepare me – "liberty bodices," kid gloves and a leather satchel and a huge panama hat (bought in a sale) which nearly drowned me. I was in the "D" class but as we were all young ones it was not considered a disgrace. I am not sure how I coped that first term but Gordon gave occasional help with the homework.

Christmas 1929 was spent at Chesterfield and soon afterwards, while staying with Aunt Aggie at Longcourse Farm, Gordon and I developed scarlet fever. Alan was about seven and the twins three. The main concern seemed to be to avoid them being taken to the isolation hospital, so Gordon and I were taken back to Sheffield, probably by public transport!

We were then reported to the doctor and duly taken to Lodge Moor Fever Hospital, miles across the City and out on the moors, an old army hospital I think, huge wards with a large stove in the centre which did little to warm the beds or their occupants. Visitors were only allowed on Sunday and then only to the windows. They stood on forms outside in snow or rain and tried to talk to their offspring inside. I felt guilty because my mother brought me new-laid eggs which had cost her 2/6[25] per half dozen. Auntie Ada sent me a bar of chocolate inside a letter. I was told I should give it to the nurse but I think I ate it instead.

I was in hospital for eight weeks. The discharge procedure involved a journey to a City hospital where we were bathed in strong

---

25   That was 12.5 pence in new money, with no allowance for inflation.

disinfectant, dressed in our own clothes and handed over to our waiting mums.

Soon we were off to live in Preston in Lancashire. At the Central School *[in Sheffield]* I was told that I should not have taken the place there if I was going to move – as if it were my fault!

The Park School for Girls in Preston had a small junior department which was much more home-like. We had gym every day and my posture improved enormously. But by the summer we were on the move again, to Maidstone in Kent.

Shortly after Mum had written this piece, in October 1989, she and I spent a weekend in the Chesterfield–Sheffield area. We visited Longcourse Farm at Duckmanton, where she had spent so many happy holidays. She found it much the same, although running water to the cottage must make life easier; she recalled that her Auntie Aggie had had to carry every drop down the steep paddock from the pump by the farm.

A small housing estate had been built on the site of Woodhouse Farm, Bolsover, where Mum and I had stayed in 1944. The pit was still in operation but the overhead hoppers had disappeared and the slag heaps had been grassed over.

We were quite surprised to find all the houses of her childhood still standing: the Mellor home at 118 Derby Road, Chesterfield and the houses in Sheffield where Mum spent her childhood, 21 and 23 Brathay Road, with their little back-yards shared between three or four families. They had been modernised of course and those in Brathay Road had recently had an external facelift under a Council scheme, but they were basically unchanged over the sixty years. Owler Lane School in Sheffield didn't look much different either, Mum said.

On the Sunday afternoon we visited Lily Lister (née Cree), Mum's second cousin from Bolton-on-Dearne, who then lived in Sheffield. Doris Cree, the widow of another second cousin, was there too. They are members of a branch of Crees with whom our branch had lost touch in the 1930s. Mum had never met Doris or Lily. She vaguely remembered visiting someone who was stationmaster at Bolton-on-

Dearne when she was a child, and they were able to tell us that this was George Harman, who had married Pattie Cree, a cousin of Mum's father Sid. All in all we had an enjoyable afternoon catching up on seventy years of family news!

Mum and Dad are now Quakers, whereas Lily and Doris have a long family tradition of staunch Methodism. We were discussing the rarity or otherwise of the name Cree when Lily told us that, during her first teaching post at Sheffield, in about 1946, she was embarrassed to notice some prominent posters for the General Election advertising a Communist Party candidate called Lieutenant Cree. She had to explain to her Head Teacher that this was no relation. After she had told us the story, over forty years on, we had to explain that he was indeed a relation; Lieutenant Cree was Mum's brother Gordon and therefore Lily's second cousin!

At various times Mum filled in some of the gaps in her memoir. It was in 1929 that Annie was elected to the Central Committee (CC) of the Communist Party of Great Britain (CPGB) along with three other female members, Kath Duncan, Miss Phillipson and Nellie Usher.

George Fletcher was also on the CC and Mum told me, "George Fletcher had a close relationship with my mum. They went to the theatre together."

In 2016, the year before she died, Mum wondered out loud if her mum had had an affair with George Fletcher. She said nothing to back up this conjecture, except that they used to travel to London together to CC meetings. The CPGB would pay for them to stay in a hotel and Annie would tell the family in detail what it was like to stay in a hotel. At some time, perhaps much later, Mum said, "Mum went to Russia for a visit. They gave her a gold watch. Later I lost it. I _was_ sorry."

Times were bad during the early 1930s. Grandpop, Sid Cree, lost his job as a fitter and turner, and moved from one job to another for a while. When Mum was about 12, Grandpop moved to a job in Preston, Lancashire. The family was soon on the move again, however, this time to Maidstone, Kent. She told me that when they lived in Maidstone, Gordon had a bicycle. "I wanted one too so we bought one on hire purchase – not a very reputable thing to do."

Sister and brother, Kath and Gordon Cree, Maidstone, May 1931.

I discovered that the petrol company, Russian Oil Products, where Sid was employed, had a depot at Aylesford, which is only about 6 kilometres (4 miles) out of Maidstone. The initials ROP are clearly visible in an aerial photograph.[26] So, that explains why the family moved to Maidstone. A website says this about ROP:

This UK company with Russian trade connections was set up in 1924... A released Home Office file (HO 144/17917) deals with concern that R.O.P. Ltd. were engaged in dubious activities circa from July 1932 to August 1933. Officials were concerned that this company was being used as a base for communist political activities leading to espionage and sabotage... Probably stimulated by its unpopularity re 'dumping', there was a campaign in the 1930s conducted by a national newspaper to boycott Russian oil being offered in the UK by Russian Oil Products through a subsidiary in the Medway.[27]

The family soon had to move again. Sid had been fired by ROP, and Mum said there was some mystery about the reason.

He got a job as a fitter and turner, the trade for which he had served his apprenticeship, at the Southern Railway Company's locomotive

---

26 'Britain from above' website, extracted 4th December 2016
27 *Russian Oil Products Ltd* in 'Blisworth Images and History' website, extracted 4th December 2016

works in Brighton. At last he had steady skilled employment and he worked there until his retirement in about 1946. The Cree family lived in central Brighton and then on Montpelier Road.

It seems likely that Dick Pennifold[28], a Brighton CP leader, had some influence in getting Sid the job in Brighton. Dick was a railwayman at the Brighton Locomotive Works, a militant member of the National Union of Railwaymen and President of the Brighton Trades and Labour Council. He was the same age as Grandpop and, like him, a founder member of the Party.

After her short stints of grammar school education in Sheffield, Preston and Maidstone, Mum was able at last to settle in to some sort of continuity at Varndean School for Girls in Brighton, where she did very well in the matriculation examinations, even though she was a year younger than her classmates. She started in the Sixth Form, studying History, English and French. She continued her memoirs as conversation (where "Mum" refers to her mother of course):

Mum looked in the paper and found a job in Boots pharmacy. I hurriedly left school in about February 1935. I sought advice from Brian O'Malley, an apprentice pharmacist at the Co-op. I knew him through the YCL. He said, "Get yourself qualified." I was Brian's girlfriend from 15 to 17.

I found my matriculation was good enough to become an apprentice pharmacist. My mum went down to Brighton Tech and I went back to Boots and asked if I could become an apprentice if I got the first exam, but the Tech said I couldn't take it.

So Mum attended Brighton Technical College taking physics, chemistry and another subject that she couldn't remember, although it was probably mathematics. "The course was for a year," she explained, "but I failed and had to repeat the year and passed."

---

28 Dick Pennifold. was a veteran trade unionist, pacifist and founder of the Brighton Communist Party branch. See also pages 27 and 538.

Brian O'Malley was quite keen on photography, judging by some photographs of Mum that he took at that time.

In the 1960s Brian's nephew, Dennis O'Malley, and my brother David Spathaky were fellow pupils at a Quaker boarding school. In 2019 they were in touch again and Dennis wrote to Dave:

[Brian] and your Mum were a couple for a while before she ran off with a certain Mr Spathaky. I think Brian was very sad about this and it seems he married somewhat on the rebound to Sheila. None of us liked her and I suspect he'd have been much happier if he'd stayed with your Mum.

* * *

The stage was thus set for the meeting of these two young people, Kath Cree and Ron Spathaky, of very different backgrounds but having in common a burning idealism, a belief that they can and must make a difference, make the world a better place where material inequality is much less than in the world they had so far experienced, and where the evil of fascist dictatorships would be defeated. This idealism was set in the ideological framework of Marxism–Leninism.

Their adherence to this ideology and to its organisational expression, the Communist Party, had come to my parents by different routes as we have seen. There was an inherent tension, therefore, which they no doubt resolved through the idea that the achievement of communism would be brought about by an alliance of the proletariat and the intelligentsia. The meaning of the word 'intelligentsia' here is that employed in the Communist Manifesto – the "portion of the bourgeoisie which goes over to the proletariat", that is, those "bourgeois ideologists, who raised themselves to the level of comprehending theoretically the historical movement as a whole."[29]

Dad's communism was a belief that he had come to in his late teens, reinforced by his experience at Sheffield University, but ultimately as the rational decision of an adult mind. Mum's belief was something she had imbibed at her mother's and father's knees. It was a 'given' of her family upbringing from her earliest years and continually reinforced in her early married life, when she lived in Brighton, through contact with her parents, her brother and sister-in-law (my Uncle Gordon and Auntie Doris) and other communist activists.

We shall see from the letters how the beliefs they held in common, as well as their different upbringings, played out in the wartime years. As the letters that have survived are almost entirely Dad's, we must allow for the fact that we are reading his words not Mum's, observing his world-view directly, and hers only through him. I think, nevertheless, that the letters are revealing of the fault lines and strengths of his character and also, more importantly, of the ups and downs of their relationship over the prolonged periods of separation which wartime imposed.

---

29   *A Dictionary of Conservative and Libertarian Thought* by Ashford and Davies, pub. Routledge, 2012

Chapter 2

Summer Schools

Leaving Sheffield, I went to Brighton to teach and was put up in lodgings in Dean Street with Sid and Annie Cree and their daughter Kath. I was put in touch with them by someone in the Communist Party.

Dad was in his nineties and talking about his life after leaving university over seventy years earlier. He started his teaching career at Brighton Intermediate School in 1936, where he taught French and English. He was there for about four years before being called up by the Army. He was remembered by John Cecil (of Oregon, USA):

I was at Brighton Intermediate School during the war years. I remembered the Headmaster Mr. Cooper[30] and Messrs. Hills, Schaerer, Coxhead, Webb and Spathaky…

Dad might also have taught Eric Feast, who wrote in 2007:

I went to the school from 1936-1939… Boys entrance was in Pelham Street, Girls entrance in York Place… We had some pretty tough teachers, and the Prefects were minor tyrants. Nevertheless a good school.[31]

Dad continued:

---

30 Actually Dr Cooper, also mentioned by Dad on pages 53, 73 and 468.
31 'My Brighton and Hove' website, extracted 7th December 2017

I used to have lunch at Ma Egan's, in Dean Street but further towards the Front *[than the Crees]*. She used to serve some sort of meat courses. I remember Ma Egan's because when I'd finished at the Intermediate School I'd walk there for dinner and then back to school for the afternoon session. It was only a ten-minute walk.

"When did you first start going out with Mum?" I asked.

I used to go to Communist Party meetings in the rooms which were dead opposite the house. Nan and Grandpop were leading members of the Branch. There were social activities in connection with the branch – regular dances in the rooms on the first floor.

* * *

When I asked Mum how she met Dad, she said:

My boy-friend Brian had then done his apprenticeship and went off to work in North London. The day he left, I went to a CP meeting and Ron walked in. That was in August 1936.

Ron had just come down from University and knew all about passing exams. So when I took the exam in December I passed, much to my amazement. I started at Boots in about January 1937, having signed up for a three-year apprenticeship. I worked from 9 to 7 but with Saturday afternoons off.

We were married in December 1937. We lived with my parents in Dean Street but soon moved out to a flat, 47 Old Shoreham Road, Brighton.

Her mother gave her a five-year diary, writing in the front, "To Kath from Mam. With love / July 1936."

Mum started using her new diary in 1937, although she may well have kept a diary in 1936 and earlier. She stopped after a few weeks but had written enough to show how actively she was involved in left-wing politics. The references to Brian and Ron are worth comparing:

January 1. 1937 Friday.

    Finished Pre Sci Prac yesterday.

January 3. 1937 Sunday

    Ron came home last night.[32] He was delightfully pleased to see me 'tho tired. L.P. conference[33] in afternoon – interesting Social in evening.

January 4.

    Helped Ron type Party programme for Brighton.

    He is having dinner and teas here during hols.

January 5. 1937 Tuesday

    Branch mtg – Ron absent at Co-op mtg.

January 9. 1937 Saturday

    Co-op conference – usual standard.

    Free social in evening.

    Results of Pre Sci – I've passed.

    Charles Tiptaft down in Chemistry.

January 10. 1937 Sunday

    Went to celebrate at flicks.

    Jessie Matthews "It's Love Again."

    Peter Lorre "Crime & Punishment"

    latter very good – wrote letters in evening.

January 11. 1937 Monday

    Went to Tech to inform & thank everybody.

    Went to Ron's – tidied up there.

    Listened to "Man of Destiny" by G.B. Shaw on radio – quite good – Whittenbury called. Read German with R. Letter from B. Wire Catter *[=later/latter?]*.

---

32 Possibly from visiting his parents and grandmother in Warrington, Cheshire, over Christmas.

33 Not the Annual Conference, which was held in October 1937.

January 12. 1937 Tuesday

R. went back to school – Received letters of congratulations from David, Brian, Grandma. Doris wrote – she's failed in London doing revision course. Letter from Turmey*[?]* & R.S.D. Last branch mtg.

January 13. 1937 Wed.

Read the whole of "Out of the Night" by Muller[34] – very good view of the future from a Biologist's point of view. Cleaned bike – started "Spain in Revolt" also good giving background of Civil War. [35]

January 14. 1937 Thurs.

Went to Tech. Molly Renville is back there. Arranged for Zoo*[logy]* lectures on Monday evenings. Spent evening at Ron's reading & writing to Varley asking that my scholarship be held in abeyance.

January 15. 1937 Friday.

L.B.C. mtg. J. Matthews on "Theory & Practice of Socialism" at Union Church. V. good, 50 present. Sold 15/- lit. & 18 tickets for Tom Mann's mtg.

January 16. 1937 Sat.

8 o/c Press comttee dance Co-op Hall 1/-.

Went to Tech Dance – not many there but had enjoyable time. Very tired

January 17. 1937 Sun.

J. Burns B.Sc. Hitler & the British Empire.

Labour Club 7.30.

Brian came down[36] – Moulescombe for dinner and stayed for tea. Called on Ron before tea.

Went to mtg – quite good speaker too general.

---

34 *Out of the Night: A Biologist's View of the Future* by H J Muller, pub. Victor Gollancz, 1936
35 *Spain in Revolt* by Harry Gannes and Theodore Repard, pub. Left Book Club, 1936
36 Brian, here and on 11th ('B') and 12th January, may have been Brian O'Malley, Mum's ex-boyfriend, even though he was now working in London. He may have been visiting the Pennifolds at Moulescombe. Although the sentence about Ron is slightly ambiguous, I think it was Mum rather than Brian who called on Ron.

January 18. 1937 Mon.

Unity achieved between S.L., I.L.P. & C.P. What will the L.P. do now?[37]

January 19. 1937 Tues.

Mtg with SL. Youth. Food Ship to Spain.[38]

January 20. 1937 Wed.

YCL[39] mtg.

Co-op Party I.M.S. Discussion on 'Russian Co-ops'

745 Labour Club. G. Hoskins leading disc.

January 23. 1937 Sat.

R. Pennifold on 'United Front' at Co-op Hall, Portland Road, Hove. R. Spathaky chairman[40]

January 29. 1937 Fri.

L.B.C. mtg 8 o/c Union Institute[41]

Quentin Bell – Progress of Fascism[42]

January 31. 1937 Sun.

Sadie Span[43] – Study of Marxism

Queens Place 7.30.

February 3. 1937 Wed.

Tom Mann – 60 Yrs of Labour Movement

& Film – Defence of Madrid

7.30 Co-op Hall 6d. Steward[44]

---

37 This is a reference to the historic pact between the Socialist League, the Independent Labour Party and the Communist Party to launch the 'Unity campaign', a united front against fascism.

38 It did not take long for practical action to start on the Unity campaign!

39 Young Communist League

40 Dick Pennifold – see page 20. R Spathaky was Dad of course.

41 Left Book Club

42 Bell was a Quaker and a nephew of Virginia Woolf, whose biography he wrote.

43 Founder member of the Communist Party in Glasgow

44 Tom Mann was a founder member of the CPGB. By then aged 80, he was a veteran trade unionist and a popular speaker. The film was directed by Ivor Montagu for the Progressive Film Institute. "Steward" probably means that Mum was a steward for the meeting.

February 7. 1937 Sun.

L.B.C. Rally. Albert Hall, London.

This was the last entry. For me, the surprise in Mum's 1937 diary is that Dad was clearly not a lodger with the Crees, although "having dinner and teas here" until he returns to his teaching job for the new term is a definite clue to the development of their relationship. The six references to Ron suggest that her romantic allegiance had definitely switched from Brian, who gets only two or three mentions. So it seems likely that Dad did not become a lodger at 17 Dean Street until later that year.

I asked Mum once (in her '90s) what it was that had attracted her to Dad when they first met. She said it was his guitar playing, but I think that was a cover-up. Dad has said that they met at a Party social, but both Mum and Dad have been vague about this. They had both lived in Sheffield and that would have been an initial talking point. But allegiance to the Communist Party must have been the main thing they found in common.

Mum eventually decided to spill the beans to me in July 2016. She told me that, when Dad moved to his teaching job in Brighton in 1936, he was recommended, presumably by a Communist Party contact, to try Sid and Annie Cree's as a possible 'digs'. This implies that Dad became a lodger in their house immediately, but we have seen that it could not have been before 1937, so Mum was aged 18 and Dad 22.

Then she dropped the bombshell:

Ron seduced me in the bathroom at 17 Dean Street. The result was that I became pregnant. I had an abortion. Mum arranged it in London. I still wanted to marry him. And Mum thought it was the right thing to do. She was quite old-fashioned in that way. I have never told anyone this before.

Wow, I didn't see that coming! That might explain why there were no further entries in Mum's diary. Her life was in turmoil and things were happening that could not be committed to paper. Abortion was illegal then, for one thing.

It was settled that they would marry soon. There was a potential problem in that Brighton Technical College, where Mum was enrolled on a pharmacy course did not allow married women as students.

In those days the route to becoming a qualified pharmacist was a four-year course. This consisted of a three-year apprenticeship – which Mum took at Boots the Chemist in Western Road – followed by a year of study at college and then the examination of the Pharmaceutical Society. Following such a career was something her parents would have strongly encouraged, as her mother especially was a fierce advocate of women's equality.

We have just one letter from the time before their marriage. It was the only occasion that I know of when Dad started a letter with the words "Dear Sweetheart." It was written while he was attending a Summer School at Godalming, Surrey, in August 1937. It appears that he cycled the 50 miles there from Brighton on Mum's bike, "that awful tin can of yours."

These 1937 and 1938 Summer Schools were organised by the Left Book Club.[45] *The letter describes the glittering galaxy of lecturers. They were broadly socialist rather than exclusively communist, despite Dad's mention of a Teachers' group organised by "the Party faction."*

Dad wrote both the letter and the envelope in pencil, incorrectly placing Brighton in Surrey:

Hillside Guest House,
Farnecombe,
Godalming,
Surrey,
26/8/37

Dearest Sweetheart,

Your card made me feel still more guilty about not having written. As you feared it <u>was</u> a job getting on that awful tin can of yours all this way. My behind felt like a toast rack when I arrived. However that soon disappeared, and a nine hour ride was a good night-cap.

---

45 See *Victor Gollancz and the Left Book Club* by Neavill, Gordon B, in *Library Quarterly*, 41(3), 197-215, 1971. It is an article that portrays brilliantly the atmosphere of the political circles in which Mum and Dad moved in the late 1930s. (www.researchgate. net/publication/255982596)

The School is very efficiently organised and although there was only one person I knew when I arrived (Max) I now have a fairly large circle of acquaintances, mostly Socialist teachers or students. There are not many students altogether and none of the University Labour Federation giants whom I used to know.

The general scheme is a lecture in the morning, on the River Wey canoeing in the afternoon and a lecture in the evening followed by a social. I find the lectures extremely useful for the facts, though the methods and general theories don't seem to have made more than a moderate advance since I had my last period of going all highbrow. We started with a masterly analysis by Campbell[46] of the Spanish situation, followed by Levy on Dialectical Materialism.[47] The latter was extremely good for the simplicity of his examples of how new qualities are derived from old, but did not touch on the historical side. He was followed by Prof. B Farringdon,[48] an extremely lovable personality, who talked on "The Separation between Intellectual and Manual Work in Classical Times." This apparently "old-fashioned" subject proved to be one of the most human and vital of outlines of how people lived in Greece and Rome. He proved that the real Marxist is a real humanist, i.e. he is best able to appreciate the essential triumph and tragedies of Man's ancient struggle against Nature and his fellow man.

Next there was one on "Goya – Master Artist of the Spanish Progressive Movement," by one of these intellectual sponges who write brain-cracking articles in Left Review. Since I didn't ever remember seeing a picture by Goya till this lecture it left me a bit cold, but apparently it was very clever.

Then there came an equally masterly performance by a psychoanalyst, Trist, who cleared up a lot of the vague ideas I had as to what

46   John Ross Campbell, author of *For Joint Action on Behalf of the Spanish People* in International Press Correspondence, v17-26, 1937

47   Hyman Levy FRSE (1889-1975), philosopher, Professor of Mathematics at Imperial College, London, member of the Communist Party and author of *Aspects of dialectical materialism*, pub. Watts, London, 1935

48   Benjamin Farringdon, Professor of Classics at Swansea, Irish republican and Marxist.

psycho-analysis really is.[49] Today we have been listening to Prof. Needham of Cambridge on "The History of Biology."[50] He gave some extraordinarily interesting facts, but, like most of the profs of today, only just about reached Darwin's time.

I should have been much more interested in J. D. Bennet this afternoon had it not been for two glasses of cider which I drank just before lunch which promptly sent me to sleep in the middle. Nevertheless from what penetrated the veils of sleep it seemed a worthy piece of work. Tonight we've got Haldane[51] and Strauss.

There has also been a useful Teachers' Group organised by the Party Faction.

I went canoeing the first day with a Jean Macfarlane, a teacher from Scotland. <u>Please</u> don't be angry with me when I say that I flirted with her a <u>wee</u> bit. I soon stopped because it was curiously mechanical and distasteful, at least on my part. So apparently you are absolutely part of me, now, and I can't look at no-one else no more, even from curiosity. Therefore if you've stopped loving me while I've been away I <u>shall</u> be in a mess. <u>Please don't</u>, not that I think you will!

I hope that the week has not been too boring and that you've taken advantage of my being away to get about a little bit socially (not that there's much time for that, yet, blast it!). Has mother been all right, or has she been miserable by herself?

Incidentally I went boating yesterday with a bloke and tipped the canoe over. We were both only in shorts, but it just about did in the old guitar, which had been a riotous success.

Must go now – shan't be long now, before I am seeing your lovely face and your intelligent eyes, before I'm holding you where you

---

49   Eric Trist, a young psychologist, interested in Marxism, who became a clinical psychologist at the Maudsley Hospital, London, treating war casualties, and later deputy-chairman of the Tavistock Institute.

50   Joseph Needham (1900-1995), fellow (and later Master) of Gonville and Caius College, Cambridge, a biologist with left-wing sympathies and an interest in Chinese science and its history.

51   J B S Haldane (1892-1964), British-born Indian scientist who worked in physiology, genetics, evolutionary biology and mathematics, and supported the Communist Party.

belong – and where you're going to be for good, as soon as I get back.

Love and many many kisses,

Ron

Please be better than I am and write by return.

"... Where you're going to be for good, as soon as I get back" suggests that Mum and Dad were definitely committed to getting married. They were indeed married – on 21st December 1937 – within four months of that letter and two days before Mum's nineteenth birthday. The story of their wedding is well-known to all the family – they married at Brighton Register Office in their lunch break with two of Dad's colleagues from the Intermediate School as witnesses, and everyone went back to work in the afternoon. Mum was working at Boots the Chemist on Western Road. The marriage had to be kept secret so that the authorities at the Tech didn't find out. Her parents knew about it, she confirmed, although they did not attend the ceremony. She agreed that her father must have given her a letter granting his permission for her to marry.

She said her mum, being quite old-fashioned in her views in such matters, was very content about the marriage. So maybe Mum was doing what she knew her mum would wish. But in the last year of her life, when the illness affecting her mind made her disinhibited at times, she told me wistfully, "I think it was a mistake for us to get married."

"Well, I'm glad you did marry him, Mum," I replied, "because otherwise there would have been no me."

There is more than meets the eye to Mum and Dad's relationship over the 75 years of their marriage. She dropped hints on many occasions about turbulent times.

In the August following their marriage Dad again went to the Summer School. This time it was in Hertfordshire, so I guess he didn't cycle from Brighton! Meanwhile, Mum went to a YCL (Young Communist League) camp. The mention of 'the university year' in this letter is puzzling but can only refer to the fourth year of Mum's pharmacy course, the first three years being an apprenticeship at Boots the Chemist in Brighton. She would have been just starting its third year when this letter was written:

Digswell Park,
Herts,
1 – 9 – 38[52]

Dearest Kath,

You will be glad to know that the School is even better than last year's.[53] The house is a huge place with big classical pillars in the façade. There are about a hundred and fifty people; a solid core of the old guard Marxists (Levy, Farrington and Gollancz[54]) and a very promising crew of labour and unattached men and women. Jean McKinley is here, but I haven't seen much of her; also a girl from the LBC, a school-teacher. I've played tennis a lot and sung with the scratch choir Alan Bush is getting together.[55] The biggest attraction probably is the grounds. In front of the house is a very wide lawn, beautifully kept, with a graceful, tall clump of cedars forming a patch of shade which you can follow round on the hot days. All the lectures so far have been held out of doors.

The lectures do not seem quite so scholarly, in the scientific sense, as last year. They are probably better adapted to the human wax-tablets that the lecturers are trying to write upon.

I was thinking today, as we sat in the heat on the lawn, that all that was needed to complete the picture was you, sitting next to me in a deck-chair, relaxing and blossoming in the environment, as you do in any company. I don't say this just because I am married to you. Neither do I say it in the <u>first</u> enthusiasm of healthy amorous

---

52 The date is an error – the postmark reads "2 AUG 1938".
53 Neavill, ibid. (footnote p29 above) wrote, "The club provided some outstanding lecturers. Among the thirty lecturers at the 1938 summer school, when there were three one-week sessions, were Richard Acland, Sir Norman Angell, R. Page Arnot, J. D. Bernal, Maurice Dobb, Benjamin Farrington, Wal Hannington, Allen Hutt, Hyman Levy, Dr. Joseph Needham, and Barbara Wootton. Victor Gollancz and John Strachey also attended."
54 Victor Gollancz (1893-1967), British publisher, pacifist and socialist
55 Alan Dudley Bush (1900-1995), a British composer and pianist, was a committed communist.

impulse. I say it because you're biologically and philosophically linked with me. Politically also it would be a great gain for everyone connected with you, because you are just at the point of great inspirations, the "spring-board" age, from which to jump and become a great woman.

Please keep on your valiant work, please, and then regard the university year as one in which you can relax. It may be a hard exam year, but at least it is a change from eternal rushing hither and thither of political life in Brighton.

I don't feel physical desire for anyone here, which you will be glad to know.

Please write if you have a moment to spare (not if you are busy). I should like to know if the distribution of the March leaflets has turned out to be a serious problem. It is the one load on my conscience at the moment. Is there any development in our domestic economy or housing prospects? Please tell me. When we get into the new place I want to take much more part in the running of the place. You are so very efficient that my slowness at learning such things is somewhat unfairly shown up.

Now I must go to Prof. Levy's Vaudeville Show. Tell me how you got on with Brian and what the YCL Camp was like. And believe me, I am going to make a better go at things next year!

Love – Ron

On the reverse of the envelope a 'stamp' has been stuck, advertising: "Help the Basque Children / Donations to 53 Marsham St London S.W.1".

That letter of September 1938 implies that Mum is to undertake a "university year." It also indicates that they are considering moving into their own place, but the envelopes show that for a time Mum and Dad continued living at her parents' house at 17 Dean Street.

The following year Dad wrote from Eastbourne and I think this was a different event. It is addressed to Mum at 46 Old Shoreham Road, Brighton – the 'new place' he had written of the previous year. It is still, in 2018, one of a terrace of rather smart-looking three-storey houses rising up a fairly steep hill. The 1939 Register confirms they were there in September 1939.

What is surprising to me is the total absence of any mention of the "hush over all Europe" of which Churchill had spoken the previous day. The letter was written less than a month before Hitler invaded Poland and war was declared:

97D Langney Road,
Eastbourne,
9/8/39

Dear Kath,

At the end of the first day's work here I don't feel too elated by the results. I had prepared a good speech for an open-air meeting in the evening and it sluiced rain down all night. However the speech will work for another time and I dug out some interesting facts. For example, the share of World Trade of the United Kingdom since the War:

1913	1924	1925	1936
28%	26%	25%	14.5%(!!!)

(Encyclopaedia Britannica and Statistical Abstract)

The first night a student Party member from Queen Mary's College, London, put me up. He was quite an interesting though somewhat sedate chap. Last night the long-suffering Bleezes stabled me. Jessie Bleeze is certainly a vigorous individual, she talks about this organising job for N.U.P.E.[56] as though she doesn't mean to let anyone put anything over her. There is a slight wistfulness mixed with the cocksureness. I don't know where it comes from. I don't know where she came from for that matter. She seems a curious type of woman for Lew – not unsuitable but of wiry mental contours; Lew is more spongy and possibly more absorbent.

Incidentally Jessie Bleeze is having to give up the NUPE job. The Doctor says it's either that or permanent diabetes. It meant a lot of travelling every day and I don't think Lew did even the amount of

---

housework that I attempt. She was up at 6 a.m., I fancy, and rarely back till 8 p.m.

In spite of bad weather I managed a quick dip yesterday.

There's not much bathing from the beach, because the Council are more straight-laced about undressing. You feel like Lady Godiva, immediately you take your socks off – centre of all eyes.

I hope you are enjoying the change of my absence. Have a good time and don't sleep with <u>too many</u> people for your habits' sake and not too openly for the sake of socialism (and possibly myself). I shall get over the possessive attitude towards you which I evinced in our famous conference of three De Possibilitate Copulandi.

Please let me know if Finer[57] can be at Newhaven at 4 p.m. Bleeze will not be coming, but you needn't tell him that, unless you want to.

I enclose the list of Jews, which I have brought with me by mistake. Perhaps you will put it where Sylvia, or anyone else you <u>might</u> mention it to, can get it and type envelopes. I will drop her a line and ask her to see you.

Tell me a) if you are well (I feel fine)

b) what you think

c) who you talk to

d) what you think of them

e) what you are reading

f) anything about next year

g) anything about the party.

This report <u>must</u> be in by the end of the quarter.

With very much Love and affection, / Ron

---

57 Probably David Finer (1908-2005), a Jewish friend who was a dress designer and ladieswear merchant in Brighton. See page 254.

Dad, Mum, her parents Sid and Annie Cree, her brother Gordon and Gordon's wife Doris (née Knight); taken on Gordon and Doris's wedding day in September 1939, three days after the Declaration of War on Germany.

At this time Mum was very focussed on her career. In 1989 she told me:

By September 1939 when war broke out, I still had three months of my apprenticeship to do. I asked Boots if I could go to College now. They agreed to this and I went to the Tech that month. I completed my final year's course and took my finals in 1940 – and failed. I had a re-take in September. It was the first weekend of the Blitz and I took the finals in London – and I passed. I stayed in a YWCA and we went into the basement at night. The windows of the exam room had been blown in.

So, in spite of being 'outed' as a married woman, Mum was allowed to sit the final examinations of the Pharmaceutical Society in London, allowing her to practise as a qualified 'chemist and druggist' and to write MPS after her name. I have her certificate from the Society.

Dad was called up soon after that and applied to join the Army Educational Corps (AEC). His next letter suggests he was being assessed as to his suitability. It's the earliest letter we have that was typed:

As before.

Add, "A" Coy., Hut 13.

20.8.40.

Dear Kath,

I think I did very well today. They told me afterwards that I had got 85% and all the other dozen candidates were below 60.

The only bother is that the decision now rests with the War Office. You know what that may mean.

I am typing this on an old Oliver typewriter, the famous old field typewriter of the Army, so if it appears a little curiously spaced at times please don't mind. It's the simplest way of getting down my thoughts.

Thanks very much for having bought a new book for me. I assume it's the one by Werner.[58] If it isn't I shall be a bit concerned as to where that one has gone to. I have the chap's address and shall write to him to find out. Or is it the long expected edition of R.P.D.'s book, revised to bring it up to date?

The Chairman asked me some amusing questions today. He wanted to know all about the Co-operative study circles I had organised. The kind of speakers we had to them, the subjects I had dealt with myself and the way I had dealt with them. He asked me where I came from and said he thought it was a good thing a smoky place like Sheffield had been bombed.

I replied that I thought that it might have been transformed much more peacefully and harmoniously without such a tragic upheaval. I instanced the city of Leeds, quite a comparable city, which had been cleared of quite a lot of its slums by 1936.

He then asked me whether I favoured "the provision of technical education for the selected few, or the provision of background

---

58 *The Military Strength of the Powers* by Max Werner, (transl. Edward Fitzgerald) pub. Left Book Club, 1939

education for the many." I said that in all situations I could think of I should try to mingle the two policies, but if I had to choose I should favour the background for the many.

He asked why. I told him that I thought a nation or force that was united could prevail in the long run over a nation that might be technically superb but not unified.

That knocked 'em. They had to think a bit about it.

So it all rests in the lap of the Gods (of Whitehall), so let's hope the A.E.C. has some sensible men in it.

Now as to Saturday. Unless I wire you or phone you to the contrary I shall meet you at the station at the time you suggest, 9-30 I think you said. I have the letter somewhere in the living huts. If by any chance I am not at the station, leave a message with the R.T.O. *[Radio Telegraph Office]* people and go and have something to eat and drink; then come back to the station.

If anything does happen to go wrong I will send the wire to the shop rather than to home, so you will get it if no-one is in.

I will phone John[59] at the Tech tomorrow (Friday) and leave a message for him if he is not there.

I shall have to make separate arrangements with him if my little timetable is to work.

Well, I'm very tired. Herewith find a little verse I copied out of an anthology called "The Compleat Lover" (!) Getting sentimental in my old age! (huh!)

Love Ron

As Dad had reached the end of the page, the verse must have been on a separate sheet, which has now gone missing.

---

59   Thought to be John Jordan – see Appendix 1.

Chapter 3
Basic Training

It was on 20th March 1941 that Dad finally joined the Army. He sent the following postcard on arrival at Aldershot, Hampshire, addressing it to Mum at 49 Hangleton Road, Hove. The address is very familiar to me as it was my home too for the first four years of my life, just up the road from Portslade Station. My guess is that Mum's parents, known to me as Nan and Grandpop, had moved from Dean Street to Hangleton Road. Mum and Dad would have given up their flat, and Mum would have moved in with Nan and Grandpop while Dad was in the Army:

> 254248 Pte Spathaky
> ~~Foster Squad~~ Block E2,
> MTW
> No. 12 Training Battn (Supply)
> Buller Barracks
> Aldershot
> 20/3/41

Dear K,

Journey quite pleasant, with fellow school-teacher from Portsl[ade] NUT. Truck took us to barracks; nearly all civil servants or teachers. Got most of kit, then saw squad "passing out" after their month's training. Dinner good; tea ditto. All very interesting. Unfortunately no chance of leave for first three months according to blokes passing out – Love Ron

P.S. Let me know as soon as you get Army allowance.

Dad followed the postcard with this letter two days later:

254248 Pte Spathaky,
~~Block E2~~ M.T.W.
Burrard Squad, E2.
No. 12 Training Battn (Supply)
Buller Barracks
Aldershot
22--iii--41

Dear Kath

The kit is fine. Army underwear is very good quality (a lot of it is Co-op!) so that I don't need any more of my own. The other pair of pyjamas will be welcome.

I'm sorry if the fake holiday meant a step backward for you at Boots. I fancy there must be more to it than what you write in your letter, since from your account alone one cannot see what else they could have done, if the dispensing job was the only one suitable for the poor bloke. However, I seem to remember you saying there <u>was</u> something else he could be given.

Buck up! You're not in the Army!

Now as to leave. We are free to go anywhere within the Aldershot Command, the extent of which I cannot tell you. The hours when we can be in Aldershot are (roughly) 2 p.m. to 9 p.m. and with good reason we can get a late pass till 12 midnight.

The only thing is that a soldier <u>is liable</u> to get an order to do work at any time, so that he may get it on Saturday night. The way to get round that is to persuade someone (presumably a bachelor) to do your turn for you.

So I suggest that I ring you up one evening and we plan a Sunday out. We have a phone-box in the barracks. Perhaps you could let me know your first Sunday off by letter.

Incidentally most of the people around me are university graduates or civil servants, so it's rather like being in the Senior Common Room at one of the lesser universities. To me – who has always had little contact with my colleagues, this is very interesting. We have to work bloody hard. – Love

Ron.

This confirms that Mum is now working at Boots the Chemist. She told me it was the large branch in Western Road, Brighton. Just three days later Dad writes again, squeezing in a PS at the top after he has written the main letter which makes it clear that they have a definite arrangement to meet on the following Sunday, 30th March:

PS Bring some rags for dusters, and Engels (if poss)

25 – iii – 41.

Dear Kath,

Thanks very much for the money. Polish and stuff for cleaning our equipment is rather dear and I was getting low though not bankrupt. I hope you will consider sending a liberal allowance to Warrington[60] when the Education Cttee money comes through. It is the first real opportunity of doing so and will probably not last long.

As regards next Sunday, the arrangement I mentioned will still be possible, i.e. I shall not be free till 2 o/c or so, but then need not return till late. I could probably get digs for you if you did want to come on Sat. evening, though I cannot see any advantage. I will ring as arranged if I cannot get out of duties – I probably can.

The cleaning is a bit wearing at the moment, but the arms-drill is very interesting and I mean to stick to it. I have just heard that I have passed the Trade Test and so the total pay will be 3/3 a day.[61] We are definitely all booked to be Clerks, which actually seems to be a quite responsible job in the army. When we've "passed out" after the first month we go on specialist training for this position, but you are wrong in your guess about possible movements.

---

60 Dad's parents had been living in Warrington, Cheshire, for some years.
61 Three shillings and three pence, or about 16p

Amongst other things it looks as if I shall be able to learn some shorthand, which is always an asset.

The bloke next to my bed, Jordan, is an L.C.C. clerk and a thoroughly good fellow. I explained to him the two marvellous chapters from Engels' book today; Introduction and Basic forms of Motion.[62] Being something of a philosopher he understood it thoroughly, though he opposed, for instance, the dialectical concept of "flux," proposing a different description of time in the universe.

Yours with more love still – Ron.

XXXXXX

The next letter was written on a Thursday and confirms that Mum had travelled up to Aldershot for the day on Sunday 30th March:

3-4-41.

8 pm.

Dear K,

Sorry you had such a journey of tribulation on Sunday. It must have taken all the gilt off the gingerbread, assuming that there was some on!

Certainly it was one of the best experiences of my life. It is strange that our life together should have improved so much as the world outside has grown more dangerous. I hardly thought it was <u>possible</u>, though I knew it was the <u>attitude we should adopt</u>. Perhaps it's a case of achieving most reasonable things if you adopt a positive attitude towards them; make them "part of your blood," so to speak (if I can use the phrase without being suspected of Nazi philosophy) "As we live so we think"; but when we have reached certain stages of development we can also say that "as we think so shall we live."

Just as you feel proud that I am forging ahead still, I also feel that it is part of myself going ahead when I see how determinedly you now tackle the problems of living. In the space of two years or so you

---

62 *Dialectics of Nature* by Friedrich Engels, trans. C P Dutt, pub. Lawrence and Wishart, 1940

have changed from immaturity into a real woman, capable of being radiant and poised, without being self-conscious. Your achievements in clothing, reading, thinking, working and health are only signs of this general transformation.

The only danger is that you might not be aware of the great changes you have brought about.

I have had a considerable minor triumph today, I got the top score in shooting in our first trip to the range, out of thirty men, and I'll show you the target later. It's like this:

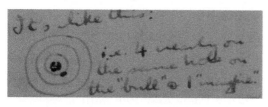

i.e. 4 nearly on the same hole on the "bull" & 1 "magpie." It's got me quite a reputation in the room. I'm thinking of going to Chicago and deposing Al Capone. Of course I may do badly tomorrow on the open range, but I feel quite confident about it.

I haven't been able to get out to Aldershot since I went with you but I'll definitely get the room fixed up in time.

Now I must get on with the job!

Incidentally I can honestly say that Sunday and Monday were completely fine as regards our short trip to bed. It is the first time in my life that I can say this with truth at all. I'm looking forward to closer and closer intimacies, warmer and richer experiences – with you –

Love Ron.

Three days later, Dad wrote again:

6-4-41.

Dear K,

I went to see Gordon[63] the other evening and he put me on to a woman with a nice place between Buller and Farnborough. She has agreed to put you up Saturday night and on Sunday (if you are free and want to stay). You don't say whether you will be free on Monday but

---

63   Gordon Cree was Kath's brother. "D" was Gordon's wife Doris.

please stay as long as ever you are able! The arrangement is absolutely informal and changeable.

She refuses to discuss £sd but Gordon told me that she does it for Toc H and after D and he stayed there she just asked them to pay what they could afford. Perhaps you could find out exactly what that was.

I could possibly wrangle a sleeping-out pass, but don't build hopes, as leave is "in the air" and officers are probably listening to thousands of phoney stories a day.

I shall most likely be able to meet you at Aldershot station at 8-30 pm. Saturday (or any time earlier after 2 p.m.!???). If I can't you can easily catch the Farnborough bus to the barracks and get the first fellow you see to take you to E2 and get me out. Even if I am CB you can probably see me in barracks, unless I am in a lecture or actually parading. If you keep close to one bloke fellows will not shout out requests for copulatory cooperation to you. Otherwise they may try to "get off" in a mild way.

(Written in between the pudding and the wash-house – this 6th day of Grace, 1941, ink run out) –

Love

The word "Love" is followed by a stick drawing of a man with large boots sending the letter X in semaphore, although the X is drawn as seen from the rear of the signaller, which is not the normal method of portraying semaphore.

Dad sent a telegram at 7.56 on 10th April 1941, addressed to "Cree, 49 Hangleton Road, Hove":

GOT PASS SATURDAY NIGHT TILL SUNDAY EVENING VOUCHER POSTED RON

The 10th April was a Thursday, so the Saturday and Sunday mentioned were 12th and 13th April. The following letter is undated but mentions that it's a Tuesday, so it was probably written on 15th April 1941. It is partly typewritten but mostly hand-written on thin typing paper:

Dear K,

Have had a bad cold since I saw you, due I think to putting on some socks which were not quite dry. However I have now made my mistake and shall not do it again.

I hope you didn't lose the 19.30 at Brighton, it is lousy going to work on a Monday after having a very late night and a strenuous weekend in addition (and how!).

The cold has only bothered me in the sense that I couldn't remember my Organisation stuff on Monday morning and have felt a general disinclination for study or even serious thought.

However it seems to be passing off now and the fact that we have little generally to do on a Tuesday evening gives me chance to get over it. Quite a lot of the other blokes have mild colds including our instructor.

I imagine that this letter will cross posts with one from you, but as I haven't a great vein of inspiration at the moment it doesn't matter. Have just been reading I.E's "Downfall of France"[64] which is certainly very interesting. It is amazing to read something by a foreign neutral who has wandered over both Zones, seeing all developments.

My room-mate has taken part of L M to read, the one on the development of combine control. I shall give him the other book after that, as he seems a real enthusiast for nature-study.

I'm sorry we had so little time (comparatively) together. Also I think that a drama with a crisis at the beginning cannot reach the heights of one with it in the middle or at the end, but we discussed that and drew up our conclusions – emotional and technical, didn't we?

I shall try my hardest for 48 hours leave in the near future. Or perhaps next time I get a sleeping-out pass it may be better for me to come home. I could travel on Saturday afternoon. Passes are few and far between however.

To divert, I cut the enclosed out of the Evening Standard (!!!) It may be all balls, but if he has tried to write books on Preventative Medicine

---

64   *The Fall of France*, pamphlet by the Russian novelist Ilya Ehrenburg (pub. London 1940)

and Epidemiology he is better than the usual medical author. Perhaps you could send to the PS[65] for one or two of them.

Perhaps you would like to write to him for a job!? I once wrote to A S Neill[66], and got some interesting advice. If you like I'll help draft a letter.

Well, now I've settled your future *[?career]* for you, I'll go on parade. The Colonel has just sent his Adjutant to request my presence! (Perhaps)

– Love R

Dad writes again three days later, starting in pen and switching to pencil mid-word when the ink ran out. STW may be the Services Training Wing:

> *[Address]* Temporary but usable
> STW No. 12 Training Batt. (Supply)
> Burrard Squad,
> 58a Cowie Square,
> R.A.S.C. Buller Barracks,
> 18/4/41.

Dearest,

Thank you for your frequent letters. The language books will be very useful, though I should be glad of "Les Matérialistes de l'Antiquité" by Paul Nizan[67] when you have time, also the book on law which you ordered. I shall have some time for study in STW, though not much.

Glad you enjoyed going out to tea. I suppose it was either "Figaro" or Johnnie's "Eine Kleine Nachtmusik" (Little Night Music) which you heard. Both are brilliant and restrained. You will probably revel in "Peter and the Wolf." It is natural that you should prefer robust hopeful themes to decadent types of ballet, being of robust hopeful nature yourself.

---

65 The Pharmaceutical Society
66 Educationalist and founder of Summerhill School
67 Pub. Les Éditions sociales internationales, 1938

To pass to permissible soldiers' gossip: we got through the ceremony quite well, in spite of changes of instructions. I hear that the stuff given out in STW is quite intelligently dealt with, though it has the usual limitations.

I have met several fellows I know in the squads coming in, including a former student from Sheffield in my year – not a particularly creditable fellow but quite a friend of the boys.

One interesting occupation has been to note the methods used by the various NCO instructors, criticising by the standards of four years teaching. The instructors divide themselves surprisingly evenly into good and bad, the good being who encourage and generally "get in touch" with their squads; the bad are perpetually surprised at finding backward men and bawl at them to improve them, thus setting them back a long way.

If you can possibly come at the next [sic] of next week please do. I could probably get as far as Diana's at a pinch, or possibly Horsham. Another alternative would be to meet at a really rural spot and see some real country.

With all my love and respect – Ron.

Again, there was an interval of three days before Dad sent a letter and a postcard on the same day. I think the letter was first:

> S/254248 Pte. RVS
> Basic Course 87
> HQ Coy STW,
> Cowie Square
> Buller Barracks
> Aldershot
> 21.4.41.

Dear K,

Sorry you didn't see Peter and the Wolf. I have nothing to criticise in your friendship with Winnie, though I believe it would be she who gained out of it. This coddling of the children is mere laziness and will probably ruin them.

I'm afraid that I cannot tell you about the things I am learning, since <u>everything</u> about a soldier's work comes under the "Security" heading.

Now let me get off my chest about Sunday. Here is the <u>most probable</u> timetable for us:

SAT: School 9 – 12-30
              Lunch 12-30 – 1-30
              FREE? 1-30 – Midnight
SUN: 9 o/c – 12-30 Church Parade. (St Georges)
              12-30 – 1-20 Dinner
Free   2 – Midnight (in practice till 9 o/c)

The only tragedy could be a 14 mile route march, which may be put in place of the Church Parade and would keep me until about 2-30 pm.

The worst thing would be the putting of the Route March <u>on Sunday afternoon</u>, in which case we should not be free until 4.

You see the whole thing is fraught with reefs and eddies, but <u>PLEASE COME IF YOU POSSIBLY CAN</u>. I am not ashamed that I need you, to see you and talk to you, though it is only for an hour.

<u>I have written to ask Mrs. Burgess if she will put you up Sat. night.</u> I don't think there would be a Church Parade <u>and</u> a Route March, so we should have some time together. Please wire me if you want me to make any alterations. If I am taken for a lot of time you can find some lovely country only five minutes from the Barracks along the canal bank to the left.

I will call at Mrs. Burgess's as soon as possible.

If I can see you for only an hour I have a lot more interesting things to tell you, since we have now started the real experience of Army life.

You ask how to improve your style, though I think it is good and will be better. The answer is, don't strive after any particular effect at all, or any bright way of saying anything. Just say what you want to say. After a longer experience of writing you will then find little airs and graces creeping in without having to search for them. Once you become very conscious of searching out a special expression your style will suffer.

Of course the best letters perhaps suited to the leisurely days of Lord Chesterfield or the Paston merchant family must have been the result of considerable thought beforehand of what the writer wanted to say. If I am worth your time to think about, then you will develop as time goes on more complex ideas which you want to let me know of, whether they are emotions of joy, collaboration, disappointment or despair. If you really want to express yourself adequately then 90% of the "writing" can come in the thought beforehand, chewing over and remoulding your ideas.

This is not a waste of time, because it is an aid to the art of thinking itself, applicable to other spheres of life; meetings, interviews or propaganda.

Concerning your books – can't you apply for the catalogue of the Pharmaceutical Society's Library and get some books from there?

Take care of your eyes now that you are doing more reading. Try to have the light coming over your shoulder and focus your eyes frequently elsewhere. I know you know all these things.

– Love

– R

Next is a postcard postmarked 7pm on 21st April:

Please come on Sat. evening if you are not too tired. I may or may not get a pass but in any case I might be able to get off on Sunday morning.

Love R

Three days later, this letter was written on a Thursday and, it seems, in some haste:

24/4/41

Dear K,

Herewith the travelling warrant. Mrs Burgess is just as hospitable and willing, but apparently I can't sleep there myself – no passes! I will meet the 8-15 at North Camp.

I am also afraid that there will probably be a *[five words deleted]* on Sunday morning and failing that Church Parade or spud-peeling. The ~~Doctor's~~ *[deletion but probably correct]* would take longest.

But we can have the following time together:

SAT   8-15 – last bus or walking time
SUN   12-30 or 2-30 – your train
– Love Ron

And now there is a long letter typed on the Tuesday after they had met over the weekend:

Aldershot,
29-4-41,

Dear Kath,

Hope the late return didn't mar the earlier part of the week-end. I really think we should write and ask Diana if we can meet at her place next time. It will cut down the time of travelling (if I can get a sleeping-out pass, I mean) and we shall be able to meet a little earlier.

Thank you very much for the shaving cream.

I managed to get our instructor into conversation today and asked him if the possibilities of an instructor's job were very rosy. Naturally he gave a very general reply, but I think it would be very possible if I swotted hard and got a high percentage. Actually I find the work quite easy, provided you sop it up by heart. I've never learned a "definite" subject since I left school, since I've been concerned with subjects involving a lot of speculation and hypothesis. It is a change to have to learn things off by heart and vomit them up again: the whole thing presupposes no intelligence whatever but a high degree of concentration on little details. However I must not get over confident and careless or I shall have a fail. My results in typing today were quite good. You will see from the enclosed that I get quite a high speed (26.8 and the speed we have to reach by the exam at the end of next week is 20). So the other subject is the thing to concentrate on.

By the way isn't the moral side of the document charming and reactionary. So are most of the typing extracts, of which I will enclose some more if I can rake them up.

If you see Gordon or have any communication with him, I should like to have back my book by Max Werner[68] some time. There is no hurry. Also it might be useful to find out what the titles of Wintringham's books are, since the one which is in Gordon's bookcase (which I have read).[69] Perhaps if some of our friends are going up to London it might be possible to find out?

J'ai lu un peu de mon livre "Les Matérialistes de l'Antiquité."[70] Cela m'interesse beaucoup. Il y a des passages de Lucrèce qui ont l'air et le style des scientistes modernes. Plusieurs de mes camarades sont des enthousiastes pour la philosophie et j'espère faire des prosélytes pour la matérialisme.[71]

One thing I didn't discuss with you the other day was the possibility of tackling the hospitals in the nearby counties systematically so that you get a job. It would be possible to get all the directories of the big towns in Sussex, Surrey, Hants and Berkshire and find in the beginning the sections showing the municipal institutions. Then a circular letter could be sent to all of them. I have to spend my evenings practising typing and am allowed to type anything I like. If you would send me a draft I could type some real bullshitting letters with all the commas polished and the full-stops doing right turns and left inclines.

I remember that the objection to a circular letter before was that there were only a few hospitals in the district where you wanted to stay. Now presumably you could (as long as you don't go too far away from Aldershot) roam a little further.

Incidentally while I am thinking I notice a tree outside the clerks' School window which has definitely got a mist of light green leaves on it. Isn't it grand to have any signs of new life in a world which

---

68 Supra, p38, Chapter 2
69 Tom Wintringham (1898-1949), soldier, military historian, journalist, poet, barrister, politician and author; joined the CP in 1923.
70 *Les matérialistes de l'Antiquité: Démocrite, Épicure, Lucrèce*: by Paul Nizan, pub. 1936
71 "I've read a little of my book *Materialists of Antiquity*. I find it very interesting. There are passages of Lucretius that have the feel and style of modern scientists. Several of my comrades are philosophy enthusiasts and I hope to make some converts to materialism."

might appear given over to Death completely if we didn't know from our hard-won knowledge that the appearances of Death are balanced in the long run by the signs of life bursting out all around. However, perhaps that's a little vague and mystical. One is so limited by the censorship of these letters.

I've just had a good warm shower "in my own time." It was luxurious. The bath-house was filled with songs from the other blokes, a little home-sick and dirge-like, but that was better than a dejected silence.

Et maintenant, chère camarade, il faut finir car l'école va se fermer, Lehman et moi allons à la NAAFI causer et manger un peu. Donnez mes salutations à la famille et à mes collègues si tu les vois. J'ai l'intention à écrire à Cooper si j'ai le temps mais je suis affreusement occupé à présent. Et il me semble que je ne rentrerai jamais à l'Intermediate, donc l'inspiration manque. [72]

Courage. Study hard. Think more. Write somewhat, and please believe that I never thought I could be so deeply in love as I have become.

Yours, R

.

Three days later Dad starts a letter on the Friday which he does not finish until the following Wednesday:

2/5/41.

(cont) 7/5/41

Dearest K,

Your cold will almost certainly be over by now – congratulations! (Condolences also, just in case it hasn't!)

It seems to me that it wouldn't be a bad idea to write to such a bloke as the one mentioned for a job. After all, aiming high is in itself

---

72   "And now, dear comrade, I must finish as the school is about to close. Lehman and I are going to the NAAFI to chat and eat a little. Greetings to the family and my colleagues if you see them. I intend to write to Cooper if I have the time but I'm terribly busy at present. And it doesn't seem to me as though I'll ever return to the Intermediate, so inspiration is lacking." (Dr Cooper was the Headmaster of the Intermediate School. See page 23)

a useful experience, even if it should be used sparingly. Perhaps he would recognise practical ability, knowledge and clarity of vision when he saw it! – I do!?% (I mean that!)

Before I forget, if and when you get a letter for me from Eleanor Rath in London, please bring it <u>with you</u> at the weekend.

(Cont) Not much time this week at all. I will probably get a day pass for Brighton on Sunday (6 a.m. – 12 o/c) Will you write and tell me what <u>you</u> would prefer to have us do. Perhaps we could meet somewhere nearer Brighton, then pop home for a meal, and I could get the last train. – Love R.

P.S. Will 'phone Thursday evening at 9-45 p.m.

If Dad got the day-pass he mentions, they would have been together in Brighton on Sunday 11th May. The next letter we have was written on the following Monday week:

HQ Coy – STW – Course 28D
19/5/41

Dear K,

I rang up yesterday, in desperation at such a nice day, to see if I could come to Redhill and meet you. But you must have been out to dinner; I suppose with the family (or with Len !%?½X!!) There was no reply. So I took a room-mate down to Heysholt to see the sights.

Incidentally, I was a wee bit disappointed about the kissing bout you described over the 'phone. I thought you were serious about the individual sex-love, the Sunday before. Or is that just an ideal? Or haven't you decided for whom the love should be? Or was it a raped kiss?

Anyway how did he take having to "love you for yourself alone?" Does he wear his puce-coloured pants under the RAF outfit?

If you <u>were</u> talking about love for me, surely you should have attempted to convince him of the rightness of your views. Or doesn't he believe that women should propound theses – but only melt?

I should like to ask you to do something. There are several reasons why I feel much more need to see you this week-end. <u>Can't you beg,</u>

borrow or steal Saturday off to come on Friday evening? Perhaps the manager would let you pledge one day of your summer holidays. Or can't you pay a locum, or get S to sign a cert, saying I'm ill and therefore you must come? Surely the others take or obtain days off sometimes and you haven't had many.

Please put on the thinking cap and see if you can't wangle something.

We'll find some new experience this week-end. The last was sharp, exhausting and terribly lyrical, retaining memories of pine-scent, the crackling of cones and your face laughing with the crisis of pleasure from the wood floor – Love

Ron

From the collection of Dad's poems we find one dated the following day:

The Voyagers

Sunbeams pour down upon the forest floor,
Making us languid though our senses burn.
Your face, among the grasses and the fern
Is lit with triumph, felt to the heart's core;
The song of growth throughout your burnished limbs,
With fire of ecstasy – growth of desire,
Though marred at times by hidden questioning.
Your face looks up into a future higher
Than even the scarred bright clouds hold promise of.
I bend to grasp you, pluck you, since I cannot sense at ease
The heightened movements leading to the dance of love.
And so, the struggle done, we see each other there,
Our hearts, like knees and thighs, revealed and bare,
While perfume of love and pine-scent rise as one.

Ron 20/5/41

Again it's ten days between letters unless we are missing some. This was written on a Thursday:

SD28 – HQ Coy

29 May 41

Dear K,

This week has been a bit of a push. I have at least the satisfaction that I have swotted as hard as I possibly could, and I think that the result was quite creditable. I seem to be picking up on the memory side of swotting, though I haven't made up the leeway.

Now re the week-end. I have just tried to phone through & been told that it would take possibly 3 hrs. Also I'm afraid I haven't done anything about the week-end, since I funked bothering the Burgesses & hadn't time for anything else.

I have two alternatives to suggest:

a) that you meet me at Redhill Sta on Saturday afternoon at 3 o/c and that you put up at Holmbury St Mary on Sunday night. Then I can come back if we have Monday afternoon off. OR

b) If I manage to book a room for you on Sunday evening I will wire.

I will try and wire you about this, but unless I hear from you to the contrary I will come to Redhill.

The hostel is 6 miles or so from Redhill.

No time for more! I hear a sweet voice hailing me, with quaint obscenities!

   – Love R

Mum has used the blank space at the foot of the letter for some sort of list, perhaps a budget:

Frock woollen	11
" Silk	7
Skirt	7
Cambknick (2)	8
Stockings (6)	12

Gloves	2
Shoes (2 pr)	10
Jumper	<u>5</u>
	62
Lining	<u>3</u>

Dad's next letter was written in pencil, but neatly, on the following Thursday:

28SD – STW

5-6-41

Dear K,

Trust you arrived back without too much ado about it. I am very well except that I have a very heavy nose-cold, for which reason I am at present hiding from the attentions of the gym instructor. So if this letter suddenly breaks off I shall be in irons.

This week continues to be very pleasant, ominously so I imagine. They generally give you condemned man's privilege before piling something bloody on you.

I have not managed to get my compassionate leave for Warrington with the reason given that we are changing to the new company and will be entitled to put in for 7 days. When is it you want me to get it if there is any question of choice?

It is raining hard today, so I imagine there will be fun and games this afternoon.

I went out to Tregolls yesterday to try and find Gordon, but he had just gone out. Jove what a palatial residence! It is in a posh suburb of Farnborough and has about four acres of ground around it. Old manor houses, mahogany panelling and ghosts! Neither could I find Arthur, though I left a message for him.

We had a splendid discussion in the class yesterday afternoon, as to whether space is curved or not. This morning I feel browned off, but no doubt shall recover w. breakfast.

Like me to meet you at Redhill Sunday, or somewhere else?

xxxx – Love R

This letter was handwritten and dated Tuesday 9th, with no month or year. I had a problem dating it as it was in an envelope postmarked 22nd August 1942. However, the course number was the conclusive pointer; 9th June 1941 was in fact a Monday:

HQ Coy. STW – Course <u>28SD</u>.

Cowie Sq etc.

Tues. 9th

In Haste

Dear K,

Thanks very much for the letter. Have extra busy week so may only send scrappy notes.

Here's a big surprise! Have been offered a similar thing to Gordon! <u>Not in what we've just finished, but in what we've just started!</u>

Would carry possibilities of "permanency" and living out, <u>with you if it were possible on your side.</u>

I think this is all Censor would allow, but will discuss with you Sat. week.

Naturally subject to disillusionment at any moment.

– Love

Ron

The next letter is typed and is a long one, not dated. I originally placed it in late March or early April 1941. But it happens that the poem Dad refers to has survived, dated 12th June 1941, and clearly refers to the walk from Dorking, hence the letter was typed after he sent the poem, and on a Saturday, so should be dated 14th June 1941. Here is the poem, followed by the letter:

Summer Song

Thunder still rumbles faintly over the hills
As raindrops mark the storm's retreating force
In single heavy plashes on the sand,
While Dorking town lies dreaming in the sun.

Of June's young Summer strength the thrushes sing
Of June's fresh Summer gown and then of you,
While Dorking town dreams its medieval dream
And thunder marks the storm beyond the hills.

Three songs I sang to you
Three songs you sang
As thrushes told the new green gown of June
In quaintly wooded nooks on Ryan's Hill;
A song of life, of living planned together,
A song of love of lying down together,
A song of songs, of reading odes together
On Ryan's Hill, in nooks of stilly woods
While birds amid the grass watch what we do.

12/6/41

The undated letter was probably typed on Saturday 14th June 1941. An envelope postmarked "Aldershot 8.45 a.m. 16 JNE 1941" probably belongs to it, and it contained two newspaper cuttings:

Staff Duties Course
Clerks' School
12 Training Bn (Supply)
RASC
Cowie Square
Buller Barracks, ALDERSHOT

Dear Kath,

I have just received your telegram, and by a most curious coincidence I was on duty and entered it in the books! Naturally you give no hint as to why you have a full fortnight. I thought you would have just a week; but then you know how I have a habit of mistaking things like that.

Anyway, we shall presumably be able to go to Warrington together, so there only remains the problem of how you will spend the other week. Do I understand that the first week has been given to you for moving purposes? It would probably be best to use the week for that purpose but I don't suppose they want to move you as early as that. Perhaps you could come and stay in or near Aldershot and help to look round for a place, but naturally enough it's your holiday and you will have to choose yourself how you will spend it to the best advantage for yourself. I haven't had time to look around at all yet, but things may be a bit easier next week. I have started various odd bits of teaching, as I hinted to you the other day, and on Monday I expect that I shall start in real earnest.

I enjoyed ever so much our little walk out from Dorking. I think it must have been a combination of the weather, the spot, the time and the moods we were both in, neither too serious nor too flippant. The whole thing was magnificent. We both got back quite early, and there was no "aftermath" for either (I hope). I hope you got my little poem about it. I really felt like that so it will be really worthy of a place in my Selected Works (Short Edition for Schools and Ladies' Seminaries) 5 roubles, pub. Salmon and Gluckstein.

Trust you have been delving into your book on Preventative Medicine, or planning our future, or reading old Frederick,[73] or one of the other things which you do so well and talk so charmingly and elegantly about (when the mood is on you and you succeed in being just yourself and expressing yourself).

I'm afraid my present surroundings are not conducive to very entertaining thoughts or profound reasoning. I can't say very much about what I am doing, except that I am in a very dusty place littered with the bureaucratic accumulations of years, with a young private under me who is browned off because he wanted to get into the Navy and couldn't. He put down Wages Clerk on his original registration form so they grabbed him for the RASC whereas they let others who just put Clerk go into the Navy. I am his sole arbiter and slave-driver till 0800 hrs tomorrow. Till then he sleeps near me on the dusty floor, goes and gets his supper, in exactly ten minutes (which he has just done) and generally acts as my shadow. He is a good-looking though slightly slow youth of about 24, with slightly auburn hair and a good figure. Perhaps I shall have a chance between now and the end of our

---

73 Friedrich Engels

seclusion at 0800 hrs tomorrow (Sunday) to make his acquaintance, drop a little of the military mask of official impassivity adopted for the delivery of orders to subordinates, and show him that even Lance/Corporals are human. I doubt if he will really believe it, merely on the evidence of one Lance/Jack, all the same.

Max has gone on his week's leave, and I have asked him to try and pick up one or two cheap books for me and carry out various other small commissions in London. He looked very fit and bucked with life. Who wouldn't?

I shall go out to Mrs. Burgess's on Monday or Wednesday night and book you for Saturday night of next week. I expect she will wonder where we have got to. I was out at Farnborough last night, but did not find the person I went to see. I don't know whether our phone conversation when he was at home was not clear, but still, I shall go out again as soon as possible and see him.

I have got out various books from regimental institutes; "I Found No Peace", a book by an American reporter which you may remember Helen Hoskens reading and being thrilled about.[74] It was actually very good of its kind. Another one is an anthology of modern German verse which John Dancy lends me when I want it. I also struggle on the Frederick and a copy of "Hamlet" which someone has just given me as a present. Also I have out a novel in the Penguin series, or rather an autobiography, called "Wild Oats" by Muspratt.[75] He seems to be a very anarchistic and very honest, if somewhat lazy super hobo, who has travelled all around the world, mostly on other people's money and petrol.

Otherwise my diet consists of official publications in connection with my course, which though very entertaining are not fit subjects for the innocent ears of a damosel of 22, who has never seen a gentleman's bare legs and thinks that babies are born through the navel. I refer to your sweet self.

Well, this is the Yaffle B[r]oadcasting Service and Pigbreeders' Bi-monthly. We are now closing down. Il y aura maintenant un

---

74 *I found no peace: the journal of a foreign correspondent* by Webb Miller pub. Simon & Schuster, 1936
75 Pub. Penguin, 1940

programme sous la direction de la Compagnie de Bile Beans de Londres. Vous écouterez des chansons, la musique de guitare, and the broadcasting of the soup course from the Astoria-Waldorf Hotel in Honolulu. Good awfully neet, everybuddy! Unsere Program ist beendet. Geschlossen die Sender Bremen, Hamburg, Kootwijk, Luxemburg und Breslau. Hier folgt eine Rede des Führers. Hitler nieder!

    Love,

    Ron

    xxxxxxxxxxxx

A few days later, on the Wednesday, Dad wrote again (reverting to pen and ink):

Clerks' School

Cowie Square

18/6/41

Dearest K,

    I sent a letter with a stamped addressed envelope to Mrs Burgess, have also got a sleeping out pass and hope very much you will be able to come on the 8-15 p.m. Please say you want to make love with me – and ever such a lot, because I feel in a condition to break the bed-springs, to bust the floor-boards, to rock the house, with mightily flood-like copulations. Excuse the frankness, but love and hot weather take their toll.

    I am just snatching a few minutes for the reading of John Donne's Love Poems, which I thoroughly recommend to you in either the full Oxford edition, uniform with my Chaucer, or in the 1/- [76] Zodiac edition published by Chatto & Windus (sold by Ward's, no doubt)

    Although Dean of St. Paul's he was a bloody good materialist (for the 17th C). Some passages seem to me to contain considerable truth. For example:

---

76 One shilling (now 5 pence)

If ever any beauty I did see,
Which I desired, and got, 'twas but a dream of thee.

I think every man is impatient when he is young, however and sometimes says, with Donne:

For God's sake hold your tongue and let me love;

There is such a lot in the song on p. XVIII of the Zodiac edition that I don't know what to quote, except

Let not thy divining heart,
Forethink me any ill,
Destiny may take thy part
And may thy fears fulfil;
 But think that we
Are but turned aside to sleep;
They who one another keep
 Alive, ne'er parted be.

This theme is found also in p. XXXIV

Dull sublunary lovers' love
(Whose soul is sense) cannot admit
Absence, because it doth remove
Those things which elemented it

But we, by a love so much refin'd,
That ourselves know not what it is,
Inter-assumèd of the mind,
Care less eyes, lips and hands
 to miss… etc. etc

Yet you will see he is absolutely conscious of the bodily basis of the most refined sex-love, by the "Ecstasy" (p XXXV)

But O alas, so long, so far,
Our bodies why do we forbear? (i.e. deny)

. . .

We owe them thanks because they thus,
Did us, to us, at first convey.

. . .

On man heaven's influence works not so,
But that it first imprints the air,
(i.e. has a tangible manifestation)
So soul into the soul may flow
Though it to body first repair

. . .

So must pure lovers' souls descend
T'affections and to faculties,
Which sense may reach and apprehend,
Else a great Prince in prison lies.

. . .

Love's mysteries in souls do grow,
But yet the body is his book.

Which seems a good place to stop! – Love R
    PS I'll get a reduced fare voucher!

The next letter was written a week later:

Clerks' School
25/6/41.

Dear K,

Glad the canoe (and the salad) have left pleasant green memories. It was nice and cool wasn't it?

I think you will be very wise to rest a lot during your holiday, though if you could rest at other people's houses some of the time it would be useful.

I'm sorry to say a cloud has appeared on our horizon. I've been ordered to go up for an interview by train tomorrow, in connection with the qualifications I mentioned. They tell me it's a much better job than the present one, but that's no recommendation. However I don't want you to cry about it (yet) because quite a lot of people get similar interviews and nothing comes of them. And if you cry at this little cloud, we may be assured of much bigger ones later – so economise in lacrimal salt! I'll phone you tomorrow from somewhere – probably around 1 o/c.

Please realise that I can't do anything about this business at the moment. The only thing would be weaken or conceal my qualifications which somehow seems impossible to do.

Thank you for such a lovely letter. It has been glorious seeing you. I still feel a bit bothered about the distance but let's hope we shall set up home together. Love – Ron

Chapter 4
Getting of Children

*From Dad's military service record it appears that he was posted to join
Spears Military Mission with effect from 27th June. That's what the
interview he mentioned would have been about. General Spears, who
was Churchill's personal representative to the Free French Government,
was a fluent French speaker and was probably interested in recruiting
Dad for his fluency in French.*

*Nothing more is recorded about the posting to Spears Military
Mission and Dad never mentioned it. The next letter we have was dated
12th July 1941, sixteen days later, though almost certainly written on
the 11th. But Dad was now on the move, initially to a "dispersal billet"
in Weybridge, Surrey, prior to a more permanent posting on 17th July
to the HQ Western Area, Royal Army Service Corps, near Frome in
Somerset.*

S/254248
Pte. Spathaky
No 5 Section, "C" Coy,
No 1 Holding Bn, RASC,
Weybridge, Nr. Woking.
12 – 7 – 41.

Dear Kath,

After a series of disjointed arrivals and departures, too depressing
to describe to you, I am at the above place. The temporary "dispersal
billet" is a moderately large house in this "large villa" district. It has
been a curious thing, as is usual in military matters, that the whole

thing takes place in a most delightful setting. I don't believe I have ever seen a district with more profusion of trees, while most of the villas are large without being pretentious. I have met a few former acquaintances, who went through the original squad with me.

I was lucky enough to meet a kindly-disposed woman in the street at Weybridge, who offered to put you up tomorrow evening. I will meet you at WEYBRIDGE station (right near my billet) at 2 p.m. tomorrow (Saturday). If I'm not there the address is

Mrs Pattison, 33 St Albans Ave., Weybridge.

It is not far from the big church with a spire, or if you get further down the village street it is not far behind the "Ship Inn."

If I'm not at the station by 2 o/c go to Mrs Pattison's and ask if she would mind you staying till I come. If you want to go out leave a message for me with her. Even if I'm not off duty Saturday evening I shall probably get quite a lot of Sunday off. Enough to make it worthwhile anyway.

Please mark all letters for me with PLEASE FORWARD till I tell you otherwise.

Love Ron.

The following letter was written on a page of a notebook and probably enclosed with the above letter, presumably with a travel voucher:

Dear K,

Valid <u>from</u> Frid onwards. Trying for a sleeping-out <u>and</u> week-end pass. Only threat is similar one to recent week-end. That is why I am so anxious for you to come early, on Fri if it could be swung. <u>PLEASE TRY.</u>

Will phone if poss. Fri 10 p.m.

Yrs. love

Ron

The next letter was written from Frome on the following Friday:

Headquarters,
Western Area, RASC
Nr Frome,
Somerset.
18 – 7 – 41.

Dear Kath,

As far as I can tell from 24 hours' inspection, I have fallen on my feet again.

Imagine the richest meadow and elm-tree countryside in England, with deepest valleys in which little lakes abound with moor-hens and near which philosophical cows stand munching. In the middle of this picture a noble estate, five miles square, with its own ponds, paths, thickets, gardens, flower-beds, plantations, shrubberies and outhouses. The crowning feature is a moderately large mansion, solidly built in a style combining late medieval, Renaissance and seventeenth century styles.[77]

A quarter of a mile away is a Medieval church, with a Norman font and some small gargoyle-like figures, probably of Saxon origin, homely and realist. True the tombs are most of the knightly family of Champenys (Champenois? Man of Champagne?) but the family is so old that it stretches from the early feudal period, the progressive phase, right through the decline of feudalism to the rise of industrialism and the Napoleonic wars. Most of the family are warriors, as the wording shows:

HIC JACET MARIA UXOR JOHANNIS CHAMPENYS, ARMIGER. NATUS 1606 OBSTAT 1642.

(Here lies Mary, Wife of J. Champ., Knight. Born 1606 Died 1642.)

Round the church is an extension of the lake, a sort of moat, which makes the church and its neatly-swept garden into a little island. Probably this had its strategic value in periods when churches, as in Spain, were often the strongest buildings in the village.

---

77 The estate is Orchardleigh in the village of Lullington, two miles north of Frome. See Wikipedia: Orchardleigh Estate.

I have just gone out to the edge of our copse before turning in, and down at the bottom of a light green slope are the dark waters of a tree-fringed lake with ripples blown towards the shore to where the nodding sedges and flags nod warning to them. Although the sun has gone in, I am reminded of one of the most beautiful Latin poems I ever read, Catullus's poem to his home lake of Sirmio:

> Ridete undae lacus ~~Sirmio~~ Lydiae
> Et quidquid domi cachinorum est
> (Oh laugh, ye waters of the Lydian lake,
> Resound with laughter such as dwells at home!)[78]

The fellows are of a type I have never met in the mass. They are typical West Country men from the sturdy little country towns. In the mess today a majority were dark, which is to be expected ethnologically. They are of good physique, but more intelligent than the real peasant fellows of South Wilts that I met at Weybridge. They speak rapidly and with a fair vocabulary in the purest Somerset dialect. "He did win tuoopunce vrom I thiz eevenin. Finally Oi did give ooviir playin, Oi did."

Apart from the fact that I am away from you I feel greater possibility of happiness than at any time since I joined the Army. The countryside has won me, and I don't mind.

In fact I think we shall still be able to see each other. We get a week-end off regularly each month, with a pass. Perhaps I could get as far as Chichester or Southampton. Also leave is regular every three months.

Of course there is little possibility of any active service here, since I am in the Home structure of the Army.

I will tell you as much as possible about what I do in my next letter.

Meanwhile courage. Think hard and make the most of the undoubted cultural advantages of being in the civilian work.

All my love,

XXXXXXX Ron

---

78 Sirmio is actually a promontory on the shore of Lake Garda. Dad has almost remembered the lines correctly, but in the wrong order. The original reads: "… *vosque, o Lydiae lacus undae, / ridete quidquid est domi cachinnorum.*"

In this whole collection of letters there are just three written by Mum to Dad. It's not that she didn't write – clearly she did, as Dad frequently refers to her letters – but simply that hers have generally not survived. Dad may have kept these three because of their life-changing significance. Well, I regard them as life-changing!

The last letter above, dated 18th July 1941, will have cross-posted with Mum's two letters dated 17th and 20th July, which she posted together because, as she explains, she did not have his address to start with.

The underlining in these letters is in pencil. It may have been done by Dad on reading them but more likely by Mum at a later date, possibly years later.

The letter seems to end abruptly at the end of a page numbered "2". A new page apparently starts another letter three days later, but the opening sentence suggests that it is a continuation of the previous one. The page is numbered "3", which supports this:

Thursday 17/7/41

My dear Ron,

I have just written a long letter to your Mother in which I enclosed £1 as promised. Also I have written to my Grandma[79] who is coming to see me shortly. Mother has been able to obtain a permit for her to enter the area so if your Mother would like to come we could probably obtain one for her. What about trying to get her to come during your leave then I could have you here all the time. I realise that it will be difficult for her to travel but I offer the suggestion for what it is worth.

Did you manage to find my letter? Actually I gave it to the postman who was going to collect the letters from the box so perhaps he lost it on the way. Let me know if it did arrive eventually.

Work is very pleasant this week. The dispenser is on holiday so I am back at my old post for a while. I find I am not too rusty thank goodness. I have applied for two jobs in London both manufacturing. It was really to gain experience in applying and interviewing for jobs. It will depend on you whether I accept the jobs if they <u>are</u> offered to me.

---

79   Annie Mellor, who lived in Chesterfield, Derbyshire

Thanks for letting me know so quickly about your move. It feels better when I know that you will let me know as soon as possible and letters do tend to be delayed when news is wanted most vitally.

I have been considering the desirability of having a child next Spring. I should like a full dress debate on the subject at the earliest possible opportunity. If an adverse decision is arrived at I will shelve the subject for another six months. I reasoned from the very beginning i.e. Do we want children? There are always drawbacks. They are a handicap and a great strain financially. Nevertheless I think that we do want them. In which case when do you think is the best time.

Answer:- Before I am thirty and since I was married young the earlier the better

Question – Will conditions alter considerably in the next five years?

Answer – Yes but the next year will probably be the best of the five and there is hope for the next generation.

Q. Can we afford to have one decently?

A. By saving hard during the next 3 months we could save enough to carry us over the first 6-9 months. After that I could go back to work to help to maintain it and I have in mind someone who might be able to look after it satisfactorily during the day.

Q. Will it cause a rift in our relationship

A. You must help to answer this one. I do not regard it as an end of my creative activities, it may be the real beginning.

Sunday 20/7/41 (3

Dear Ron,

I can't post this letter until I hear your new address so perhaps I can elaborate my theory somewhat. The problem of food and general war conditions can be faced and the risk taken if we think it is worthwhile. Personally I think it so. They are not the end of life but contribute to a full and balanced life.

I must confess that my last point (P.2) is the problem to me. I know that it will depend on my attitude to the child & life generally as to what

<u>your attitude will be.</u> I don't expect a binding and legal declaration on your part, conditions will probably prevent its fulfilment anyway, but I do want as complete an understanding as possible.

I love you and I want to have a child by you. I feel that you would like one too but the problem that you raised during my holiday of <u>restlessness etc</u> must be faced now. If it is serious <u>will it be improved or worsened?</u>

I have been looking up old friends this week. Everyone is anxious to see you if and when you come home on leave. Renée[80] has been up here to tea today. I think she is maturing. She is really a very interesting companion but she is studying hard else I would see more of her. She tells me Eileen[81] is going to have a baby sometime in the Autumn. It is rather a coincidence as I had been thinking over this matter all week. She is leaving at the end of this term.

Doris[82] and I cycled into Brighton this morning. I think I shall cycle to work occasionally if the weather keeps fine. It will save money and give me some exercise.

Where is Frome? Shall I be able to come down for August Bank Holiday? I shall probably get the Monday off so it would be worthwhile.

Think hard and write soon.

Much love

Kath

There follows a card from Dad postmarked "FROME SOMERSET 12.15 PM 22 JLY 41" and addressed to "Mrs K Spathaky, 49, Hangleton Rd, Hove." The card is pre-printed with their home (Hove) address and phone number. Dad has crossed through this before inverting the card to type his message. His typing has faded badly after the first couple of lines so there may be a few transcription errors:

---

80 Renée Shulman, a friend of Mum and Dad whom I remember from my childhood in Hove as Auntie Renée. Mum and Renée kept in touch until well into their 90s.

81 Percy Ireland was Dad's former school-teaching colleague. He and his wife Eileen were Mum and Dad's close friends.

82 Doris was Mum's sister-in-law.

Dear K – Could you, at leisure, send me some bits of my travelling household, i.e. the Penguin novel I left at Arthur's or Frank's, my Elementary German book (not the one you sent before), Leanniov's[83] book if you can spare it, the Dutt[84] book when it comes, a book by Werner[85] when it comes, and if room a novel by Gustave Flaubert called "Salembô."[86]

I have written to Dr Cooper[87], and will write again to you as soon as I have received any of your recent letters.

Love,   Ron

[Then handwritten in black ink:]

P.S. Also my dance-shoes and guitar-tutor (book)

[Inverted:]

Phone: Portslade 6084

49 Hangleton Road, Hove, 4.

It is clear that Dad had not yet received Mum's letters of 17th and 20th July when he wrote that card on 22nd July. By the following day he certainly had, and he typed a long letter at once. The title "Cde" stands for Comrade:

Subject: Getting of children, Domestic Relations

TVS/123/G Dom.

23 July 41.

From: Pte Spathaky, R.V.

No. S/254248

To: Cde Kath Spathaky, M.P.S.,

Thanks for writing to Ma. I have also written, so they should not be feeling too bad about things. I have also been thinking about the way

---

83 Probably refers to Aleksei N Leontiev, Soviet developmental psychologist.

84 Rajani Palme Dutt, leading theoretician of the Communist Party of Great Britain

85 Max Werner – see p 38.

86 *Salammbô* by Gustave Flaubert, pub. Michel Lévy, 1862. It has been described as 'erotic, sadistic and decadent' and was written soon after his much better known *Madame Bovary.*

87 See page 23.

it will mess up my leave for both interested parties if I try to go to both places. It would be better in a way if I came to Brighton for the whole of this leave and then went to Warrington for the next one. Still another alternative would be for me to have my Mother down here for a short time. I could spend the whole of the evenings with her and she might find something to do during the day. What do you think of this idea?

Your letters are quite admirable, stylistically and from the point of view of bright ideas. If you want to accept a job in London or Reading go ahead and do so. Obviously you don't want to remain in the same place for the duration of the War. I suppose you didn't hear about the Reading job. I came through there on my way here and spent a few hours in the Public Library, which unfortunately was a rotten one.

I'm afraid it would be impossible for you to follow me around, at least until I had been in a place for quite a long time and was thoroughly settled. Even here there is an element of uncertainty. Yesterday the Major whose clerk I am asked me whether in view of my qualifications I would like to be transferred to the Army Education Corps. This would entail a rank of Instructor-Sergeant, if I managed to get it, and a short course of about a fortnight at the Wakefield Army School of Education. But lord knows where I would be posted after that, though it would probably be in the West Country, since I seem to have become a part of the furniture here.

Of course if you would like to give up working in a shop for a time and come here clerks can live out in Frome. It would mean getting a bike and cycling in every morning, but there would be no hardship in that. I had better get to know about the AEC business first.

Now as to your new thesis, appearing with all the explosive suddenness of revolutionary conceptions (rather apt!); I certainly would like to have one, but under present conditions even more than earlier times, the burden falls on the woman, and this cannot be avoided. Therefore it is largely a matter for yourself. I agree with your little Socratic dialogue about the subject, although I don't quite see the strict logic of "Before I am thirty and since I married young the earlier the better." I feel that it <u>should</u> be the sooner the better, but taking your opening words, it seems to me you might equally well have said, "Before I am thirty, but because I was married young there is still quite an amount of time." However, I agree with the conclusion even if I don't see the exact point you are making.

The plan would also depend a good deal upon this idea you have in mind of someone who could help to look after it when you got a bit tired of doing so and wanted a change or wanted to keep your pharmacy ideas up to date. What have you in mind?

I never did consider in your case that it would mean a cessation of creative activity. I agree wholeheartedly that "it may be the real beginning." I suspect in your case that it would, since you have already been so sensibly and not sentimentally interested in children. You also know my view that in spite of all your obvious progress and development during the last two years you still seem to suffer occasionally from some occasional repression. I hope you won't misunderstand this; don't forget that dull hopeless people don't have any repressions, since they have nothing to repress. It is often something which accompanies a complete volcano of emotions of various kinds underneath the surface. I don't think you are exactly a volcano, but I have always been acutely aware of the contradiction between your energy and common sense, and what I called your restlessness, which might also be a sort of lack of permanent interests. Like all contradictions, it can be resolved, and then your undoubted energy and brain-power will continue, but at a higher level.

3.

(continued later) I have mislaid the first two pages of this letter during the last 24 hours and have spent quite a long time searching for them among the official correspondence, remembering the whimsical heading which I gave to it.

I rang up home this afternoon to get my Registered Number on the Board of Education Teaching Certificate and Diploma. i.e. <u>my registered number as a teacher.</u> I hope you will find the correct one. It is plainly marked, the only thing is that there are rather a lot of numbers on the various documents I have.

If you find from this letter that you have sent the wrong one, please send the correct one by letter. It is my state number, Board of Education, that I am concerned with.

The reason why I want it is that the Major had just brought notice from the next "higher-up" that I should apply to become a Serjeant-Instructor, which, as I said, will probably entail a short course at Wakefield (only eleven days, I believe) and then a posting to a very responsible job somewhere in this part of the country.

I have also just had (a) your letter which went to Weybridge and (b) a letter from My Old Man (my Father), the first I have ever had from him except when he wanted to chew me up for not writing to my Ma. He has asked me to try and find somewhere where they could come and stay down here. It'll be a bit difficult, however, because our lives are a little centred on the estate and it seems an awful pull to get into the nearest town, Frome.

It never rains but it pours. A Corporal who was a colleague at Aldershot has just written to me to say that the Captain i/c Clerks' School at Aldershot wrote the day I left Aldershot asking for me to go back there. However, it seems best that things should take their course here, since I shall probably arrive at the rank of Serjeant quicker by this route (if things go well).

I will finish now as I am tired with the day's work, Love, Ron.

Here is Mum's third letter:

Monday 28/7/41
36/1956

Dear Ron,

The number above is that of the Board of Education reference now used instead of registration and it is the only possible one. All your other certificates were numberless. It is the same one as on the telegram.

Your letter arrived this morning so apparently the post takes longer and we must make due allowances. Thanks very much for your answer. You say you want one but do you think I ought to in view of your absence and general war conditions? I am not frightened of taking the decision, indeed I have already done so for myself, but I want a mutual decision so that the mistakes of so many of our friends will be avoided.

Sorry my arguments got mixed up. I felt that since I was married young I would be ready earlier both physically and emotionally to have children. I shall still have enough youthful energy and courage to fight for my child.

It was Doris who I had in mind for looking after him (or her). She suggested that she could leave her job if there were two to look after (her own and mine). She now informs me she was half joking so I will have a further talk as to the possibilities. Of course many things may happen before then. There may be many more nursery schools by then.

I could not understand your reference to a job in Reading, but I remember now it was a hospital job. I never actually applied for it. I applied for 2 different jobs in London but I was turned down for both. Probably because of lack of experience in the manufacturing side.

The A.E.C. seems quite promising. Denis has just finished a course at the school. It is very intensive training but very interesting. Better I should think than Aldershot but you will be in a better position to judge.

If we are lucky I should leave the shop in about 3-4 months' time and I should be able to come to see you more easily until it was born.

I gave myself a lecture yesterday on thinking about this subject for such a long time but now we are decided I can settle to do other jobs. I was able to do about 2½ hours real studying in the afternoon.

I called to see ~~Arthur~~ Frank but he could not find your Penguins. Can you buy another copy or shall I try? I will send you the books when I know the first parcel arrived safely.

When are you going to get some leave? Can I come half way this next weekend as I shall have Monday off.

I am so looking forward to seeing you again. It will mean so much more if we cease avoiding the natural result of love making.

Much love, Kath

In spite of Mum's comments about making allowances for the post being slow, Dad's next letter is dated the day after hers and is clearly a reply to it. It was written on a Monday so they were planning to meet on the weekend of 2nd-3rd August:

Headquarters,
Western Area,
Nr. Frome,
Somerset,
29.7.41.

Dear Kath,

From one or two remarks in your letters I notice that you are doubtful about the above address. Let us agree therefore that unless I say otherwise, the addresses I put on my letters will henceforward be adequate ones. Since this is a Headquarters I don't spread around the actual address, though you could probably find it from some official quarter in Frome by showing your dependant's papers, should you ever arrive there in a hurry.

I have not made any helpful suggestions about next week-end yet, for the simple reason that I haven't quite known what to do. I want to see you, the same as you want to see me, but it's a bit of a puzzle. All leave has been stopped I mean just over the Bank Holiday.[88] Therefore I cannot <u>this</u> week-end come half-way and meet you.

Incidentally the idea of the youth-hostel at Winchester sounds very good indeed. The place is very nice, so I hear, and is almost exactly half-way between our two locations.

I believe there is one advantage of being here, even if it is rather a negative one. Trains on the Southampton, Salisbury, Westbury line are relatively fast, not like the Puffing Billy you used to spend hours on between Dorking and North Camp. Westbury station is a mere stone's throw from Frome. From Frome however, we are about three miles out, or rather less I fancy. The best way is by the <u>Bath Road</u> as far as a pub called the Ship and then ask the way to the address you will have gained from somewhere in Frome.

---

88   In those days the August Bank Holiday was the first weekend in August.

However to come down to brass tacks, I shall probably go off pop if I don't see you, but I am very dubious about asking you to come all the way to see me, though I could probably get most of Monday off as well as Sunday, and a sleeping-out pass for Sunday night. But it's a real long way – it rather depends on how very much you want to come and see me. I shouldn't like to influence you at all, though of course I should be overjoyed if you came. I should, however, love you just as much if you didn't, if you see what I mean.

I shall in any case ring you or wire you just before the week-end, letting you know how I stand re duties (I know I am duty clerk all day Saturday and till 9 o'clock Sunday morning, but that is all the more reason for me being off completely on Sunday and Monday). We may quite possibly get a complete holiday on Monday.

You will have to take into account the possibility of trains being overcrowded, since they are not putting on any extra ones.

I have been out with the Education Officer all today, seeing at first hand the work which he does. According to what he says I am as good as booked to start away from here on AEC work in the middle of August. I shall probably have the School course at Wakefield (more school! don't I ever stop being "educated.") and then come back to this area, although not inevitably. Then we shall start again with our seemingly endless discussions about living together.

Still, don't start calling me Sergeant-Instructor Spathaky till I tell you, otherwise I may get in jail for assuming bogus military rank! Of course there is also the possibility of an AEC Commission if I can do well at Wakefield.

I'm tired with the fresh air now, and with being driven about by a smart FANY,[89] so terribly sleep-making, my dear.

Hope to see you soon, I will ring as soon as I can find some provisional digs in Frome. In case you decide to be "<u>daft</u>" and come! (I don't mean it.)

Love

Ron

---

89   First Aid Nursing Yeomanry

Dad drew two cartoons in pencil, one at the head of the letter and one at the foot. The top one is labelled: "This my new camouflaged bicycle. Like it?" A stick figure appears to be crawling towards a sign which says "Pub Camouflaged". The other one portrays a vehicle travelling down a hill towards a caption: "Camouflaged Town". The vehicle bears the initials WD and a hammer and sickle insignia, and is flying a flag bearing the letter V. No, I don't understand them either!

It is so pleasing to me that we have these three letters of Mum's amongst the hundreds of Dad's, together with his replies to them.

It is almost always the case that a series of letters that has been preserved for many years represents only one side of a correspondence. So for most of these years of love and war we just see Dad's side of things, his point of view, his view of Mum and of their relationship. (It is some compensation that we have her memo of Chapter 1 written many years later.) Here, for just a couple of weeks, at a crucial juncture of their lives, we see Mum in the driving seat on the issue of starting a family. Dad is now reacting to her wishes, reluctant, I sense, to put his full weight of approval to the decision as she wants him to, writing first about the decision he has made about his army career, which just at this moment is a distraction from the main business she wants him to commit to with all of his heart, mind and soul.

There is now a gap of two weeks in the correspondence, possibly because Mum was able to get to Frome:

Dad wrote the following poem, which he dated "11.8.1941".

Two Faces

Very old are the woods,
But the buds are young
And the grass is full of a surging youth
And the sunlight red with maturity.
The roads are old, but the paths are new;
Paths in the morning striking sheer
To the heart of Adventure's brave new land.

Very old are we men
But the blood in us
And our thoughts
Have the icy tang of the pool
The vigour and song of a bird-watched dawn.
Age-old is the earth
But the world is new
Each time that the charted track is left
And the foam curls round a rebel prow.

Two days later he wrote a brief note, written on a page torn from an exercise book:

Frome
6.30
Wed 13th Aug

Dear K,

The E.O. is moving his office to

49 Convalescent Depot
Sherford Camp,
Taunton

tomorrow. I move with him. This will be my address.
Mother isn't coming.
My interview re Sjt-Instr's job is Wed. 20th
Writing later,

Love, Ron

Chapter 5

Army Educational Corps

Dad is now firmly committed to moving to the Army Educational Corps. He has moved about 50 miles west of Frome and is based at Sherford, a suburb of Taunton. The AEC personnel seem to have been based at a number of Convalescent Depots (or Condepots) during the War.

His next letter is written on the same paper as the last. It is undated but Mum has inserted the date "14-8-41" at its head – her dates are usually when she receives the letters:

(Written standing in High Street)

No _ _ _ _ _

RASC att. S.O. (Edn) W.Area

49 Convalescent Depot,

Sherford Camp,

Taunton

Dear K,

Written after pleasant day travelling down in the car (E.O., "Fany" and self). Her home is on the way and she took the Maj and self in to tea. So I had tea with the Great Man (Blast his eyes, damn his soul . . . . !) He's very decent, rat him!

Being attached to a Convalescent Depot is going to be a cinch. I sleep in a pleasant room, on a new flock mattress, go without gaiters, walk about slowly (like a convalescent) and serj-majors smile sweetly and say "How are you feeling, old man?" To which I murmur: "Better, sir, better. Of course I get a twinge now & again." (Of conscience?)

I think I'm going to like Taunton!

– Ever so much love

Ron

The next letter was also written on pages from the exercise book. This time he has torn out the centre double page. He has again left the letter undated, and Mum has inserted the date 17-8-41, a Sunday, which would have been the date she received it. Dad refers in the letter to "tomorrow (Sunday)" so it was probably written on 16th August. There are two mentions of a John whom Dad misses almost as much as he misses Mum it seems. Was I named after this John? It seems likely to be John Jordan, who is mentioned in an undated letter of July 1943 (and also many times earlier simply as John):[90]

No. S/ _ _ _ _ _ _ _ _

N.B. R.A.S.C. att Edn Offr W Area,

Sherford Camp, Taunton

Dear Kath,

I have just returned from the phone; it seemed a very short three minutes. Perhaps they counted the time when they were ringing me.

The Taunton Library has some quite good books, including most of the Nelson Discussion series. I have out "The Adult Class" by A. Ratcliff,[91] which is thought-provoking, even if the philosophy beneath it is not very deep. Also I have Liddel-Hart's "Dynamic Defence of Britain."[92]

After going there I went to a small but attractive snack-bar and had a moderately dear tea (1/8) *[8 new pence]*, discovering to my disgust a large and friendly Services Club ten minutes later. Then I bumped into Owens, one of the Sergeant-Instructors at a camp four miles away from here. He took me to tea at a cinema café and we talked Army Education. I shall certainly go into the job with a maximum of previous knowledge on the subject.

---

90   See Appendix 1.

91   Pub. Nelson, 1938.

92   *Dynamic Defence* by B H Liddel Hart, pub. Faber & Faber, 1940

Following that I saw him to the bus and walked back to the camp. There is quite a clean and pleasing office, on the edge of this large new camp, which I can black-out and lock myself in at night. Then I can write to you, study or do any Army Education work to my heart's content. I never felt as full of a single purpose. All that I miss is you and John.

The camp is only about one eighth full of convalescents, and the new clean buildings, on the edge of the country, are quiet tonight. There are tall cedars at intervals in the lines and half-neglected flower and grass patches.

I suppose you couldn't phone John and persuade him to come over to Southampton on the Saturday afternoon? Then he and I could have part of the evening and part of the morning together and I could leave him and go off with you about 11 o/c.

Thus:- SAT: 4 p.m. – 10 p.m. Ron & Jno.
                10 p.m. – 9 a.m. K & R (multo cum copulatione)
        SUN: 9 a.m. – 12 a.m. all three of us.
                12 a.m.   your train K & R

John would probably be glad to get back earlier to see Marie. Of course it seems a bit of a cheek to ask him to do this, but you might test out the ground, if only for a future occasion. I shouldn't mind paying at least some of his fare for the privilege of seeing him. Also it has other value. I want to make some proposals of a practical nature. Please try!

I don't quite know what to do tomorrow (Sunday). When you are starting in a place it is the most difficult time to fill in. Most of the chaps get right away from their billets and if you are just breaking ice of new acquaintanceships you are left stranded high and dry.

Possibly I shall study in the morning, except when N.A.A.F.I. is open, then go for a country walk in the afternoon and go and hear Harry Browne (IB) speak in Taunton in the evening. I saw the advert for the latter in the Taunton Gazette today.[93]

---

93 Harry Browne (1919-2009), author of *Spain's Civil War*, pub. Longman, 1990, was a member of the International Brigade – obit. in *The Guardian*.

The rest of the time will be rather difficult to fill in. One can hardly study all the day, though I seemed to be able to do so in 1933-4-5.

Love
Ron

The following formal-looking note about his qualifications was probably enclosed with the above letter, no doubt in connection with his application to join the Army Educational Corps:

URGENT
Subject: Degrees and Diplomas
Candidates – A.E.C.

<u>CONFIDENTIAL</u>
WA/3970/G Edn.
16 Aug. 41.

To: Mrs K. Spathaky, M.P.S.,
49 Hangleton Rd. Hove.
From: Edn. Office, W. Area.

No. S/254248 Pte. Spathaky, R.V. – R.A.S.C.

May all degrees, diplomas and certificates in support of the candidature A.E.C. of the above soldier be sent to this office, not later than Tuesday, 19th. Aug. 1941.

R.V. Spathaky Pte.
Clerk
Edn. Office W.Area.
Sherford Camp,
Taunton.

Dad followed this up with a telegram the following day:

17 AUG 41

TAUNTON

SPATHAKY PORTSLADE 9084 =

SEND ORIGINALS DEGREE DIPLOMA HSC SORBONNE BOOKLET

The planned weekend together duly took place in Southampton on 23rd and 24th August, with Mum, Dad and the still mysterious John. It is of interest to me as it must have been when I was conceived. Dad wrote about it, firstly in a short letter on the following Tuesday and then in a longer one on the following Saturday:

"A" Coy,

Hut 13,

26.8.41.

Dear K,

Glad you got home early. It will make the week go so much better if you get a good start. I enjoyed the weekend ever so much and I have been ever so busy since.

Werner's book is splendid. He must have been a soldier for many years at some time, since he knows how to describe a campaign as though he "were on the inside."

Hope you feel duly inseminated after our efforts. If you're not then I shall have to try other methods – possibly a garden syringe. Please let me know as soon as there is any news.

I am rather busy now, so I must cut this short. Am writing Mother tonight. All going well here.

Love Ron

Next is a long letter, closely handwritten in pencil on four sides of foolscap (13 x 8 inches) grey notepaper. Like the last, it refers to the momentous events of the previous weekend:

"A" Coy. Hut 13,

30 – 8 – 41. (Sat)

Dear K,

It is a lovely night tonight, a continuation of a splendid day. I have come back to the office where it is dead quiet and far from all intrusion to open my thoughts to you. I feel very strongly the joy of being able to do that. Surely that is the dialectical part of a true marriage. Two people can become one in the sense that male and female are complementary, yet they remain individuals bringing their own store of fresh energy and ideas into the "Oneness."

Let me start by paying you a well-earned compliment. When John and I were alone last week I asked him how he thought you were getting on generally. He replied almost spontaneously that he had seen a big change in you during the last months. He didn't mean particularly as regards politics (because he didn't see so much of you as before) but you had surprised him by commanding attention in some gathering or other.

This seems to prove the old saying that "we are our own best critics." You said that you had felt a new confidence and poise when with the people you move amongst.

He added that "she looked often before as though she were worried about something, rather pale and tired." I wonder what that was?

Talking of men and women and their relationship; I have just noted a saying by la Rochefoucault

The desire of the man is for the woman.

The desire of the woman – is for the desire of the man.

What do you think about that? I fancy it is true, about the women at least that I have met, and to some extent <u>you</u>. I also know that it's highly respectable and supposed to be praiseworthy. The funny thing is that I don't like it. I should like you to love me because I was developing mentally and/or physically, not because I would make a good husband and do the right thing by you. Do you agree, or do you think it's impossible, or that I'm wrong?

I hope you will go ahead with the job in the Hospital. I think you were cut out for something better than retail work. My leave will probably come soon however, and I hope you will find out from the Essential Work Order, or some such document, what is the position as regards taking time off. I'm quite certain that in factories this occurs, so how much more should it in a non-vital industry.

What did you think of our love-making in war-scarred Southampton? I think it was the very best yet – a marked development in quantity and quality on former times. It was a fine moment when you lay arched upon me, face upward, and I could caress the whole front of your body as we moved, particularly as that made it possible to caress your tightly-stretched breasts, stomach, "mons veneris" and groin. May I make a suggestion, which I hope will bring suggestions in return from you?

I think it is a case of "controlling development," or of something turning into its opposite, of balancing extremes. The problem with most of us, with our inhibited upbringings, seems to be to give ourselves up to love-making sufficiently. I think you and I have learned that fairly well now. The only thing is we have produced what I think is the first phase of abandon – an anarchistic and impersonal frenzy, a spasm in which the bodily joy is just shuddered away with closed or fixed eyes and convulsively-twisting limbs. Which is as it should be – for a time!

Do you think I am being completely idealistic if I propose that we both try to make the crescendo and the finale much more personal and related to each other. I want an orgasm in which I don't <u>just</u> produce ejaculation by effective rubbing of my foreskin on the glans by the cunningly serrated muscles of your vagina. I want one in which I <u>realise</u> something about you (I can't define it more yet) at the crucial moment; face, breasts, back, legs, I want all these to be integrated so that something new appears, some fusion that was not possible before, something that was prepared for by long stages.

Perhaps there is a key to it in the <u>relative</u> shortness of time we take. I think it would probably be worth while preparing ourselves for a couple of hours or more, physically and mentally, for such an event. Please keep me to this as well, if you agree to it. And I <u>do</u> like us to talk while we're doing it.

(Sun. morning)

Gosh! I was full of the rising sap last night. However you don't mind a few of the earthy details occasionally? I'm not becoming completely D.H.Lawrencish.[94]

I rang up home on the off-chance on Friday night, but you were at Portslade. Perhaps Pop didn't tell you that I invited you to ring me at Taunton 2698 Ext 13 on Saturday afternoon at 3. I stuck around the office on the off-chance, but I concluded you were too busy or something.

It's boiling hot again today, and I shall go a long walk this afternoon. There are some hills which look about 4 or 5 miles from here and I shall try to reach them. I don't know very many people at this camp yet, though there are a young architect and an economics student who are moderately interesting. The bother is that I tend to wait for my transfer to the A.E.C., though I understand that the staff at the Army School of Education at Wakefield is mostly on leave at the moment and the courses are not recommencing at present. Pop probably told you I was the only one of the <u>thirteen</u> finally recommended by the Board of Officers.

I took another class on Friday afternoon. I chose an introductory talk on "Economics" and showed them what commodities, booms, slumps, capital, money, values etc were. They seemed quite interested. I have now got permission to organise some French and German classes, and if I can get rid of a very temporary fit of lethargy which has seized me, probably due to a chill, I shall do some posters to put up in the NAAFI today.

Called round during the week to see some of our friends[95] in Taunton. They were quite pleased to see me and we shall probably get on quite well together. I hope that Wakefield business starts soon, however, since I am a bit tired of the uncertainty.

Well, I have locked the office so that no-one can come in. I have a bed-roll of Maj. Swyer's in here, and I think I'll have half-an-hour's nap. I haven't received those socks that Ma and you talk about, so they are either lost or following me around.

---

94 D H Lawrence was the author of *Lady Chatterley's Lover,* not published in Britain until 1960.
95 This will refer to Communist Party members.

Please "keep on going where you're going." Remember 1) lots of real friends (like John), 2) study and think, 3) not <u>too</u> many meetings, influence people outside.

Don't get too mooney about having a kid. We shall probably have to wait about three or four years now!!? Have you ever thought of returning to your Eton crop style for a time? I have your photo on my desk and I still think it's <u>grand</u>.

Ever so much love, Ron

I would love to have seen Mum's reply to that letter! Dad's next letter comes a week later, written in pencil again. It is headed by a pencil drawing, mainly of railings and a gateway, secure-looking gates with spikes on the top and an arch over it bearing the words "Welcome to Sherford". There are buildings behind the fence. In front is a sentry box and, just appearing over the lower edge of the drawing, what appear to be the helmet of a soldier and the bayonet of a rifle:

"A" Coy,
Sherford Camp
11 – 9 – 41

Dear Kath,

I am fed up with this leave business. They ought to put up the date when we are going and have done with it, instead of having all this going on as to whether one will be first on the rota or whether a week-end pass will alter the chances of "privilege" leave.

I shan't try for a week-end pass this weekend for the reason that I'm gambling on real leave or nothing.

It was interesting to hear about the Brighton town meeting with the Mayor's greetings to Yalta. Under whose auspices was that?[96]

Nothing very remarkable has happened, except that I've done a lot of reading. You may remember me buying "Spartacus," at 6d. in the Jackdaw Series.[97] All about my famous ancestor (!?) It was jolly

---

96 Yalta is a resort city in the Crimea, which was at that time threatened by the German invasion of the Crimea.

97 *Spartacus* by J Leslie Mitchell, pub, Jarrolds Jackdaw, 1937

good. I've also finished "Holy Deadlock" and lent it to the NAAFI girl I told you about.[98] Have you read Pritt's shilling book on "Our Ally"?[99] I've lent that to her as well. She's a very demure girl of 28, who was housekeeper to some old dame in the heart of Exmoor. I only see her over the NAAFI bar (you'll be pleased to know) since she's off in the afternoons and I'm off in the evenings.

I tried to get some French classes going recently but for some reason which I haven't really analysed correctly I didn't get the response. I think fellows are too unsettled in a Convalescent Depot. However I'm going to take some others soon over at a neighbouring barracks.

Sorry if this writing is bad. It's just that I feel lazy, full of unexpended energy and browned off.

Love RON

Above the "Love Ron" is a pencil sketch of three gloomy faces, a hill with two sets of what I guess might be stick soldiers firing at each other, and then arrows pointing to the far side of the hill where there is a caption: "END OF WAR".

Dad writes again the next day, much more neatly, in pen, on notepaper:

Taunton, 12 – 9 – 41

Dear K,

I have been told by the C.S.M.[100] that my 7 days will start "within the next week." I know this is vague but it seems more certain than anything else I have had. I shouldn't make any arrangements until I actually wire or phone.

Please let me know immediately when you know anything on the "Biological Front."

I have written acknowledging receipt of my socks to Ma. I also got the 10/- O.K. Thank Percy[101] for me about the bonus-query. I see from the

---

98   *Holy Deadlock* by A P Herbert, pub. Methuen, 1934
99   *The U.S.S.R. Our Ally* by D N Pritt, pub. Frederick Muller (1941). The author was an MP and barrister and will have a part in this story later.
100 Company Sergeant-Major
101 Eileen Ireland was then pregnant (see page 72).

"Chronicle"[102] that I can expect another 10/- a week, or is that "Pie in the Sky" as far as Brighton Council is concerned? Perhaps it will balance up the Income Tax a bit, will it? I have been doing a little more Pyccku ma bvencorockapoë lately.[103] I never got very far with it, but it's coming back.

I'm afraid I've been getting a bit lax with my main duty recently, but if I could have a bit of leave I could think about it and come back refreshed. The great difficulty is places, though I have not tackled the problem yet on really hard-thinking lines.

I don't know if I told you but I composed the entire report on Education for the Area this quarter. Should probably get £8 per week for that kind of job in civi life. It's probably at least up to the standard of old Sawbridge's work. (I hear he's got called up? Commissioning I suppose?)

I think I should almost certainly be sent from Wakefield back here. They seem to have taken a fancy to me. It may not be actually at the Depôt, but I may be a "pool" instructor and travel round the county, or along the North Coast. It's a tiring job waiting for news of this business.

Met an interesting Frenchman in the camp yesterday who is in English uniform for some reason. He was in Berlin in 1928 and claims to have known Thaelmann[104] personally. Lived in Alsace-Lorraine, was in Spain during the Civil War. But I suspect he was a member of P.O.U.M. so I'm steering clear of him.

Je suis allé danser hier soir à Taunton. Rencontré deux de nos médicos (R.A.M.C.) accompagnés de trois fillettes de la NAAFI. Je me suis attaché à la compagnie.

Je lis quelquefois un peu de l'allemand. Toujours le même livre.[105]

Have you had any more interesting science books? I hope you will keep an interest in such things even when you "go all maternal."

I think I shall try and do a little writing this evening, on the lines of the discussion the three of us had when we met. One tends to get a

102 *News Chronicle*, a daily newspaper generally supporting the Labour Party and the left.

103 I do not have a clue what that means or even what language it is.

104 Ernst Thälmann was leader of the Communist Party of Germany, later imprisoned and shot by the Nazis. P.O.U.M was the Workers' Party of Marxist Unification, a Spanish Trotskyist party.

105 I went to a dance yesterday in Taunton. Met two of our medicos (R.A.M.C.) accompanied by two NAAFI girls. I joined the group.

   I sometimes read a bit of German. Always the same book.

bit lazy in Camp because everything is so self-contained. Also being convalescents the chaps don't bother to walk far.

(Cont. in our next!)

Love Ron

Dad had his leave and must have spent it with Mum in Brighton, as he describes it in a letter typed on the Friday week after the last:

"A" Coy, Hut 13.
30 – 9 – 41.

Dear K,

In reply: a. I have never heard of a child psychologist called John Rickman.[106] b. I have seen "Love on the Dole" and I think it's marvellous.[107] c. I shall not be able to get a week-end off for a little while. We are unusually busy, with all the Tech and other school sessions opening up.

I was a bit disappointed with my leave. It was my own fault (and partly yours, perhaps). The old reason. I spent half the time in a dull brutish stupor, during which my only fear was that I should meet any of our friends, since I should appear too daft to speak to them. It also tired you very much, since you were not a bright conversationalist, except on one or two occasions when you woke up.

It was a horrible contrast with some of the good times we have had on "short leave."

Still, that being disposed of, we can discuss other matters. I must confess that I have felt one or two misgivings lately, as to whether you would become too much child-centred. I hope you won't. Study of the matter is good and that is obviously what you are doing, but I hope you won't dream about it and occupy yourself in chicken-like broody dozings about what a dream-child it <u>might</u> be.

Think of it a few times when it's roaring its bloody head off and you'll get a sense of balance.

---

106 John Rickman (1891-1951) was an eminent psychoanalyst and a founder of the therapeutic community movement. In 1941 he was editor of the *British Journal of Medical Psychology*. He was a Quaker.

107 Film about working-class poverty in the 1930s in Salford – with Deborah Kerr.

Tell me as soon as you want to come and live down here. I can start looking round for somewhere. Harold, one of my friends on the staff, has got his wife down. She is an awfully nice kid, as proletarian as they make them and with an intellectual interest that I think may be very deep indeed.

I have been over to a neighbouring location to teach some troops in training. It was quite interesting to see another place (it was a big one) and observe conditions a little more like my training place. There are also French lessons starting here under my aegis on Wednesday, though I don't know whether sufficient chaps will come and make it a go. The bigger demand seems to be for German so perhaps I may rub up that and give a few lessons. It is quite easy to teach in the elementary stages.

Have not had any time for reading during the last few days, but I mean to go down to the local library soon and have a "Field Day"; pay all my fines (which are not many) and get all the books I have been wanting to get. I hope we get old Dutt's book soon.[108] I think it's a bit of a swiz not bringing it out within a reasonable time. After all the ordinary publishers of books don't have all this fuss and I can't see why a man like Dutt should either. Conditions were much more difficult when he started writing it.

I hope my clothes have arrived home by now. I felt a little loth to leave them in the cloakroom as I did. However, I had a moderately satisfactory day in London and hope that much will come of it.

Well I must go to work now, so I will make this a short note and write further to you tomorrow or the next day.

By the way, please tell me whether you have told my Ma that I have had a full leave, because I have had a letter which asks why my last letter was posted in Brighton. Unless you have told her why I am just going to say that I have had a long week-end. It sounds as though I shall have to go and see her sometime. She gets a little wistful these days as to why I haven't been.

Yours with much love,
[signed with a flourish in pencil] Ron

---

108 *India Today* by R Palme Dutt, the leading theoretician of the CPGB, was published in 1940.

The next letter was dated three days later:

> (Moving into Taunton soon.)
> "A" Coy, Hut 13
> Sherford Camp.
> 3 Oct 1941

Dear K,

I did not tell you over the phone, but depression, now fast disappearing, also arises from a temporary lapse connected with my work. I am actually handling work of considerable responsibility and I made a slip connected with the appearance of a lecturer to a unit. It was a mere matter of overlooking some correspondence – you know so well how these things can happen.

I didn't get into a row about it, but it will teach me not to be so cock-sure as I was getting beforehand. After all, the worst mistakes can be learned from. I shall have to give more time and thought to planning the working of the office, its files, lists and other features. It isn't as though it were an uninteresting job, but it's difficult to make one's contribution to a great scheme from the confines of one little room. I do all the spade-work and others reap the effect; courses, discussions, craft-work, evening-classes etc.

Still, I am rapidly emerging from my despondency, as my stomach returns to normal.

I am just preparing a discussion on the "fourth chapter." On Tuesday we have a discussion down at the Education Centre, led by a friend of mine, under the auspices of the Army Education Scheme.

I forgot to ask whether my civilian clothes finally returned to Brighton, under the kindly eye of D. Incidentally I have very much changed my opinion of him. You may remember that when I saw him at first, at Johnny's, I was rather conscious of his "middle-class" appearance.

I think now that this was just prejudice on my part or guardedness on his, and I find him a splendid chap to talk to.

———————

It is a curious thing to say in the Army, but I am in a quandary about my very sedentary habits once more. I need exercise and an occupation for my hands. I think I shall have to look around for a guitar once again, and also go to the swimming baths a few times. My recent jaundiced view may have arisen from lack of exercise.

––––––––––

Please tell me how you feel personally about the child-to-be. Don't think because I warn you against broodiness that I don't want to hear about your thoughts. It would be impossible (and unwise if possible) to go through one of the greatest creative acts in the universe without realising it to the full & rejoicing in it.

Do you feel any different? – fuller, or maturer, or more cautious, or what?

There are some interesting people here; Gaier, the Frenchman, Seegelonde, also French; a member of the Non-Combatant Corps; a nice girl in the NAAFI, the NAAFI storesman, a decent young bloke in the massage-department called Wellet; James in the Q Dept., Dickie the masseur. Hope to get week-end leave this or next week-end.

– Love, Ron

Four days later Dad writes again, in pencil, on four sides of yellow notepaper:

"A" Coy, Hut 13,
Tues Oct 7. 41.

Dear K,

I've been overworked during the last week or two, organising the Short Course for Education Officers, but I hope you don't think I'm forgetful of you – and of what's going on.

The Padre of the Depot has asked me to serve on a sort of discussion group committee he's got going. It is quite interesting. He's very like all the other priests I've met, well-meaning but probably completely blind to the real world. However there's a virtue in his trying to start any discussions whatsoever. I'm opening the first "group" on "Can Democracy be Made Efficient?"

I think I shall take an evening off tonight, or go a long walk before seeing Harold and the others. I need some exercise and inspiration.

Would you mind sending me "Mathematics for the Million," please?[109] I know it's rather a big book, but I'd like to get a hold on the subject, which still baffles me a good deal.

I shall be glad when I've thrown off the foggy feeling engendered by the difficult spell of work. At such times it seems hard to grasp the real humanity beneath the mass of institutions, the Army Forms, the queues, buildings, the formalities. After all they are all aspects of purposeful <u>human</u> activity, aren't they? The war itself is a <u>human</u> activity, planned and achieved for human purposes, even if many of them are base.

But it seems hard to realise that when you are in it.

I remember the impression of a man in the last war, who said that a few months after war broke out all purposiveness seemed to disappear. He felt that the War was just a disease, something that grew and attacked you or families in London, or a thousand miles away.

Yet this is not the case. There are main laws of causation and purpose behind war. The only thing is it is difficult at certain times to discover them.

When I was in London I bought a book at Foyle's called "Feldpostbriefe von Schweizerische Deutscher" (Field-Post Letters – by Swiss Germans)[110]. The writers were ordinary Swiss soldiers, telling their families what was happening to them. It was one of the most touching things I have read. Yet even they did not seem to be gripped to the extent that we are.

Mother has not written to me since I explained about my letter being written in Brighton. I don't know whether she suspects about it and is really annoyed. It is a bit thin to expect her to believe that I haven't had any leave and I deserve any suspicion I get for being such a bloody liar.

---

109 *Mathematics for the Million* by Lancelot Hogben, pub. Norton, 1937
110 *Feldpostbriefe von Schweizer Deutschen* by Charlotte Grünberg, pub. Orell Füßli, Zürich, 1916

Well, it is now a quarter to four, and when I think that in pre-war days I should nearly be finishing work I could grind my teeth in envy of those left in the civilian world.

I think I'll walk out of the office and get a bit of sunlight for a few minutes.

Love,
Ron

On the following Sunday, Dad wrote in pencil from Bristol. He must have been tired, as he said, because he made more than one error!

Sherford (as before)
(written in YMCA Bristol)
Sun. 12th Oct.

Dear K,

I'm terribly sorry I didn't phone you as I promised. When I finished work today I was too tired to find a phone-box in the black-out. I acted as clerk to a conference of officers at the university and it was a rather gutty business. I had to run around and carry things for them, at the same time as I tried to look after the finance of the Conference (and you know how good I am at that).

Still, I got something of the intellectual measure of these people, and it was not very great, I can assure you. The result of my tiredness is that I am not buggering off to the edge of the city where my official billet is, but I'm going to stay here at the Y.M.C.A and blow the 3/6 expense. There's a nice little room here and it makes a great mental change. I only wish you were here with me.

I have not been to Bristol since I was about seven or eight years of age, and can recognise nothing but the famous Clifton suspension bridge. Last night I slept in a house next to the famous Clifton College (a real public school), now an O.C.T.U.

No-one seemed to know I was coming and I was rather coldly and uncomfortably lodged, so I shan't go back.

Discussion at the Conference was rather like a student teachers' weekend school, only very elementary. The worst contribution was made by an A.T.S. female officer, who didn't seem to understand her girls or their psychology in the very slightest. She was obviously a middle-class snob.

The best parts of the meeting were the two civilian lecturers, one on the historical background of the war and one on the economic aspects. The second was mainly concerned with transference problems in the labour supply field and on how to pay for the war. He said nothing about technical reorganisation, concentrating on improvement of production by consultation with the workers.

Well, I'll read a few lines of Longfellow's translation of Dante's 'Divine Comedy' and then to sleep.

Love

Ron

There followed a telegram dated "17 Oct 41", addressed to:

CREE BOOTS LONDON RD BRIGHTON
ARRIVING ADDINGTON 7.15 TONIGHT PHONE YOUR TIME
RTO PADDINGTON

The last line is clearly a correction of Addington. Mum must have still been known as Cree at work. Anyway, they obviously met up:

Hut 7, "A" Coy,

20-10-41.

Dear K,

I enjoyed the week-end very much. We were still not at our best, and still won't *[be]* until we've solved the usual problem, but we were obviously determined to enjoy each other's company and the determination (environment helping) won through.

Kew was even better than last time. The touch of dampness made it more attractive than the heat. Every tree and plant seemed moist, friendly and alive.

I seem to have balanced that blinking budget for the Course, after several fits. I'm beginning to see that maths is something like politics or the arts – determination is half the battle.

I have been working overtime tonight, so have not been able to do much else, but tomorrow is the A.E.C. discussion. "Democracy in U.S.A. and U.S.S.R," which should be very interesting. I have been asked to be Chairman, so I shall have a chance to guide the discussion fruitfully.

It's rather a bad subject, involving as it does comparisons between nations supposed to be allies, but if we play our cards carefully we can avoid invidious comparisons too much.

I have not had time to reply to my mother's letter of about a fortnight ago, so will close now and write again soon.

Love,

xxxxxxxx Ron

A week later, again on a Monday, Dad sent the following letter:

"A" Coy, 114 as before

27 Oct 41.

Dear Kath,

Confusion and chaos! We have been moving office! – though I am still in the same billet. Took all Sunday morning shifting files and boxes on to the Major's little utility truck. Then had rest of the day off. I went to the A.T.S. Company Office to try and interest the A.T.S. officially in our discussions. The subject of the one tonight is "Can Women Replace Men?" I succeeded in persuading an A.T.S. Serjeant to open it. We don't start for another hour or so; I don't know whether she'll come, but I rather think she will not dare to back out.

Today we moved [the] rest of the stuff to the new place in Taunton. It is rather a gloomy place, but no more so than the place at the camp. The bother is at present that I have to do a hell of a lot of walking up and down from the camp. This may be remedied within the next few weeks. However, when the files etc have got into a little order we shall tackle the private problems of the lower personnel.

I feel very tempted to ask you whether you will not give up the job and come and live out with me for even the (possibly) short time before I am transferred. It might be long time, on the other hand. What do you think of this? I might be able to find a furnished room or something of the kind and get billeting allowance.

Must run away to the Discussion (A.E.C)

Yours with much love.

xxxxxxx   Ron

The strain of living apart is showing further two days later when Dad writes again:

A Coy, Hut 7,

29 Oct 41

Dear K,

Fraid I've been a louse at writing again lately. Turmoil in the Office and increase of the other work in the evenings is still the reason.

I have met two or three more special friends in Taunton, including somebody in the A.T.S.

Being particularly browned off through not having time to think, I have been plotting to bring you down here to live, in spite of my temporary position. Don't you think we could afford it for a few month or two *[sic]*, or would it be asking too much to ask you to a strange place when I am working so hard? I am thinking while I write rather than doing any systematic planning, but what do you think about it?

Sally, Harold's wife, will probably be here for quite a time and you would almost certainly get on well with her.

I have recently been negotiating to get my meals down at Nunn's Field, near the office, so I shan't be so browned off next time I write.

Love

Ron

I think the following typewritten note was enclosed with the above letter:

Dear Kath,

I am absolutely in the thick of it at the moment, preparing an opening of discussion for an official Conference on Education that takes place tomorrow, but I can't resist the chance to slip a note in to say that I love you very much and want ever so much to see you.

As soon as the Conference is over I will take a big sheet of paper and tell you all about the exciting things we are doing (within the limits of the censorship law). I keep on trying also to get off a packet of cigarettes for my mother but I can't seem to get time to pack it properly.

Love,

Ron

Another two days pass before Dad writes again:

A Coy, Hut 7,

31-10-41.

Dear K,

The new office is a rather dingy second-floor suite over a cleaners, but being in the centre of the Town, in the main square. We have been hard at work getting straight since we came there.

Tonight I finished about 5.30, hopped out and bought a few buns from the NAAFI opposite, and by the time I got back a truck was waiting to take me for my weekly lesson to the camp just outside the town.

It was a pleasant change doing elementary French with the five people I have. I had a look at their NAAFI and inhaled the general atmosphere of the place each week. It is much more soldierly than our kind of Depot.

When I finally got back to Camp I was too tired to do much, except go down to the NAAFI bar, have a half a pint of shandy and eat a supper of rabbit & chips. Then I took some books along to the

Church (which is also a Quiet Room) and started to read. After a minute who should come in but James, the Economics student from Bristol, with a friend of his. We spent a pleasant ¾ of an hour putting some democratic ideas into the friend, who pretends to be a thorough pessimist, though he really isn't half so bad.

(Fri 1415 hrs)

This morning, for the first time since we moved, the office work seemed to go with a swing. We have a new set of telephones installed and are quite a little exchange on our own. I have not got thoroughly used to the slickness required to "keep calls on the line" while speaking to extensions and that kind of stuff, but I am pleased to find that I am not half so dud as I thought. And if you can operate a small switchboard you could have a smack at a big one in a pinch.

I'm sorry about the Brogan book. I lent it to Harold for the discussion we held and have only recently got it back. However, here it is.

I am a bit alarmed to hear about the parcel I sent. Hope my Army shirt, some handkerchiefs and several pairs (at least) of socks were in it. There was no letter. In future I will see that a list goes with any clothes I send.

Well, I have to start work now,

That letter ended abruptly with the comma. The next we have is dated 15 days later, on a Saturday:

Area Education Office,
6 Fore Street,
Taunton
15-11-41
(Tel 2215)

Dear Kath,

I think it might be simpler and speedier for you to address letters as above from now on, as they are much more under my own eye than if they went to the other place. If you send them as above you <u>can</u> put just Mr. etc.….

I put the scheme for the Education Centre to the O.M as soon as I got back and he agreed. So we have called a conference of pips from each unit and a number of civilians (including WEA and NUT) to discuss the scheme. Once again I am to open on it.

Have not yet done any flat-hunting, but will get the local paper today and see what's to be done. Also Harold, Sally and I are going out to a friend's house for tea (having got permission from the Major to leave early.) I may get some advice from the friend.

Have been very improvident as regards books recently. Bought
"The Remaking of Italy – "Pented" (Penguin 6d.)[111]
"Taxes on Knowledge" – Collet (Thinker's) 1/3[112]
"Splendeur et Misères des Courtisanes" – Balzac 2/6[113]
The bother is that the office is almost next door to W.H.Smith's and another fairly modern bookshop. So when I go down for my morning break the temptation is enormous and I fall. However I shan't buy any more, at least not for a bit.

I feel a bit homeless here at the present time, and would very much like a place with a bright light and <u>COMPLETE</u> SILENCE where I could study, think and write. Did an article for a London paper this week and one for Somerset County Gazette – submitted to Command for permission to publish.

– Yrs. with love
Ron.

On the following Wednesday, Dad sent a letter, closely written in pencil on the back of a flyer from the People's Press Fighting Fund, appealing to comrades for funds for the fight for the removal of the ban on the Daily Worker. The flyer was signed by Violet Lansbury:[114]

---

111 *The Remaking of Italy* by Pentad, pub. Penguin, London, 1941
112 *History of the Taxes on Knowledge* by C D Collet, pub. Watts, 1933
113 *La Comédie humaine: Splendeur et misères des courtisanes* by Honoré de Balzac, pub. Edmond Werdet, 1838-1847
114 Lifelong active member of the CPGB, daughter of George Lansbury

6 Fore Street,

Wed 19-11-41

Dear K,

I'm so glad that you have decided to come on Wednesday fortnight. I answered two adverts in the Press today which offered accommodation. Shall call them during the dinner-hour.

Today we had that Conference I told you about. They agreed to a general meeting to draw up the plan. It will be held on Dec 5th and should be a very important step in advance.

I am trying to think what you can do here. The first thing will be to have a rest from work, then to get to know a few people. I think you will like Sally and Doris Lorler of the A.T.S. What you want to do during the day-time depends very much on you. If we get the "Centre" going pretty quickly (before you become shy and retiring – if you do) perhaps you could preside over it a little bit. But I don't want to suggest you should help with my work too much, because you always get the dirty jobs piled on to you if that occurs. Or can we avoid it?

Have you ever thought of "borrowing a baby" for a few days to see how you could look after it, or do you think the experiment would be too risky?

If you see John will you remind him to put his name down for the Regional Cttee on Education of H.M.Forces c/o Staff Officer for Education, Military Area (Brighton), S.E. Command. If he can't find the people over there, couldn't he get released for a few weeks work in our Area. I think the Bristol Regional Cttee would welcome him and would certainly reimburse him to some extent.

Love Ron

A week later Dad typed the following letter:

6 Fore St.,

26 Nov 1941.

Dear K,

The address of the digs is:

The Manse,

14 Silver St., (off East St.,)

Taunton

I believe that buses go all the way to the corner of the street, but it is practically certain that I shall be able to come and meet you at the station at 5-14 p.m.

I will try and get time to call in and enquire about bed-linen and crockery and the other things you have asked me about. Sorry if I haven't replied to these things very promptly, but I have had a spell of increasing business, which will reach its high point about December 15th and then die down again.

The Old Man has asked me to open that discussion at the Bristol University course for officers. This is on the weekend of 12-15th at the University hostel. There is a dance on the Saturday evening and he has asked me to bring you, as well (I imagine) as to the rest of the course.

Will the time for retreat from such public exercises have arrived by then, or will it be possible for you to come? We shall have to pay your fare to Bristol but the accommodation and the course will be buckshee! What do you think?

(Thurs morn) Went to dance at the Empire Hall in town last night. It was fair to mediocre; I left at 10-40.

The Major has not yet come, so I have a few spare moments. Arrangements for the Conference on the Taunton Education Centre are fairly well in hand, except for a general circular which HQ seem a long time duplicating. We are getting a duplicator of our own at any time now, so we shall be able to turn out circulars as quickly as the Cause demands.

Have written several articles on Army education lately, for submission to HQ Publications (for vetting purposes). It's a terribly slow business, however, and they will probably have been passed by the time they are out of date.

I seem to have heard of this Naomi Jacobsen person you talk about. Is she Jewish, because if she is she has at least that advantage over ordinary Englishwomen. I have very rarely read anything by a woman novelist that I liked, but that may be my lack of contact with the world of feminine affairs. But stop! There is a Vicky Baum, who attracted me when I was about 18. I still read her with pleasure. She has just brought out two new books, I believe. One is called "Results of an Accident."[115]

Well, I shall have to start work now. Will send you details about the digs as soon as possible. We can always move out if the room is too small or we don't like the woman.

Love Ron

The next letter is also dated 26th November, so it was probably enclosed with the one above. It is typed as if it were an official letter but we presume it was sent to Mum to legitimise her attendance at the conference at Bristol mentioned in the last letter. There is a more personal hand-written note on the back:

Area Army Education Office,
6 Fore Street,
Taunton 2215.
26 Nov 1941.

Dear Madam,

Your attendance and advice are invited at a conference to discuss the running of a Taunton Army Education Centre, to be held in the Public Library, Taunton, on Friday December 5th 1941 at 7 p.m. This applies to any of your friends who have an active interest in such activities.

The Army Education Scheme is planned to foster lectures, discussion-groups, musical and art clubs, hobbies and a general interest in the democratic anti-Nazi cause of our armed struggle. It is realised that there are large numbers of soldiers with developed interests in various occupations, who have discontinued them since entering the Army. We feel sure that we can consult with you as to the means of reintroducing such pursuits and even linking them with the main fight that is going on.

---

115 Vicky Baum (1888-1960) was an Austrian-Jewish writer who migrated to the USA in 1938. She wrote *Incident in Lohwinkel, Results of an Accident* in 1930.

There is no suggestion of cutting down or overlapping with activities that are going on in several units, but only a Taunton Centre can take advantage of the facilities offered by a County town, draw in experienced civilians, co-ordinate unit efforts, maintain lists of speakers, and organise week-end schools on discussion-work, hobbies and other topics.

There are considerable difficulties in the way of such an idea, planned in war-time. Other armies, however, have set up vast organisations for dealing with the morale and "ideology" of their troops. Surely we can produce a "core" of people in this Area who will avoid regimentation of ideas and yet sustain and even create enthusiasm for the War effort.

Yours sincerely,

[signed] RVS for S.O.(Edn)

AREA EDUCATION OFFICE

On the reverse of this letter Dad has written:

P.S. Could you send or bring a large bottle of Drene (blue) shampoo for Sally (Harold's wife)? She will pay us.

That was the last letter Dad wrote in 1941. There are no more letters for a couple of months, probably because Mum came to live with him in Taunton for a while.

Chapter 6
Sergeant Instructor

Dad celebrated the start of 1942 by writing a poem:

Fleeting Glimpses

O pardon if
We press along the mountain path of war
And glimpse the foxglove only as we run,
The misty glades,
Glow-worms and laughter, music and the dance,
The slow record of wisdom if we scan
But hastily, as runners dressed to fight.

Such things were fit
For deeper musing, keener glance, the peace
Of book-lined rooms, the measured voice and tread
Of friendly argument beneath the stars,
The calipers and gauge, the plotted chart,
And certainty of scientific ways,
Yet we left them and sought the bitter fight.
Still they shall be
The buried seed-like plantings in the heart
To lead to reaping with the victory;
The sun-sprayed glades,
The fir-tree candles will be there to laugh
And nod to us in scented mountain breeze,
In victory and peace,
In victory.

RVS. 1.1.42.

The end of January finds Mum in Chesterfield, staying presumably with her Aunt Gertie – one of her mother's formidable five sisters. She knew them all well from her childhood in Sheffield as she would often go and stay with them, especially Gertie.

Dad has been posted to Wakefield in Yorkshire for a week or so, to train as a Sergeant Instructor in the Army Educational Corps. The next letter was written on a Saturday and it seems that Mum and Dad had met at his parents' house in Warrington. She then returned to Chesterfield while he went back to Wakefield, stopping to see the Chinese Vice-Consul in Manchester on the way:

Sjt. R.V. Spathaky, A.E.C.,
Army School of Education,
Parliament Street,
Wakefield,
31 Jan 42.

Dear K,

I hope you arrived safely. My journey seemed surprisingly short – as I saw the signs "Wakefield" on the seats I had to grab my kit and run.

The Chinese Vice-Consul in Manchester was quite helpful, though I don't think he had been to his own country for many years. He gave me a few useful things and let me read a lot of useful stuff. I was quite glad I went and I think the personal method of obtaining information (à la Haldane[116]) is always the best complement to book knowledge.

We won't post-mortem the Warrington stay, as agreed. I give it 55% as a "mark." What will you give it?

The School is quite nice so far. There doesn't seem much to do till Monday, but I don't feel like getting away from these blokes, since I may not even see fellow A.E.C. for a long time.

Will write developments,

Love

Ron

---

116 J B S Haldane, a well-known scientist working in genetics and related fields, and mathematics. He joined the Communist Party in 1942.

The dates of Dad's letters are often a problem. I have come to the conclusion that Dad got the month wrong in dating the next one and it was actually written on 3rd February 1942, a Tuesday (3rd January was a Saturday):

Army School of Education,
Wed. 3 Jan 42

Dear K,

Unfortunately the course has now been reduced to one week. I am posted back to Taunton, there being no vacancies at all where I wanted to go. They also refuse to consider week-end leaves from the school. So I shall be catching a train about nine o'clock on Saturday back to the jolly old stomping-ground.

It looks to me from a rather small-scale map here that Chesterfield is not too far off the London LNER[117] south from Wakefield. I shall go to the station today to enquire as to the possibility of breaking my journey there for a couple of hours. I would ask you to come to Sheffield for a little talk, but I don't think you ought to go about by train more than necessary – always admitting that you know best.

However, I will send a telegram to you today or tomorrow, as you suggest. Please don't think of leaving Chesterfield if it is nice there.

Love,

Ron

P.S. I opened the <u>only</u> discussion at the School. Not bad. The Capt. Instr. said it was very good and showed a "depth of knowledge."

We have only a few surviving letters written <u>to</u> Dad during the war. This one is from Mum's parents, Annie and Sid Cree, founder members of the Communist Party of Great Britain in the early 1920s. I am sure it has only survived because Dad used the back of it as page 3 of his letter of 15th February 1942. The letter is on headed notepaper in Annie's handwriting:

---

117 London and North Eastern Railway

PHONE:

PORTSLADE 9084

49, HANGLETON ROAD,

HOVE, 4.

Sunday 1st Feb

Dear Ron,

Enclosed find book as Kath requested, also W. N. & Vs[118] with an article on Army education which I thought you might like to see.

We are so glad that you have at last got a fair chance and I am sure you will come out O.K.

We are keeping the flag[119] flying as well as we can so the boys won't be ashamed of us when they come back.

Good Wishes,

Mam & Dad

The following Friday, 6th February, Dad addresses a postcard to Mum at her Auntie Gertie's house, where she was somewhat snowbound:

[To:]

Mrs Kath Spathaky,

132A Derby Road,

Chesterfield,

Derbyshire

A.S. of E.

6 Feb 42.

Dear K,

Will be catching 8.50 L.M.S.[120] Wakefield Saturday a.m. Shall probably be able to break my journey at Chesterfield for the night. I shouldn't come to the station, however. I will get a bus out to the address. If I can't manage it at the last minute, I'll wire from the Wakefield P.O. on Saturday morning.

---

118 *World News and Views,* a Communist Party periodical
119 Red of course!
120 London, Midland and Scottish Railway

Thanks very much for the jolly fine letter, which I have already read and reread several times. Do you feel alright? I expect you will be healthy if snowbound.

We have got some sort of a musical show or lecture this evening – "Music for the Troops" – Love Ron

Dad was to be based at a convalescent depot at Sherford, near Taunton, Somerset, to look after the educational needs of the convalescing troops. He received a promotion to Sergeant on 8th February 1942, although there is no reference to this in the letters we have until a month or so later.

Here is the next letter we have:

No S/254248
114 Condepot,
15-2-42. Sunday 6 o/c

Dear K,

I am writing this in the Reference Library where I am recovering for half-an-hour from the week's work. It has been a pretty tough job and promises to be still tougher. But I'm not chained to a typewriter. There's human material to deal with, which makes all the difference.

I now find that the day-time Educational activities exist very much on the margin of the medical parades and regradings – almost like a big divisional ante-room, but it's worth it for all that, since we may be able to evolve something more fundamental to the life of the Depot. The evening voluntary activities promise to be good – as I always thought.

Jimmy[121] is still slipping off most week-ends to continue his protracted courtship. Why they don't go and have a good cut off the joint I can't imagine. I'm sure he wouldn't feel half so "metaphysical" about the whole business. At least they would know where each other stood, even if they didn't like that knowledge quite as well as they thought.

They had already arranged a debate when I came – on "Idealism or Materialism" with Taunton College (or rather Queen's College).

---

121 Jimmy is mentioned over a dozen times in Dad's letters (on pages 116, 119, 121, 133, 160, 161, 177, 196, 199, 200, 220, 236 and 534). We learn that his surname begins with A and that his wife is named Vera, but no more.

I'm sure this is well above the heads of most of the fellows, but since they have started it they will have to see it through. This takes place on Tuesday next.

I have got a bunk[122] to myself at the moment, though there is another empty bed in it. I have not yet succeeded in lighting a fire in it but I shall do so one evening this week if I want to stay in & read.

There is rather a lot of handicraft about this job and I shall have to learn it as best I can.

Could you please send: 1) some tooth-paste 2) some money – I missed pay-parade 3) Sooner or later Capital[123] & the guitar.

Hope you feel O.K.

Love,

Ron.

Dad writes again three days later. It's a measure of how fast and reliable the postal service was then that the money (and I presume the toothpaste) had already arrived:

Condepot,

18.2.42

6 p.m.

Dear K,

Thanks very much for the letter and the money. As you may have guessed, I missed pay parade. I shall get it this week instead. I will return the 10/- if I can. Did not think of cashing a cheque (if I have one – haven't looked) till after I had written.

Have just sewn on two buttons and strengthened the stripe on one overcoat arm. The fire in this bunk which I share with another bloke has been a bit troublesome this evening. It is a little Army pattern coal and coke stove and objects to being fed with coalite dust. However, it's roaring away now. I am sitting at the regulation table-cum-desk at the

---

122 Dad uses the word 'bunk' throughout his letters to mean his room, not his bed.
123 *Das Kapital* by Karl Marx, (Vol. 1) pub. Verlag von Otto Meissner, Hamburg, 1867

window and looking out over the other serjeants' hut and (if I shift a bit) the hills at the back (near where we walked several times).

I have been mainly concerned in a whirl of administration as yet and not much teaching except Current Affairs and supervision of the French and German (native) language instructors. Also the voluntary work in the evenings.

In my last scrappy note I forgot to answer your interesting question about music.

Music, like drama, has certainly been divided into descriptive (Romantic) and the more formal (Classical) types. Our old "Tyl Eulenspiegel" of Richard Strauss or Debussy (in a strange way) were examples of the descriptive, and Mozart (generally) or Bach of the formal. It strikes me that where modern music combines both, like old Beethoven did ("Moonlight Sonata"?) or Shostakovich, it is on the right lines; where it claims to be a departure from both it is probably all balls! The stuff with lots of discords claims to be very revolutionary but it's probably anarchistic balderdash, though one must allow for genuine experimenters, obviously (Debussy, Honneger? Duke Ellington in jazz, George Gershwin in Rhapsody in Blue, American in Paris, Dog Ballet[124] – I believe the last name is incorrect).

The letter from Thomas is quite interesting, isn't it. Even though I make it a rule never to acquire new correspondents (and even to shed old ones – if they're not "good"!) I'm afraid I must reply to it, since it contains a request for information and it would be mental dishonour not to give this.

Perhaps there's a genuine clue there on how to get me to write.

If you see any interesting books in Hove Library on simple utilitarian war-time poster-work, leather-work, book-binding, or map-reading you might let me know the titles and I can get them through the Taunton P.L. I know the Dryad series and that's all.

Hope you and he/she (?) are well

Love

– Ron

---

124 I think, since ballet was a main theme of the film, this refers to a number called *Walking the Dog* in the film *Shall We Dance*.

Dad wrote again five days later:

23, Feb 42

Dear K,

The evening work here is voluntary, both on the part of the patients and of the A.E.C. staff (blast it, my fire has gone out!). I expect to get quite a lot of support from the chaps I know, when the preliminary stages have been passed (calling of committees, drawing up of plans in conjunction with the W.O.I etc). Jimmy is certainly of little help at the moment. Unfortunately I haven't seen much of him since I got back, though we went to the pictures once together.

We have got the R.S.M. to agree to one concession, which will be important. I have permission to go into the Men's Mess and Canteen to contact them. This means a hell of a lot in this camp – though the patients' own mistrust has to be broken down.

The learning, and then teaching, of a little handicraft is inevitable. We are going to attend the local Art School for one afternoon a week, Ind[125] taking carpentry and myself leather-work. I don't object to this by any means at all. It will perhaps balance up a bit.

Very sorry to learn about Doris.[126] Give her my love and tell her to cling on – she's not in the Forces yet!

I will certainly send the back pay when I get it. I shall get, presumably, 8/9 a day or £3-1-3 a week. What will your allowance be? What do you suggest I send home out of my part? (Don't be shy about it!)

It seems fairly possible that I shall be able to have my leave just after the baby is born. W.O. I Ind knows all about the position and is quite a reasonable kind of cuss. He'll pilot the pass through safely if he can.

I'm just going to collect my thoughts now for the discussion group, which is on "Japan" tonight.

– Love Ron

---

125 "Ind" is the surname of a colleague – Warrant Officer Class 1 Ind.
126 Doris was Mum's brother Gordon's wife. Like Mum, she was nearly six months pregnant; my cousin Helen was born ten days after me.

The cringeworthy music lesson continues:

114. 1-3-42.

Dear K,

I have not got your letter here (at the Kriegers') but I remember most of it and they have turned off the radio, so I can think up a few answers to the questions you ask. First, about Classical Music: this was a feature of the increasingly tyrannical feudal despotisms of the 18C and of the sycophantic courtly salons that grew up. Emotional lives, like all other aspects of existence, became formalised, stately and conventional. Music was a matter of mathematical exercise rather than anything else. But the position was complicated by the fact that some of the patron-oppressed musicians refused to express the trite ideas of their masters.

Beethoven was really the first to break free from the conventions that restricted Haydn and Mozart.

It is true, however, that Beethoven's work has a <u>structure</u> – it is not an uncoordinated urge like some of Schubert's (I understand).

Within the old convention much great music was written, in spite of what I have said. Bach infuses a rich dignity and even gaiety into the stiff texture of his fugues and canons.

Romantic music brought freedom, however, and was probably a progressive factor. Many of the Romantic compositions are associated with the French Revolution. (?Schubert)

Compared with classical music it has a sense of elevated emotion, intensity, idealism. It is directly connected with drama (or real life) like Richard Strauss's Tyl Eulenspiegel. In this sense you are right in saying it is nearer realism.

But Strauss's stuff meanders very often and hasn't the enormous control over the figure-patterns that Bach had. It relies more on richness of <u>tone</u> than on <u>pattern</u>.

I should think the world would be best served by the musicians who welded what was best of Romanticism (the feeling & "colour") with the pattern and learning of classical music. Personally I have never met anyone except Beethoven who did this, except possibly Shostakovich, but I wouldn't be certain of the latter.

As to your point about the source of inspiration of the Classical composer, he would probably have replied that he gained inspiration through study of masters of earlier ages – Scarlatti for instance.

The Romantic would claim inspiration from life.

I heard the actual programme that you listened to – the Lohengrin is good isn't it?

A good book is Percy Scholes' Handbook of Music & Musicians[127], or the Encyclopaedia Brit article on Music. There's a very good series on the wireless on Tuesdays at 1-30 p.m. called "The Orchestra Speaks." You would find these very helpful if you want to learn to pick out the various instruments of the orchestra.

Thanks very much for the Drene. The only thing I could do with is a good electric light bulb for my bunk. Have you still got the ones we had in Taunton?

I may get some 48 hrs leave in 3 weeks' time.

Love
Ron

Dad's next letter was dated 7th March and postmarked "TAUNTON 8 MCH 1942", which was a Sunday. It's lucky it was kept in its envelope for over seventy years. It was addressed to:

Mrs. R Spathaky,
49 Hangleton Rd,
Hove, Sx.

Mum has written in pencil on the envelope: "Finance letter". It seems a little weird that he is writing this letter later on the day they parted – according to the following letter, dated 8th March – and it was therefore possibly posted in the same envelope.

---

127 Although Scholes wrote several books with similar titles, such as *The Concise Oxford Dictionary of Music,* I cannot find a reference to this one.

Sat. 7.3.42.

Dear K,

Sorry I have slowed down the rate of correspondence a little. First, as to actual questions:-

(1) I'll leave the guitar till my leave. Thanks a lot for the heavy tome. The clock will be welcome, though I struggle through.

(2) It is not "physical considerations" that prevent me coming home, but the fact that we have hardly turned over the soil of this depot. I can't at the moment lay myself open to the fault for which I blame Jimmy.

(I think "Anne Gwendolin Spathaky" is perfectly bloody, especially the Gwendolin, which sounds like a cross between a mandolin and a Welsh mountain.)

I can probably get home for a 48 hours on the 21st-22nd March, unless the W.O. goes on his privilege leave that week-end, but I'll make you a promise – I'll write a really long and detailed letter, much better than I've done before, and within the next fortnight.

(3) I will send Brogan's book on U.S.A[128] home at earliest opportunity, also the "Short History," which I have been trying to exchange for the French edition for months.

(4) I'm afraid the Budget is not quite as good as your Budget Speech made it appear, Mr Chancellor. I should have been paid this week the extra, but wasn't. The Coy have promised to publish it in Orders today. In the Pay Warrant my rate seems to be laid down at 8/3 a day (not 8/9) – the reason is that War Pay or something is not paid now. I'll go into it deeper when I can get a look at the Warrant. This gives:

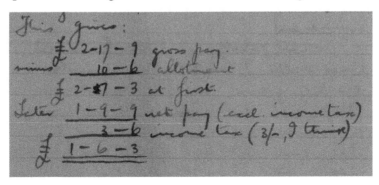

128 *The American Political System* by Denis Brogan (London, 1933)

Actually I have the form from the office whereby, as soon as it is published in Orders, I can increase your allotment. I can carry on with the same amount as I have been getting, 12/6 a week.

So actually our combined gross income is £3-5-9,[129] from which 11/- income tax has to come, leaving £2-14-9. If I draw 12/6, you will have £2-2-3d (always remembering that the income tax is, I think, 3/- & not 3/6d.)

If you want to consider items to be cut down on your Budget, I suggest

	OLD	REVISED
Light and heat (Summer)	4-0	2-0
Insurance	1-6	6
Fares	2-0	1-6
Entertainments etc.	3-0	2-6
Clothes	4-0	3-6
	14-6	10-0
Saving		4-6

Also I think you ought to reinvestigate the 30/- for housekeeping and rent. If the Sgts. Mess has their way this would be my Budget:

Income	Expenditure	
Pay 12/6	Beer	12/6

But I'm rapidly becoming T.T due to the sight of the hogs swilling it down.

By the way, I never suggested Michael John, and I don't like it – I suggested John Michael.

Congratulations on putting on weight! I hope you don't feel too distressingly like a barrage balloon. Don't forget that, like a wart on your nose, it always feels 10 times bigger to you than to others.

---

129 Mum has entered a correction to this figure. There is an arrow in blue pen from the £3-5-9 to a space on the right where the figure £3-15-9 is written, also in blue and in Mum's handwriting.

Jimmy, Yahoda[130] (a Czech), the Kriegers and self are going to the flicks this evening. Tomorrow I'm preparing a couple of sessions of a special kind I'm addressing next week-end.

More soon,

Love Ron

P.S. Have Coxhead and Shilton returned books?

As mentioned, the following letter was written on the Sunday, the day after they had parted, unless Dad is referring to the previous Saturday (28th February). That seems unlikely as he made no reference to it in his letter of 1st March:

S/I, Spathaky, A.E.C.
114 Convalescent Depot,
Sherford, Taunton, Som.
8.3.42.

Dear K,

For some reason I felt glummer about our parting on Saturday than I have felt on any occasion. I think it was because you looked so fit and happy, and there was all the possibility of a happy couple of days – except the permission to have it.

Not that I'm anything but glad at your obvious perkiness.

I arrived uneventfully at the Depot at 11-45 p.m. and slept in James' bed so as not to rouse the blanket-storeman. James was on a week-end pass.

Today they have shifted me into the Serjeants' bunks, with three other chaps who are in the P.T. line. I haven't actually seen them yet since they have not been in the room, but the P.T. Corps are generally pretty decent.

R.S.M. Laidlaw is moving out today and I have a new boss, an old regular who looks quite a sensible fellow, though our qualifications are curiously varied. We shall probably get on well together after further acquaintance.

---

130 Gustave Jahoda, psychologist and author of *A History of Social Psychology: From the Eighteenth-Century Enlightenment to the Second World War*, pub. Cambridge University Press, 2007. See also pages 125, 130 and 177.

I have not been in touch with Swyer yet, but on the face of it I am one of the two full-time education personnel of the camp. This will entail quite hard work and I doubt if he will be able to draw me into the office work much. The Depot needs an office-apparatus of its own and actually has one.

Met Harold accidentally this morning and he carted me off to lunch at Mary Street. Sally looked as blooming as ever and Dickie came in in the afternoon. I presented your love to him and he said he wished John Michael were here to dangle on his knee.[131]

We listened to a wireless concert, including Beethoven's 4th and César Franck's Variations Symphonique, both of which I recommend. The 4th is much lighter and more lyrical than the 5th which we had. Apparently old Ludwig was muchly in love when he wrote it (According to Dicky).

I must finish now and write an answer to my Ma's letter. Letters etc. had better be sent to the Convalescent Depot. I shall certainly be quartered here for a time.

Please keep on loving me. I think the kiddie will probably mean "the first signs of daylight" as regards some of our problems, even if other (and higher) ones take their place.

Love,

Ron

A week later, Dad writes again:

March 15 42.

Dear K,

I'm sorry I didn't come home this week-end, but we had something special on hand and I just couldn't drop out of it. On the other hand the W.O. I suggests I try for 48 hours during the week. Since a good deal of my work is done at the week-end there seems no good reason why I shouldn't. If I can get it backed by the O.M. within the next fortnight I may surprise you by coming in <u>one</u> Tuesday or Wednesday night. Will you warn John?

---

131 How did Dickie, or Dad for that matter, know I was going to be a boy?

I have received my increased pay and it has been duly registered in orders, so the form to the Education Office will go off straightway. You should get at the same time as this £8 (money-order) which is the back pay since I got my stripes i.e. since Feb 8th. I suggest in future I get a paying-in book at Barclay's bank if I have any such financial transactions.

I have also sent in the form asking for 2/3 of my pay to be sent to you (two-thirds of total). This is the limit according to regulations, but I will send all except 15/- in practice and if you want me to cut my own amount down don't hesitate to say so – I <u>could manage</u> on 5/- or so at a pinch but it would be a rather narrow existence. I should enjoy it if it meant you or the babe were getting something you needed, however.

As I have been working solidly for most of this last week I am thinking of going down to the pictures with the Kriegers this evening. Sally says thank you very much for the Drene and wanted to kiss me (so that I could pass it on to you) but as Harold was there and I might have enjoyed it too much the scheme for repayment was abandoned. But joking apart, she was jolly glad of it and it put us all in a good humour.

I do not find my sexual desires exorbitant during this period of abstinence. There is however the inevitable mounting up of desire and secretion of spermatozoa, which is automatic. The result of this is that I masturbated on one occasion, but the only self-defence I can think of is that I don't seem to have nocturnal emissions, which are the normal way of disposing of the fluid. I think it is important after a certain time (a month of two) that it should be got rid of, though I am not certain and don't like the idea of masturbating.

I have been reading quite a lot – Bill Rust,[132] L. Research, P and Nat Front, Volunteer for Liberty,[133] Victory in '42, LM[134] and WNV,[135] so I spect I'm as up to date as most of you people. I am beginning, with the spring weather, to feel as fit as a fiddle, though one week-end

---

132 William Rust, Editor of the *Daily Worker*
133 Journal, *Ejército Popular de la República*, Brigada Internacional, XV (Madrid 1937-1938)
134 *Labour Monthly,* a publication associated with the Communist Party
135 *World News and Views*, a Communist Party publication

a little while ago I had a slight touch of "incipient flu'" which sent me to bed for an evening.

How do you feel? Do your colds lessen? You must try and get every bit of spring sunshine that you can, so that the somewhat inevitable dangers of the winter are repaired.

This is not the long epistle which I promised, but a trial run before I really burst into it. After lecturing to the "boys" all the week-end I should not be able to sustain a high note for very many pages.

Tragedy – I have lost (or had pinched) one of my pairs of woollen pants. I don't know whether to get a new pair from the Q.M and pay, or wear my pairs of running shorts alternately with the other pair, or have I another pair at home. Have you any advice? To cheer you my money will be 8/9d a day. I don't know whether any of the pay revisions recently announced will benefit us, but I hope so.– Love, Ron

There follows a letter dated 23rd March 1942 to Dad from the Brighton Borough Treasurer's office, claiming that he was overpaid for February and telling him they would be withholding his war allowance "until the total overpayment has been recovered." The Borough's involvement must be related to the fact that they were his employer before he was called up. Dad sends the letter to Mum with this comment in the margin:

This looks pretty blue. I'll write and ask them to do as they suggest.

The issue crops up again in his letter of 12th April. Meanwhile he sends a pound note with his next letter to Mum a few days later:

Enc: £1

28.3.42.

Dear Kath,

Just a short note to be followed by a longer one. The W.O. has been on leave ever since I came on leave and it has been one huge scramble. Next week I hope to have a little more time and will write more.

Jahoda and I are sitting in the Reference Library of the town, to which we have fled from the camp. We have just been talking to one of the librarianesses – a rather flirtatious but very young (and probably gullible and shallow) girl of about twenty.

The bother about the W.O. being away is that we generally share out the jobs to be done. He does all representation to higher authorities, contacts with the outside world, finance. I do all the interior economy – instructors, apparatus, registers, Current Affairs, stock, organisation of new classes.

This appears to be a good division of work, but it is a hell of a lot for one person to do. However, it's been grand doing it and the voluntary instructors work like blazes.

I still have the whole of my £2 in my pocket from last week's pay-day. I think I had better get a crossed P.O. or a money order, since it seems very difficult to get down to the bank.

There were two evenings of this week taken up by social events (compulsory) in the Sergeants' Mess. They are both terribly boring and I came away half-way through the second – a dance. The company of a Somerset Light Infantry mess is terrible somehow and I can't understand why it is. The specialist sections of the Camp, P.T., Medical, etc. (except Education) avoid the place. Perhaps it is their fault because they allow the show to be dominated by the old Somerset "sweats."

I want to take this evening off for reading, if I can make it. Otherwise it will be a week of hard work but not much progress intellectually.

Hope you are well,

Love Ron

The next few letters are typewritten on lined paper torn from an exercise book. This one was written on a Monday:

30 Mar 42.

Dear K,

I hope you got my last scrawl safely, together with the £1 enclosed. As soon as I can get down to the bank I will put in another 12/- or so.

Will that be alright for this last week's money? I imagine you have not got your increased allotment yet, but I would like you to let me know as soon as you have received it as I want to stop them from paying me too much at the Depot. The Pay Office work here on the very empirical system of paying a man the same as the preceding weeks on his pay-book, until they get a violent jab from someone, either the man or the P.M.

Have just got in from a discussion opened by Dicky, which was very interesting, on "Recent Films." He is a little sectarian and high-falutin' in his description of art and all that, but he was helped in a way I was not in my student days by his legal training which makes him explain things very clearly.

Your news about the Government leaflet is rather disturbing, although it is the kind of thing we ought to expect. I personally don't think there will be all that danger during the next few months, but as someone pointed out in the press recently, we have a habit of underestimating the Nazi strength. I should really consider the possibility of going to the farm for a few months. Organised maternity services may not be so hot in Chesterfield but if you could get in touch with a really good midwife or doctor through your relatives it might be worth the risk. I'm very sorry to have to say that I must leave it to you to work out for yourself. It depends on several things that I can't estimate from this distance; the attitude of your relatives to your coming, the expense, your commitments with the Brighton medical services and the commitments you have with your Ma, but I wouldn't think the latter would stand in your way if you felt safer further North.

Remember the old rule; talk it over with your most trusted friends, listen to all their objections and advice, and then make up your own mind. I wish I could be with you to give what little protection a man can give his wife. I know you will have courage, however, whatever happens, and while you have that you need never regret what you do. Also you will be certain that you have my love – more than ever these days – I have staked a claim to your love which can't be lightly waved aside.

The W.O. has been on leave ever since I came from Brighton and I have had a really hectic time. The job is a terrific one for one man, but I have had a lot of help from all kinds of people on the Depot. The voluntary instructors in the Depot have been splendid – and have very often received scant treatment after hard work in charge of a particular section of the place. But Ind has come back, almost as I put this in the post and things should be a bit lighter. I shall have a bit more time to prepare my Current Affairs.

Sunday evening I got an invitation which I prized very much. One of the former staff of the Queen's College opposite took me over to a special service at the College. A mixed boys and girls choir sang a Bach chorale, a service in Latin. It was impressive in the extreme and shows one of the things in bourgeois art that is worth preserving – the music of Bach.

Please forgive these short letters, I promised you a long one didn't I?

Love Ron

Dad wrote the following poem, which he dated "2.4.42":

Wartime Spring

Along the sunlit Sherford street
Trees blossoming
Make April gentler than loving hands.
Against the glare
Of painted sheds buds glow
And catkins nod.

I have seen dawns that beckoned me
Beneath grey clouds
To where bright bars of light
Glowed over cool hills;
An omen and a promise
Of days to come.

So spring leaps in,
A dark-haired boy with merry classic face,
Smiling at death and age,
Sturdy with pride
In his own energy and gracefulness,
To laugh our solemn faces all to shame.

The next letter is dated nearly a week after the last. It is now April, and Mum has moved back to Brighton from Chesterfield. With the baby due in May, Dad starts thinking about how life will change. There's some erotic sex talk again in this one:

5-4-42.

Dear K,

Was rather worried by reports of a S.E. town being blitzed, but I imagine you are all safe and sound. Hope you are not frightened by the nurse's comments at the hospital. You always had rather brown patches under the eyes, even before you started the jolly old breeding business. Just like these ruddy people not to tell you anything that might lead to confidence but to concentrate on some little detail that they probably don't know anything about, anyway.

I don't know whether I told you when I last wrote, but I ate some hard dinner in the middle of last week and have had some bad attacks of indigestion and browned-offness ever since. I have just got some large size vegetable laxatives from the MI room so I am hoping to be back fit and fresh in the old educational harness tomorrow. It is annoying not to feel absolutely on top of the job. Still, even small respites, such as the indigestion (plus Easter) forced on me, have had their recompense. I have had time to think about the job and am turning over in my mind a memorandum to give to the Old Man on the state of the Educational Centre.

Glad to hear that you went to Eastbourne and breathed a different atmosphere for a short time. Wish I could force myself to get a train to Weston or somewhere for an hour or two – but I have been thinking vaguely about doing that for the last six months. There are also the Quantocks, which are within walking distance, but which I never seem to get to.

Enclosed find £2, which I have devised no means of getting down to the P.O. to change. I will try and register money from now on. I have sent a second Army Form 0 193 to the P.M. to get your allowance increased. You know that there is a slight increase on top of <u>that</u> from the recent Scale Changes? It's not more than a bob or two a week I believe.

I have also sent an AF 1483 to ascertain the state of my credits (or debits).

I am thinking a lot about you these days. I suppose I shall undergo quite a lengthy eclipse when the baby arrives – what a blow! Or is that another bourgeois legend? You don't seem to view me with any different feelings so far, so that I can only hope that I will still play a part in your feelings. You'll have to make an extension to your emotional life, rather than put a partition up and cut the accommodation in two. Is that possible?

I know all this will be merely theoretical to you at the moment (as it seems to be in a way for women at other times) but I must confess that unfulfilled physical desire just about eats me up during the last week or two. I reflect with the most inflamed sentimentality upon the hearty fucks enjoyed by us in the past – and out of 500 odd I think you'll agree there must have been quite a number of good ones. If a woman were to offer herself to me on a platter, so to speak, with no technical problems, no sentimental bargaining and no possibility of an aftermath, I should probably fall.

But since such persons probably only exist in the throbbing minds of adolescents and expectant husbands there seems to be no danger. Especially as you know I am erotically lazy and find myself rapidly cooling off at the very thought of having to pursue a female, or <u>make arrangements.</u>

Anyway, this is just to say that I hope you will not have lost an interest in <u>this</u> side of the love instinct, when you have rested from your present labours. How long did you say a woman has to wait?

You say opinion on the war seems divided between the "can't move-ers" and the "already won-ers." I think most ordinary people's opinions are in agreement that something could be done on the Continent; it is only the Munichites who hold us back. Just imagine what a mobilisation of resources and of opinion would have taken place if the eastern ally had been another imperialist power, in whose territory our own capitalists had large-scale holdings. Can one imagine that more would not have been done?

With all my love

Ron

A week later Dad typed another letter:

12.4.42.

Dear K,

Your epistolary style seems to progress from height to height as your matronly burdens increase. I like hearing of where you've been in Brighton, who you've seen, what's different in the town and what's the same. I see, for instance, that old Frank Ingham kicked the bucket the other week. It seems quite a fixed rule among these hardy bathers to die of heart failure, doesn't it?

We had last Monday off. I can't just remember what I did but I don't think it was very important. I think I just went a walk with Jahoda, our tame Czech (now just posted) and argued about Haldane's book "D.M. and Science."[136] I don't know whether you've seen it. It's a 3d. L.M. publication and one of the best things I've read.

On Tuesday I did some big Current Affairs classes during the day and inspected the Map-Reading class of one of our convalescent corporals during the afternoon. He was quite good in his manner of presentation but did not chop the instruction up into small enough bits – the old fault of amateur tutors (said he priggishly!). He took the criticism very well, however, and will probably take notice of it.

---

136 *Dialectical Materialism and Modern Science* by J B S Haldane, published in four parts in *Labour Monthly*, June, July, September and October 1941

Tuesday more Current affairs and a voluntary lecture on "Epstein" by a professional sculptor in the evening. Unfortunately not many people turned up to the latter, but there was, as always, a jolly good explanation. Instead of going to it I had to attend a Quiz competition at a neighbouring unit, to act as Questionmaster. This was quite amusing. Wednesday a double dose of Current Affairs and in the evening the preparation of a talk on India for the voluntary discussion group (shifted to Friday this week). A group of debaters went down to the local Toc H to debate the subject of "Equal Pay for Equal Work" this evening, and thoroughly trounced them – Dickie and James well to the fore in the trouncing, as usual.

On pay afternoon I can't remember what I did – oh, yes I can, I went to the Gaumont with Dickie. There was a good and long show: "The Bad Lands of Dakota" (a real old Western but done in a modern style, i.e. with a few ideas in it). Then there was a jolly good Soviet film – "100,000,000 women."[137] Then a good March of Time about the Argentine[138]. Then lastly the main picture, but for the life of me I can't remember the title of it or a single thing about it.* However, it was good, I think. In the evening I went on with the preparation of the discussion on India.

Friday I got notice from the O.M. that I should have to spend a few days in the Office while Owen was on leave. It was quite interesting to do this, to see what had changed since my absence – and what hadn't! I have to go in tomorrow morning as well, but after that I shall not be needed.

Since I started this letter I have heard something that rather changes my outlook. I may have to go and work in the country not far from Taunton, and serve quite a number of units, using a motor-bike as transport. This will be quite interesting in a way. I shall certainly like to ride a bike, as it will at least be a step towards understanding that most important of things in a modern way, the internal combustion engine. The organising work, from all points of view, will obviously be much less certain and less schematised, but it will be a bit freer in other ways.

137 An 8-minute film by the Soviet War News Film Agency (1942)
138 *The March of Time: The Argentine Question* (March 1942), an American short monthly film series sponsored by Time Inc.

I'm putting in for a pass this next week-end. I may not get it, but on the other hand they may allow it. If you don't think we can afford the outlay for the rail fare say so in your next letter and I will probably hitch-hike, or at least part of the way. In any case it would probably be almost as quick as coming by rail – the trains wait such a dickens of a time at Westbury.

Dickie and I went a bit of a stroll round with Peggy and Molly, whom you know (I think), the other evening. I hope you don't mind – or rather I know you won't, but I always tell you whenever I have anything to do with any woman, however slight the acquaintance may be. We drank a coffee in the "Three Mariners," which is a tea-shop in the High Street (the one that leads down to the Park gates). Actually there was a particular reason for our little confab, which I will tell you about.

The Brighton Borough Treasurer has apparently revised his views on what he should and should not give me. I've just had a letter telling me that from April 1st 1942 I have an Army increase of 3/6 per week. Therefore I must now repay the amount in respect of the period from 8th to 28th Feb 42 – £6-5-5. This is minus the amount payable for the month of March – 15/8. Total repayable – £5-9-9. So I shall write immediately and offer to pay them 5/- a week; then I can do it out of my money this end. Actually I will try and pay it into the bank or send it to you. Then you could perhaps send it in to the Steine.[139] What do you say about this?

Hope you are still well,

Are people still trying to frighten you with old maids' tales?

Love Ron

*Will Hay in "Black Sheep of Whitehall"[140] – Quite good.

---

139 The Old Steine is the main street in Brighton and presumably where the Borough's offices were located.

140 *The Black Sheep of Whitehall,* Ealing Studios comedy (1942)

Dad was home on the weekend of 18-19th April and wrote again the following Sunday:

26 April 42.

Dear K,

Thanks very much for the early letter this week. It was almost there when I got back, so to speak.

Monday I had my annual Tet Tox[141], went to bed all Tuesday and felt putrescent all Wednesday. It is only at the end of the week that I really feel human again.

As you will have gathered from my telegram (I hope), I expect to get home about Wednesday noon for leave, and start back about the noon of the following Wednesday, so will you make definite arrangements with John for some time suitable to him?

Please look up some decent pictures and other shows for us to go to. I do not want to go out too much, but I should like to be in a position to go if we feel like it.

I think some leave will do me good. I am a little bit stale, though I could carry on willy-nilly for quite a long time.

It looks as though our circle of friends is to break up badly. The other boys are due out of their respective courses etc within a week or two and Jimmy is in a higher medical category at the moment and fretting for a whiff of grape-shot.

I have nearly finished that book of old K.N's that I took back with me. It's jolly good. I want to do quite a lot more reading when I get home, so please unlock all these mysterious and rather dubious stores in which you have no doubt hidden away the thing that makes life enjoyable.

I must hop outside now and see if the paper-man is selling his wares near the cook-house; then I shall get the bike and distribute some adverts for the discussion to all the huts. So I have quite a morning in front of me.

Yours with love,
[signed] Ron

---

141 Tetanus toxin vaccine

The week-long leave Dad has mentioned would have been from Wednesday 29th April to Wednesday 6th May. Two days after getting back, he writes a postcard in pencil addressed to "Mrs K. Spathaky, 49 Hangleton Rd., Hove, Sx." and postmarked in Taunton on 8th May 1942:

Fri 8 May 42.

Dear K,

Got back OK. Hope everything alright your end. I shall probably be static for a week or two, so I shall apply for compassionate leave forthwith. All the folks send their regards – Peggy, Molly, Sally, Harold, Dicky, etc. etc.

Courage, mes enfants!

Love Ron

On the Sunday he starts to type a fairly long letter, which he finishes on the Wednesday:

10 May 42.

Dear Kath,

Work has been quite good since I got back, and I have the prospect of remaining in the camp for a week or two more. Yesterday I walked around Taunton with Dickie and Molly in the afternoon, then went to the Empire in the evening for a dance. It was lousy, though I enjoyed it for a time. Really the women seem quite frightful in this place – those that look even passable are as bucolic as could be and remind one of all the novels of farm life one has read. But perhaps I malign the sex in writing thus.

This morning (Sunday) I have been round to various parts of the camp to fix up the adverts for a meeting tomorrow on "Photography." Then I typed a stencil for the fortnightly Educational Bulletin, and am hanging around in Dickie's place waiting to catch an Educational Officer, so that he can sign it, then I can get it duplicated. This afternoon there is a meeting at the Gaiety Cinema in town and in the evening we are hearing some music at the Hadleighs'. I don't feel like going but I suppose I shall feel more like it when I get there.

Dickie is reading the novel about Welsh life called "How Green is My Valley."[142] He thinks it's very good and I shall try and get it out of the camp library when I can. I believe you have read it, haven't you?

Leave was jolly good really, though I seemed to get a touch of sluggish digestion from not getting around enough. That was obviously my own fault and laziness – I have recove*[re]*d now and feel quite fit. Hope your "condition" (as the Victorians used to say) is continuing satisfactory – no vapours or migraines? You were certainly as little affected by the whole business as ever I can imagine anyone being – just as it should be. In fact if I may say so it seemed to have added a certain stimulus to you to keep up to the mark with your other interests. I think you will probably be very glad you have gone through all this, and would have become very miserable and nerve-wracked if you hadn't. Like I am when I don't have a bed-companion, only worse.

I will give in my notification in the near future that I shall be applying for compassionate week-end leave some time on Saturday, Sunday or Monday. Do you think it's wise to do it like that? Then when I slip the actual application in at the last moment they will not have to run around like a lot of marmosets.

(Continued 3 days later!) Will you please let me have by return a certificate saying that you are going to have a baby and when it is expected to arrive. Also please say in your reply to me when you think it would be best for me to get leave.

I shall not be able to finish off this letter completely as I should have liked, because we are very busy this week preparing an Exhibition and one or two other special jobs, but I know you will believe I am with you in my affection and mind during this week. Please stand up to it!

Love Ron

P.S. I have not had time to study your last letter yet, but à propos:

---

142 *How Green Was My Valley* by Richard Llewellyn (London: 1939)

It's true that out of all the thousands of composers of music very few seem to have been women. On the other hand many of the very finest players (interpreters) have been women (Myra Hess, Sidonie Goossens, Ida Haeckel,[143] Marie Wilson[144]). Which would seem to suggest that women prefer to commune with the world of music through a masculine mind rather than express themselves. I think that one day this position will be levelled up as between the sexes.

It seems from the next letter that maybe I am expected to arrive pretty soon; but in fact I hung on for another ten days! This letter was not posted until at least 24th May, due to an oversight by Dad which he grovels about in the subsequent letter:

16 May 42.

Dearest Kath,

I don't know whether this will reach you before the balloon goes up, but I hope it does. Please keep up the old courage and use all your moral resolve to numb yourself to the pain and not give way to it. I know you'll be all right and that the child will be a jolly fine one and I am dying to be on the spot and see it. I haven't felt how near the whole business was till just the last few days and now I want the whole thing over so that we can start remodelling our life in line with the new necessities.

Funny how it makes a lot of difference to even two people who are only allowed to see each other on a leash for quite a short time each year. It means that there is something that can never be forgotten – even when life is at its drabbest and at its most dangerous.

I have made all the preparations for leave that I possibly can, but I am in an awkward spot. They have some information in the Depot about my moving but somehow they seem to be delaying

---

143 Ida Haendel CBE (born 1928) is a Polish-born British violinist.
144 Marie Wilson (1903-1959) Violinist in the BBC Symphony Orchestra 1930-1945 and then in the newly formed Philharmonia Orchestra

matters and I cannot just understand why. There seems to be nothing that should stand in the way of me moving off straight away.

I have not seemed to find as much work to do during the last couple of weeks. Perhaps it's the inevitable sensation of being on one's last legs in a place.

I hope the new position does not add any train time on the journey to Brighton – and how I wish I could get posted to the Sussex area.

The country around here is just surging into full spring with a suggestion of early summer. The fields are full of thousands of buttercups and daisies and the trees and hedges smell like all the world's romances rolled into one. Our child will have a lovely natural world to be born into, even if the man-made side of it seems a little awry at present. He/she will be able to roll in the long summer grass and put its face in the buttercups and dandelions.

The boys are quite excited by the prospect and keep on asking me about it. I shall have quite a few people to notify. Perhaps I'd better buy some postcards tomorrow and get ready.

So long for now,

Love,

Ron

This postscript was scribbled in blue pencil on a small scrap of paper:

P.S.

1   Mr Ind's wife seriously ill ∴ my posting put off till about Tuesday.
2   C.O refused my leave on account of just having had privilege leave. May get it later.

Courage, mon amie!

Love

– Ron

Another eight days on and I have still not been born:

24.5.42
Taunton

Dear K,

Hope this reaches you in time to explain my "manifold sins and wickedness." I have just discovered to my horror that I didn't post that letter of which I spoke to you on the phone. I was so certain about it when you suggested I had forgotten that I didn't bother to go through my pockets. Today I was looking for something else and it slipped out from amongst about a dozen pamphlets, notes on meetings, etc. etc.

Very sorry. But I <u>did</u> phone quite a bit, didn't I?

I shall not be going to Weston-super-Mare until Mr Ind comes back, and he has got a week's extra compassionate leave because his wife is ill. He comes back on Friday 29th. On Saturday I shall go down to the Area Office and arrange my posting, so that the machine will probably work by about Wednesday of the following week. This has given me a new lease of life in this place, and I have buckled into the work a bit better than the week previously.

There are certainly some very important conferences on this week-end, and I wish I were in a position to take part in them as in the old civilian days. But perhaps someday soldiers will have their political rights restored to them and will play the part that is their right and heritage in moulding the effort of the nation.

The fact that these conferences coincide with such a crucial moment on the Continent will make them all the more important. I wonder what the huge meeting in Trafalgar Square will be like. If the weather's at all fine I bet it will be monstrous.[145]

I have been reading some good books recently: "The Stars Look

---

[145] "Moscow rallied popular support in the Allied countries as well. In May 1942 a demonstration in favor of a second front attracted some fifty thousand people in Trafalgar Square" (*Normandy: The Landings to the Liberation of Paris* by Olivier Wieviorka, Harvard, 2008)

Down,"[146] "Berlin Diary" by Shirer[147] and I have been critically estimating that book "Russia Fights On" by Maurice Hindus.[148]

The Exhibition was a considerable success: we managed to get together quite a lot of work which the lads had done at various times, and it added up to a considerable amount when all was gathered in: a woodwork section and sections for leather-work, bookbinding, art and poster-work, landscape-modelling, A.B.C.A[149] and clay-modelling.

This week we have in the town the Southern Command Continental Orchestra, organised by our Corps. I have been busy selling tickets for it. They are playing a rather middle-brow programme of Grieg, Strauss, Brahms, etc with a bit by the unspeakable Ketelby "In a Monastery Garden." But on the whole the effort is worth supporting and I think it will be a fair success.

I am going down to the town in a few minutes to sell tickets round the N.A.A.F.I.s etc.[150]

Sorry nothing has happened yet, but I am told that the first one is often a bit late.

Courage,

Lots of love, Ron

XXXXX

[and then in pencil:]

P.S Call it John Brian? or Eve or Margaret

Telegraphic Address 114 Condepot Taunton or Taunton 2697.

---

146 By A J Cronin, fictional account of repression of coal miners in the North-east (pub. Gollancz, London, 1935)

147 *Berlin Diary: The Journal of a Foreign Correspondent, 1934–1941* (pub. Knopf, New York, 1941). William L Shirer was an American journalist who was in Berlin before and after the outbreak of war.

148 London: Collins, 1942

149 The Army Bureau of Current Affairs was an organisation set up in 1941 to educate and raise morale amongst British servicemen and servicewomen with a programme of general education for citizenship. ABCA organisers and teachers seem predominantly to have been left-wing and the organisation is generally regarded as a factor in the landslide Labour Party victory in the 1945 general election. See article in Wikipedia.

150 NAAFI (Navy, Army and Air Force Institutes)

Chapter 7
New Arrival

*At last I make my entrance!!! I was born on Tuesday 26th May 1942.
Dad received a telegram the next day and, probably as soon as he heard
the news, sent Mum this telegram back:.*

Envelope:

POST OFFICE TELEGRAM
NO CHARGE FOR DELIVERY
SPAPHAKY MATERNITY HOME BUCKINGHAM CRES
BRIGHTON

Telegram:

[Time stamped:] BRIGHTON SUSSEX 27 MAY 1942
SPAPHAKY MATERNITY HOME BUCKINGHAM CRES
BRIGHTON
= CONGRATULATIONS SEEING YOU SOON LOVE = RON
+ SPEPHAKY TU/T

*The telegram has "12.55" scribbled on it, which must be the time it
arrived at Brighton Post Office. For me, the misspellings of our surname
at one day old started a lifelong saga of such errors.*

On the same day Dad typed and posted a letter:

Taunton,

27.5.42.

Dearest Kath,

I was ever so thrilled to have the telegram; I went about for a time in a daze, rather a golden daze, as the picture of both of you presented itself to me. I hope you will be well enough to read this letter – I'm afraid I don't know much about these things, for instance as to how long you will be before you can read and generally sit up and take notice. Needless to say I shall be thrilled to death to get the first letter from you. There is so much one would like to ask. Was it terribly and horribly painful, or can you bear to tell me about it? Is the kiddy very nice, or is he just red and inexpressive like most babies when they are first born? Does he look happy? What does it feel like to feed a baby yourself? I should like you to share all these secrets with me if you will.

Most of all, do you feel very weak, or will you be absolutely all right in a few weeks? Is there any danger about the stretched tissues that you were rather apprehensive about when I last saw you?

The Taunton Army Education Centre has got a discussion on this evening on "The War – this Round." I have been asked to take the chair and Dickie will open the argybargyment. I wish you could be here to take part – it is for civilians as well as troops. Still, when I get moved to Weston-super-Mare I shall probably be able to have you there, if we can afford to live out. When you are better perhaps we can go into a financial huddle and decide. It would certainly be a jolly fine place for a kiddy to live in during the War, wouldn't it?

I have to go down and comb the canteens at the moment for people to attend the discussion, so no more except to say how much I love you (I suppose that will have to be plural now).

Lots of kisses

XXX Ron

Further congratulations quickly arrived at the Sussex Maternity Home. The first one was printed on rather colourful 'Greetings Telegram' stationery but was undated:

GREETINGS SPATHAKY SUSSEX MATERNITY HOSPITAL
BUCKINGHAM ROAD BRIGHTON
CONGRATULATIONS AND BEST WISHES LOVE =
MOTHER DAD DORIS

(Doris was Mum's brother Gordon's wife.)

Next came a postcard from Mum's mother, postmarked "BRIGHTON &
HOVE SUSSEX 915 AM 28 MAY 1942":

Mrs K Spathaky
Sussex Maternity Hospital Buckingham Rd
Brighton

                                      Hangleton Rd

Dear K,

Just a line to wish you good morning. We were glad to find you looking so well, and baby so fine.

I have tonight written Mrs Spathaky[151] telling her how you were and what her grandson was like. I told her you thanked her for letter received. I thought she would be glad to have a little more news than a telegram and you may not feel like writing for a day or two. We forgot the bag so I will try and fetch it on Friday night.

Do you want the baby registering? You will miss coupons if it is not done very shortly.

Love Mam.

Hope to see you Friday.

Then there was an envelope addressed in carefully penned capital letters.
It is postmarked "ALDERSHOT HANTS. 11.45 AM 28 MAY 1942". On
the reverse of the envelope is a pen sketch of a bow tie, drawn with some
care, together with what I assume is a sketch of a baby's face below it.
The letter was from Mum's brother Gordon:

---

151 Dad's mother in Warrington

Farnborough
Wednesday 27/5/42

My dear Kay,

I understand from a P.S. on the outside of the latest letter from Doris that you have pulled the deal off O.K.

And what a deal – male heir to the family estates and all that – well well!

Congratulations old thing – Mother and Boy doing well I hope? Was it worth waiting for?

Now you must buck up and get better because Doris will be waiting for your bed.[152]

Cheerio and the best of luck to you both. Love Gordon.

X Kiss from Uncle to nephew

Mum was clearly fit enough within a day or two of the birth to write to Dad. He then typed a letter to her:

Taunton, 29.5.42.

Dear K,

It was lovely of you to write so quick after the event. The little bit after Doris's writing was absolutely terrific. I always imagined people were knocked out for long enough. Perhaps if that is a gauge of your returning vitality you will be up and about earlier than the classical time? I know nothing about all this.

Mr Ind will probably be back tonight (Friday) and I shall be posted away either just before the week-end (e.g. Saturday morning), or on Monday or Tuesday when the week-end feeling of the Posting Office has disappeared. Whenever it is I shall try and get in forty-eight hours between the two stations in order to see you.

I haven't asked much about the new arrival yet. So he has the same shape head as myself, has he? Does that mean he is going to have some brains, or not? What has he got of yours so far – your practical ability and constitution, I hope! And your affectionate nature. And your physical attraction, mixed up with a bit of my shape when I was eighteen. (Swank!)

---

152 Their daughter Helen was born just ten days after me!

The work has been pretty terrific during the last week or two, but the uncertainty about going away has meant that it was all consolidation work and not very much expansion at all. Before I go away I shall have to try and get at least one man who will keep the Discussion flag flying, because I think the whole business has been very helpful to convalescents and has given them a new slant on the army.

It was jolly good the DW resolution getting through the LP conference, even if by a small majority.[153] It will show whether Morrison[154] is willing to submit to the dictates of his own movement or whether he has gone "right over." What does everybody think about it in Brighton, including your Ma and Pop?

Harold and Sally have now left the town, for where I don't know. They are probably still on leave making whoopee before Harold is posted to some important job with two or three stripes attached to it.

I have not heard from the folks at Warrington since the event, but I must write today and confirm the telegram which your Mother so kindly sent. I have not had a single moment to do so before.

Dickie is also posted away, as I may have told you, and he has gone to one of the biggest centres of Army life in the country. He will be able to make lots of friends and throw his weight about when he has got settled down.

My washing has got into a putrid state since I last saw you. Since I expected going I have not dared to send in anything at all, for fear of not being there when it returned. The result is I am in my last ditch as regards socks. I think I'll wash some this week-end, or else start at the beginning and wear them all again.

Please tell me all about the kid, and yourself, and the Event, when you are fit enough to write.

Love,

Ron (excuse this, no pencil)

P.S. I have sent 10/- to B Edn Cttee, damn them!

---

153 DW – *Daily Worker*; LP – Labour Party
154 Herbert Morrison, Labour Home Secretary in Churchill's wartime Coalition Government.

"Excuse this, no pencil" is because Dad usually signed his letters and this time only typed his name.

Although there was no indication in the last letter, Dad must have paid a lightning visit to Brighton, since it was he who registered my birth as John Michael Spathaky on 1st June, the following Monday. This is confirmed in the first sentence of the following postcard, written the next day when he was already back in Taunton:

Taunton,

2 – 6 – 42

Dear K,

Too busy to write a letter at the moment, cleaning up things I left half-finished when I came away.

I'll write a really good screed the first free evening I get. How's yourself and J.M.?

– Love

Ron

By 2nd June he had still not been posted to Weston-super-Mare or wherever he was going. In fact he was still in Taunton on 7th August. The next letter confirms that I was known as John Michael, the names which Dad had suggested back in March, as I know from my birth certificate. I still use them on official documents. It becomes clear later in the month that the decision was still uncertain as between John and Michael as their preferred name for me. Two days later he typed a long letter and re-used an envelope which was then postmarked 10am on the 6th:

Taunton,

4 June 42.

Dear K,

Thanks very much for the letter. Don't be too introspective about "how you should feel and talk about the baby." I know you have enough modern common-sense to become either too goofy or too impersonal. Just feel what you want to feel about him and say what you want to say.

Work is held up a lot at the moment by heat and small numbers. Doesn't seem to be holding up the war, however, does it? The Cologne and Essen raids were good efforts, it seems to me. I don't think they can possibly make up for the lack of a land front, but they are better than none at all.

I hope the hospital routine will not be too exasperating. You will immediately recover from that feeling of going back to school which you seem to feel, as soon as you get back to your own home and room. Also you will feel as though you have really done something, I should imagine, and are not just one of a crowd.

Been finishing Shirer's "Berlin Diary" today, the diary of an American journalist in Berlin during the last period of appeasement and the beginning and present period of the war. It is jolly good for a middle-class young man's point of view, the sort of bloke who has no idea of the general forces at work behind appearances, but who is exceeding*[ly]* good at his trade of recording impressions.

Is the baby feeding better now, and dealing with his windiness better? Or is he still a bit blue about the gills at times?

He's probably too busy thinking about the political situation to bother with a little practical thing like feeding – like me of course!

This is all for now. I will write over the week-end.

Love, *[signed in pencil]* Ron

My cousin Helen was born on 5th June, but there is no mention of that event in Dad's letters. He types another on the Sunday:

Taunton,
7 June 42.

Dear K,

I suppose this is the last letter you will get in hospital, and then you start living your own life again, not quite so much at the mercy of routines and timetables, except those made by J.M.

I'm afraid I've been suffering from "movingitis" during the last week or two, but not quite so much as before and in fact there has been a little more activity than previously. Dickie has safely arrived at his new post and it appears to be a bit more interesting and responsible than appeared at first sight.

I've done a lot of sun-bathing during the last week, which has not contributed to the cause very much, but also some P.T. (voluntary) which possibly does constitute some contribution.

Still reading Shirer's "Berlin Diary" which I mentioned to you quite a time ago. It is rather a long book, but very good in some ways. Also dug a little more into old man K.M.'s huge tome, which I am now in about my fourth or fifth year of reading. I am only reading it in a general way to get the hang of it this first time. Then I want to set to work and study it properly.

I am sitting in our own centre at the moment, everyone else in the place being off on Church Parade. This part of the establishment is deserted and it is very nice and cheerful. I have been doing a "skin" on my typewriter for the monthly Educational Bulletin.

A solitary A.T.S is walking (fairly smartly) across the big parade-ground. It is Joan, the Despatch Clerk, I can see from her walk. She has a fairly tough job something like I had in London, keeping tag on all the letters that come in and out of the Depot.

Now I can see old Bimbo Smart, Orderly Room Sergeant-Major going across the "Square." He is the Chief Clerk of the place and belongs to the local regiment – you know, the people with the distinctive way of wearing their hats. He is a gross baboon of a man, with enough narrow practicality to make him feel he is no end of a fellow. His anecdotal manner is positively elephantine and he roars like an ape at his own coarse "humour." However, it takes a wide spectrum of types to make up the working and lower middle-class. Of all the spectrum, however, I think some of these local regiments must have produced the most primitive fellows.

Went to a dance at the Empire Hall last night with Spiegler, who is the latest Alien Company we have at the Centre. He is a cheerful and sincere little sprite, with a rather feminine manner, but apt to get a bit too perky with the girls when he's known them only a short time. At least that's what a girl I danced with told me, a girl who lives next door to the camp and who incidentally has borrowed "Man's Worldly Goods"[155] from me and seems to understand it. She is about 20 and quite a nice kid. She is good looking, but has the misfortune to have a deformed hand. It just doesn't seem to be completely developed, which must be very annoying for an otherwise attractive girl.

Spiegler and I met her at the Taunton Centre at the joint discussion which we hold weekly with the W.E.A.

Well, I shall have to go and get the signature of the Education Officer for the stencil, and then for a bit of cleaning up in the bunk. You will be amused to know that I successfully washed four handkerchieves, a pair of pants cellular, a towel and four pairs of socks. Vive le progrès.

Love

Ron

Mum must have stayed in the maternity hospital for about a fortnight. She would then have moved back to her parents' home in Hangleton Road. On the Thursday Dad typed another letter:

Taunton,

11.6.42.

Dear Kath,

Very bucked to know that you are out of the hospital atmosphere again and that you are modelling your own routine (in so far as you do not have it modelled for you!)

I am a bit browned off at the moment. I suppose I miss Dickie and Harold, but I must simply get to work to replace them by two other friends who will mean as much to me. Also, as I explained to you, there is inevitably less to do at the moment.

Still, the W.O. is quite a reasonable kind of cove, and falls in (at least half-heartedly) with any sort of suggestions that are made. I have

---

155 *Man's Worldly Goods: The Story of the Wealth of Nations* by Leo Huberman (Harper, New York: 1936) (American socialist writer)

proposed that I should take over some of the actual map-reading. The ordinary instructors are a little below the ordinary calibre at the moment.

When I say I miss Harold I should add that he is actually back here for a day or two at the moment, since his new posting is not settled. So we have had a few chats and strolls together.

As the weather is pretty gloomy today, I propose to run down to town straight after work and pop into the flicks.

Rory, who has been in this town for an interview re pips called up to the Depot this morning and had ten minutes chat. It was a great pity he couldn't stay longer, but I liked to see him again, he is such a jolly nice fellow and so sincere, as Bri is also. I may catch him in town this evening before he starts back and have a cup of tea and talk over old times.

On the other hand he may have to catch an earlier train to I.[156]

We are trying the effect of another ramble this weekend. I don't know whether we shall finally make a success of it but you know we have been trying to get them going for months.

I am told (words are straws) that I am the next in the county to be made up to WO 1 or WO 2. Owen and another geezer (with more service than myself) have both been made up. It would be quite useful to get 16/- a day, wouldn't it?

That reminds me, have you sent in for the increased allowance yet? Also I saw in the Press something about being due for maternity benefit? Are you insured with an approved society? I'm not presumably?

Love,

Dad's name must have disappeared off the bottom edge of the page – or he just forgot to sign this letter.

Three days later he typed another:

---

156 Probably Ilminster

Taunton,

14.6.42

Dear Kath,

A state of browned-offness, while not presenting chronic symptoms, still persists. I feel ill-at-ease, intensely aware of the shortcomings of the members of the Mess and stuffed up with emotional and physical sexiness, sometimes fused together, sometimes one or the other, generally co-ordinated in a desire to have you with me, sometimes twisted into an erotic urge towards anything with skirts on that happens to cross my path.

Part of it may be due to the need for some physical toning-up. I don't do P.T. as often as I should; so I have my own way forward there. But mainly I think it is a temporary feeling of frustration as regards the war. I'm doing precious little that contributes to a Second Front at the moment – a few talks occasionally that's all. I should like to get some better training in arms but I suppose that's impossible.

Today we have organised a ramble from camp to Stapley Lawns, some low foot-hills about 6 miles from here. Invites have been sent to a few girls' clubs in town, but I don't know whether any will send members. It is difficult to invite too many outsiders in case few convalescents decide to come. The W.O. and myself would look queer leading a score of young women around the local villages.

I have finished Shirer's "Berlin Diary" and "Battlefields and Girls," the little book of poems the Central Books are putting out.[157] They are jolly good and are only 9d. If you get them tell me what you think of the poem called "Twenty-second of June." I like this description of the 1917[158].

---

157 *Battlefields and Girls*; poems by David Martin (W. MacLellan, Glasgow: 1942). David Martin OA (1915-1997) was a Hungarian-born journalist who had served in the medical service of the International Brigade during the Spanish Civil War. He later settled in Australia.

158 22nd June 1917 was the date of the Third Battle of Ypres in WW1.

"But I rose. My fetters shambled
Like the typhoon-shattered dyke.
Treasurer and master trembled
At my power titan-like.

No more usury and plunder
Of my force. The serving beast
Burst the cursed yoke asunder,
Rose a human! – in the East.

Free and master of my mission
On the world I pressed my seal,
Cast reality from vision
Liberty from brain and steel.

Sun is high, the grapes are growing.
Toast my health and drink my wine.
Poet, see my tractor mowing,
Grain and bread and fields are mine.

See the last mobilisation,
Reason and humanity
Challenging in tank formation
Armies of insanity."

I had a couple of posters done by one of our convalescent artists, illustrating some of these verses. Unfortunately he was not quite up to it – though they are passable.

They have had some parades in town today in connection with United Nations Day. I didn't seem to get any information of what they were doing, so the posters didn't mention it. But the local Press has quite a lot of adverts about it so I suppose some of the patients will go. It was my fault for not seeking out the information.

I'm sorry if J.M. was a bit of a handful when you first got him home. Has he stopped excessive yelling now? Have you bathed him much, and is he definitely checked up as being all there? Have his eyes changed colour, or whatever they do? Does he move about much yet, especially when he's angry or hungry? I hope you haven't discarded any of your theories yet in face of the overwhelming fact of the practice – or have you?

What about yourself, are you quite reduced to normal size now, and all healed up and fit? Mind you start taking some exercise soon. You remember that you said you would get the bike fitted up and really get out and about.

I am typing this in the Church Hut, which is one of the few quiet spots in the camp on a Sunday morning. The bunk was for some reason too cold so I brought the typewriter along here.

There is a P.T. Sergeant in the next bunk to me who works in the same office as the O.M. He is quite a decent bloke, but looks more depressed about being in the Forces than anyone I've ever met.

He knows quite a lot about politics, having been apparently at college at the same time as old Cornford[159] and Haden Guest[160]. But he says that he "wondered if they really meant it, at that time. They certainly did, it has been proved."

Yours with much love,

Ron (sorry, no pencil)

It seems that I have decided that feeding is a good idea after all! Dad wrote again on the Thursday:

Taunton, 18 June 42

Dear K,

Glad the brat has taken to feeding properly now. It must be rather worrying not to know what is wrong when you are starting.

---

159 John Cornford, poet and communist, who had been at Trinity College, Cambridge, and was killed fighting the fascists in the Spanish Civil War. See Wikipedia article.

160 Leslie Haden-Guest (1877-1960), author, journalist, physician and surgeon, active worker for the left and Labour MP. His son David Guest was killed in 1938 while fighting the fascists in the Spanish Civil War.

My next leave will be next week-end Saturday 27th June. I will let you know definitely about this as soon as I can.

My attack of browned-offness has come to a head and passed its crisis. I'm afraid it was largely the usual type of indigestion that was causing it. I have taken a generous dose of Andrew's liver salts and feel slightly better. I shall buy a tin today and treat myself to a real course of them, together with much exercise. It is probably connected with a slackness of work.

Our discussions have been quite a success, and last week-end we organised a good ramble, which I may have told you about. (Having indigestion I have no memory.)

A dozen blokes came, with two girls who live next door to the camp. They are quite young things and I have been to a dance with one of them, or rather I have danced with her at a dance. She is 19, in the G.T.C.[161] as a potential officer, and for some years has been one of the moving spirits in a Youth Club. She is quite good-looking but has the misfortune of having one hand undeveloped – her fingers are underdeveloped.

I am not seeing her or any other girls very often however, in spite of the enforced idling, since I seem to have developed an acute social conscience and feel at least 35 and as though I had five children.

So perhaps you won't mind me talking to her occasionally.

Of course you probably will. "Nature red in tooth and claw" and all that!

I have been reading an amusing book by an American woman called "Be Your Age".[162] It deals with the behaviour to be expected from people at various ages.

I think the authoress's name is Marjorie Barstow. She develops the quite common-sense theme that people go through definite emotional phases and developments, proper to recognised ages. The thing is, they go through them at very different ages, different from the "norms," that is. Thus a woman of forty may go through a period of deferred homosexuality, going about with gangs of other women

---

161 Girls Training Corps, a uniformed youth organisation for girls
162 *Be your age!* by Marjorie Barstow Greenbie, pub. Stackpole, 1938

and raving about "beastly men," though the most likely age for that is 16-17 (say).

I'm afraid this camp is definitely not developing me at the moment. I find that I am getting bored and nervy with nothing to do. This is, I suppose, the big danger of the job. I feel like volunteering for anything from a machine-gun battalion to a mine-sweeper. But they won't take Education Sergeants! In any case I suppose the role of ideologue is my chief one.

Administration is not yet up my street.

This afternoon there is a cricket match between the Sergeants and the Officers, in which I am performing, unless it rains, which is possible.

I'm afraid I hope it does

Harold is still hanging about getting rather bored with gardening at the moment.

Sally's address is 88 Baker St., Weybridge, Surrey.

I shall be awfully glad to see you again, and (if it could only be done) to set up house again. The latest news bulletin is that I'm going to Ilminster, and soon. Of course I shall believe that when I have arrived.

We had an interesting debate with the A.T.S. a few weekends ago. One or two of them spoke quite well, but there is obviously a tough job of education and general leadership waiting there.

I have been reading the famous novel "Story of an African Farm" lately by Olive Schreiner.[163] I've heard about it for years. If you see it in the library you'll find it's damn good.

Yours with much love,

[signed] Ron

The next letter we have is handwritten in pencil and dated over two weeks later. The following letter just a day after that implies that they had been together in the interval. Here Dad refers to me as John for the first, and I hope only, time. That felt weird as I read it for the first time:

---

163 Published in 1883 under the pseudonym Ralph Iron, it has become recognised as one of the first feminist novels. (See Wikipedia.)

Taunton,

6.7.42.

Dear K,

I have not succeeded in finding anywhere yet for you to come to, but I think I shall be able to before the 18th. One of the P.T. Sgts who lives in Trull nearby has a spare room which may be available. I'll write as soon as ever it materialises.

Today I led a ramble to the Blackdown Hills from the back of our camp. We had 19 people, about half men and half girls from the local Girls Training Corps. The two girls who helped us with all our activities with civilians came – Joan and Betty. They are quite decent kids and I wish you were here as I am sure you could be such an influence on them.

They are at an age when they are just waking up to men and are rather blasé about it all in a way, though Joan is rather gone on a bloke in the Navy.

I'm afraid living on the very edge of the country has cut them off from the experience of the kind we have had, but they have the thriving Youth Club in Taunton to their credit.

I hope John hasn't been too much of a tie and that you have managed to get out once or twice by yourself. I was very unthinking when I suggested you were worrying more than acting as regards his feeding. I quite see the wisdom of the new policy and I hope he will continue to sleep.

I got another lesson on the motor-bike during the week, and feel much more confident now. I went about 45 m.p.h. on a country road and felt awfully proud of myself.

I suppose I shall be moving to Ilminster within the next day or two, so if I do I shall get straight on to the job of finding a place there where we can stay. Needless to say I have no idea what the conditions of the new job will be except that I shall probably be living out in billets.

My W.O. is coming back tomorrow, which means there will not be quite so much to do. I have had quite a hectic time while he has been away, but it has been interesting.

Will write a longer letter tomorrow –
Love,
Ron

He did write the next day – a typewritten letter:

Taunton.

7.7.42

Dear K,

I hope the combined exercise which the Press reported the South Coast towns have been doing did not put the wind up you too much. They may not be indicative of anything!

I'm sorry the last letter was a bit scrappy but sometimes I can't write at all well.

My W.O. has now returned from leave and I once again await the word to fold my tent and depart. I wish I could be out of it all, with the war over and the tasks of home-building in process of solution by both of us. It must come very hard on you to deal with them by yourself. I feel inexpressibly remote from rents, ration-cards, napkins, feedings, civilian doctors, thermometers, washing of baby clothes, and other things that must constitute an eternity for you at the moment.

It is still pretty certain that I shall go inland to where I told you.

Last night I walked around Sherford village and tried to find a place for your week's stay, from the 18th onwards. Unfortunately the people were either too old or had their rooms filled already. Tonight when I have finished with the Dancing Class I shall go to Trull, which is a little on the other side of the camp, and I am a bit more optimistic about finding a place there. One of the P.T. Sergeants has given me the address of a farmer in the village who occasionally puts people up.

Before I can get there I have our Dancing Class, however, which, having started in a moment of enthusiasm I must keep on, since it has become one of the great functions of the week. I have two sessions 7-0 p.m. for complete beginners and 7-30 p.m. for the second lesson – for those who came last week.

Very little is being done during the day in our line, but I have managed to keep the evening work going and that balances things up a little. I found out today that another unit near here is keeping small livestock, so this may be a possible activity. The only difficulty is that convalescents are rather uncertain people and if a whole crowd were discharged suddenly their animals would probably be left to starve unless they were discovered in time by the staff.

Did our love-making satisfy you, or was it too soon to start? Next time I shall not need you to be quite so passive, I imagine, and you will have regained a more lively interest. Or do you feel a bit dubious about it now? The babe must be very tiring and must seem a complete world in himself without having husbands intruding and making more physical demands.

If the war were not hanging like a shadow over it the Somerset countryside would be most fascinating at this time of the year. Even in the small doses of it which I get on the weekly rambles, it is a constant anodyne against the almost physical pain of the camp, the grimly utilitarian huts and cookhouses, the raucous bellow of the wireless in the Sergeants' Mess, the boozing and bamboozling which goes on week after week.

One can cast off all this and restore eyesight and mind with the rich damp green, the steep little wooded hills, the crowded grain fields, the old-fashioned (if unhygienic) country houses, the everlasting leafy song of the trees. The one advantage of waking in my bunk is that the birds always sing in some big ash trees near the window. In contrast there is a bird with a most unpleasant croak which always utters a machine-like note, harsh and malevolent, at bed-time.

If we can get a week together, either here or at I.,[164] I will show you how nice the Blackdowns can be.[165]

Still, it was very nice to come home for a few hours last week, and get a touch of the real Brighton sunshine and a sight of the Downs. This is the country of darkling hedgerows, of damp recesses in the small woods, of cattle stamping in the mud down by the streams.

164 Presumably Ilminster
165 The Blackdown Hills are now (2017) an Area of Outstanding Natural Beauty.

The sun bears down with a strong and panting ray. In Brighton, by contrast, the air seems like wine and the turf up by the golf-links seems crisp and bouncing. One's feet are led on to run and the wind calls one to activity.

Or am I idealising it?

Well, I must go and have a wash now and see whether it is getting near time for the old dance-lesson. Then I shall be able to take this letter along to Trull and post it when I have succeeded or failed to find somewhere for you.

Love,

[signed in pencil] Ron

[Then, also in pencil:] Later – Sorry. No luck in Trull so far. R

Dad pencilled another letter a week later. The date has been changed from 13.7 to 14.7 and the time has also been overwritten, but Dad neglected to change the day of the week. The 14th was a Tuesday:

Taunton 14.7.42

Mon. 1015 hrs.

Dear K,

Hope it's OK about Friday. It's just a little country house, but the room with the double-bed seemed clean and they don't take in lodgers regularly. Cost will be £1 a week if you bring your rationed food (or let me get it in Taunton, bringing or sending some of it).

It is only a quarter of an hour's walk from the Camp, but still further out in the country

The address is

Mrs Rowsell,
Staplehay,
Nr. Trull

[Here Dad drew a sketch plan showing the Camp, Trull and Staplehay with the location of the house indicated.]

I've had a return of my indigestion, but I am losing it with a variety of aperients from the M.I. Room. It makes me feel very flat and woebegone but I am alright as soon as I cure it. I am rapidly coming to the conclusion that I should not eat anything after tea, as supper always seems to start the trouble off, especially a big meal of sandwiches.

To revert to the digs: there is no bathroom but there is a wash-and-stand and she has a small bath if the hand-bowl is too small for the baby. She also promises to let us have plenty of hot water.

Joan and Betty, those girls who help with the camp rambles, would probably help with care of the kid. Shall I ask them to come along on Sunday morning and see you?

You can have your meals with the old couple, or in the front room by yourself. She looks a quite reasonable type of individual, a typical countrywoman. The old man is deaf and very subdued.

I will go tomorrow and hire a taxi to meet whatever train you get in by.

I hope there is one getting in between 4-30 p.m. and 6-30 p.m.

Do you think you can manage the inconvenience of the journey?

Love

  Ron

Mum and I came to the lodgings near Taunton, so there were no more letters for nearly three weeks. The next was dated 3rd August which was a Monday, although Dad says in the fourth paragraph that it's a Sunday. The stay did not turn out well!

            Taunton,
            3-8-42

Dear K,

Thank you very much for the telegram and card. I shall be anxious to know if J.M. and yourself have returned quickly to good health and normal routine after the impossible conditions of that horrible house.

Of all the places we have tried to live in while I have been in the Army I think the room in Hampstead was the only nice one.

However, I shall be home at the end of this week, probably on Saturday afternoon. I shall be very glad to have a week off since I have never at any time felt so frustrated as during the fortnight of this play.

We have had every evening taken for rehearsal since I saw you. This afternoon (Sunday) is the dress rehearsal with orchestra and during the week, at various times, come the four performances.

However all things come to an end.

Jimmy[166] and I have not been too idle as regards the general situation – as you know. We have scored quite an important point during this last week.

I have been to a couple of dances with Mostyn over the holidays. I think really I feel the better for them – if only in that I don't want to go to dances again for a time.

I bought a rather interesting booklet by Jack Owen yesterday, called "War in the Factories" (1/3)[167]. Have you seen it? It is published under the auspices of the old DW.

Well, for the first time since I have been in the Army I overslept and missed breakfast this morning. So I'm pining for the NAAFI to open.

Have you managed to get to the Library at all, or out on your bike?

Ever so much love,

Ron

Although Dad dated that letter 3-8-1942, a Monday, he refers to "this afternoon (Sunday)" so I think that, in his frustration, he did not know the date and was probably writing on Sunday 2nd August 1942.

In fact he did not get home the following weekend as the next letter, typed on the Friday, explains:

---

166 See page 113.

167 *War in the Workshops* by Jack Owen, pub. Lawrence and Wishart, London, 1942. Owen was a leading trade unionist for over forty years and a life-long communist.

Taunton,

7 Aug 42.

Dearest K,

You will have received my telegram by now. I'm very sorry. It was the smallest thing that stopped it. A special conference next week which all instructors have to be present nolens-volens. However I shall be able to come next week, so it won't seem very long.

I hope the kid and yourself are all right. I am quite sure we did the right thing in packing you off from here when we did.

The atmosphere of that place was terrible. But it was a ruddy nuisance that the SO dragged me into the play the very week I was hoping to be with you. I am quite certain we should have had a much better time if it hadn't been for that.

The performance went off very well. My little part seemed quite O.K. Peggy and Molly played a joke on me by sending a greetings telegram to the theatre and I received it when all the stars of the show were in the Green Room. They all expected that the messenger boy was looking for them, but he came to me, the humble super and handed it to me among the roars of the cast. However I managed to survive it with good grace.

I don't suppose I shall bother to stay in London for the night when I come home on leave. As you suggest, I shall call at the bookshops and possibly go to a foreign-language film, if there is one, during the two or three hours of Friday afternoon. Or if the journey has been too boring I shall come straight home.

You will be pleased to know that our various bees, quizzes, discussions etc. have been going pretty well lately. We have as many as 40 people at some of them. Mostyn is still here and has been very helpful as regards the evening part of the work.

I went to a dance at the Empire Hall with Jimmy last night. It was hellish crowded but we had quite a good time. We had a drink with one of our trans-Atlantic cousins and a useful preliminary chat about speech, habits, beer, and we were just getting on to the other subject when the dance finished.

I'm glad that you feel so much recovered, since you looked pale and strained during the first part of the time here, though you were better later on.

Please arrange my little evening (or whatever it may be) with John. I have quite a lot to chat over with him. Perhaps we could push the pram over the by-pass road one day (if we started early enough).

The ramble is on this afternoon. I don't know who will come; nurses, convalescents, staff, negroes, white Americans, NCOs, girls from the town etc. It will be a bit of a job to keep them together, I think.

The news continues to be terrible in the extreme, doesn't it? It seems as though the Government are only getting the wind up at the very last moment, when the Russian bargaining power is probably their desperate position in the Caucasus. I expect the Russians are now saying: "If you don't help with a second front now, then Iran and Iraq will go up the spout, with India following..." or words which express that feeling.

And yet political feeling seems to be relatively impotent in this country. It is more widespread than even at the height of the Popular Front period, but it lacks almost all the means of expression in existence then. Certainly a removal of the newspaper ban would change the whole position.

Could you collect as much news of what is happening in Brighton and district for when I come home, so that I can get in touch with the civilian world again for a short time and not have to spend too much time in questions to people before I start discussing with them.

Will see you next Friday.

With love and great eagerness,

Ron

Chapter 8
Glider Pilot Regiment

The next letter is undated but we know from the last one that Dad expected to be home on leave from about 14th to 20th August 1942. He has moved to Bulford, the huge military base on Salisbury Plain in Wiltshire, so it must date from about 25th August:

Temporarily: S/I Spathaky A.E.C.
c/o District Army Education Office,
Bulford, Wilts.

Dear K,

My forecast was incorrect and I am still in transit, on my way to A.D. I shall probably be on French teaching work, almost all day and on a highly organised basis. To tell you the truth, however I am glad to be starting work in a formation that I think will be efficient, even if I am a bit more straight-jacketed for a time. It will get the taste of Condepot and its petty feuds out of my mouth.

I will give you a fixed address as soon as I can. Anything to the above will trickle through to me in time (i.e. in two or three days extra time).

The news in the paper about S. and S.E. coast raids on Saturday morning was rather disturbing. Do you keep some little bits of cotton wool to stick in J.M.'s ears if bombing comes too close? I should do.

It looks to me as if I shall be very much a part of the new unit, to the extent of taking part in their special training, but I shall have to wait for next week-end leave to tell you about that.

I had quite a number of train changes after setting off from T. All my trains seemed to be "stoppers" and I wandered round the immense camp for several hours before finding somewhere to lay my head. Finally I ended up in the blanket store of an odd unit who were prepared to accept my tall story and also give me some breakfast.

I am writing this in the well-appointed A.E.C. Library in Bulford, with two rather curious accompaniments. One is the heavy artillery, who in a field nearby are practising and nearly blowing the roofs off – the other is the chord-practice of a W.O. I (A.E.C), leader of the Command Symphony Orchestra, who is in the next room.

I have not managed to write Mother. If you could do so and explain why, I should be relieved. Embrassez Jean-Michel pour moi!

Love

Ron

There are several problems with the next letter. Firstly it is not dated. As Dad is asking for "my clean pyjamas", its date would probably be after his home leave and therefore about 28th August 1942. Secondly it appears that he has moved again but is unable to say where he is. The problem with this is that the following letter seems to be from Bulford:

No. 254248 Sgt, Instr. Spathaky, A.E.C.

1st Glider Regiment,

Army Air Corps,

Home Forces

Dear K,

I shall apparently be here for quite a time, <u>here</u> being <u>miles</u> from everywhere, but somewhat nearer home. The surroundings are very invigorating, and the chaps seem grand, so far as I have seen them.

There are two other members of the Corps here, teaching Maths, good fellows both, though the senior is rather the aggressive type of Yorkshireman and tried to assert his seniority a bit. My work will be almost completely separate from theirs, however.

I'm afraid I shall henceforward rely on you very much for one or two things, since the purchasing of simple things is so very difficult. Here are two things I am very much in need of at your earliest leisure moment:

a. My watch mended. <u>It has never at any time gone satisfactorily for more than six hours</u> and is now completely hors de combat. I should be very blunt with the shop about this. Failing this I would have the little clock.

<u>b.</u> A new type-writer ribbon.

Also if in Hove or Brighton Library or in Wards you could see and <u>tell me</u> the titles, authors, publishers, price and year of publication of some books from time to time I should be very pleased. This is a terrific problem. E.g.

"France" – General Physical and Human Geography. Also "The Netherlands" or Belgium and Holland separately

These books must be up-to-date (post 1930) and should preferably be <u>regional</u>.

If you can get some publishers' lists sent direct to me it would help, e.g.

Harrap & Co. Ltd 82 High Holborn W.C 1

Nelson Parkside Works Edinburgh

(others from Wards)

It will not be useful to have any European geographies with these countries included, as I should already know most of what is in such books.

Lastly, if you see any magazines, periodicals or newspapers, with interesting photographs of the countries mentioned, either from the geographical, social, landscape or any other point of view you might

a. Buy the publication & send me the photos <u>or</u>

b. Send me the title, date and publication address so that I can get it.

I will now have my clean pyjamas please and anything else I left in the way of kit.

Love – Ron

The dating problems are even worse with Dad's next letter. Why on earth did he date it 9th January? The attempt to light a fire fits January better than August, but he was in Wakefield then and the first paragraph shows it was obviously written in Bulford. I would suggest it was written after the previous one, probably on 30th August, that being a Sunday, as he thanks Mum for the pyjamas. What a puzzle!

Sun 9 Jan 42. *[sic]*

Dear K,

Thanks for several letters and pyjamas. Who do you think came along Bulford main street just as I was out for a walk today? Nobody but Bernard S. – the Bernard in poierson![168]

He is actually here in the bunk while I am writing this letter, ferreting among my books and making sarcastic remarks about the fire which we spent half an hour lighting.

Having recovered from our mutual surprise we discovered we were both at a loose end. He had just arrived here and I had had a class cancelled this afternoon. So having nothing better to do we took the bus to Andover. The sun was shining brightly and life seemed much cheerier somehow. This impression continued even though the sun disappeared and we ran into fog at Andover. The town had a reasonable number of civilians in it and was not too bad. A bit square and plain, but honest in appearance – like the very word Wiltshire.

We went into a chapel that was giving teas to the troops and had a jolly good tea putting 6d each into the box when we left the place. In the canteen we had an amusing chat with two Americans. One of them gave me his address in Brooklyn (New York) and asked me to go and see him. So if you ever get to New York, call on Sol Greenberg, 61 Bay 32 St., or phone Esplanade 2-4816.

Bernard seems unchanged, except that he is a bit subdued and will need "opening up" a little. More soon.

Love

Ron

The next dated letter was typed on 4th September and written from his new location, HF (Home Forces):

---

168 Bernard Stone, Dad's colleague at Brighton Intermediate School

H.F. 4 Sep 42.

Dear K,

Thanks for the two letters, which arrived at the same time. Michael seems quite a good name for the lad. Personally I don't care if it is twisted into Mike. The book names were useful. If you come across any others I can always make use of them.

I am just settling down to the vagaries of this job. It is totally different from the other. Above all I am glad to be away from Ind, the W.O. I have just drawn a bicycle from the QM for certain external work I have to do, so I shall get the chance to see a little of the countryside. Also I have exchanged my old "bondhook" for a more modern Lee-Enfield rifle. This is all to the good.

I think I told you by phone that I managed to tack myself on to one of the squads and do a little rifle-shooting the other day. I didn't do so badly although naturally I was out of practice.

I get the chance to do a little Current Affairs occasionally, though not so much as before.

We are having a dance at the Sergeants' Mess tonight. Apparently they bring wagon-loads of A.T.S or W.A.A.F.S. or something out to this "edge of beyond," go on the razzle, then the wagon disappears and everybody returns to pale-faced austerity for another month (we hope).

I have given a big order for papers and journals to the local newsagents, including the paper. I don't know whether I shall get it delivered, but I'm going to have a darn try. Please keep Sept. 7th's issue and subsequent ones, till I come home on leave. Otherwise I may miss it if I don't succeed in getting it delivered. I hope there is going to be a terrific sales-day on the 7th, is there? Our people deserve to have their heads chopped off if they don't give the thing a good send off after the triumph of last week.[169]

I went into the local market town recently. There were lots of troops about and quite a number of civilians, it being National Day. Since I arrived late I couldn't go to the pictures, but I managed to

---

169 The ban on the *Daily Worker* was lifted on 27th August and it resumed publication on 7th September. (Source: *All Propaganda is Lies, 1941-1942* by George Orwell, ed. Peter Davison, pub. Secker and Warburg, 1998.)

acquaint myself with the centre of the town and various canteens. In the streets I actually met one or two chaps who had been patients in the old depot.

Well, all for now. I have to get on with "swenken[170] and toil."

Love

[signed in red pencil:] Ron

So Michael it was! At last I have a name, rather than being called "the kid" or JM. And I did "twist" it into Mike fourteen years later – without any knowledge of this discussion – although my wife Marian calls me Michael, but that's another story. The "local market town" was probably Devizes.

Dad typed another letter two days later:

H.F. 6.9.42

Dear K,

Unfortunately I have been given a talk to do next Saturday morning, which rather bungs up the idea of week-end leave, unless I can manage it from Saturday after duty i.e. about 11-30 a.m. until Monday midnight. I will apply for it, anyway. But if it doesn't work I shall just have to put it off until the following week-end, which will be a nuisance but not such an unmitigated calamity for us.

I forgot to mention something to you in my last screeds. I wrote a letter to the new S.O. recently, in which I raised two personal matters. The first was the question of that emergency commission I was recommended for. I told him that in view of the importance of the unit I am at present with and the job I am doing I wanted to withdraw my name from the list of candidates. The second was an enquiry as to my recommendation for promotion to W.O.1, which was made by the O.M. to higher authority before I left the other place. I asked if my transfer to the present unit cancelled that. He was very decent about and said that he would forward both matters to higher quarters, so I suppose I shall hear sooner or later.

---

170 *Swenken* – a Middle English word for physical labour.

Thank you very much for the descriptions of Michael's latest developments. He seems to be a model baby and I shall expect to hear that he is talking by at least the age of one year and reading dialectics by the age of 7.

I haven't got a lot of time just at the moment but I will write a long letter during the week some time.

I <u>should</u> like the diary, though I can wait till I come home at a pinch. Thanks awfully for the parcel, including the clock. Everything was professionally packed and in perfect condition.

Please interest yourself in all kinds of things and go on developing as you have done so much in the last few years!

Love,

[signed in ink] Ron

The next letter was typed on a Thursday nearly three weeks later. Clearly Dad did manage to get home for a while, for one or other of the weekends he had mentioned:

H.F. 24.9.42.

Dear K,

Thanks very much for the old "oxgun" which you sent, I also left a copy of the "Zeitung" which I had not finished with. If you feel in a mood for sending it some time I shall get a good 3d worth of reading out of it.

I received my promotion to Warrant Officer (Second Class) today, and though I didn't quite catch the date to which it is backdated, I have a strong feeling he said May 17th, so at 3/3 extra a day I shall have quite a bit of back pay. I will buy a few books and send the rest unless you think I should let it stay in my credits for an emergency. I shall probably have to stand a few beers in the Mess but I won't go beyond a few bob.

So my address is:

W.O.II.[171] Spathaky, A.E.C.

and I am not called Sergeant-Major. Verbal address should be "Mr. Spathaky."

More later,

Love, *[signed in pencil]* Ron

Dad's next letter was written in pencil four days later:

W.O.II Spathaky, A.E.C.

28.9.42.

Dear K,

Nothing new transpired during the week, except that the work has developed a little. I am still held up in my Current Affairs by the need for a good detailed geography of Flanders and the Netherlands, but I may find one when I go to Salisbury next.

I went to the nearest town last night with Sgt. Lane, the younger of the two maths teachers who are here. The other man was on leave. We walked around in the afternoon, seeing the town, joining the Library and generally winking at the girls in the canteens (with uniformly poor results!). In the evening we went to the troops hop in the local Corn Exchange. Lane met a W.A.A.F he knew, so I was left out in the cold somewhat – consoling myself with the virtues of marital fidelity however.

When the dance was over I proceeded to the "Passion Wagon," but he saw his Waaf to the station, thereby losing both the battalion trucks. I expected to see him land in about 4 o'clock in the morning, footsore and fagged out. But fortunately he caught the P.W. of a nearby unit and was in bed only a quarter of an hour after me.

I'm afraid all this sounds like fiddling while Rome burned, but when there is no encouragement given one to work hard it is difficult to study hard all the while, or do P.T.

Lane is a very promising bloke – I suppose it is his proletarian origin in Abertillery before he went to Teachers' Training College. Of

---

171 Warrant Officer (Class 2) is the lower of the two warrant officer ranks. Warrant officers are the highest group of non-commissioned ranks.

course he goes dutifully to Methodist Chapel on Sunday evenings and has a rather sentimental streak in some things but I have long ceased to bother about people's minor characteristics – militancy is found flourishing on the queerest trees.

I have just heard from Mother – she speaks of a very attractive sounding parcel of fruit she is sending – I hope it's not already the property of the Post Office, the Black Market, the regimental postmen or other multitudinous middlemen.

It looks as if Stalingrad will hold on doesn't it? I have always imagined Timosh[172] had quite a lot of reserves up in the Urals and the main problem (I should think) is whether he will have to use up them prematurely at Stalingrad. He will want them for the big attack which Werner[173] predicts for the end of October. If a Second Front can be opened immediately then the Nazis are gripped in a vice. If not then the whole thing will mistime and we're in the soup.

Please tell me all about M when you write. I love the way he looks shy when he laughs. This seems to show that normally he is a bit afraid of me and is shy of expressing himself.

Love

Ron

Three days later Dad typed another letter:

H.F. 1 Oct 42.

Dear K,

Everything going jolly well. Have just had a game of baseball with the "battle-boys" and find I'm moderately fit. It's a jolly fine game and I can't understand why we haven't played it more in England instead of the insipid game of cricket.

Just received your nice long letter. I don't mind Renée[174] showing my effort at a poem to the bloke. Much good may it do him.

---

172 Marshal Semyon Timoshenko, Soviet commander of Stalingrad in 1942.
173 Paul Werner, a Swiss journalist who followed the German army into Russia. He wrote *A Swiss Journalist in Russia* (pub. 1942).
174 Renée Shulman – see footnote, page 72.

Unfortunately it was written during the first part of the war but I don't think that there is anything in it that is incorrect.

Went to a dance with boys last night, at a R.A.F. camp. I have much sterner business to be about in the near future.

Mother's parcel of fruit arrived today. I drew 30/- pay day but my field allowance (WOs only) has not yet been published. It is 6d a day (back-dated), bringing my total pay to 12/3 a day (including the 6d extra under the new government rise) and all back-dated to May 27 except the

The rest of that letter seems to have been mislaid. The next one is dated nine days later:

10 Oct 42.

Dear K,

I'm sorry you haven't had a line for a few days, but I think you'll admit that it seems a long time because I had been writing more than once a week before *[the]* last letter. Now a lot of work has piled on and my correspondence has slackened off. It is likely to be in waves like that.

I still like the job. I have a much more clear-cut rôle than in any other place. Here it is a case of teaching languages and current affairs, and as I have always wanted to combine these two I don't know what the Army could offer me more. There happens to be a man in the camp who thinks I should also teach flight and navigation but I'll soon see about <u>that</u>.

Re Pay: (ah! says Kath, that's more interesting!) I was promoted WO II w.e.f. 27.5.42 and the rate is 11/9 a day. My Field Allowance has not yet been published in Orders but it is completely separate from the ordinary pay for all purposes, as it is supposed to make up for the discomfort entailed by Field positions, such as sleeping with mere Sergeants instead of having a bunk of one's own. It is probably not subject to income tax on that account.

Incidentally your new allotment rate comes into force on 12.10.42 so make sure they pay you as from that date.

All this means that I shall have a sum around £14-0-0 in my credit, so I shall be able to buy a few books. I should suggest that on my next leave, which won't be too far ahead, we have a short time away somewhere, either staying in a hotel in London or anywhere else you like to suggest. I suppose you wouldn't like to ask Henry Corke now that we have a baby? Anyway perhaps you would like to make some suggestions. I certainly think we should enjoy a <u>little</u> of the increase, even though you may wish to put the rest of the money to more long-term or altruistic motives. If you insist on a large proportion of it being invested patriotically I think we should put half of it into War Bonds (or Savings or whatever the things are) and loan a few quid to the "Daily Worker." I leave you to make some suggestions, being the Finance Minister of the family. I'm in favour of a little jaunt to London, poissonally"

I think I've left something out of the pay business. I can't be certain of the details but I fancy W.O.s wives get an increased basic allowance, in addition to the allowance from me. They'll tell you at the Post Office. Needless to say your pension rates are going up so it'll pay you to have me bumped off as soon as possible, unless you fatten me up to be W.O.1 and then live the rest of your life in luxury.

Of course I don't mind you going to a dance. I shouldn't go myself if I expected you to remain at home.

The food is much better since we have changed our Mess Cook. Been reading Douglas Reed's "All Our Yesterdays." [175]

He relates how one big newspaper tried to get him to write an article on the "Bomb the Russian Oil-Wells" theme just before Dunkirk.

I hope you are now getting lots of exercise and won't get all stuffy and maternal at your age. Strengthen up the old stomach muscles, won't you! (By legitimate methods!) I go on a cross-country run quite often with the boys and one day (as I think I told you), I had a game of base-ball.

I sent a letter yesterday asking for my name to be taken off the list for a commission. I gave my reasons; that my present Div and Corps

---

175 *All Our Tomorrows* by Douglas Reed, pub. Jonathan Cape, 1942. (The title was inspired by the more well-known work *All Our Yesterdays* by H M Tomlinson, pub. Harper 1930.) Reed was an anti-Nazi but also an anti-Zionist.

combined the two sides of warfare, mental and physical, in a way that I don't think could be found elsewhere.

I've met quite a lot of friends about here. Things are humming nicely and though the general situation re the front etc is gloomy the position nearby is very promising indeed.

Lots of love,

[signed in blue pencil] Ron

Eleven days later, on a Wednesday, Dad typed a short letter from which it is clear that he had been home at the weekend:

H.F. 21 Oct 42

Dear K,

Arrived back quite punctually at dusk so that I caught my bus and was able to do the little bit of work for the morrow that was needed.

I enjoyed the week-end very much and hope you did as well. Tomorrow I may do a hop over to somewhere on the coast, on business. So I hope the cloud conditions are good and the barometer in a kind mood.

The books I bought are of great use and I am very glad I have something to plug away at and keep my own reading from becoming rusty with.

Very busy at the moment. All sorts of new aspects of the job opening up; for instance today I had three other people taking blokes at the same time as I was – under my general tutelage.

I am just going at the moment to write a note to Ma and then have a look at the "Caucasus."

Much love,

[signed in ink] Ron

On the Sunday, four days later, Dad wrote:

25 Oct 42.

Dear K,

Thanks for the note, which arrived in time to be considered "before the week-end." I also wrote to Ma, sending her that 10/- and telling her about our suggestion about the next leave. I did say Nov. 13th, though whether it will be exactly that week I can't say. From Smuts[176] and Roosevelt's statements this week it rather looks as though things might be moving, doesn't it?

You seem to expect prodigious gains for Michael each week. Don't expect too much of him. Remember children (at least bourgeois children) always break their mother's hearts. Then, prepared for the worst, you can enjoy anything over and above that.

I have been reading Tutaeff's "Soviet Caucasus"[177] for the last week, and enjoying it thoroughly. He must speak English almost as a natural language, since it is charmingly written.

Yesterday I went for a bike ride over to Trowbridge, where I have not been before, and visited the library. It is a quite pleasant country town, not very different from Devizes (or Horsham).

Still full up with work, and I am thinking of asking for an assistant soon, as I shall not be able to cope with it if the thing grows much more. It now involves quite a lot of travelling about and consequent waste of time but it makes it more varied from my point of view.

The "flips"[178] are jolly fine and I have caught up a little on the advantages of our modern technical civilisation, a thing I had always wanted to do. I only need to have a bit of car-driving experience and I shall be the complete modern (bow-wow).

---

176 Jan Smuts was a former (and a later) Prime Minister of South Africa. In 1942 he was a field marshal in the British Army and a member of the British War Cabinet. F D Roosevelt was US President.

177 *The Soviet Caucasus* by David Tutaeff, pub. Harrap, London, 1942

178 RAF slang for joyrides

So Krupskaya is good, eh?[179] I imagined the human touch would appeal to you. Does it tell you all about what a model flat companion he was in Switzerland, or is that period not dealt with?

I shall have to write to Mother now, and thank her for nice parcel of apples and cake which crossed post with my letter.

Cheerio, all love,

[signed] Ron

The mention of Trowbridge strongly suggests that Dad is stationed on or near Salisbury Plain (but not at Bulford). This may be Fargo according to Alec Waldron's book.[180] *He previously appeared to have been inhibited by the censorship regime from revealing his location since being posted there around the end of August. But this tallies with his mention of Salisbury on 29th September and his earlier description of "here being miles from everywhere."*

The next letter is dated on the Friday nearly two weeks later:

H.F. 6.11.42

Dearest,

It must seem a long time to you since I wrote, and it is nearly a week since I rang. However, I suppose you are a little inured by now. The lulls do not represent fluctuations in my affection, as you know.

I rang up Dad's office at Warrington at the same time as I rang you, and as luck would have it my Mother was there. She said she would like to come and I am about to write and suggest she comes on Monday, Nov. 16th.

The parcel with pyjamas was received with great rejoicing.

---

179 Nadezhda Krupskaya was Lenin's wife, a Russian Bolshevik revolutionary, politician, and Soviet Union Deputy Minister of Education from 1929 until her death in 1939. Mum had probably been reading her *Memories of Lenin*, published in English in 1930. Krupskaya and Lenin lived in Geneva from 1903 to 1905, returning to Russia as the 1905 Russian Revolution was getting underway. They returned to Geneva in 1908 but it appears soon moved to France. Her *Memories* throw much light on the relationship between the working class and the peasantry and other aspects of the revolutionary movement in Russia.

180 *Pacifist to Glider Pilot*, by Alec Waldron, pub. Woodfield, 2000, p129

I have quite a circle of friends here nowadays and have all my work cut out keeping in touch with them, since we are not strictly near each other.

Have heard from Jimmy in Taunton (or rather Jimmy who was in Taunton).[181] He is just going overseas somewhere or other. Seems to have become quite a fit and keen fighting man. Mostyn also sent a note. In fact if I replied to everybody I had made friends with in the last year I should need a secretary and another couple of typewriters. So I'm afraid I cut a few out, such as Gustav Jahoda, who is quite persistent, however, and thinks that he will get a toot out of me some time.[182] It is very encouraging to think that such fine men exist, even if one cannot be with them. They can obviously only develop one way, as a mass, seeing their inherent qualities.

By the way, I may fulfil my plan of making one or two calls when I pass through London on my way to leave. I have never managed to carry out this idea so far but it is really more necessary at the moment.

Much virile desire bubbling up at the moment, by the way, however, that seems out of place in a world war so has to be treated with aloofness and philosophy.

Camp is dreary at the moment, oceans of mud and very few places to go where one can read, except the bunk. The rank-and-file of the regiment get out of the place as soon as they can. This is unfortunate as it does not go to breed a community regimental spirit. I am turning my attention as much as I can. There will shortly be certain radical reorganisations which will allow a solution of the problem.

Glad to hear you have been seeing Eileen and Renée[183] lately. Did the latter borrow my poems and has she promised to get them back later from the bloke in question? I shouldn't like my works of art to be lost to all posterity. Such a loss to mankind, my dear, don'tcher know!

Bought recently Tutaeff's "Soviet Caucasus" (I think I told you) and have been reading it. By the way, have you read the anniversary

---

181 See page 113.
182 See page 121.
183 Eileen Ireland and Renée Shulman – see page 72.

number of L.M., particularly P.D.'s usual notes?[184] I felt a real glowing of the old heart-cockles with pride as I read them. Read, mark and inwardly digest. If you don't know them thoroughly when I come home I'll divorce you – and that's some threat from a man with a W.O.'s salary (you lucky little soul!) ?&"/@£&'()¼.

I have to have an inoculation (one of the routine ones) tomorrow morning, so I shall probably be out of action all weekend, I shall have to catch up a little on my study and possibly on letter-writing.

I hope you can imagine me at the present. This hut stands right in the middle of the plain. It has a good light, and there are quite a number of blankets if I want them. It is dark outside and just a few planes low overhead. I am sitting without a fire (fuel economy – I have got quite used to it) typing away quite quickly to keep myself warm. This afternoon I cycled a total of 16 miles visiting one or two outlying classes. I was lucky enough to have tea with a unit that was having its dinner at teatime and so I managed two dinners today.

Well, I'll let you know as soon as the leave is fixed up. I'm a bit uncertain as to whether they may not put it off till the following week, but if they do it's only a week's difference, isn't it?

Tell me when the young Spathaky begins to speak, won't you. Then as a professional linguist I will draw up a word count for him, so that he can learn correctly (perhaps!).

Love,

[signed] Ron

It feels weird to be typing Dad's words about trying to keep warm while I am in a Sydney heatwave. A week later Dad typed this:

H.F. 13-11-42

Dear K,

I'm very sorry to have to delay a week, but certain rather important developments have made it inevitable. On the other hand there is just

---

184 L.M. is *Labour Monthly*; Rajani Palme Dutt was a leading journalist and theoretician in the Communist Party of Great Britain.

the faintest chance that I may be able to come during the week. If I can I will send you a telegram.

I will also write and suggest to my mother that she comes on the following Monday. I will bring all the spondulicks with me.

The news certainly seems to be pretty good and I can't think they would dare to be too optimistic if they hadn't very good reason this time. People were so put out after the last debacle.

I wrote a poem to you the other day and went and left it in a note-book I was using, like a silly sap. When I retrieve the note-book I'll let you have it.

Is there anything we can do together for Marjorie (or any other part of the business) when I come home. I could hold a discussion circle or stick stamps, or do anything that was useful. Or I'll take Mike for a walk while you do something if you like.

More next time,

Love,

[signed] Ron

Mike indeed! That's interesting. I don't remember anyone calling me Mike until I was fourteen. I was always Michael until then.

I believe that the poem Dad referred to is the one below. Although it is dated 6th August 1942 this is belied by the title and he probably wrote it on 6th November:

Autumn Camp

The earth grows dark before the stars appear;
No lights are found in garrison and camp,
In dripping dockland, silent city street –
But only iron-clad boots of million men,
The vast new Spartacus, reborn at last,
Who shook with slave-burned limbs the gates of Rome
And threw revolting legions at the angry rich.

The modern Spartacus, with English face,
With earthy soldier's joke, and cigarette
With questioning – how long, when will it end,
What will they do when bugles sound the peace?

What shall we do with them, deluded fools
That follow Hitler, modern Crassus, till
The People show that they too fight with flame,
With lead until the very cities weep
And women beg for peace, and land, and bread.

Still vague, these questionings, though for the few
The mighty pattern of the times unfolds
And makes of history a splendid book
Of workers' anguish, of the peoples' hope,
The short-lived victory, the final page;
The certainty of life from out of death.

So does a boy build up a shining boat,
To sail the creeks of Thames in summer time,
But fails at first, the skill not in his power
And tries, and learns what other men have taught;
Until the dawn, when swallows skim the weir,
He launches out and sails for distant shores
Where Marlow sedges murmur in the stream.

The next letter was written nearly three weeks later – clearly Dad had returned from leave. It was handwritten in pencil:

H.F. 26.11.42

Dear K,

Things in a whirl when I got back. I had dug myself in during the first few days here, but during my leave all sorts of other departments had encroached on my premises and my work had been carried on pretty badly by my substitutes.

However, having been evicted from my premises I am trying to settle down in some new ones and do some instruction at the same time.

Leave was jolly good, and I thoroughly enjoyed our dance and the few walks we had. It was also good to do a few jobs in the old way. During my next leave I think I shall do something like offer Marjorie all my mornings and devote my afternoons and evenings to you. I think both parties to my attention would gain by my planning my time. And when Michael is weaned I suppose you will be able to plan yours a little more freely.

Please let me know if Ma (your Ma) was able to do anything about my letter to Willie in London.

Now I'm going to sit back in the N.A.A.F.I (the only comfortable place in the camp) and relax for an hour or two.

Love – Ron

Chapter 9
Salisbury Plain

There has now been a gap of nearly two weeks since Dad's last letter:

HF 7th Dec 42
10 p.m.

Dear K,

The spirit is very willing (as regards writing) but the jolly old flesh feels very weak at the moment. I have been working quite hard and I feel as if I had a touch of flu coming on. I shall go sick in the morning unless I feel better. The bunk is not too bad – the one into which I have just moved, I mean. It is small and crowded with my stuff, including a table and a bicycle, but it is better than the horrible box I had until a few days ago.

This evening I tried to light a fire for the first time this year, with some damp wood and some stuff called "peat-coal." I struggled with it for about two hours and then gave up in despair and retired for a fairly big supper in the N.A.A.F.I. to warm me. When I got back ten minutes ago the whole mass of peat-coal still glowed dully in the middle, and it looks as though it might go on glowing for the next week, giving out about 2 calories an hour. Still, even a wisp of smoke rising from the ashes is a bit more cheerful than a bare grate. It is not even very cold but I thought I would exorcise my cold by a little more warmth.

Still, instead of that I'll go to bed, so Goodnight, darling. Love to Mike.

Love,
[signed] Ron

Three days later Dad writes again. This time, unusually, his letter is written in blue ink. The P.S. is written upside-down at the top:

P.S. Thanks for parcel

H.F.
10.12.42.

Dear K,

I doubt whether I shall be able to get home for Xmas, but I'll try for a week-end as soon afterwards as possible.

Sorry my last note was so doleful. I duly reported "sick", for the first time in my military career, and took liberal doses of Mist. A.P.C (whatever that is!).

I feel a lot better now, especially as my present bunk is very comfortable. For 3/6 a week I share with some other W.O.s the services of a batman, who lays the fire, sweeps the room and makes my bed, gets coal on the day of issue and does anything special. I don't think there's any exploitation in it, since he doesn't rely on our money to live and his own Army job is a bit of a sinecure – he looks after the Company bath-house! Necessary but not arduous!

I agree with you that "Soviet Caucasus" is a bit choppy; likewise the book on "China", though I think the second is jolly good to have. I still like the picture of all those little figures peering cheerfully out of the walls of a temple-cave – the Lohans, domestic gods or something.

Thanks very much for Denny's address. I will write to him as soon as possible. He isn't far from my people.

Glad to hear our two Ma's saw Uncle Bill. I shall get her to tell me all about him when I see you next.

Raining like hell outside. Wish I'd brought those big boots back with me now!

Classes going well. I'm teaching German quite a lot. I shall really have to learn that language before long, or I shall meet someone who knows it better than I do!

Love, Ron

Two days later, on the Saturday, Dad wrote again in pen. There's an interesting mention of a "phonetical apparatus" – purely science fiction of course in 1942:

H.F. 12.12.42

Dearest K,

I had a rather bad time with the cold, but it's gone now. Also had a rumpus with one of the bosses over a small point but nothing worth worrying about.

Have got a jolly good library going in this place. Also a wall newspaper, "*The Lineshooter*," which has some jolly good contributions and a rattling good editorial (?) by yours truly.

Please congratulate Pioneer Michael on the new clicking-sound. I will duly record it on the phonetical apparatus I am perfecting (perhaps?!!) and use it to build up his first words.

Incidentally I didn't think of it, but perhaps we could meet somewhere for a week-end just after Xmas. What do you think about it? We could perhaps book beforehand in a hotel in Southampton or some such place. The only bother is I don't get time to look up all these things; times of trains, buses, fares, hotel-bookings and the like.

Little sex demons running up and down inside me lately. Find myself making eyes at innocent (?) A.T.S but not too much and never so far with any effect. The Army seems anxious to help matters: I have to instruct auxiliaries occasionally – completely impersonally of course!(?)

Planning a "do" for Xmas in the Sgts' mess. I am on the Entertainments Cttee and am producing a sort of competition sketch like they had at the dance we went to in Ditchling Rise – remember?

Took a Current Affairs talk this afternoon – the blokes lapped it up. They are very interested in the career of Darlan[185] and also in the Beveridge Report.[186]

---

185 Jean Darlan was commander-in-chief of the French armed forces under the Vichy régime but went over to the Allies in 1942 in return for continuing control of French forces in North Africa.

186 *The Beveridge Report* was *the* key report, published in November 1942, which led to the founding of the welfare state in the UK.

I have not managed to get any more flips lately – for which I suppose you will be glad.

Still reading Hart's "Expanding War"[187] and I think it's very good indeed though I don't think he does justice to the Russians completely in the sense that 90% of the actual grappling has gone on in Russia. Our share has been in sea-warfare but that doesn't win wars and occupy countries, though it helps.

It's raining like hell outside. Imagine a dark barracks in the middle of an anthill, a little tidy room (yes, believe it or not) with green-painted brick walls, typewriter, table groaning with books, a fire which smokes a little, a bed, 4 sten boxes with library, a rifle, kitbag and me perched on it all. Love Ron

Dad's last letter of the year was written on Boxing Day, a Saturday, so the "next week-end" he refers to is Saturday 2nd January 1943. "Ma" refers here to Mum's mother, who would have had her Party contacts to thank for getting what I presume was the Beveridge Report:

H.F.
26 Dec 42.

Dearest K,

I imagine I shall be able to get away next week-end for either short-pass or 48.

Could you tell me a train that will get me back to Bulford (or Salisbury) by noon on Monday morning? I have local timetables here but not one that is readily accessible which stretches as far as home. Incidentally I should get the 2.50 p.m. from Salisbury coming, which gets me in for about 6.30 by the southern route.

Thank Ma for the report. It makes very interesting reading indeed. I have advertised it as being available for chaps to read in my bunk.[188]

---

187 *This Expanding War* by B H Liddell Hart, pub. Faber, 1942
188 This will be *The Beveridge Report*. See footnote on the previous page.

I went on the range firing this afternoon and my average was not too disappointing for a man who has not done a great deal of the business. I still feel a bit deafened by the explosion of my old shotgun (actually it isn't so old; I have a much newer one than I had before).

Love to Michael, with many "clicks",

Yours, *[signed]* Ron

Three weeks after this last letter, Dad wrote about a house he had found for Mum and me to live in, near where he was based on Salisbury Plain:

H.F.

19 Jan 43.

(in haste).

Dear K,

I will come and get you on Saturday. Presumably we can return on Sunday. I have phoned the owner of the house and accepted on a <u>weekly</u> rent basis of £2-5-0 a week. I am sending off the cheque tomorrow morning some time. So if there's anything crops up, send me a telegram and I'll stop payment of the cheque.

It's rather a drab place on the outside, rather like an Army building, but the inside is quite nice. There are the following rooms:-

Kitchen scullery pantry bathroom dining-room two bedrooms.

Furniture (as far as I've had time to look):- beds (with blankets but could find no sheets, also with eiderdowns) tables in kitchen and dining-room. Sideboards and pantry cupboards, ideal stove and electric cooker, geyser in bathroom. (He is having the geyser seen to.)

Crockery etc.:- (not much) two dishes, pie dish, washing-up bowl, 4 saucepans, 2 frying-pans, strainer, two flat-irons, 2 kettles, pail, buckets, brooms, large enamelled water-jug beaucoup de bogpapeur!

At least the important black-out boards are there, I'll check them as soon as I can have another look. Bulbs – in most of the lamps, not in some.

Plenty of chairs, including some very nice easy ones in dining room.

I'm getting some coal and will go in when I have some time off and get the place thoroughly cleaned up and the blankets etc aired.

If you want to send me any instructions as to preparation please do so either by wire or express letter.

Hope both well,

Love, *[signed]* Ron

There is a gap of almost six weeks until the next letter that we have, no doubt because Mum and I were staying in the house which Dad had rented for us. However at some point we probably returned to Brighton since we visited the Forest of Worth in Sussex. Dad wrote a poem and made a sketch of the parish church, which he signed and dated February 1943. Later he recalled the visit, in his letters of September 1943 and December 1944, and in another poem dated March 1945:[189]

The Forest of Worth

Red berries light the way in Worth's old wood,
Where serf and knight rode in for sanctuary.
The moss reflects the green of Sussex ash;
The birds sing loud, in spite of February.

Freedom is here, the patient olden striving,
And calm of heart, the senses washed anew.
The Saxon church still gives its ancient shriving,
The stream flows on.

Feb 43

---

189 See pages 242, 379 and 403

By 1st March, Mum and I were back in Brighton and Dad wrote this:

1 Mar 43

Dearest K,

Arrived back to find Cyril had not really done a hell of a lot. He seems to lack initiative. I have been mainly preparing for the course, brushing up my French and getting things duplicated.

Met several friends in the unit who have come in from the dromes and outside stations.

Unfortunately Fanny[190] and wife will not be able to come down on the particular weekend promised, as she has gone on a course, but I will try and come. Perhaps he will come also.

The wretched little shanty down the road haunts me, when I am in the classroom and when I go and get my newspaper. I half expect to see your apron-clad figure come out at the back, as before, or the pram parked in the garden.

However, together with the advantages we must remember the rotten range and the fact that it was tiring to be without proper facilities.

Of course for me it was lovely; You may not have realised it, but it is the longest consecutive period that I have spent with Michaelopolous. He actually knew me by the end of my leave.

I don't exactly know why I started off badly when I came back, but that period is nearly over now and Fanny and I are planning vigorously a great new programme of work in all directions.

I didn't know you dropped interests because of me. Which?

Anyway, it looks as though the war is dragging on towards its end. Nations could not stand as many years of war again as we have had

---

190 Fanny was the nickname of Alec Waldron – see Appendix 2.

already, I feel sure. Then we shall be able to start a scheme for home-building (or <u>family-building</u> is perhaps the better idea) and profit by mistakes and successes of the past.

I am going off to the YWCA for an hour now for some French conversation with Margaret who I have discovered to be an expert. There is however, *pas de scandale*, I assure you.

Love
Ron

Dad's next letter was seventeen days after the last and typewritten. Clearly he has been home to Brighton on leave since then:

H.F. 18 Mar 43.

Dear K,

Considerable changes in the work since I came back from leave, though nothing radical in my own position at the moment. I have had a considerable number of flips lately, including one in a big bomber which was quite exciting.

Hope it wasn't too much of a strain having Fanny and Hilda with you. Did you get him to do any of the work? He is not a bad bloke, though a little flyaway in his ideas. Full of lots of bubble and squeak, backed with considerable ability but sounding almost too good to be true.

I have been thinking of trying to get into the flying side of the Regiment. By the time this reaches you I may have given way to my (Hitlerian?) intuitions and had an interview about it. If you have any strong views about it perhaps you would send me a wire. Actually I may not apply as soon as all that, so there would be time to argue over the thing in a letter. You see, I fear that if I don't I may be sent out of the Regiment at some time, and posted to some darned Convalescent Depot or Mobile Bath Unit. I don't fancy the job of amusing patched-up heroes with talks on how the war should go or lessons on the common irregular verbs.

I don't suppose there will be a lot to do this weekend. Is there any chance of meeting you anywhere, say on Sunday morning

This photograph of Ron Spathaky in February 1943 shows his Army Educational Corps cap badge, Airborne Division shoulder flash and Warrant Officer II sleeve badge.

(or on Saturday, staying the night somewhere if it can be managed). I could hitch-hike a lot of the way and possibly back. It is just a case of it being rather a long way to come the complete way. I suppose you don't feel like coming as far as (say) Chichester or Winchester or Southampton? I suppose you'd have to bring Michael, and I don't think you should come if it's likely to do him harm but I just suggest it as a possibility

Love

[signed] Ron

[Handwritten] P.S. I'll ring up Sat. morning if I can.

It looks as though Mum and Dad did meet that weekend as he wrote a brief note on the Tuesday (23rd March 1943):

23rd

Dear K,

Got back safely. Much more work to do, therefore afraid no time to do more than carry out my promise as you closed the door.

F is still cheery and lots of discussions going on. Hope to write a long letter at the end of the week.

Love

[signed in red pencil] Ron

The next letter we have was written five weeks after the previous one, in lovely clear black ink, handwriting that is a pleasure to transcribe over seventy years later:

As before
1 May 43.

Dearest K,

Have had a quiet day since I took my last period at 3.30 p.m. I had a shower-bath and went up to the local Army Library to return some books handed to me by people who have been sent away suddenly. The place was closed, but I met an interesting Canadian lance-corporal of Artillery, a man of about 35, who also wanted to get into the Library. We finally gave it up and went to the local Y.M.C.A. for a tea and a chat. Later we were joined by a Clydeside gunner.

The Canadian had some very interesting ideas on social development. He came from British Columbia a land of wide open spaces, small but very crowded cities and a good deal of "Beveridge" democracy.

He was that rare specimen in the 20th century (rare in this country, anyway), a real follower of old Adam Smith, of *Wealth of Nations* fame (see our two volumes in the Dent edition – or your volumes). His big bugbear was the overcrowded stuffiness of big cities, the lopsided development of industry at the expense of the countryside. His remedy smacked rather of Walt Whitman, a return to the noble savage, but enlightened by books, good boots, a Bukta tent[191], primus stove (and, I suspect, 200-300 dollars Canadian in his belt-roll).

I managed to convince him that we'd got to build on the framework of a modern industrial society, at least in this country, though he was a clever arguer and had a good sense of humour. His weak point was that each of the "simple" commodities that he wanted to retire into the prairie with were the things the whole trouble is about in peace-time, boots, shirts, waterproof good books, heating and a house.

Still it was refreshing to meet a man who, like many of the Americans in this country, had a strong idea of personal freedom and

---

191 I remember this type of tent from my early camping days!

a slightly baffled feeling that so many Englishmen will "take the kick lying down and like it."

Not that it is representative of Englishmen as a whole. It is merely a result of Baldwinism and Chamberlinism.

(Sunday)

Went a terrific hike with the P.T Sergeant today. By leaving out the beginning and end of it, for security reasons, I can tell you about it. We got to a village called Shrewton, turned south along a pleasant road for about four miles, then struck over country, undulating Wiltshire hills, with copses every mile or so, towards the hamlet of Staple Langford.[192] Arriving there at 1245 we called at the local inn, a surprisingly pleasant one, drank a pint or so of cider each, ate our ration of bread, butter and meat and pondered awhile.

I forgot to say that coming down the hills into the village we hailed a pleasant country-girl driving a firewood cart. The horse was going at little more than walking pace. The girl was quite a simple but well-spoken lass of about 17 or 18. Her father made a living catching rabbits. Her job, when rabbits were in season, was following him round and taking the bodies from the snares.

Leaving Staple Langford we had a bit of a job crossing the straggling branch of the River Wylye, but managed to climb a steep escarpment and get into the extensive glades of Grovely Wood. The trees were in their new summer dresses, bluebells and primroses were everywhere and if the weather had been a little sunnier it would have been ideal.

By vaguely making use of the map-contours we struck the right end of the Wood, that nearest Salisbury. At Wilton, between the edge of the trees and Salisbury we had a rather meagre tea in a teashop (PRHA – People's Restaurant Hostel Association (?)[193]) Then we nipped on to a bus for Salisbury, where we really stoked up in the best canteen in the town.

Booth is a young chap with a very good sense of humour and a fair knowledge. He is conscious of doing an important job and doing it well. He seems a bit (relatively) soft intellectually after Fanny's wiry polemics.[194]

---

192 OS: Steeple Langford
193 There was a BHRA – British Hotels and Restaurants Association – at that time.
194 Sgt/Instr. Alec 'Fanny' Waldron, departed on 13th April for North Africa with the advance party of the Glider Pilot Regiment, which was to plan the Sicily Landings – see Appendix 2.

However, that doesn't prevent him from being a very congenial companion, and an important cog in the HQ staff.

I don't think I shall be able to get home next week-end (8th-9th), but the following one will probably be all right. What do you say? I probably could move a few mountains next week if it were really preferable, but I don't like to alter plans once started.

Hope Michael has thought out a new syllable by now. We shall see all kinds of dialectical leaps in his speech soon, I hope.

Love to you both,

Ron

The next letter from Dad was dated on a Saturday, just a week after his previous one. Mum and I were still living with her parents at 49 Hangleton Road:

H.F. 8.4 5.43.

Dearest,

It has been a hard struggle not to nip onto a bus and come home this weekend. Only during my last few visits have I realised what an enduring yet ever-varying institution a home can be. We must definitely try and get a home of our own if and when this packet finishes.

But the precise things I am doing this week-end may have long-range effects, so I could not deliberately and cold-bloodedly (or rather hot-bloodedly!?) cancel them. Talk of hot-bloodedness! Forgive my primaeval materialist conception – but what is the biological bulletin re next week-end?

I organised a dance for the Battalion last week, and, barring the somewhat cramped quarters which we had, it was even more successful than the one you saw at the other place. We are going forward now from success to success. It may seem a small thing, in the terribly urgent situation, to be doing, but these blokes develop an attitude towards their amenities almost like a woman's attitude towards her home. They grieve if there aren't facilities for hot-washing, plenty of beer and cigarettes – and you can't blame them, with the job they've got.

There's no definite news of F yet, though we are able to write to him. If you ever feel like doing so (repeating your alluring promises in the event of my senility) the address is:-

No 2596687 S/Sgt A. Waldron,

1st BN The Glider Pilot Regt.

Army Air Corps,

c/o A.P.O. 4605.

I gave the weekly lecture to the whole Battalion last week. This involved a dickens of a lot of preparation, maps etc., but it was work I was very keen on. Most of the officers attended, and I felt that it went down very well. The title I took was "Inside Europe." After that I had part of a day to recover, since it involved a big expenditure of energy.

At the moment I am sitting in the mess, while the wind whistles like a thousand fiends around the huts. We have forced the Mess Caterer, under threat of lynching, to provide successively fire, cake and tea. Four of the pilots are playing pontoon and a fifth, a Durham man, is watching them. After every "hand" they move round the table so that one of them is brought closest to the fire.

Another man, a rather amiable but colourless chap, is reading a crime novel near me. A very intelligent Scottish lad has just asked me if I have a stamp to sell.

A few more are dropping in now, from their supper in the garrison or their pub-crawl in "town."

The evening news is excellent. Tunis and Bizerta.[195] The German news in English afterwards was very subdued, and made no excessive claims.

The shuddering wireless, the bane of all messes, is booming some jazz about "You'll Smile Another Day."

When I have finished this letter I shall have a few more minutes with Charlotte Haldane's "Russian Newsreel" (very poor) and a warm, then I shall dive between those blankets as soon as I possibly can. One of the new officers is coming to consult me about something tomorrow. He's only been in the camp a few days and I can't imagine what it can be.

---

195 The two Tunisian cities nearest to Sicily. They were taken by the Allies on 7th May 1943 and this effectively marked the end of German–Italian presence in North Africa.

Hope you feel your world is one worth persevering in. Don't wish for the wider horizons of male warfare. They harden and temper, but you have the chance to expand democratically at your own tempo – Love Ron

(Cont   Sunday 9th. 9.25 p.m.

Read this morning. The officer did not come. Probably could not find this hut in the vastness of the camp. I have gone to the corresponding hut (exact in its likeness down to the screws on the door) in the next Squadron "lines" before now and scrabbled at the place where the key should be, cursing my forgetfulness before I realised that the secreted nail was not in the appropriate place.

This afternoon I saw Margaret for the last time. She got through her interview and is going on to pre-OCTU.[196] She'll make a splendid officer, there's no doubt about it. After having tea in the YWCA I bussed over to A[197] and had a real meal in the big canteen there.

I hope you got the £4 I sent by Money Order, I drew £6 but kept £2 for various things I needed, e.g. a pair of shoes I bought from a bloke for 12/-, in quite good condition.

Could you possibly get my other pair of brown re-soled?

Love, Ron

P.S. I shall almost certainly get 48 hrs next week,

By the Tuesday of that week, "almost certainly" had turned into "I shall not be able to…":

As before 11.5.43.

Dearest K,

It looks at the moment as though I shall not be able to manage this week-end, since there has been a tremendous development in military history. For some unknown reason I have been put on Church Parade !%?½! After two years! Lord knows where I shall fall in, what I shall

---

196 OCTU is Officer Cadet Training Unit.
197 Possibly Amesbury, but Andover seems more likely.

do when I do "get fell in" or how I shall return. Still, it will provide the lads with a laugh. I could possibly get a pass which would get me home at 9 p.m. Friday and let me catch the 5.8 p.m. back here (on Sat.), but it gives such a short time at home.

If you want me to try for this very much, send a wire immediately. If I decide independently to try it, I'll send you one as soon as it's granted or refused.

It seems weeks and weeks since I saw you and the lad, though in fact it is only just over a fortnight, so we can't grumble. I'm afraid that plethora of passes in the Bulford period spoilt us.

I've been reading up my geography of France recently. You probably remember the big geography book in French which I had, a relic of my school trips to France, I believe. It's quite a good one and the subject is ruddy interesting. The lads seem to like it as well. Well, this is not a proper letter, but just a note on the leave situation.

Love,

Ron.

The next two letters are rarities, being written by third parties. The first is from Mum and Dad's good friend Alec 'Fanny' Waldron and the second from Jimmy A, probably his friend Jimmy from his time in Taunton. It seems just possible that Mum had responded to Dad's request, in his letter of 8th May, to write to Alec:

S/Sgt Waldron

2596687

1st Bn, The Glider

Pilot Regt.

B.N.A.F.[198]

15/5/43.

Dear Ron and Kath,

It may seem that I have deserted you from the point of view of letter writing but such is not the case. As you can see from the address

---

198 British North Africa Force

we are now in North Africa which was my guess. It's not bad out here. The weather is warming up towards the hot season which is just starting, reaching its peak in about July. The people are French, Arab and Spanish. All personnel are now very appreciative of their past lessons with you. In particular Bill Denham wishes to thank you for past assistance in learning French. Although news gets through OK it is, generally speaking, very deficient of news about the 'home front.' Main military moves are traced with great care but potential issues at home are more or less ignored. Out here it is almost impossible to gauge the inner feelings of the people. Politics are generally speaking an unhealthy subject and it is wise not to broach it at all unless particularly friendly with a particular native. As a matter of fact I have a standing invitation to the house of a French barrister who is improving my French, in return for which I am teaching him English. Johny Wordwark also had friends here and is doing quite well.

Discussion groups as far as we are concerned are completely out of the question. I can't tell you why exactly, but believe you me I am doing my best.

I have got quite used to the changed life and am doing my bit to maintain my 'vitamins.' I am in excellent health owing no doubt to good food and exercise.

I shall be very pleased to get any copies of the D.W.[199] as old news is better than none at all. Unfortunately I'm not with Bill Ritchie so cannot utilize his excellent French.

Well I suppose I must close and get this posted. Thank you both for the happy time which Hilda and I spent at your home. It was the happiest few days of my life – and I mean exactly what I say.

I look forward to the time when we shall all meet again but business first?

So cheerio to you all. I hope all at 49 are well including your son and heir. [200] Many of the lads wish to be remembered to you.

So all the best from North Africa,

Fanny.

---

199 *Daily Worker*

200 49 Hangleton Road, where Fanny and Hilda had spent such a happy time. "…all at 49" would include Grandpop, Nan, Mum and me. See Appendix 2.

Next comes another letter written by Dad's friend, Jimmy A, who was also serving in North Africa. I insert it here as Dad refers to it in his next:[201]

> 5675125 Cpl. James A.
> GD, Defence Coy
> Advanced HQ
> 1st Army BNAF
> 2.5.43.

Dear Ron,

It's such a helluva time since I heard from or wrote to you that I ought to find a few things to say for once.

Of course there are lots of things I'd like to tell you about which the censor would scratch.

a) We had a cold winter and lived the worst of it in tents, and out of them of course.

b) It's so damned hot and 'buggy' now that only the novelty of it keeps us from wishing for the return of the great coat days

c) I am waiting for a pre O.C.T.U. which is to begin as soon as the campaign – or rather the battle is over.

I haven't contacted any of the people you know.

We have a company library and when possible a Wall News Paper. We have adopted Base Ball from our Comrades in arms.

Water is not as scarce as it might be, but the necessity of constant laundering and bathing puts rather a strain on the system. We have been issued with a "utility" outfit of K.D. *[=khaki drill]*. We have no hats but continue to use "F.S" and "Helmets Steel." I think that perhaps this is a false economy as headaches are none too rare. Perhaps they're caused by something else though.

My sister, strange to say, is developing a critical faculty in directions a little unexpected in view of her calling. My father is becoming a frequent visitor to the old Book Shop at Exeter where he has discovered some interesting stuff.

---

201 Jimmy A is probably the Jimmy Dad referred to over a dozen times without ever giving his surname. On 6th November 1942 Dad had written, "Have heard from Jimmy in Taunton (or rather Jimmy who was in Taunton). He is just going overseas somewhere or other." (See page 177 and also page 113.)

Betty Norris wrote to me from time *[to time]* and has offered to send me out some of Locke's literature which she seems to admire. It will be very welcome anyway as I have nothing of that sort with me that isn't hopelessly out of date.

So far I have proved impervious to the ailments which are all too common among the population of this charming country. This is no doubt a tribute to the R.A.M.C. because as you know I have been the envy of valetudinarians in my murky past.

I am just at the end of a week as Orderly Sgt. and I've had a busy enough time to be glad it's nearly over. It's a welcome change at first, but it rather falls off when you begin to be haunted by cries of "Ord'ly Sergeeent!" in your sleep as well as by day.

A fly has just stung me more viciously, I feel, than was really necessary. Adding insult to injury the little barskit did it on the end of my already somewhat vermilion nose.

One of the blokes was saying in the dining tent that he though*[t]* the end of the war would take him by surprise and that he'd be bewildered. He said, "I won't know what to do first, whether to dump the C.S.M. under the tab or... or..."

"Smack 'im on't bluddy nose" cut in our Yorkshireman.

I'm getting too hot to write much more so I'll pack in and wait for a <u>prompt reply</u>.

Yours,

Jimmy

Dad's previous letter to Mum was dated 11th May; his next is five days later on a Sunday. Dad wrote a postscript at the top, so the transcription starts with that:

Could you send for that birth certificate some time please? They have 2/6 of mine already.

As before, 16.5.43.
1800 hrs.

Dear K,

I duly bulled all yesterday evening and appeared on parade in a curious line of my own, called "Supermunerary", or is it "Supernumerary" (I must look it up – the latter is correct, I think!)

The actual evolution of the parade was quite smart. I am won over in general to the idea that men who are fighting or will fight together should do a certain amount of this bucking, prancing and curvetting on ceremonial parade. When done well it does bind them together. But when one does it with regular monotony it becomes a weariness of the spirit.

I enclose Jimmy's letter which you may like to read. It's quite amusing, though it sounds the slightest bit heat-tormented. I notice he doesn't mention his own girl in it, but only Betty, of the Betty and Joan duo. I wonder if she's failed him under the stress of a year's absence? I find difficulty in remembering what she looked like, though I get the impression of someone dark and rather shallow.

The enclosed poems are copies of contributions to our wall-newspaper. The first was written by someone in an obviously rather reactionary frame of mind. The other is my reply. It is the first bit of polemic verse I have tried, at least for a long time.

I think, further to our phone conversation yesterday, I shall definitely have to postpone this business of leave until next weekend (and cut out the middle of the week).

Have you got any further with your enquiries about crèches. One town was claiming in the press that it had the finest system, but I'm damned if I can remember where it is – a London borough like Hackney I believe.

How about trying to find another woman pharmacist (by advert) and doing half-a-day's work each. You might find one quite near. In fact there might be one with a baby.

Love, Ron.

I believe the poems Dad referred to are these, found among his other papers:

VICTORY.
(Sent to "Fargo" by an unknown contributor)

I am so proud
To be allowed
To die.

So very proud
The State has vowed
That I
Shall fight until the Reich declined,
Still yet another treaty signed
And prouder still in twenty years or more
When these our sons march to war.

* * *

DEFEAT.
(An imaginary reply)

"We are more proud,
As, heads unbowed,
We Czechs die.

So very proud
That men have vowed
That they
Shall fight until the tyrant falls
(The torment of Lidicé calls)
And build a world where nevermore
The best and bravest march to war."

Note:- The Editor accepts no responsibility for the completely opposed views expressed in these two poems

Dad's next letter is dated almost two weeks after the previous one, in which he hinted that he would be home on the intervening weekend:

Attd. "A" Coy. (as before)

29.5.43.

Dear K

Very nice letter at hand. It is a curious reflection on our conduct that we seem to be able to express ourselves better by letter than when we are together lately. Still, it all starts with the heat!

I had a War Office wallah around to see me do my stuff recently. I got quite a nice bouquet about it, although apparently my S.O. thought I was getting a bit too much of the old limelight. Still, it was good form – the class were on their toes and strained considerably to make a good impression.

Afterwards he had a good argy-bargyment with me about method, and I was able to score quite a number of strong points.

I have not done quite so much reading this week, though we have done quite a good week's work. In the evenings it has been a bit hot to settle down to it. Once I am accustomed to the change in the weather I shall go on "stimulating the neurones."

Looks as though things are boiling up, doesn't it? Have you thought any more about this "town with the best crèche?"

I think you said something about leaving it until after the next set of M's injections, didn't you?

I should like to feel if I went into action that the gun I was using <u>might</u> have been assembled by my wife, or even that the drugs had been pounded by her! But I submit entirely to your ruling on that and once you make a decision on it it's best not to think vaguely about what you might be doing. I really don't know enough of the entire circumstances to offer advice.

(Sunday 7-40 p.m.).

Today has been rather uneventful, barring several interesting conversations I have had including one with S/Instr. Booth, A.P.T.C.[202] In reply to your poser about "boots or shoes" he thinks that shoes would be better for a kid, for the same common-sense reason you mentioned – if we are to strengthen our ankles with crutches why not strengthen our legs with leg-irons and so on *ad absurdam*.

By the way, assuming I don't get moved beforehand, the S.O. had asked me to go on a course at Oxford – lasting a week on "International Affairs." If I got it, what a difference that would be from Army life – like a vision of the future, or a glimmer of the past! Not that I idealise it, but I think it could not fail to have a regenerating effect on anybody's brain. It will probably be about August 14th. or thereabouts, so I shall get my leave in first (other things being equal – which I don't suppose they will be!).

I have just been listening to the first ones of a set of Linguaphone records on Hindustani. Jolly interesting – wish I had time to do the whole set!

Have posted a letter to Ma at long last. Last week's little trip to Arundel wasn't bad, was it? We were chumps not to take a map however. I saw as soon as we got back where we went wrong. We ought to have turned further left in the town, after crossing the river bridge. However, that's what comes of insufficient thought beforehand.

Love, Ron

The date of Dad's next letter is uncertain but, as he normally gives a few days' notice of a change of address, I guess it's about 2nd June:

W.O II etc. 1st G. – P. – R.
c/o Hengistbury R.A.F Station
Christchurch, Bournemouth
(Letters posted up to 6.6.43
After that as before)

Dear K,

Writing this on a large pre-fabricated bungalow frame which serves as table in this "P.T. Camp" where I have been sent, mainly as

---

202 Army Physical Training Corps

a change. I needed it badly and the sea air is doing me marvellously well. This morning I went with four or five chaps along the coast and we first of all climbed (with the aid of short linked "toggle-ropes") a mud cliff about seventy feet high. Then we strolled along to a headland and lowered each other down to a half-way point on a 90 foot drop. Having got half-way down we repeated the process. But the last man has a tough job on both halves of the climb. On the second half I was last man. The only solution is to lower the last but one man, throw the rope down, then come down as best you can.

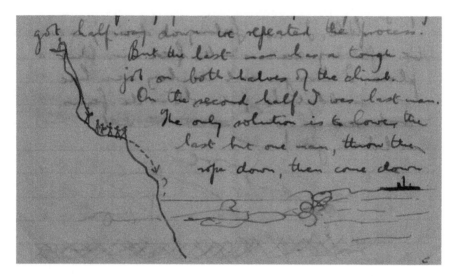

Then I got to the edge of the very steep part and – well, there is no particular technique except to keep your behind and head back to prevent yourself taking a header. If you do take a dive you probably slaughter the four or five blokes who are trying to break your fall, – but whizz!!X%½ ?! I did a lovely toboggan run in my denims and airborne smock.

I can tell you this because it was not part of the official training – that hasn't started yet.

Suffice it that the location is perfect, the weather is perfect (by patches) and the company (including S/I Booth, A.P.T.C my tent-mate) is loyal and co-operative. I may possibly do one or two talks down here in the open but my main object is to get fit. After 24 hours I am certain I have gone a little way towards that.

The prospect of a weekend is rather slim, Whitsun being taboo, but I'll have a shot

That letter ends there, in mid-sentence at the end of the second side of the first page, so there was at least one further page that is now lost.

The next letter was written while in transit to… well, he's not allowed to say where. In these conditions Dad failed to date many letters. Mum would usually write the dates she received them on the envelopes, but I think at least one letter has been stored in the 'wrong' envelope. By examining the paper used, postmarks, and internal evidence from the letters themselves, I think I now have them in the right order.

The first letter is written in pencil on blue-grey notepaper. It is undated, but the words "Received July 2nd" are written in Mum's hand on the matching envelope. I provisionally date it at about 13th June 1943. It was probably written on board ship for North Africa, as it is postmarked "Maritime Mail". A label stuck to the envelope reads, "OPENED BY EXAMINER 3999". The envelope is addressed in pencil to Mum at 49 Hangleton Road, Hove:

> 254248 W.O II Spathaky,
> The Glider Pilot Regt.,
> RNWZW
> British A.P.O[203] 5095

Dearest K,

Received your very speedy reply (concluding with the little quotation from my poem – for which flattery many thanks) This will really be the last note for some time, but whether long or short I don't know. In any case I'll write as soon as we touch anywhere.

If you could send an occasional note to Warrington, it would help me with the job of writing there, though I realise a little the arduous nature of a mother's day. Perhaps it will be better as soon as he can be left without too much danger of him cutting himself with knives or picking up pieces of live coal.

---

203 Army Post Office

It certainly seems as though babies have a remarkable system of balance (within their limits). I noticed at Southbourne how when he fell he carefully threw his head forward at the last minute in order to guard the back of it.

See you soon (I hope)

Love – Ron

Chapter 10
North Africa

Rodomontade in Algeria

In desert Africa this burning sun
Has shone upon both conqueror and slain,
The pyramidal fire, the victory feast
Of Hamilcar, the tents of fierce Mahoud,
Striving to call its mysteries their own,
While giant Atlas with his cool green cloak,
His hair of clouds, is ever on the watch
As nation wears down nation in the sand.
Here mercenaries in their legions toiled
To wring the olive-groves from fellaheen.
Atlas has long outlived them, nor the fire
From skywards puts one wrinkle in his brow
Deep-creased by subterranean travail.
He stands his guard and doubtfully lets pass
This latest army bringing liberty.

15.06.1943

I doubt if Dad wrote this poem before he arrived in Algeria on 27th June 1943, so the date must be wrong.

The following letter is on the same blue-grey notepaper with matching envelope as the previous one. It was postmarked 17th June 1943 which, according to Dad's military record,[204] was the day he embarked for North Africa. The tone suggests Dad is feeling serious about his situation, perhaps for the first time in the war:

> 254248 W.O II Spathaky,
> The Glider Pilot Regt.
> RNWZW
> c/o British A.P.O 5095

Dear K,

I am writing this just before we start and I don't know when it will reach you, probably some days after I have gone.

I hope you don't feel too badly about the whole business. After all, you have a couple of million colleagues. Remember it is very good mental hygiene to be cheerful – and often through the practice thereof one actually does feel cheerful. You may be sure I will write as often as I can and will tell you whatever I can within the drastic limits of security.

I have managed to take away quite a lot of books, including a few of my own, and the typewriter. I hope you got the bicycle pump I sent off.

To while away the time at the moment I am reading "A House Divided" by Pearl Buck. Quite good so far. Au revoir! <u>Please</u> write even if you don't get any letters from me. I will answer them all when the opportunity arises. Remember you are doing good anti-Nazi war-work when you write, because it will make me more efficient.

Also, if you ever get into a jam, remember the various funds you can pester, in addition to the regular Ministry.

1 The A.E.C. Benevolent Fund,
c/o Education Section,
War Office (A.E.3)

---

204 Military service file, ref. D/APC/HD/39300

2 The Airborne Security Fund
address: (see adverts in papers or write to c/o
Command Education Officer,
Southern Command,
H.F.

3 The N.U.T. Benevolent Fund
c/o Mr. Suckling
173? Ditchling Road,   – see old letters
Brighton

There is also the Serving Soldiers' Airmen's and Sailors' Association, whose address I think you have, (the one that is advertised in R.T.O.s offices everywhere).

I have made a will and left my immense fortunes to you and nominated John Jordan executor.[205]

Please send that birth certificate on as soon as you can, with W.N.V

Love to both of you

Ron

The next letter is again undated but Dad writes that he is "en route" (and it is postmarked "Maritime Mail"), so I assume it was written on the ten-day voyage to North Africa, that is between 17th and 27th June. Mum has written, "Received in week ending July 3" on the envelope. We know from his military record that Dad arrived in Algeria on 27th June. He then travelled overland to Tunisia.

A signature, "2/Lt C.P. Scott-Malden", is scribbled at the top of the letter and also on the envelope. I would guess that this is 2nd Lieutenant (later Captain) CP Scott-Malden (1918-2001) acting as censor. He served in the Glider Pilot Regiment in Tunisia and Italy at the same time as Dad and was wounded at Arnhem. He was from Portslade.

Most of the first line of the address at the head of the letter had been neatly torn off using a ruler, possibly by the censor:

---

205 This is the only reference to John Jordan that gives his full name, but I strongly suspect that he is the good friend referred to simply as "John" in many letters. See Appendix 1.

254248 W.O II Spathaky,
The Glider Pilot Regt.
RNWZW
British APO 5095

Dearest K,

This is written en route. I have managed to get quite a lot of my work going and have taken an early opportunity of brushing up some of my own qualifications.

There is a number of interesting people about, including a young padre of the (Presbyterian) Church of Scotland with whom I argue on Hegel, Feuerbach and others. He is very young and very idealistic, having spent the last nine years going from one university to another. I find him and a colleague of his very simple and sincere.

[There follow several lines which have been crossed out. Whether Dad thought better of them or the censor deleted them, I cannot tell.]

Near me the R.S.M is writing a letter with great beetling of brows and glares of concentration. He is an Irishman of a very intelligent and practical type, always smiling, with good teeth, a high domed forehead and hair which is thinning at the front.

Even though he fulfils the traditional requirements of an R.S.M, strictness and extreme smartness, he is known by all members of the Regiment as a real man. Certainly he is as fair a man as I have found in the Army.[206]

More as soon as possible.

254248 W.O II Spathaky,

Love, Ron

The next letter is not dated. It was stored in an envelope postmarked 4th July and addressed to Mrs C Spathaky (Dad's mother who lived in Warrington) but at Mum's usual Hangleton Road address in Hove, Sussex. This could be a slip of the pen.

As she often did, Mum has marked the envelope with the date received – 3/8/43. This letter includes the sentence, "I have written one before this one since landing." However the letter after it is dated 4th July 1943 and is headed, "Letter II"; it is an Air Letter (so needs no envelope) but has no postmark dated on despatch. I remain confused:

"A" Coy – The Glider Pilot Regt.,
c/o 5 BN. No.1. I.R.T.D.[207]
B.N.A.F.

Dear K,

Arrived here yesterday, after quite a pleasant journey. Have spoken to a few local inhabitants. The sea-coast is magnificent, with water as blue as can be. One could sit in it all day away from the fierce heat if there were time.

It is amazing to a foreigner to see how every species of plant and animal is different from the English ones. I have not even seen any grass like ours, though there are numerous splendid mosses and the trees are quite ubiquitous so far. Some very small birds with quick-moving wings flit around like large-sized bees.

---

206 Probably RSM Michael Briody, described in even more glowing terms by Alec Waldron in *Pacifist to Glider Pilot*.

207 Infantry Reinforcement Training Depot

Nearly all the population of N.A. live quite near the coast. The coast Arabs are cheerful coves, but look very down-at-heel. I hear their clothing problem is somewhat serious.

To the rear of us rises a crest of Atlas foothills, not yet the "mighty Atlas"[208] but a tolerable imitation. They are well-wooded, with sharp crests and are very impressive, somewhat dignified and mysterious; not much like the domestic smoothness of the Sussex downs.

At night the birds make noises unlike English birds. There is one which emits a continuous whistling note something like a railway train whistling or letting off superfluous steam.

It is curious to think that nothing lies to the far South of us except three thousand miles of desert, until you get to the Congo and then the "civilised" South Africa. At present I am lying beneath a small wild-pear tree and the scene (which I have altered very slightly) is like this:

By the way, the address which I give is not a very good one for postal purposes but it is the best I can do. I shall possibly not get a letter from you for a fair time, but please go on writing. I have written one before this since landing.

I hope Michael is well. I dropped a line to Mary (Jack's girl) in London, when we touched shore.

It is getting lovely and cool and I must get on the bathing parade so as not to miss "de-sanding" myself. I hope that you are well and that Michael is growing (and crowing) lustily.

Love, Ron

The next letter is dated 4th July, the same date as the postmark of the previous one. This is an Air Letter (not an Airgraph) and, although Dad labelled it "Letter II" at its head, he also wrote a figure "1" on the front. It was addressed to Mum at Hangleton Road, Hove, and has then been re-addressed in her mother's handwriting to "c/o Mrs Clark, Woodhouse Farm, Castle Estate, Bolsover u Chesterfield, Derbyshire." So, Mum and

---

208 "Mighty Atlas who holds aloft on his shoulders the heavenly firmament..." Virgil, *Aeneid*, Book VIII (trans. Day-Lewis)

I had gone to stay with Mum's Auntie Aggie. It bears a Brighton and Hove postmark of date "10 JUL 1943":

> 254248 W.O II Spathaky A.E.C.
> "A" Coy 1st BN Glider Pilot Regt.
> 5 BN No. 1 I.R.T.D.
> B.N.A.F.
>
> 4.7.43.

Letter II

Dear K,

Yesterday I managed to get to hear André Philip[209] speak. You remember him as de Gaulle's right hand man who came from the underground movement in France to contact de G about 6 months ago. He was very good, though necessarily very general on some points, for the sake of the unity of the French National Committee of Liberation.

I manage to get one or two local French papers, but if you can send me anything out it will help, especially an LM or World News. Occasionally one gets the radio bulletins.

At one time during our wandering I managed to spend a few hours in a small town. It was in the evening, and the white buildings were modern and cool. A British regimental band was playing in the square and soldiers and sailors of all colours (and almost of all nationalities) were walking up and down, making eyes at the local girls. They are a bit handicapped by the language difficulty, but many acquaintanceships seemed to be in the process of formation. I had a few glasses of "Vin Orange" in a pub with some old 1st Army chaps. I made certain, however, that I made them drink two to every ½ + water that I had. Near the "Grande Place" was a small public park with desert cacti, statues and a balustrade overlooking the river. I had a few words with a girl who was reading a novel by Henri Bordeaux. She said her "only enthusiasm" was reading. She had left a boarding-school the year before and was glad she left because "the other girls

---

209 André Philip was a socialist politician who had become Interior Minister for the French Committee of National Liberation (CFLN) in July 1942. He had been a leader of the SFIO (French Section of the Workers' International).

were stand-offish." She was not particularly well-off and only the company of a few other girls helped.

"Now I spend all my time with Maman and my married sister." She indicated Maman and sister a little further along the balustrade. I bowed to the old chaperon and the young pretty matron. After teaching her a few English words to help her in the walks with an English chap I drifted off. The band was playing the three national anthems and everyone within sight was standing stiff and erect. The sun dipped beneath the Med. I found my jeep, with some weird commando individuals crowded in it, and we drove back along the coast road at a hell of a rate, making the already cool breeze feel cold.

Men from Burnley, Sheffield, Lanark, Exeter and everywhere else trudged along the sandy road, shouting, singing, walking silently or reeling slightly, thinking of difficult days in Tunisia, when it looked as though the numbers would be too few and the panzers too many.

I have swum each day since our arrival, and have written to Ma once or twice. Perhaps you would ring Warrington 500 some time and make sure Pop knows I am all right so far?

You can use these Air Mail letters to write to me, though I think they cost a little more than out here. I have not heard from you yet, but the first letters are only just arriving, so I shall wait patiently.

Today is marvellously cool for N.A. It will probably arrive at the gasping stage towards 5 p.m.

Incidentally it would be interesting for me if you could possibly keep these letters, as I may be able to piece together something from them in later days. It is unwise to keep a diary at the moment.

Today I have been rearranging my kit so that I can get at the most needed things easily. Everything is covered with sand, but it shakes off easily. I shall have to go and do a bit of work now, in connection with my normal duties. These are only just beginning, but I have good hopes. Please send that birth certificate when possible. Keep well. Courage.

Love, Ron

The next letter is postmarked on the letter itself – 9th July 1943. It is also headed "Letter III", so we seem to have the correct sequence. It's written on an Airgraph form, which has a panel for the address and a fixed space for the text of the letter. Dad's writing is quite small here, with limited paragraphing:

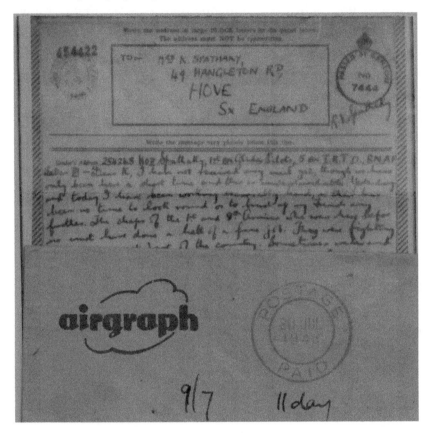

TO: – Mrs K Spathaky
      49 Hangleton Road
      Hove
      Sx England
Sender's address: 254248 WO II Spathaky, 1st BN Glider Pilots, 5 BN I.R.T.D. BNAF[210]

---

210 Airgraphs were photographed at a Kodak centre in Algeria and sent as negatives on microfilm. They were then printed in England from the microfilm, placed in window envelopes and posted on. The postmark on the envelope thus shows the date of posting after processing in England. A postmark on the letter itself shows the date of the original posting.

Letter III – Dear K, I have not received any mail yet, though we have only been here a short time and this is understandable. Yesterday and today I have been working reasonably hard, so there has been no time to look around or brush up my French any further.

The chaps of the 1st and 8th Armies who were here before us must have done a hell of a fine job. They were fighting in the very worst part of the country. Sometimes water and even ammunition must have been scarce and brought up on precarious transport such as mules. We are comparatively luxuriously off. This is the old story of the pioneer and those who follow on – the epigones. Perhaps we shall be upgraded to pioneers as time goes on.

Needless to say everybody is hoping for action. The whole country, French, British, Americans, Arabs (an Arab is a town councillor in Algiers and another is a member of the French Council of Liberation) have all one question upon their lips – when? Please send me any magazines or papers that are of interest, without making it a burden on yourself.

Give my love to Michael. Tell him I'll bring him back an elephant, if I can push him across the Alps. Or perhaps he would like a nice stretch of desert to play in, with a few date-palms and oases? I must now get ready for a spiffing parade, with much elbow-grease in the cause of smartness. Hope you are well. Make it a long letter –

Love, Ron

A major event of the war was about to take place: the first attack against the Germans and Italians on the European mainland. Dad writes an Air Letter on 10th July 1943, the morning after the night-time attack on Sicily. The postmark confirms the latter was posted on the 10th and Mum has noted the dates of sending and receiving as usual, namely 10/7/43 and 19/7/43. The letter is numbered "2":

254248 W.O II
A Coy 1st BN Glider Pilot Rgt.
5 BN I.R.T.D., <u>B.N.A.F.</u>
10 July 43.

Dear K,

You will see by the morning's news that Sicily has been invaded. Everybody is agog with this, though no details are available. It makes one feel that things <u>do</u> change and one will get home some time, even if it is a long time ahead and via Rome, Florence, Milan, Marseilles, Paris and all stations to Berlin.

I have by now seen a little of the North African coastal hills. The forests of cork-oak are quite pleasant. Undergrowth is dense and of a vivid green, mostly menthol bushes and various semi-desert grasses and flowers. One or two of the wadis have water in them even as late in the summer as now. Occasionally one comes across an Arab farm, with a small donkey braying and pulling at its tether, a group of children in rags playing in a field (cleared with difficulty and always on the point of returning to forest) and the farmer comes out, look at our helmets and murmur "Hammidulilah" in their own language not wanting to commit themselves to any European tongue in case they use the wrong one. It has struck me several times that in some of the most backward villages some people may not be completely clear as to the fighting having finished in N.A.

But perhaps, like so many "superior race" theorists, I underestimate the local Arabs. They probably have their own institutions, their advanced individuals, their militants and their own means of news-transmission.

I sent an ordinary letter to Fanny[211] yesterday, I don't know when it will get there. I mean to write to Jim as soon as I can in addition. I may bump into one or both of them sooner or later.

There is an intense interest in news from home here, together with a serious lack of means of supplying it. Please tell me anything and everything when you write and try and send some parcels of periodicals and papers, I prithee. But don't put the ordinary letters

---

211 Fanny Waldron – see Appendix 2.

in with the papers, so that if the papers get lost the letters will not necessarily "go for a Burton" with them.

This morning I am recovering from a piece of military training I took part in. I cannot say anything about it except that it was novel and rather strenuous for me. If I get some more exercises of a similar kind I shall be as fit as can be, albeit somewhat lighter than usual, due to sweating.

I think there is no objection to our friends knowing that I am in B.N.A.F., but my unit should not be mentioned in the same breath. If anyone asks who I am with, say the "Airborne troops" or the "A.E.C." I should like the blokes at school to know if you should ever see Percy.[212] I often think of the old School and the pleasant (if somewhat complacent) faces in the Staff Room). Also I keep on remembering the B.E.C.S.[213] and our numerous acquaintances in it. If I ever get a chance I will write to the Sec., of the M.C.Cttee.

Tell Michael I think of him a lot and will bring him a camel at least, but perhaps some macaroni will be better, since it will indicate progress – I am always thinking of your dear self.

Love
Ron.

The next letter was written on 14th July and labelled "Letter V". This numbering in Roman numerals now (since Letter III) seems to apply only to the Airgraph format of stationery. Dad says he had written the day before, and that must have been Letter IV, but it has not survived:

Letter V. Sender's Address WO II Spathaky, A Coy 1st BN Glider Pilot Regt. A.E.C. B.N.A.F.

Dear K, I wrote yesterday (13.7.43) but as I have a couple of spare airgraphs and am just packing my kit I thought I would dispose of them. I am keeping very well. A number of English out here suffer from stomachic complaints until they become acclimatised, but I

---

212 Percy Ireland – see page 72.
213 Brighton Equitable Co-operative Society.

have been relying on the old endocrine glands and regular doses of Andrews' liver salts.

The midday heat is the problem of this climate. It provides the temptation to drink water, and water on an empty stomach here has an appalling effect. On some days the flies are rather bad, but occasionally there is a day with weather of European type, and then one feels fine.

Please remember that you can get airgraphs or air-mail letters to send to me (I don't know which). They are much quicker. I have not received anything yet from England, but I feel in my bones that the problem is going to be a very difficult one, at least from England to here. So we shall have to resign ourselves to it or get Bill to ask a question in House. – Love, Ron

"Hurrah!" cries the transcriber. A typed letter at last!

254248 W O II Spathaky, A.E.C

"A" Coy Glider Pilot Regt

Army Air Corps, B.N.A.F. 21.7.43

Mrs K Spathaky

49 Hangleton Rd ,

Hove 4 Sx

Dearest Kath,

By a most unusual chance I am enabled to send this letter to you quickly. I am full of beans and fitness, though in rather an out-of-the-way place. It can hardly be described as isolated, however, when there is a whole army round about.

I hear that the Press gave a good account of the doings of our Regiment after the Sicilian landing. It's quite a thought – that one is in the unit that opened the Second Front[214]! There were deeds of

---

214 It is interesting that Dad refers to the Sicily landings as the Second Front. I have not seen the phrase used for the Italian campaign by any other writer. Within British politics the Communist Party was the leading proponent of the 'Second Front Now' campaign, but this referred to an attack on German-occupied north west Europe, not on southern Europe. The campaign reached its peak when forty thousand people assembled in Trafalgar Square on 31st March 1942.

enormous heroism; unfortunately they cannot be told for a short while, but will be released in the near future. As I write the Allies have occupied about a third of the island, including most of the towns (like Caltanissetta and Ragus).

The heat is difficult to get used to. I realise now that I used to read the letters of Jimmy and others in N A, but did not picture to myself the conditions that exist by about 4 in the afternoon, when the earth is throwing it back as well as the sky and one lies very nearly panting for breath and waiting for the short time from about 6-30 p m until dusk and 8-30 p.m. when civilised life is possible. There is also a period of about 2 hours early in the day when it is bearable. It is mainly for this reason that I should be glad to set foot in Europe again and start the long path which will lead back home.

Many of the towns around here suffered badly in the bombings. Native and other life became completely dis-organised and there have been outbreaks of typhus. Curiously enough there are some people who attribute the disease to the defects of the Arabs themselves! First we smash their villages and destroy what systems of water supply and sanitation they have (when I say "we" I mean "Europeans"), then we throw in their teeth their lack of cleanliness.

However there are certain sections of organised opinion in N.A. which guard the worst excesses and press for a better treatment of the "indigènes."

I haven't received any mail yet, which is rather a nuisance, but I am confident that you will have written.

I must catch this unusual courier now, so I will start the day's work and hope that I get a letter with some home news soon,

Love RON

Dad typed another letter (another "Letter V"!) three days later:

W.O.II Spathaky, A.E.C.
"A" Coy 1st BN The G.P.R.,
B.N.A.F.   24.7.43
Letter V

Dear K,

Still no mail, but in hopes. It generally takes 5-6 weeks and then you get about ten letters all at once and read them as a serial.

I half wrote a letter to you last night but was overtaken by the swift African twilight. Unfortunately I put it down (still in deep dusk) and today I cannot find it anywhere.

This afternoon we all went on trucks to a very decent beach to bathe. The water was hotter than I have ever known it.

It is most pleasant, though very enervating if dips are prolonged.

You will be glad to know that F took quite an honourable part in the Sicilian operation.[215] I cannot say much about it yet, though we have just received the news that Palermo has fallen and there is a strong likelihood that the rest of the island will fall in the near future. Unfortunately I was able[216] to take a single risk in company with these splendid boys, due to being a "static B---," as people in stay-back occupations are called by the "veterans." However that might possibly be remedied in the end.

Needless to say I shall be jolly glad to get a foot into Europe, since it will be a foothold nearer home. It is not because I dislike this country, or its inhabitants, unlike some of our racial-theorists, whose scorn of humbler foreigners is generally due to his lack of real experience of them. But to be in Europe will be a symbol – that we are on the ground which stretches all the way without a break to Dieppe, and almost Brighton.

As I type, F is building his bed out of some old boards he has scrounged from somewhere. It will be about the first time I have

---

215 "F" refers to Sergeant Instructor Alec 'Fanny' Waldron, who had a leading role in the landing of troops by glider in Sicily. Due to lack of communication about changes in the wind speed off the coast of Sicily, obviously vital data for glider pilots, there were heavy losses of life. Waldron was pilot of a glider that landed in the sea. Through his skill the troops aboard made it to the shore, while Waldron himself, a non-swimmer, clung to the floating aircraft for seven hours before being rescued, hospitalised briefly in Malta and then returned to Tunisia.

216 He must have meant to write 'unable'.

not slept on the earth (with my ground-sheet under me, of course). Boards are a bit harder, but I think the general feeling of being off the soil and a little further from the beetles and (rare so far) snakes is a compensation. F and I have been doing some washing today. One has to work for three days here and then do a day's laundering. There is no other way out if one wants to remain moderately clean.

There is one considerable compensation in this terrific climate, the fruit. We are just in the season of ripe melons, figs and grapes. I have seen quite a lot of lemons about also, but so far have not been able to buy any to send home. I will do so as soon as I can, though I don't think much of their chance of getting there. It would be good for Michael to have one drink of real lemonade not made from Lease-Lend juice.

.... (later) The dusk overtook me again, and I am continuing this as the early afternoon heat mounts up. The cicadas will soon cease one by one their "reel unwinding" act and the olive-groves will be drowsy and empty except possibly for some Arab labourer caught during his day's work by the heat, laid out rigid under a tree, in the position in which true Believers hope to die, laid out straight with his arms folded over his chest, his fairly heavy robe pulled completely over his head and shoulders.

You will see by this that the old typewriter got out here quite unharmed. I was very surprised. Most of my books (those used for work, that is) got out also. But if you ever get a chance of a cheap typewriter for the post-war period don't let the above stop you from snapping it up. I don't believe the miracle of transportation will be repeated.

When you write please tell me all about Michael's development, won't you? I shall be very interested to hear about his first attempts at speech. Remember he made no attempt to connect any sense with the sound at all when I was there last. I hope you are persevering with all those common-sense ideas about education you had. I have no fears that by being brought up by a mother alone will give him any particular inhibitions, though I should be very concerned about such a prospect in the case of any other woman.

I have been teaching myself quite a lot of Italian. It is a lovely language, and I hope I have the chance to use it somewhat more than I have used French.

Well, I'm afraid the real heat is coming now, and the keys of the typewriter are becoming hot to the touch. I shall settle down and read a French novel "On se bat sur Mer" until I fall asleep. F has gone swimming but I feel I haven't the time and in any case I don't want to be enervated during the later part of the day.

Yours in great good humour,

Love, R O N

The next letter is dated 1st August 1943 and is handwritten up to and including the first paragraph. Dad then switches to typing:

Letter V ?

W.O II... 'A' 1st BN G.P.Regt.,

B.N.A.F.   1.8.43.

Dear K,

Work thrown back a little bit last week by me going sick on two days. I overate melons or something unromantic. For a day I was "iller" than I have ever felt in my life, but, except for an occasional reluctance to eat a meal, I am cured. (Going over to typewriter – quicker.)

The news about Italy is great isn't it?[217] There must be a very great development going on among the Italian people. It makes one wonder very much which forces are taking the lead and coming to the fore as regards the future of Italy. For all we know this is Italy's Kerensky period.[218]

My illness made me a bit browned-off with the eternal olive-groves and heat, but I am objective enough to know that this is "the voice of the stomach." I have met Frenchmen who told me of the real interior where heat is heat and men have even overcome Saharan conditions, by careful training and determination.

---

217 This was presumably the dismissal and arrest of Mussolini by King Victor Emmanuel III on 25th July 1943.

218 The implication is that Italy might soon have a communist revolution. In Russia's October Revolution of 1917, the Bolshevik communists took power after the brief period when Alexander Kerensky's more moderate socialists held power after the February Revolution.

Still, I can't help thinking with intense nostalgia of a good sweet Brighton rain-shower (with no flies and insects to follow) or a day with light sunlight on the Undercliff Walk.

During the last few weeks I have not had much contact with the local inhabitants, having been in a rather more isolated place, but I hope to see a few French people on a little sort of outing I am taking to a sea-town not far away. I have got a lorry and some grub and am taking some of the "administrative company" of the Regiment, so that they can get a change from their normal rather routine work.

(a few hours later). Well, the trip was quite a success. The town was quite a pleasant little resort, untouched by the war, with good bathing and some natural attractions a bit more varied than much of the usual N.A. coast. However I mustn't describe it in detail otherwise I would be giving away where we were, to others besides you.

I have just received letters from you dated 20 June and 4 July. This seems to be bucking up a bit. Would you mind very much letting "SWN" know my new address at 519-21 Grand Buildings, Trafalgar Sq, W.C. 2. It will be much better than me wasting an air-letter on them. We only get one a week. Perhaps you could also tell the Sec., of the Co-op M.C.C.?

I have been learning quite a bit of Italian. I shall certainly hope to make use of these various things I have picked up because of the darned war. Would I could have picked them up in some other way, but there. I mustn't indulge in the dangerous philosophy of Shakespeare's character:

"The world is out of joint. O wicked spite!

That I should be the one to set it right."

I am hoping to get permission tomorrow for an Iti prisoner to give me a bit of dope[219] tomorrow. Straight from the horse's mouth so to speak.

I'm glad Bernard[220] called in. I bet he was surprised to hear I'd beaten them (or quite a lot of them) out abroad. Hope I beat many of them back too, but that is a bit of a forlorn hope, I suppose.

---

219 'Dope' – information, especially that which is not generally available.
220 Bernard Stone, colleague of Dad's at Brighton Intermediate School

I have seen during my travels some of the towns in the war zone. Several have been frightfully mangled. When they had been in enemy hands they had been left without A.R.P. shelters, blast-walls or any protection. The crowded native city, beneath thick but crumbly walls right in the centre of one town had simply been reduced to a mass of rubble. In the thick heat of afternoon the whole thing seemed alive with stench and typhus signs were up on many walls. There's nothing like an Oriental town or hamlet for the breeding of malignant diseases as soon as any disorder or disorganisation occurs. They have such difficulties with sanitation in the normal way that the problem becomes intolerable when life itself is thrown out of gear.

I believe the French population of the war zones has had a hell of a time. According to the press the resident General of Tunis went down to some of the worst areas last week, but apart from the distribution of a few token gifts he was unable to do very much. The basic economy of the country has to be got going, and that must be a hell of a job, seeing that the bulk of its commerce was with France, Spain, Italy and only a little with G.B. and U.S.

Well the last evening flies are making meals of my arms at the moment, so I will hasten to cover them up as comes in the gentle hour when the flies disappear and the mosquitoes and other dear small beasts take over the night shift.

Yours with ever so much love, and ever so much for Mike, Ron.

Next we have a letter handwritten in ink on seven sides of lined notepaper. The date should be 1943, not '42:

Attd. "A" Coy 1st BN G.P.Regt,
B.N.A.F. 11.8.42.

Dearest K,

After a few weeks of camp in some moderately pleasant but rather monotonous olive-groves, during which time I worked fairly hard, we have been sent to a rest-camp for a few days. This is on the coast in another part of N.A. There is a splendid bay with silky white sand,

and a sea of brightest blue which a fierce sun beats upon, tempered only by cool breezes. Inland, once through the luxuriant gardens of the white colonial villas, there is a well-blessed region with a variety of plant-life I have not often seen out here. Tall cypresses that make one think of Italy, fig-trees, nasturtium hedges, and quite a number of big white flowers of definite African type.

At one end of the vast bay, pointing out into the Mediterranean like a jewelled and pointed dagger, is a native town. It is much whiter and cleaner than the plague-infected villages we have seen. There are many trees in its squares and gardens, and, terminating the promontory on which it stretches into the sea are the suitable contours of an old, long and low-lying Spanish fortress.

I am sitting, naked except for some gym-shorts, under a respectably-sized tent open at both ends and tied on to the trees of a tall hedge and earthen embankment on one side. Beside the 3 beds and mosquito-nets of Fanny, Booth[221] and myself we have quite a smart table. It is made from three big Italian motor tyres and a very large circular metal plate which fits the tyres as though it had been made for the purpose. There is even a slight camber from the centre downwards and a rim at the edge which prevents plates and mugs falling off.

The villa in the grounds of which we camp is, despite the successive sojourn of several sets of troops, magnificent. It is gleaming white among the cypresses, firs and African pines. The roofs are flat in the usual French-Arabian style, and the windows are square, with the most elaborate iron-work grills outside.

---

221 Fanny Waldron and S/Instr. Booth APTC (see Appendix 2).

Some of the furniture has been left by the owner (a Harley Street specialist, I am told) and in its solid dark mahogany and teak-like qualities it sets off the white walls to perfection.

Only the arcades outside the ground floor have modified-Moorish arches. In a courtyard on the sea-side is a stone swimming-pool, which can still be illuminated at night by big electric bulbs beneath the surface of the water.

In my travels I come across various interesting relics of the "war that has passed over" the country. One evening I was reading some personal letters that were left by a German who was in a hurry. Here is an amazing (or is it tragic) bit from one of them, written by a woman.

"It has come to pass at work that we have to work all hours that God sends… but I must answer something in your letter of 5.4.43. It is true, Fritz, that I slept twice at Röhr, but what's wrong with that? I sleep with nobody – believe you me! I wrote this so that you shall know what I do when I go to Röhr. The Kitzelberger Family, Stüttgart-Röhr, Schönbuchstr. 5. – that is my answer."

She then defends herself against the charge of staying out late by saying that she works 14-15 hours a day "at the Firm." "When would I have the time to go out?" Also he had accused her of going alone with soldiers to the pictures on 26.2.43. She refutes this as a lie etc. etc.

It's queer sitting here in Africa and reading these disconnected fragments of someone else's life. I feel completely detached from the bloke who received it – as though I am watching him from another planet. Thus does a front-line cut a world into pieces.

A chap also found in the grounds a copy of the Italian paper "Corriero della Sierra" for April. It was pretty poor fascist propaganda. Its great theme was the impossibility of U.S.S.R agreeing with the "pluto-democracies." (e.g. "Stalin will never agree to the Atlantic Charter") and the "irreconcilable" quarrels between de Gaulle and Giraud. All this has been proved false by the facts.

I have talked to German prisoners from time to time. They admit the existence of vast dissensions within the Nazi ranks and freely describe the rôle of the S.S. troops in Poland, though they made the usual claim that the Wehrmacht had no hand in this – only the trained thugs.

You will be pleased to know that I am fit from sea- and sun-bathing, my digestion has recovered from the far too prevalent dysentery troubles and I am quite happy, though longing for the successful conclusion of the whole thing and a return home to your dear self and to Michael.

However, we knew when we got married that this would be a decade of "Sturm und Drang" so we have been psychologically prepared for it in a way that many of our comfortable lower middle-class friends were not.

I haven't received the birth-certificate yet, or the news-papers, but I have just got your latest airmail, for which many thanks.

Love,

Ron

My research has indicated that the "splendid bay with silky white sand", where Dad spent this 'rest-camp', was the Bay of Hammamet. He wrote a poem about it which he must have mislaid since I found it on the back of a sheet of notepaper on which he wrote a letter to Mum more than a year later, on 24th January 1944:

The Gulf of Hammamet

An ivory jewel
On green waters
Lies Hammamet
The mosque sleeps

Behind the fortress wall.
A muezzin in white,
Whiter than the salt lakes at Gabbez,
Calls Islam's sons to prayer.

Within the ferengiz English lady's garden
There is a lotus-pool, with white stone round,

Beneath the coolest palm spray
Where the small fish eat the evil larvae.

Upon the Arab road, the ancient highway,
An old man with peace upon his face
Gives three locust-fruits
For courtesy
To a stranger.

Alec Waldron confirms in his book that the rest-camp was at Hammamet where, having nearly drowned in the Sicily landings, he was taught to swim by PTI Sergeant JLS.

Dad writes again a week later:

W.O II S
A Coy 1st BN Glider Pilot Regt
<u>B.N.A.F</u> 18.8.43.

Letter VIII?
Dear Kath,

I have just come to the end of a short holiday which the Army has given us. I have described it in as great detail as possible in an ordinary letter[222] which will arrive in time. Suffice it here to say I feel as fit as a fiddle and ready for another tussle with sand and eternal olive-trees. However tout passe, tout casse, and I suppose we shall get out of the country some time, but whether into Italy, Egypt, Crete, Syria, France or England it is impossible to say.

We have a discussion coming off next week on the famous chapter. It should be interesting as everyone is doing the necessary private study beforehand. There was quite a good one last night on "The Allied Treatment of Liberated Territories." Quite a bit of debating talent of a rough and ready kind was shown, with some shrewd common-sense.

As I write this the weather is quite exceptional for a N. African late afternoon. Though the sun is pouring down on the bay there is

---

222 See page 225.

strong salt breeze blowing through our tent. This letter has already been blown on to a cooking pan, as you see from the smudge (lower left).

This evening we are having a game of baseball, under the professional tutelage of Sgt. Instr. John Booth, A.P.T.C., one of the three inhabitants of our tent. Most of my time is spent reading. I have been dipping into Dorothy Woodward's Problems of the Pacific (Penguin). May I recommend the four or five pages in it on the history of China as an absolute masterpiece. Also dipped into some massive tomes in French and German by Count Keyserling, the leading pre-Hitlerian German psychologist. The latter were left here in the villa either by the Germans or by the original owner when he was dispossessed.

I haven't had any mail while I've been at this particular spot, but that's because we are away from the mail-distributing centre. I'm hoping very much that the first packet of news-sheets will arrive soon. News is perhaps the worst difficulty here. Though I have lots of two-month old "Listeners" and things I only know from a Yank unit bulletin that Gerry is evacuating Sicily and we're hitting his Siebel barges pretty hard.

Been ploughing through "Garibaldi & his 1,000" by Trevelyan;[223] – jolly good on the fight against feudalism in Italy. Now I must get down to learning a few more languages just in case various eventualities occur.

Hope Michael is still an interest and not a burden to you. As for the mention of Margaret – well, les femmes ne sont jamais satisfaites!

Love,

Ron

Dad's next letter is written in pencil on a NAAFI Letter form – like an airmail letter that you fold and stick so that the address appears on the outside:

---

223 *Garibaldi and the Thousand* by G M Trevelyan, pub. Longman, 1909

WO II Spathaky, A.E.C.

S.O. Edn HQ 1st Airborne Div.,

B.L.A. 20.8.43.

Dear K,

Hope the job is going all right and Michael. I'm not in any danger – and not likely to be, as far as I can see. At present, besides doing quite a lot of work on our "In-the-Field" job, I'm exploring the pleasant by-lanes and hamlets of the country, brushing up my French and generally diving into the local situation. The day before yesterday I met one of the leaders of the local Resistance. Today I hope to go and interview him officially.

Sitting in the fields near our truck as I write, there is no sound of plane, shell or voice, except two blokes nattering about the Naafi ration in a nearby hut. Tom is really a good companion to have, and I have great hopes for him in the future. He has brought lots of very sensible books with him and […] readily of the opportunities he has neglected in the A.E.C. We had a mumbled discussion about all these points as we slept in the open the other night.

I have apparently survived the appalling rations of the journey here, though I had the most painful "seizing-up" of the old digestive system yesterday. I loosened it up by 2 number Nines and ½ oz. of olium castorium (or what you will?).

I'm already longing for a letter from you to say how the job is going and how many lovers you have acquired in your new social world. Please write – I have only a rather restricted little milk-maid of 17 to speak to on our farm – who has never been beyond the local town and who thinks I must be a foreign millionaire since I once visited Paris. You stand in no danger of competition at the moment. But I'm sure you won't bother about me talking to as many people as possible. I should consider my time misspent if I didn't get among the people. – Lots of love, Ron.

I have dated the following letter from the barely visible postmark, showing "22 AU 43". Mum has also written that date on it, and 31/8/43 as the date she received it. The letter is written using very poor quality ink, which gets fainter and fainter until Dad dips his pen or re-fills it:

W.O II...... A Coy
1st BN Glider Pilot Regt.
B.N.A.F.

Dear K,

I am now getting your letters regularly, though very late ∴ [224] they are going through 5 BN I.R.T.D, the original transit camp we were in. Don't put anything on the address except what I put on my last letter, please? (i.e. copy the above, plus my name, for the next letter.)

I was very glad of the *Post* etc. in the bundle, and the "Time and Tide." Would you mind fulfilling an urgent book purchase for me? Would you buy me Max Werner's Attack Will Win in 1943 (Gollancz? 7/6?)[225] and Deutsche Soldatentum: a German military reader by W.B.P. Aspinall (Harrap, 1943; 5/-)

If you can send them out, and I know chaps are receiving parcels and even small boxes of books, then please tie them in your best professional manner, and then double it!! Every parcel that comes out seems to have been the victim of a steam-hammer plus a drop-forge; corners are open, the coverings are torn, in fact it almost looks as though <u>each</u> were opened by amateur looters.

Your suggestion of your taking a place of your own is certainly epoch-making. I suppose the old folk have visions of you developing into one of these 'ere Army grass-widows! Naturally you always get periods of fed-upness with the rather contracted hell of your own home. It is completely up to you. If you move perhaps you could let me know in time and I'll leave my card at your place if and when I ever come back to England. (Curse this lousy ink, pen and the HEAT!)

I'm very glad that Michael's slight bandiness is not serious. I have always heard that the appearance of such a condition in very small children is not serious, since it always corrects itself.

---

224 Dad has used the 'because' symbol, which makes sense here.

225 *Attack Can Win in '43* by Max Werner, pub. Soviet Russia Today, 1942. Max Werner was the nom de plume of Alexander Schiffrin. (See also page 38.)

I should not mention it to Hilda if I were you, but Fanny has been suffering rather badly from his old sinusitis. It will probably pass off sooner or later, but it makes him a bit lethargic and bad tempered. He was very bucked to receive your airgraph and will probably reply (pas de scandale)!

I have just sent off an airgraph to your Ma and Pa, thanking them for the good wishes of the friends who signed. Perhaps you would thank Eileen, Percy,[226] the Powells, Dick, Joe Park, Mrs. Corbett, Joe, K and George Austin,[227] Mrs Stockman and anyone else who was on the list when you happen to see them.

Love

Ron

Next is a long, typed Air Letter postmarked 30th August, two days after the date Dad started it:

W O. II S. attn. "A" Coy

1st BN Glider Pilot Regt.

B.N.A.F. 28.8.43.

Dear K,

There has been an immense speed-up in delivery of your letters since you just put B.N.A.F. on them. I received the one posted on Aug 16 on Aug 27. It brings both you and Michael a lot nearer. This is particularly welcome at a time when there seems to be no indicator of how long we shall wander around the Mediterranean and Europe. I do hope you find it possible to remember who I am and what I am like. I certainly cling to remembrances of our home life as a slight alleviation of this horrible climate, where one's life is one continual battle against the heat which upsets one's stomach nerves and head. Of course I do not mean that the battle is impossible, but it is a very difficult one.

I came back from the rest near the sea to find a permanent temperature of over 110 degrees[228] in the shade at the headquarters

---

226 See page 72.

227 Dick could be Richard Pennifold – see letter from Eileen Ireland on page 538.

228 43 degrees Celsius

camp. It is absolutely necessary to sleep all afternoon, when the "heat peak" is on.

Last week I took a hell of a lot of Current Affairs and language periods which was quite good – also one or two Discussion Groups. I also had a talk with Fred Pateman[229], of whom you may have heard.

Glad to hear you had Hilda and her friend down. She has written a letter to Fanny describing with enormous gusto the time they had. Also I am relieved that Michael's leg is not going to be permanently bandy. I couldn't imagine him being like that.

I'm afraid the slight spirit of holiday engendered by the trip to the rest-villa has now disappeared and I'm sitting in the grim and unromantic "I" tent typing this. We have now passed the hottest point of the year. The rains are due any week. One hears dreadful stories of how soldiers spend weeks and weeks in wet clothes and only dry out in the short intervals of a few days between the long showers. Perhaps much of it is exaggerated. In any case the people who work in the "I" Tent have planned to move into the tent as soon as the first shower comes. Sleeping under a single fly-sheet slung from a tree will be insufficient. The tent will be a protection against anything less than a flood.

Being somewhat fed up with the camp, I am trying to get a few biscuits, cheese and bully-beef tomorrow (Sunday) in order to hitch-hike to a French-cum-Arab town some 15 miles away. There I want to brush up my French somewhat, if I can find any French people. There are really not many left after the great exodus during the African campaign. The number has actually gone down from 30,000 to 7,000, though a few more may have come back since I got that figure.

The native citadel in the centre got the biggest bashing of the lot. I have not been in it, but I believe it is completely pulverised in places.

The Padre is holding a concert next Wednesday, so I suppose I shall have to contribute a turn of some kind; I am trying to think of a theme for a skit. It is difficult here, since themes seem to be reduced to flies, heat, food, health and a vague view of the operations going on. I suppose the latter fact seems quite strange to you. You imagine

229 Journalist at the *Daily Worker*

that we are quite near the spot and almost hear the guns. Actually the ironic truth is that you are very much nearer the nearest Germans than I am (as the crow flies).

I have just received some numbers of WNV[230] (the one in a separate envelope yesterday). They are very useful. I shall be glad to have a few dailies just occasionally. You have no idea *[how]* one hangs on the mail, as regards these fortnight- and three-week-old papers. I should be horrified if they stopped coming.

The Russian victories are magnificent. We hear tonight that they have encountered harsh resistance at Poltava[231]. Still, their sweep forward from Kahrkov is so important that I imagine they will keep on with their offensive now. Once we feel that the peace feelers in Finland really do mean something and that Smolensk, Ghatsk and Vyasma have fallen then I shall expect to see the German on the borders of Russia in no time.

Well, my dear, please keep on with your usual cheerful planning and your important school of one pupil. I wish I could be there to help with it, but there is hope that I shall be some day.

Love, *[signed in pencil]* Ron

The next letter we have is again typed and is dated almost a fortnight after the last one. However, Dad's date of the 9th must be wrong as the Air Letter is postmarked 6 September. Mum received it on the 18th:

as before
9 Sep 43.

Dearest K,

I haven't had a letter from you for a fortnight or so now, which is probably the fault of the mail system. In a theatre of war in which big changes are going on it is inevitable, I should think, that there are defects in the A.P.O. One also has to think of the effect of enemy action on ships and mail-bags.

---

230 *World News and Views*, pub. Communist Party of Great Britain
231 A bitter battle as part of the huge Dnieper offensive against the Germans in Ukraine.

There doesn't seem much hope of getting home in the near future. I hope you are not getting too bored. The best thing will be to give yourself as many interests as possible – keeping up the old work in the measure of your opportunities. I had a delayed letter from Jimmy (from the old Condepot) the other day. He is still with the advance company defence platoon of 1st Army GHQ and wrote to me not knowing I had come out here. In fact I think the letter had been all the way to the old camp in England and come out again.

The letter from your folks with the signatures of the "gang" was a great tonic. I am just recovering from two small but annoying septic places and I was rather lower in inspiration than usual. It helped to set me on the upward grade again. Of course any ruddy scratch turns septic immediately in this unhealthy country.

I have had some interesting discussions lately. Yesterday I had some private instruction on the latest German machine-gun. It was quite ingenious, full of interesting gadgets like German aeroplanes, but without having fired it I should think the Bren is still the best gun on the market.

Most of the chaps are very anxious to leave Africa now. They don't care much whether it's Italy, S. France, Spain or N. France that we go to. I fancy they would prefer N. France, but mostly on slender grounds such as the possibility of landing in England and having a 48 hours leave. Not that those are slender grounds from a personal point of view, admittedly, but they are slender from the point of view of the war.

When one sits here, in the middle of a bare patch of scrub between olive-groves, it is almost impossible to imagine home life. I'm sure we shall be all disoriented for quite a time if and when we do finally get home. It will be extraordinary to sleep in a bed – you will probably find me getting out with a blanket and stretching out on the floor, or digging a hip-hole out in the garden under a tree.

Still, I think I shall be cured of my ancient tendency to like camping, something of which you always disapproved. Youth Hostelling will still be quite pleasant, however, if the problem of Michael could be solved.

Well, I'm afraid business calls. It is possible that my letters will be irregular for some little time (especially seeing that yours have been), but please keep wanting me to come back, won't you? I want to continuously, and deeply.

Love,

[*signed in pencil*] Ron

Dad's next letter was dated 10th September and postmarked the 12th:

W.O II... (as before ?)

10.9.43

Dear K,

This is written under the stress of unexpected but welcome events. My mail may be irregular for a short time. I haven't had a letter from you for about a fortnight, but I guess this is due to bottlenecks rather than sinkings.

The news about Italy is terrific isn't it? One wonders what motives the Germans can have for occupying Rome. I thought the city was in a bad defensive position. They will no doubt find many enemies within, as well as without.

There is much speculation among us, as to how far advanced preparations for a "main job" into N.W. Europe are. I fear we can only be of nuisance value (though very great nuisance) from the South, comparatively speaking.

At the moment I am sitting in an olive grove (another one). The sun is baking-hot. We slept in the open last night and it was quite warm.

I am now allowed to mention that I have been a good deal in Tunisia, and spent a day in Tunis, where it was unbelievably hot and one could find practically nothing to do during the siesta part of the day, the only time we could be there. The holiday villa I described so enthusiastically once was near Hammamet, south of Tunis. The Gulf of H will probably be marked on the map, and possibly the native town of Nabeul.

The furthest south I have ever been is just below a town called Sousse (Susa). It was bombed to blazes.

Much early stays were at Phillipville and places like Bedja and Medjez el Bab.

Went swimming in a dock last night, when the evening had become cool. The water was slightly oily, but felt lovely and cool after the burning day. There were naval MB's and assault craft round about, the crews breathing the evening air in their white vests and shorts. The one branch of the Services that can always get it's washing done!

I have just reached a "new low" as regards my washing. When we left the last camp there was an interruption in the supply of water just before we left. Result: dirty towels, h'chieves, khaki drill shorts and shirts, everything except a few pairs of socks which I swilled through somehow. However no doubt somewhere in Spain, Yugoslavia or Italy there will be more water.

Love, Ron

Chapter 11

Italy

The next letter was again written in pencil on an Air Letter. It was dated 14.9.43 but postmarked almost a week later on 20th September. Dad has now landed at Taranto in Italy, although he is not allowed to mention the town, only that he's in…

ITALY

W.O II… Attd. "A" Coy
etc. 14.9.43.

Dear Kath,

Landed a few days ago. The town was badly bombed in one part,[232] and most of the people had evacuated the rest, but those we met were quite cheerful, in fact they were glad to be beaten. The food situation seems to be bad, probably due to general war privation and the depredations of the Germans. I have learned quite a lot of Italian and am teaching it as rapidly as possible.

News and A.B.C.A.[233] subjects are rather short, but I hope to remedy that as soon as possible. My foot-sores which I caught at the last location have started to heal slowly. My appetite is excellent, I sleep on the bare earth or a board as comfortably as if I were on a bed, and my only danger, as usual, is in feeling too satisfied and interested in language-work and general prep. while men are on patrol against the enemy a score of miles away.

232 Air-launched torpedoes severely damaged the Italian fleet in Taranto Harbour on 11th September, and fuel storage tanks in the town were bombed.
233 See note 148 on page 139..

I suspect a couple of your letters have gone astray, but that will be the result of the move. Only one packet of journals came and one separate WNV. The only paper I have at the moment is *Il Corrriere del Puglie*, dated 29th July (when Musso was still in power) Please slip a DW in with the next lot!

The address is the same as before.

The country around here is mostly olive-groves, but slightly more European in flavour than where we were before. There are one or two lanes which are fairly pleasant though I think the north of Italy is really the place to be in.

Lots of kids hang around our camp, as they no doubt did with the Germans.

There are some ship-building yards not very far away.

(Interval of one day) Have just received birth certificate and the two WNV's (via I.R.T.D!)[234] They were very useful.

Have had rampaging stomach-ache for a day, due to too many grapes and stewed figs. I know this will sound too good to be true to you, but there it is! The pain has now gone.

I have not yet managed to go from the camp down to the town but I hope to do so today.

Please don't worry about me being in Italy. I am in no danger whatsoever. In fact life has been so monotonous recently that I have been thinking of applying for a transfer to AMGOT,[235] but I don't know whether the Regiment would allow it.

There seems no possibility for me to partake in really active ops. I have tried my hardest and failed.

Love Ron

In spite of the heading of the next letter, it is only the second one that we have that Dad wrote from Italy:

---

234 Infantry Replacement (or Reinforcement) Training Depot
235 Allied Military Government for Occupied Territories

LETTER 3 from ITALY

W.O II....

H.Q. 1st BN Glider Pilot Rgt.

C.M.F 30.9.43

Dear K,

Received yesterday one of your airmails and a W.N.V. Thanks muchly.

Very comfortable here except for the flies.

I have rather a difficult problem, K, in the sense that I feel I can contribute practically nothing to the war effort, yet it is difficult to see what could be done. The boys are occupied mostly with sun-bathing, walking in the local town, buying ice creams, post-cards, and spending their inflated lire on various odd goods. I am dubious about doing the same – it rather smacks of the Nazi letters you read in SWN, "Dear Lieble, Please get me one little fur coat from Smolensk, etc."

In the meantime there is little but sun-bathing, reading, teaching Italian and talking to the local population. Tonight, however, we have a discussion on "The Progress of the War" led by the Intelligence Officer. This will be on the large flat roof of the house, with no light but fag-ends, a bit from the moon and a single small hurricane lamp.

Tomorrow I am off by motor-bike (requisitioned from the Itis) to take a couple of lessons with detachments of our Regiment who are elsewhere. I can ride moderately now. The only thing is, the roads around here are pretty bad and oh so dusty! One never sees real dust in England, the rain disposes of it too quickly. (Of course we haven't seen rain for five months now, except for a freak shower of a couple of minutes in N.A.)

Frankly I feel I am a little out of touch at the moment, both with our own blokes and with the citizens of the local town. I mean to remedy this as soon as possible. The lack of good books and periodicals is still a terrible blight. In N.A. we did have the Regiment's library which I brought out, but we sailed with very light kit to Italy and I left with the rear party (as did my typewriter). No doubt they will catch us up again in some part of the world.

Do you remember our little trips to Horsham, Worth and to Belgium?[236] I'm glad we had a few good times together before this ruddy war, because without those there would not be very much to look back to, except hard work. As it is, the men out here will never forget their civilian backgrounds. Army life never envelopes the conscript entirely. It is only the old "sweat", the professional soldier, generally without mental horizon, who gets used to the barracks and billets and general lack of cultural life in even the humblest sense. I am a bit behind with letters to Ma. Perhaps you would explain to her that we have been moving about rather a lot.

Lots and lots and lots of love to both of you.

Yours, Ron

The next letter is an Airgraph postmarked 7th October and then, on processing in England, on 20th October 1943:

WOII Instr. Spathaky, H.Q. 1st. BN Glider Pilot Regt., C.M.F.

Dear K,

Received your airgraph No 5 today. Will write a long letter as soon as possible. I have sent AGs recently to Percy, Mrs C. and Mother. Next I must reply to an AM from Renée.[237] I still receive your single copies of WNV in letter envelopes but no other packages. Glad to hear Michael is now walking in reverse. What's the latest vocabulary attainment? Hope all the "gang" are working their hardest.

I have just been given a better room, less crowded and with good light, in the library of the big house where we are. We are at the moment not in any great danger – the only possibility is a fall from a m/cycle on the bad roads but I don't ride much.

---

236 The visit to Worth was described on page 187 and also recalled on pages 379 and 403.

237 AG – airgraph; Percy Ireland, Mrs C (Mum's mother Annie Cree). AM – airmail; Renée Shulman – see page 72.

The Regiment is in good mental fettle, though their position has certain inconveniences. There is every opportunity for my kind of work. I have not been into the local town for about a week, because light and water troubles closed the shops in the afternoon. Haven't seen any signorinas worth looking at yet. If I do I'll bring you home a couple to help with the housework in the new house. (! ? %)

We shall all be damn glad to return and see our wives again. Travel perhaps broadens the mind, but it's hard on the feet! – Lots of love,

Ron.

Dad wrote a poem to me:

To Michael, with a Toy

I wish that I could fashion you a thousand shining towers.
Instead take this,
A creature born of idleness and of the wasted hours
I hope it's not amiss
That spavined are his flanks, gory his limb
His head misshapen. This will not hinder him
From pleasing you; perhaps you'll laugh the more
'Tis worth a kiss
I wis.

7.10.1943

Dad's next letter was written in ink on 8th October on an Air Letter, but it was not postmarked until the 14th; Mum received it on the 25th. The stamp has been torn off the airmail letter at some point and this has removed a few words of text on the other side of the page, as indicated by ellipses, thus [...]. The edges of the letter are also badly eroded, again resulting in missing text:

W.O.II… H.Q. 1st…..
C.M.F. 8.10.43.

Dear K,

Nothing much to report at present. We are all hoping against hope that we might be returned to England, in time for a real 2nd Front, but no-one has any real information.

Lessons have picked up quite well lately. I have been teaching about 10 lessons a week, which is quite good for this theatre of war.

I had a visit from a superior officer yesterday. He came from somewhere right up the "monkey-ladder", Army H.Q or thereabouts. He seems quite pleased with the work, left me some pamphlets and hooked off.

I suppose I shall see a "boss" in another country if we move to […]. The average […] one visit per […].

I hope you find plenty to do and are not too lonely with just the companion I made for you. I have had practically no urge to find a woman abroad, though I have found I like a bit of feminine company.

The brothels are in full swing in Italian towns but nobody with elementary ideas on hygiene or morality goes in them.

Have you had any feeling of need for masculine company (in general), or does the company of our mutual friends in Brighton satisfy you?

As for physical, as well as emotional and cultural longing for you personally, why, I'm het-up with it, honest I am! So wait for me as long as you can, won't you?

(I must now break off this letter to do an A.B.C.A. for this afternoon.)

Rather a funny thing has occurred: two of the chaps in our room went bathing off a small raft today; the tide was setting offshore and out they went, including one chap who couldn't swim. They drifted before our amazed eyes on the flat calm water for miles till they were picked up by a naval trawler. At first the naval men thought they were Germans trying to escape from Italy. Later the Navy brought them back in a launch.

We have "organised" a big packing-case today in order to try and keep our books safe in case of any future movements either inside

Italy or away from the country. Some of them are editions which could not be obtained elsewhere

(LATER) Thanks very much for the last airmail letter written to B.N.A.F. The other will now come to C.M.F.[238]

Also received Brighton and Hove Herald of Aug 18 and enclosed papers. The mobilisation of so many volunteer labourers for agriculture was a jolly good bit of work. I told the lads here about it and they were quite impressed.

I have just got quite a lot more A.B.C.A. pamphlets from an Army source, so I am set up for a time as regards things to deal with.

Much love

Ron

XXXXXXXXXX

Dad started another letter within a day or so:

W.O II… H.Q 1st. BN etc.

C.M.F. 12.10.43.

(finished 15.10.43)

Dearest K,

I have taken the day off today, and am sitting at about 4 o'clock in a small cove which is part of a terrific bay in Southern Italy. As I sit almost at one end of it. I can see the other end almost opposite me stretching away almost endlessly to the horizon, blending towards the horizon with the mountains. To my right rear is an Italian A.A. post, with some serviceable-looking guns in it. I hear from our gunners they're not so good, but that may be professional rivalry. Behind them again is an old rambling building that used to be a monastery, with a tall tower beside it used, I fancy, for an A.A. look-out post.

On the front right stretches the low coastal plain, with a coastal road and railway shown up in clear relief by the afternoon sun. The light everywhere is purest yellow, making the olives in the foreground shine as if with a green flame.

---

238 Central Mediterranean Force

In the middle distance are white villages and a town, just white chequered patterns on the hillside. On the very top of the only peak in view there is a village, just like a cairn of white stones from here. Walking on foot around the bay one would probably cross forty miles of ground; in a boat straight across the bay the distance first on water, then on land, is probably twenty miles. As for the sea itself in this enormous gulf, it stretches right away to the sunset, mile upon mile with the merest ripple on it.

When I arrived here this morning I first had a read (Frédéric Mistral *Mes Mémoires*,[239] then Evelyn Waugh *Put Out More Flags*[240]) then I met Fanny and a bloke called McCulloch and had a chat. I read while they bathed. Then they returned to camp for lunch. I went into a nearby olive-grove and lit a small patent fire-tin we are issued with. Then I boiled the contents of my water bottle in half a mess-can and added some of a tin of mixed tea, milk powder and sugar. This with some tinned pilchards, cheese and marmalade, formed quite a decent meal. After it I read again for a time, then went further along the bay to negotiate with a fisherman for the hire of his boat.

In the end he took five cigarettes and the nearly full tin of tea. So I was pushed out of the miniature cerclet of stones and rowed myself over the flat stretches, using the heavy long sea-oars, one which works over the other and with which one stands up, facing the bow of the boat. I got some good exercise out of it, and when I was tired of going out I turned towards the swimming cove.

As I neared the rocks a couple of Indian soldiers swam out and swarmed over the side, their teeth gleaming white with their pleasure at finding something to play with. Soon, with two to row, we had the boat going along in fine style, albeit with a slight tendency to describe circles. Then I stripped, dived overboard and round the boat. The water was about 25

---

239 *Mes origines: Mémoires et Récits de Frédéric Mistral* (translated from the Provençal), pub. Libraire Plom, Paris, n.d.
240 Pub. Chapman and Hall, 1942

foot deep and clear as crystal, with the chill just taken off by the sun. After a while we pulled and I settled down to write this, distracted occasionally by a sunset which would only be possible in Italy.

Kath, I hope terribly that we shall be able to see home again soon, if only for a short time. Foreign travel and Italian theatre of war and all that are very fine, but one gets sick of "behind the Front-line" activities. I would willingly go out to the fiercest Front in France if I could see your dear face within the next month, hear how Michael's vocabulary is progressing and (if I am still allowed) feel your loving white body against my now somewhat dark brown one. However, perhaps it will come, perhaps it won't!

Yours with much Love
Ron

P.S. Sent a short story to Bill Rust[241]; don't know whether he'll use it – R.V.S

P.S. Am now allowed to say that I have been at one time through Taranto. We have moved (since I began this letter).

In a little country town today I bought you a heavy silver antique ring for 32/6 (probably worth £5), 2 metres of local lace (6/- a yard) and two brightly coloured woven girdles (2/- each!) I hope I get them home. I <u>may</u> try to send them. I have also bought what seems to be a good Swiss watch and a fairly good fountain-pen.

The enclosed postcards (3) show what Italy <u>can</u> be like. I'm afraid we have seen but little of the beauty yet, except the Gulf of Taranto, but we cannot grumble!

Love,
R
XXXX
XXXX –– for Michael

The next letter is postmarked 22nd October but was written over several days, as indicated:

---

241 Editor of the *Daily Worker*.

W.O II etc.

<u>H.Q.</u> 1st BN… etc. C.M.F

18.10.43 2115 hrs.

Dear K,

Moved again. We spent a day or two in a thriving country town, in a billet right over an ice-cream shop in the main street. There were some reasonable shops, an immense fortress built by Frederick Barbarossa (Holy Roman Emperor 1105) and some interesting members of the local National Front Committee, the democratic alliance of all anti-fascist parties and individuals. I have written an article which I am sending to News Chronicle, Herald and Bill R.,[242] on the political and social situation. As I mentioned elsewhere, I also sent a story called "Near the Aqueduct" to Bill.

We are now in a modest country château (sorry, castello!) owned by a Marquis. It has a high tower, a steep hill from which to dominate the countryside and the most remarkable shrubs and trees in the estate. The R.S.M and myself share a room, in which I have a spring bed (the first since England) and I have a little (forced) leisure in which to explore the two little towns nearby. I do not reproach myself a few days of exploration, since we have had some very rough conditions, both on our first station and in Italy, As soon as I get my bearings I shall start work again full-pressure.

I hope we manage to get a brief visit home within the next six months. I suppose it is possible. A move to the Far East would be the real "blight." I don't fancy myself as a learner (and instructor) of Oriental languages!

I have had one or two differences from time to time with Fanny, but on the whole the "boys" have been carrying on the good work, under difficult conditions. I fancy Bill Ritchie will never be of much help, but other people come to the fore as shaky ones drop out.

Please congratulate Gordon[243] for me on getting the "belt of honour." I hope the OCTU has not also given him too much of the "grand manner" and verbal guff which is so depressing.

---

242 *The News Chronicle* and *Daily Herald* were national newspapers.

243 Kath's brother, Gordon Cree. I could not imagine him taking on any airs and graces, what with his loyalty to the working class and his Yorkshire accent!

19.10 43.

0930 hrs.

Good morning, Darling! Woke up today with a thick head, the R.S.M. having closed the window before we retired. However it's a lovely morning and woods and little villages on the hills around here are shining like billy-ho. I am off in a few minutes with the Major to requisition this house from the local mayor.

20.10.43

0845 hrs.

Yesterday afternoon I went a good walk with Fanny, through lots of small terraced fields, walled in something like Derbyshire fields. We were trying to find some huge caves in the neighbourhood. We didn't find them, but we found some woods just like English ones and many of the curious little peasant houses that are a feature of this part of Italy. They are called 'trulls' (trulli) and are circular huts of stone with a single door-opening and a conical roof.

I have just got your letter dated 6 Oct. Sorry you've had a fit of the blues, especially when I can't help. I think you should avoid

any comparison between Michael and Helen.[244] Boys and girls probably develop very differently during the first years and different temperaments express themselves in such varying ways. Gordon and Doris are both pretty extrovert and "wear their hearts on their sleeves" a lot. If M is enquiring by nature what have you to worry about? He who seeks shall find. You have provided your own solution to the odious comparison.

And now I must go out and bargain with the local peasants for some spuds and a turkey (delle patate e un tacchino). We are very anxiously awaiting any possible hint of a move at present. This place is devilish pleasant but no-one wants to stay here too long. We should become part of the landscape.

Lots of love to both
of you. E corragio
Ron

The next follows on a couple of days later:

C.M.F (as before)
24.10.43

Dear K,

I've just received snaps of M. They are splendid. Could you possibly let me have a really decent one of yourself, with or without him? I have mislaid the little snap of you which harks back to the Eton-crop days.

There's not much doing at the moment. Please don't give up hope that we may see each other before the year is out. If we do there will be such a lot to talk about, won't there? We have both had experience so different from our previous lives – you as that important person the Head of the Family, and myself in this strange country. I hope you have been getting some of the picture post-cards I sent off. They don't deal very much with this part of the country, but a people has to

---

244 My cousin Helen is ten days younger than me.

be studied as a whole and those are the kind of scenes that "colour" Italian personality.

Of course one never gets to grips properly with the people when one is in an army, because there is always the feeling on the part of the people that you are living an entirely different kind of life from them and cannot understand, but we get over that difficulty as much as possible. Some of our H.Q. boys played a little nearby country-town at football this evening (and got beaten 5-2!)

I received a bundle of DW's last week – the first large packet of them! It was good to see the old columns again.

You will be glad to know that my differences with Fanny have been composed a good deal. I still find his personality a bit depressing compared with how he was in England, however. Even though he is normal in his love-life his likes and dislikes of other people seem so temperamental – in fact almost physical. And in spite of his moving in high circles for a time just before the "op" in Sicily he has recently dropped a series of considerable "clangers" (as the Army calls them) on minor disciplinary matters.[245]

I wish I could get into touch with a somewhat wider set of people than we have here at present, but that is something you cannot alter when you are buried in a sea of Italian villages without much contact with other troops.

We get a fair amount of reading matter from M.E.F Cairo. It's amazing what the forces publish there. They have complete illustrated fortnightlies, something like Picture Post, monthly magazines and a fairly intelligent thing called "World Press Review" which produces the "best" from world articles, even a few from enemy sources.

I am still plugging away with Steinbeck's "In Dubious Battle"[246] (in Italian). It started rather artificially, I thought, but now it may turn out to be a more significant book than "Grapes of Wrath."

By the way, here is a very rough translation of one of Petrarch's sonnets from Italian:-

---

245 See Appendix 2.
246 Pub. 1936. The main character of the novel is an activist for 'the Party', who leads a fruit pickers' strike. A film was released in 2016.

"The sun could never shine so splendidly
Above you lulls in cloudless skies of blue;
Nor after rainy days the rainbow's hue
Change hour by hour its vision ceaselessly,
From flaming red to violet's lightest sheen
As changed the day when first I met my queen."

Nè così bello il Sol giammai levarsi
Quando 'l ciel fosse più di nebbia scarco,
Nè dopo pioggia vidi 'l celesti arco
Per l' aere in color tanti variarsi
In quanti fiammeggiando transformarsi
Nel dì ch' io presi l'amoroso incarco.

Of course this is all 14C stuff, but it gave an impulse to the whole of European poetry that has lasted up to our day.

Well, I'd better get on with a bit more Italian, but not any more Petrarch or visions of our twining bodies will be interfering with the rules of grammar.

The advent of slightly cooler weather in Italy has made me feel a bit sensuous, curiously enough, so if you feel your thighs or breasts tingle you'll know someone is thinking of you (aren't men beasts !?%).

Hum, I appear to have written this on the outside of this letter-card! How very awkward. I shall have to do a bit of judicious folding and hope for the best.

Love,

Ron

xxxxxxxx

The following six-page letter, written neatly in ink, is undated. I found it in an envelope postmarked 26th October 1943, and its size when folded fits that envelope, although a different pen and ink were used to address the envelope. Other letters from around this time are all Airmail or Airgraph letters which do not require an envelope. Dad has drawn three

long lines in place of his own address at the head of the letter. There is
no real reason to doubt that it was stored in its original envelope. A brief
note with the same three lines drawn in the top right corner was with it:

———————————

———————————

—————

Dearest K,

I think the present moment is opportune for saying one or two things that I have been pondering over. We have obviously reached a stage in our knowledge of and relationship with one another. I wonder if it divides itself up into the traditional three parts? Let's see.

First, the callow student days, when I thought I knew a lot, when I had theorized a lot about those things which are our main driving force. But I hadn't met the ordinary people who are the raw stuff of social development. As soon as I came into touch with those people, who were satisfyingly like the descriptions I had received from Messrs. Dodsworth[247] and others, I met you amongst them. We were both very much "in love with love," had both received a fairly sound but rather narrow ideological training and we just bought a ticket in the oldest lottery blindly, or guided by intuition and visual judgement, which may be better criteria than is supposed. "To every content is a corresponding form."

And lo, and behold, I bought one of the absolute winning numbers, someone on whom the rest of my life can be based, whether it's a long life or a rapid adventurous matter of a couple of years. Nothing can destroy that. It is something that goes down in the secret annals of creation. It has happened. It can't be taken away by gods, demons, satyrs or all the forces of change, progress or decay.

After the first lyric came the settling down, to an experiment of common living, a very modern idea of sharing work, domestic cares and pleasures together. The chief danger was bound to be the dead conservative past, the traditional instincts leading man to take advantage of woman. I did to an unforgivable extent – yet even in the

---

247 Norman Dodsworth, the "charismatic leader of students" of Chapter 1.

flat there were very bright moments, listening to the radiogram, the friendship with David Finer[248], the holiday in Belgium, talks at odd moments with all kinds of odd people!

No-one could say we did not see a vast number of people, though the number of days we spent together was infinitesimal compared with the time most people take to explore each other.

Then, no doubt with the stress of Munich and our speeded professional lives, came the incidents of George and Len (and even dumb good-natured little Sylvia – though she didn't count). Why was it? I don't know. I think we were just seeing whether we had really done the right thing. We wanted a basis of comparison. I think we both achieved it.

After that came the period at Hangleton Road, which for some reason is more confused in my mind. I think we were much happier, though the urgent crisis of the times kept us still much too much apart. But there must have been high points in it, for instance the time when you were doing locum for the chap down on Church Road (was it?). I remember spending a couple of hours before I came to meet you – thinking over what we would say and do, planning how I could help you, how I could best make up for the fact that you were working long hours and I short ones.

That evening I remember working my idea of the personal dialectic which I still hold firm to. The first thing in our lives is struggle – joyous or grim as we succeed in making it, against the forces of reaction. As one perfects oneself in the struggle so one develops, lives a wider life, uses the faculties, becomes more confident – therefore we seek out the "vortices" of world struggle, where we are of most use, in order to equip and enrich ourselves, in order to be more happy. This is my credo. I have had a great deal of problems in the Army, but I feel that, by and large, I have pursued these ideas – and you have helped because you believe in them, because they are true.

Of the period in the Army I cannot speak so much. It has not clarified itself enough, but the entry of Michael into our lives has certainly changed both of us, for the better.

---

248 See page 36.

I think we are different in temperament, in background and in tradition, even in our qualities and defects. It can be that such cross-breeding produces the best results. M is a third person to our charmed circle, who makes not just an arithmetical addition, but makes us like 4 or 6. From him comes no jealousy, no anxiety as to his upbringing – for that he is safe in your professional hands – he will be happy and creative. He is the promise of a future, when we shall keep ourselves young together in the response to his questioning, in helping with his problems, the reading of his books or the meeting of his friends, the doing of his experiments, and all, I beg, with unobtrusiveness. We will not force ourselves on him, trying to make him believe as some ridiculous parents do that they are the same age as he. But sometimes the young companions cloy, a boy seeks parents' company spontaneously, asks questions – because the young want to know, want to plunge deeper and deeper into the stream of knowledge. (That's why you and I are young, thank goodness!) Then is the time to strike, to inspire, never to turn aside a chance question or treat a fantastic opinion flippantly. Children are the natural poets of the universe – some of their senses are keener than ours, they are realising things about the world that we are in danger of forgetting.

This will be our adventure, our continual honeymoon. I look forward to it hungrily, eagerly, confidently. Now let me finish by thanking you for your kindness and steadfastness to me, for what you have taught me – things I will never forget, as I ask you not to forget me, though you continue these adventures with another, or alone. – Love, Ron

This note was stored in the same envelope as the above letter, but I sense that it does not belong there:

————————

————

Dearest K,
    Hope you got back safely.

Will write as soon as circumstances allow.

In great haste.

Love,

Ron

P.S. Hope you managed to see Hilda.[249] You will have such common problems to talk over.

We have no real assurance that the last short note and the long letter before it are in the correct place in the sequence. But now we come to a dated letter, with a postscript written at the top:

P.S. I don't have my letters censored except by myself!

(same address) C.M.F.

30.10.43

Darling,

No mail for about three weeks! The reason given is the weather, but we feel suspicious, since a man in a nearby unit who visits us daily had a letter yesterday which was posted on the 23rd. If mail can be brought for one man it can be for others. I rather feel that some mail-bags are languishing somewhere, at Algiers, Bizerta or Palermo.

I think it is no military secret if I tell you that I have been reduced to almost complete inaction during the last fortnight or three weeks. There has been no remedy for it – though I believe I could have been used if the higher-ups had been keener.

Thus I have been, with Fanny[250] and a few odds-and-sods (not many officers) in this very pleasant villa, in a splendid park between two country towns both of which have a certain amount of interest. Luckily an A.E.C. boss at 8th Army has sent me quite a lot of stuff to read (for A.B.C.A.) and I have bags of Italian books, but what a life! I rise at 7 a.m., go down and eat an enormous breakfast (porridge, bacon, onions, sausage, white bread and jam), then I learn Italian

---

249 Hilda was Alec Waldron's wife – see Appendix 2.
250 Staff Sergeant Alec Waldron – see Appendix 2.

for an hour or so. Perhaps I hitch into the further of the two towns ("Conzertina" let us call it) and have a coffee, call at the book-shops, interview a member of the National Front,[251] call at a military unit to try and get a job (and fail); then I roll back to the castello for an enormous dinner. And so on throughout the day, with various intervals for writing articles in between.

It's certainly a bit baffling. However it's only a temporary phase and there's just nothing I can do about it at the moment.

We have just heard that Liberty of the Press has been restored in S. Italy. There is still no liberty of political meetings under Badoglio,[252] though that may come, if the Allies press hard enough from the outside and the National Front from within.

My eyes feel a bit strained at the moment so will finish this domani.

(interval)

31.10.43 noon

Have spent the morning cleaning my equipment and my rifle and interviewing a few Iti's who came to the house for odd reasons, permission to travel south to the coast, enquiries as to whether we were going to requisition their houses and so on.

Please tell me lots about yourself in your reply to this. Do you get out any more and take exercise? Have you managed to buy any new clothes? Have you had any affairs with any blokes? Did temptation that way ever present itself? (if not, then you're not going out enough!) Do you ever want a gambolling, exciting, rolling long fuck? Do you remember particularly any of those we had? Which ones were best?

Sorry, my pen is getting a little out of hand, but it is true that one wants very much to even <u>hear</u> some sensuality from one's mate; perhaps it would sublimate the actual lack of it.

Last night, in the house of an old Socialist wine-merchant in "Bondoli" I saw a remarkable display of newspapers and other writings

---

251 At that time in Italy, this was an *anti*-fascist group.

252 Pietro Badoglio, Chief of Staff of the Italian armed forces. On the arrest of Mussolini, Badoglio was appointed Prime Minister. Having signed the armistice with the Allies in Malta in September, he and the King of Italy declared war against Germany on 30th October, the day that Dad started this letter.

of the period 1919-22. He had stored them when the left movement were made illegal in 1922. They told of the street fighting provoked by the fascists and the numbers of people killed. It was most moving. His sons are officers in the Iti army and one of them is a very ardent propagandist for the N. Front. As he has a job on the army transport inspecting different areas he manages to get about quite a lot.

Love Ron

HQ Coy. at Villa del Monte, Noci, Puglia, 12th November 1943.
Dad is furthest right in the second row from the front

Next comes an airmail letter, so the address and postmark are on the same single sheet as the letter itself. This makes the dating quite puzzling. The postmark is '14 NO 43', but Dad has clearly dated the letter 8.12.42. Not for the first time, he shows uncertainty about the numbering of the months, but the year too? And he has dated a second part of the letter, still on the same sheet, 16.10.43! I guess the whole thing was written in the second week of November 1943. There's a PS at the top:

P.S. Received four letters & stacks of papers – Thanks

As before, C.M.F.

8.12.42 *[sic]*

Dearest K,

There has been no line from you for three weeks, due to the vagaries of the post, though I received bundles of papers and letters from my people and your Ma (for which thank her very much indeed). I have now started work again with full vim and vigour and the increasing nip in the Autumn air here seems to encourage more rapid thought.

I have also sent the parcel of goods which I bought for you. There are two coatees, two little plaited belts and a undervest. I will keep the ring until I come home. Just had a good jaw (2½ hrs, to be exact) with Mac, Arthur, Bill Ritchie and Fanny[253]. You may be sure that all the old themes came up. Bill seems to be making a turn for the better. He has made considerable linguistic progress and is pretty fluent in Iti, French and to some extent in German.

Fanny spends a lot of time acting the fool these days.

I have been reading part of a famous Iti novel by Manzoni, The Betrothed (I Promessi Sposi) lately. It is supposed to be the greatest work in Italy following on the Divine Comedy of Dante. It was written in 1628 and shows the various intrigues of feudal lords and how their plottings react on the desire of a young artisan pair, Renzi and Lena to get married. I expect there is a translation in one of your libraries if you care to see the kind of stuff I have been immersed in during a few weeks when I was isolated from the blokes.

Just sent off Christmas cards to you, your Mum and Dad, Whit. and Renée.[254]

The Regiment certainly has used a lot of paper in them, but I think there are probably questions of prestige involved.

I managed to get a good hot bath this morning in the outhouse of the villa. It involved filling with tins of hot water a massive stone-bath, of the usual domestic shape, which had been fixed up somewhat surprisingly in this particular shed. Still, the weather is still very mild here, with occasional days of intense rain.

---

253 Alec 'Fanny' Waldron – see Appendix 2.
254 Renée Shulman – see page 72.

16.10.43.

Sorry there has been such a long gap between the two parts of this letter. I have been up to my eyes in work and have hardly been in to the H.Q for more than ten minutes at a time. I have been snatching a meal here and there with the outlying squadrons, sleeping on borrowed blankets in a school in a little country town which is distinguished by being 370 m. above sea level.

I snatched a day off on one occasion and travelled to Bari, which is a very big town on the E coast. It used to be the centre of Mussolini's Arabic broadcast propaganda. For about 1/8 one could get a modest meal which included an omelette. This is in contrast to most parts of Italy I have seen. In the little country town where I am at the moment I should think a third of the people have nothing to eat but 150 grammes of bread a day, a smear of meat and vegetable paste and a few nuts and odds and ends like mushrooms. The very small children seem to be perishing visibly day by day, their faces are old and wizened. It is a terrible thing to see a people on the edge of starvation. On the other side "of the fence" we are very well fed and cared for.

There is great speculation among the pilots, as usual, as to whether we shall all be brought back to Britain in time for a 2nd. Front. They are even discussing how much leave one has on disembarkation. Of course no-one really knows what is happening about anything.

I'm sorry if one or two of my recent letters have sounded a bit mad. I do long so much to see you. It's not a matter of retreating from the job in hand, because if we could only have a week together it would make me feel like facing whatever the future holds.

– Yours with love, Ron

XXXXX For M – xxx

As I wrote above, that letter was probably posted on or about 16th November. The next is dated 9th December 1943 and postmarked the 10th. It is cryptically headed 'B.N.A.F.' (British North Africa Force) suggesting he has left Italy; but his movements are otherwise shrouded in military secrecy. With France under German occupation, the route back to England would have been via North Africa; and I think the whole upbeat tone of the letter, together with what I suspect are deliberate hints (such as the final pair of exclamation marks in the postscript), suggests that Dad is headed home:

B.N.A.F.

9.12.43.

Dearest K,

I'm very sorry I haven't been able to write for about a month. You will have been writing and writing into the blue, I'm afraid. You will now see why!

I haven't received the books you sent off. I suppose I shall get them some time.

We are all quite well and in the very best of spirits, in fact we couldn't possibly be in a better state of mind.

Unfortunately the censorship prevents me talking about almost anything except my health, which is excellent, my love for you and M, which is mounting and mounting, and my work, which has been highly satisfactory during the last week.

I hope you will have got my Christmas card by now, so even though it's early I'd better wish you a Happy New Year and may it be the happiest yet!

Avec tout mon amour,

Et salut au camarade Michel[255]

Ron

P.S. Don't write any more yet. I'll tell you when!!

RVS.

Dad started the next letter on 29th November, which is before the last one, but wrote much of it on 11th December, which is after it! It is handwritten on an Air Letter but the stamp was not franked. The phrase "The worst week I spent in Italy was…" is the best indication so far that Dad is no longer in Italy. The "Happiest New Year" hint is repeated:

---

255 "With all my love and greetings to comrade Michael."

———————————

———————————

—————————

29.11.43.

Dearest K,

I am sitting in HQ living-tent with the RSM and a couple of other WO's and Sergeants. We are surrounded by NAAFI stores, our kits and contemplate our muddy boots with some annoyance. We all have 4 blankets, greatcoats, groundsheets and gas-capes, so there is no danger from the soggy ground around or from the freezing cold at night.

Unfortunately I cannot tell you where we are, what we are doing or what the future holds. This is bloody annoying, as our correspondence has been scrappy enough in all conscience during the last three weeks. I have had nothing from you in that time, though I know the reason.

Still there's a silver cloud to every lining (I mean "lining" to every "cloud"). I have had quite a bit of work to do during the last few days and have quite a lot to look forward to. This is better than being idle. The worst week I spent in Italy was when I had absolutely nothing to do except read.

This morning I held a rifle inspection for the R.S.M., one of the few little military jobs he has given me while we have been away.

(LETTER INTERRUPTED VIOLENTLY BY DAYS OF TRAVELLING IN A CATTLE-TRUCK. NO CHANCE TO POST IT)

11.12.43

Sorry about the above, darling. For the first time tonight I am able to find a table and a decent light to write under. I have also written you a separate letter by ordinary but I will repeat some of the things I have to say therein.

In the first place, all best wishes for the Happiest New Year yet!

Secondly please don't write to me for a time, as my address will be uncertain. You can be assured that I shall be as safe as one can be (under Service conditions).

Thirdly please excuse me if no more letters come for a short time. I shall be thinking of you and comrade Michael, and it is due entirely to difficulties with the Army Postal System that I shall have to dry up for a short time. As soon as I can I will let you know of my whereabouts.

I have bought quite a number of good magazines lately, including *Renaissances,* a review of political tendencies amongst the Fighting French. Also I have met several interesting characters, including a young law student who escaped from the Gestapo in 1939. He is now a notary, i.e. a public official who advises companies and individuals on all matters connected with contracts, wills, divorces, investments etc. He is also an expert on "graphology" – which is a new one on me. It is the study of handwriting for medical purposes. In some clinics they are able to gain information on nervous disorders by reference to a person's style of writing

XXXX Lots of love – Ron

Next is an Air Letter that appears to have been torn in half. The second page with the postmark is now missing. Dad has dated the letter:

13.12.43.

Dearest Kath,

For the last three days I have been living in mud, of a particularly sticky kind, both by day and often during the night. Yet curiously enough the only time when I ever got a cold was when I went into the local town and got a haircut. And I soon threw that off!

In fact I am as happy as the rather monotonous conditions allow. The work I do in A.B.C.A. is plentiful and fairly interesting – that's something.

It is becoming very annoying to be so long away from home, however. And I don't mean that I just need someone to go to bed with. I have long ago had my moments of extreme physical desire – and got over them! What I miss just as much is the general aura of yourself and the boy, the general feeling that we are missing opportunities of developing our interests and our affection for one another.

If it means much to you, I can assure you once again that all this ordeal of separation has deepened my feeling towards you. We may take a little time to get to know each other when I do return but if you will try and keep a place for me in your world.

And that is where the first page ends, the second being lost. The next letter is the last for 1943 and is postmarked 21st December:

20.12.43

Dearest K,

I hope you received the other scrappy letters I sent off recently. I nearly tore one of them up when I saw what a mess I had made of it, but I thought you would like to know I was still alive and kicking, even if you had to piece it together like a jig-saw puzzle.

I have climbed on to the peak of a high foot-hill to write this, the outer buttress of a range of mountains above our camp. The sun is shining hotly down. Below me are patchwork fields, scrub and pine-forest. Lower still are rough river meadows, a curious flat river-bed covered with stones and an untidy stream, splitting and weaving its way out of sight. The far side of the pebble bed is made up of an abrupt cañon-like earth wall, fairly straight at the top, with a fringe of eucalyptus trees along it. After that are some orchards and a main road. Finally I can see our camp. Beyond that the plain continues for twenty or thirty miles and there is another range of mountains parallel to the one I am sitting on. One giant has snow on its head.

There is not much chance of rain at the moment, but if the black cloud on top of my range above <u>my</u> foothill, does grow and burst over me I shall certainly be wet long before reaching camp. The way down is extraordinarily tricky. You take a squint from where I am and you pick the easiest path. But a little lower down brown patches that appeared to be shoulders of hill turn out to be scooped concave-fashion out of the earth. Patches of scrub (or what appeared to be such) are found to be pine-trees.

However it is interesting. Unfortunately I cannot tell you where it is but one day I shall perhaps do so.

In the meantime, in case my other scribbled notes did go astray, all best wishes for the New Year. I'm sure you'll find ways of amusing yourself and somebody to go out with.

While I have been writing the black cloud <u>has</u> been spreading, so I'm going to interrupt this letter, as usual, and try and get down to some houses about four miles below me. (INTERVAL OF 1½ HRS)

Well, after the solitude of the heights here I am again in the big marquee recreation tent, where a few chaps are playing draughts with little enthusiasm, wondering when we shall get out of here. Two or three are reading two-month old Lilliputs and News Revues. Outside in the sun, which is fiercer down here, a football match is on. That's where I really ought to be. Keep well!

LOVE – Ron

We now know from his service record that Dad embarked for England on 26th December 1943. In a much later letter (8th April 1944) he refers to having been "in the ship's sick bay 'coming back'".

Chapter 12
Military Hospital

The first letter of 1944 was a surprise to me. I wonder if Mum was equally surprised when she received it. Dad disembarked in England on 4th January 1944[256] and it seems he was in Brighton for a few days before travelling north to see his parents in Warrington. It appears from the second sentence that he became quite seriously ill at his parents' house. This is supported in his letter of 16th March 1944 which shows that his illness prevented him returning from Warrington to Brighton on 13/14th January; he was taken straight to a nearby military hospital.

A close reading of this chapter suggests to me that Dad suffered a degree of depression in addition to the jaundice for which he was treated. Whether brought on by the physical illness or perhaps the stress of his tour of duty in Tunisia and Italy, I cannot say. Feelings of self-doubt show on his arrival at the hospital in the next letter ("I am of no desperate interest to anyone, at the moment.") and seem to reach a peak with his letter of 24th January when he declares, angrily it seems, ("I wish to goodness the illness, the war and the whole damn period of absence were over."). They continue intermittently until his move to the convalescent home in February, where he seems to return to a more normal, stable state of mind:

---

256 Military service file, ref. D/APC/HD/39300

Winnick[257] Military Hospital
(Ward E.M. 4.)

12.1.44.
Winnick
Warrington, Lancs.

Dear K,

I looked with eyes trained by the stoicism of habit on this latest transformation. Swift moving, straight from the fireside at home to the cloistered anonymity and hive-like immensity of Winnick Hospital! Still, the Army will owe me a week's leave, if I can stay here for just a week. On discharge they will send me to a Convalescent Depot (shades of Taunton!) and I suppose I shall be able to claim the leave upon return to the Regiment. They generally put you through the whole gamut, though, there is the same procedure for festered fingers as for cerebro-spinal meningitis. Perhaps, however, I may miss the Condepot stage.

I feel rather impersonal at the moment, or perhaps highly personal. The Army has no interest in me (except to get me fit soon). Mum has seen me for a few days, but a large impersonal ambulance and two A.T.S. drivers have swept me out of her ken. You had become fairly self-contained in your efficient world and were able to continue that self-containedness for some more days or weeks.

So I am of no desperate interest to anyone, at the moment!

Perhaps I can manage to revel in that anonymity, for a few days. If I have not lost the faculty, I can learn for a time from within instead of from without, as one does so often with the Army abroad. As long as these thoughts are not interrupted too much by the row of the wireless in the general ward and the cheerful banter of the blokes, none of whom seem very ill, they should be useful.

The M.O. has not seen me yet, but I have been put in a small private room which is bare but not too forbidding, with a rather weak electric light in the very high ceiling. Various nurses, of varying degrees of efficiency, inhumanity, politeness and cheerfulness, have come in and subjected me to various ritual operations, taking of pulse-rate and

---

257 The correct spelling is Winwick, which Dad learns later.

temperatures, specimen of sputum, and I have now acquired at least the dignity of a medical history. But in the middle of all this, apart from a slight depression, I feel moderately well, though somewhat lazy. I keep on wondering automatically if I should be in here at all, or if they will accuse me soon of "miking!"

14.1.44

There's one thing, I have several channels open as regards my leave; failing the Hospital (or Condepot) there is the Regiment and, as a last court of appeal, the Army Education Corps, who generally stand by their instructors in such matters.

The M.O. has seen me and confirms that it is catarrhal ephitis (some form of jaundice).[258] They are giving me practically no food, which is a nuisance.

Pity, I wanted to come up to the fitness standard necessary for that curious indoor bed-sport you have taught me.

Love,
Ron

Dad's next letter was dated four days after the last part of the previous one, but was much neater, written in ink rather than pencil and using lined notepaper:

Ward E.M. 4 18.1.44

Darling Kath,

Please don't cast a momentary frosty cloud over our talk by saying it was "not a great intellectual achievement." Hoighty-toighty, shucks for your pale-faced, long-haired intellectualism. I'm afraid I've been like that for too long and infected you with it. Our talk was fine! So there.

I can only guess what you mean by "it would be good to have another two hours for real preliminaries." To <u>what</u>? Really, I divine the worst!?!

---

258 Possibly he means nephritis, which is inflammation of the kidney.

Re my splenetic liverish self – the doctor found me tootling round the ward this morning – I felt top-hole. He threatened me with the possibility of a month in hospital, but when he examined me he was forced to admit that, "it seems as if it's passing off." However, I'm afraid I won't be getting afternoons off from hospital for at least another week or ten days. As to when or whether you should come again, I still throw the choice in abject cowardly fashion on your lovely shoulders. Since I always <u>want</u> to see you <u>that's</u> nothing to judge by. But whenever you do or don't come I still think it would be nice if you could bring the boy for a week when I am hopping out for afternoons etc. But if you would become distressed through not having his toys, proper clothes, playing facilities etc. then it's up to you to reject the idea.

There's one thing, if you want to have a week or two with a bit more personal freedom to nip into Manchester or Liverpool you have two females who would look after S. jnr. and (I really believe) obey your highly rationalist and modern instructions.

I have read S. Isaac's book on the mind of the child[259] and I think most of it is just good common sense. I want to reread the sections dealing with M's age and then I'll give you an opinion on it. I didn't study books on such young children at Sheffield.

19.1.44.

Just been awakened by the stern voice of the nurse. (!?) Must get this off for 9 o/c.

The fat-free diet here is jolly good. I get an egg a day. But I hate getting hospitalised. It will take time to get used to the outside world again now. Still, it can't be helped.

Love,
R

XXXXXXXX
XXXXXXXXX

---

259 *The Nursery Years: The Mind of the Child from Birth to Six Years* by Susan Isaacs, pub. Routledge, 1929. (Diana and I also had a copy of this book on our shelves for many years.)

Later that day, having posted his letter to Mum, Dad wrote a poem, referring to me as Little Bear, as he does again in the letter that follows it:

Dream

Laughing I drew you to the garden
Where tendrils of bright ivy wove
A sunshine filter, and in there, my love,
Upon your bright skin the dappled shadows played
Like fingers laid,
While Little Bear climbed in and out the glade.

Straight as a huntress in the stream you dived
Your hair a casque of lustre on your brow
And so the live-long day, while flowers swayed
We three sought nooks and clefts where minnows play

19.1.44

The next letter is simply dated "Sunday" so must have been written on 23rd January. It is longer than usual and again neatly handwritten in ink, except that the first page has some large inkblots, for which Dad added an apology at the top:

Sorry about this page, but no words are missing, Ron

Ward E.M. 4
Sunday

Dearest K,

I've waited till late in the day before writing to make quite certain you were not coming this week-end. I hope your non-arrival is the result of policy not accident.

It's perhaps as well, darling, whatever the other reasons, since I've developed a rotten head-cold and am busy inhaling TCP(?) under a towel. I should not be very good company.

Mother came in on Wednesday and this afternoon. The Old Boy is coming tomorrow afternoon.

I have not seen the Doc since I last posted a letter to you. It seems as though the bed has claimed me for another week.

Meanwhile I'm afraid my overheated imagination keeps on solidly fucking you, darling. I hope you don't mind and don't feel exhausted. The jolly old sub-conscious builds gleaming fires, stacks piles of seductive cushions in front of them, creates your bright eyes in front of mine and literally puts us through all the 59 positions known to the oriental love-manuals. The imaginary act always takes a couple of hours, it seems, to consummate. I wish I were up to that in real life!

Sorry if all this is rather unpractical, but I'm <u>raging</u> with it. I feel much worse than if I hadn't seen you (from that point of view). If we had been able to live a healthy sex life, both working in our respective spheres and creating a technique of living I should not be writing like I am. We should have struck the balance between habit, over-easy response to momentary desire and frigidity. We should have explored the aesthetic side of it, the border-lands where it blends with quiet evening talks, poetry, music and common pursuits.

As it is, while I bear all these things in mind, the imperative need is to get an armful of you and "git goin." Which is all right for cave-men but shouldn't be enough for the period of sex equality.

The latter is the indispensable factor of our marriage. It was the bud which was growing when it was rudely interrupted by the war. It was the thing which I did not honour in the first part of our marriage but which I was learning slowly.

When I think of you, Kath, as the partner and love-friend, I feel a burst of pride in you. When there is evidence of independence in you, as there is often, I think of our marriage as a strong bond between equals. You are my superior in quite a number of things and I am glad to acknowledge it and learn from you. When you occasionally gave way to that little old-fashioned flutter of misgiving ("You <u>will</u> keep on loving me, won't you?") it introduced the old marriage back to the stage.

If you were ever in misfortune I want to defend you, as one defends one's best comrade and expects to be defended by him or her in one's turn.

As for your physical appeal, you shouldn't have any qualms about that. I now see that somehow a woman can improve herself as the months go by. Your legs, your waist, stomach, breasts, shoulders and head have acquired an elegance and grace which I'm afraid I didn't think possible for the neat little Technical student.

And if I didn't have physical charm, particularly the considerable advantage of robustness and freshness, you couldn't have turned out a little boy as wonderful as the little bear who follows you around.

I love him with every fibre in me.

Now back to practical affairs for a second.

The reasons why I have suggested several times that you should come up here as soon as I can sneak out of hospital are as follows:-

a. If the 2nd Front opened I might possibly not be able to travel on the railways in Sussex.

b. In that eventuality we should be able to spend my leave up here as well as my day passes from hospital.

c. In the case of the 2nd Front, other reasons apart, I'm afraid I would feel you were safer up in Warrington, though I don't suppose the reason would appeal to you much by itself.

Still, I'll let you know progress as soon as I can.

Lots of love and disgustingly elemental physical manifestations at the thought of you

XXXXXXXX

XXXXX

Ron

Dad writes again the next day. The letter is, as usual in this period, written in ink on plain blue-grey notepaper. On page 3 there is a poem in pencil (which I have inserted elsewhere), and at its foot he has written in pen:

Sorry, didn't see this on the paper when I started! – RVS.

Ward M 4
Jan 24 44.

Dearest K,

I'm getting slightly annoyed by this place now. If I stay in bed too long I shall be weak on my pins. Things move so slowly one's mind becomes attuned to the slow rhythms.

The doc hasn't seen me since the report I told you of. He may come in tomorrow. I shall make a strong bid to get out of bed if he does. If I am able to do that I shall be going out three times a week very soon (within three or four days).

If I get out of this place within a total of three weeks I shall miss the Convalescent Depot, which is at Stoke, of all the insalubrious places in the world! A nurse I have just asked doesn't think much of my chance of "making it." Of course it won't be so bad if they give me my leave before sending me to Stoke. That seems quite likely.

I wish to goodness the illness, the war and the whole damn period of absence were over. I occasionally dream of doing some honest work, well-planned and executed, which would put me on a basis of equality with your maternal achievements. I would just like to do a hard creative day's work and return home to you and the family.

The house I dream of would not have to be ultra-modern, but would have large rooms and be near to trees of some kind. And the things we could do if we only had time!

We could go in for physical culture, for ourselves and the children, we could take some subject of common interest and take an external course in it, listen to music, make a nice garden and learn about flowers and plants to teach the children (I think we both start from somewhere near scratch there!)

Instead of this, what do we see, or what do I see? Instead of capitalising on experience gained abroad and pushing ahead with my Army job I lie here, at perhaps the most vital moment of modern times, without a decent light to read by, with cheerful nymphs carrying bed-pans hither and thither, a cheerful Canadian with a duodenal ulcer and a too-comfortable heated room. The bother is that when you've been in for a week or two you don't mind about all this. You just snuggle down in the blankets and "take it."

However, I've nearly finished my report to the A.E.C. on my work abroad, and I've read quite a lot of stuff in French, German and Italian, as well as material for current affairs.

So actually I'm not so damn badly off!!

What I suppose I'd like to do is to show you, with the well-known masculine tendency to unload troubles onto a wife, what I could worry about if I wanted to!!

Well, the wireless is now blaring away inescapably for the evening, so not much more intellectual effort is possible till a serious item comes on and they switch it off.

Tell me what you dream of when you dream of our home that we painfully strive towards. What do you imagine us doing, to make that terrific partnership that would be possible if we were permanent partners, throbbing to the same pulse, rising to the same dawns and slipping to bed with the breath of the same flowers and moist earth in our nostrils, calm in the expectation of new joy in each other on the morrow.

Instead of me being a rush visitor, <u>doing</u> 49 Hangleton Rd., Hove, like an American visitor <u>doing</u> Paris!

Well, I'm going to have a look at an Anthology of Modern Poetry the Staff-Nurse loaned me.

By the way there's a considerable interest in the political situation on the part of the patients. Curiously enough (for me who has been in a petty-bourgeois regiment) the interest is mainly among the working-class lads. Which refreshes me.

Lots of love,

Ron

XXXXXXX
XXXXXXX

The next letter was written on 25th and 26th January:

Ward EM4

25.1.44.

Dearest K,

In reply to yours of the 22nd, penned in best Kathleen mood.

The Doc walked past the end of my bed today, in a hurry, and said, "Ha, much better obviously. The colour's going. Your urine is practically free of bile, but there is still some derivative of bile in it. I want to take another blood test." – all in one breath and was gone!

So there we are! Or rather aren't I?

Still, I've finished and despatched my report on my work. All I can do is go on reading up A.B.C.A.[260] and languages. Also the Occupational Therapy woman of the hospital has been to see me. I think that a few words with me disposed of any idea that I might be the craftsman type, but I got her to send me up a red dog which was already cut out in felt. I have the absorbing job of sewing it together. When I get out "my sewing" the Canadian man rolls up in laughter on the bed and appeals to the world to come and see "the new Spathakycraft," "Won't Junior love tearing that to bits with his teeth" and other pungent comments.

(Interval while I give a writing and reading lesson to Chinsky, a Russian Jew from Grodno, who has got into the British Army somehow.)

26.1.44.

At hand yours of Monday 24th., which cheereth me mightily. In reply:-

Mother told me the other day that they can manage the three of us at a pinch and there is no need for you to write and ask if you can come. Just come whenever you want to.

The Doc is due here any time now, so perhaps he will make some new Delphic proclamation.

Yesterday I received your registered letter to C.M.F. with "Germany's Road to Democracy,"[261] together with an old air-mail letter referring (once again) to this mysterious wooer Frank "whom

---

260 See footnote on page 139.
261 Ed. Heinrich Fraenkel, pub. Lindsay Drummond, 1943.

you have not seen for a fortnight now." I shall have to hear the full story – it's irritating not to have had Part I of the serial, but only that "by Christmas I should have got used to not seeing him." How far did he get towards the "deadly deed of midnight" – naturally the only aim of one's wife's paramours!?

Do you tell these poor misguided boys that you have a bounding boy of 20 months, or do you slyly move your wedding-ring into a purse and pose as the repressed adolescent bursting for experience?

Sorry, I'm not being sarcastic. I'm honestly ever so interested in all the phases of such an experience. But once he "whops it out and whops it in" I think it becomes much more serious for both of us. Not only because of estrangement but because of the terrific uncertainty of this V.D. business.[262] I think it's quite reasonable to believe there has been a terrible spread of it, since nearly all of the population was uprooted and transplanted.

Not that I think you would do the thing – unless the circumstances were completely unusual.

Personally, I don't think I would at all. My desires are much more elemental – a good day's work, a walk in the gently English rain, a sight of the Sussex countryside, to teach Michael some words and to learn from you a little of the old babycraft.

I've just had a letter from Fanny, written last Sunday. He found the unit unable to cope with the returning pilots, and managed to double back to Hilda for the week-end with some kind of a pass.[263] I must reply today.

Conversation among the "up" patients sitting around the fire:-

AARONS: (RAF Medical orderly, ex small shopkeeper.) Course there are channels of complaints, but it's not often you get them used in the R.A.F.

PRICE: (RAMC Orderly, back from NA; a talker, but shallow) Aye, it's the same in all the forces. If you put forward a complaint on the grub the others will leave you in the shit when it comes to seeing an officer.

---

262 Venereal disease, now known as sexually transmitted disease or STD.
263 Fanny Waldron – see Appendix 2.

AARONS: Most ordinary blokes are afraid to look after their own interests. It makes me mad. (To another patient) Don't you agree that the ordinary man in the street is pretty cowardly?

(The man appealed to, a poor talker, conscious that he is neither cowardly nor particularly brave but that Aarons is probably no hero, just nods.)

MYSELF: (pulling the old line, from bed)

What about the Trade Unions in Britain, then? How were they built up when the penalty for forming one was seven years' transportation? Surely people stood together.

AARONS: (deflated) Oh yes, that's true.

XXXXXXXXXXXXXX Love, Ron

In view of the high frequency of Dad's letters while at Winwick Hospital, we should assume that this one, simply dated "Thurs.", was written on 27th January 1944:

Ward M4,

Thurs.

Dearest K,

I am waiting for the doctor's visit at present. Thanks very much for your third letter. You are becoming quite a Lady Chesterfield – and your style is flowing, natural and with none of the jerks and strainings mine has… (ENTER DOCTOR)…

Durn the man! He listened pleasantly to all my disappearing symptoms, noted with approval my more normal colour, smiled agreeably and good-humouredly pooh-poohed the idea that I should get up.

In answer to your points about books I haven't felt <u>more</u> inclined for a continuous piece of study or writing for several years. But of course it's difficult for other people to get the books for one. If it is possible for you (when you do come or if you do come) to bring that little book on the "British Empire" by Evans which I borrowed from Hove I should be greatlih obleeged. I'm thinking of making myself a bit of a specialist on *[sentence unfinished]*

Incidentally, via the Staff-Nurse, who went into Manchester yesterday, I've bought a very complete and modern anthology of poetry The Poet's Tongue.[264] Tell me if my unhappy children are starving and I'll stop buying books! Herewith a folk poem:-

A carrion crow sat on an oak,
Fol de riddle, lol di riddle, hi ding do,
Watching a tailor shape his cloak;
Sing heigh do, the carrion crow,
Fol de riddle, lol di riddle, hi ding do.

Wife bring me my old bent bow,
Fol de riddle, lol di riddle, hi ding do,
That I may shoot yon carrion crow,
Sing heigh do, the carrion crow,
Fol de riddle, lol di riddle, hi ding do.

The tailor he shot and missed his mark,
Fol de riddle, lol di riddle, hi ding do,
And shot his own sow through the heart,
Sing heigh do, the carrion crow,
Fol de riddle, lol di riddle, hi ding do.

Good isn't it? Daft of course.

I have just finished the second of your books, the one on "Toys in Wartime." It's probably useful but I think the author must be a very "bouncy" fellow.[265]

---

264 Ed. W H Auden and John Garrett, pub. Bell, 1935.

265 *Toys in Wartime* by Hilary Page, pub. George Allen & Unwin, 1942. I am amazed to find that I still have Mum's original copy of this book. It is inscribed, in Mum's handwriting: "K. Spathaky / April 1943 / 49 Hangleton Rd / Hove". Stuck to the inside front cover is a small red sticker of "People's Bookshop, 90 Trafalgar Street, Brighton, 1".

Hilary Page was the founder of Kiddicraft Ltd. A website, hilarypagetoys.com, shows several toys that I remember having as a young child, notably the Building Beakers, the Hammer-Peg (although this was first made in 1955 so must have been my brother Dave's) and the Pyramid Rings. Finally, when we moved to Ireland in 1950, I was given an Irish version of the Counties Jig-Saw.

One good suggestion was that of painting part of a wall black and giving the children coloured (or white) chalks to scribble with. Shall we do it?

Incidentally I am reminded that you have not told me any reasons for wanting another child, except that it is best to bring children up in numbers. Are there any others?

My reasons would be, I suppose:-

a. They are so jolly and loving when they are young.

b. If some of them break your heart when they are older <u>some</u> of them may not.

c. They may give you a fish-and-chip supper, a warm by the fire and a copy of their old newspapers to read when you're old and doddery.

d. If they happen to agree with any of your ideas (which is a matter of speculation) they will certainly push them further than you did. You then have the senile satisfaction of saying. "I told you there was something in the idea."

e. They make you limit your purely sexual interests to your wife in a way nothing else (I imagine) could do.

Well, dearest, don't come this week-end if it's going to knock you up.

Love, Ron

He wrote again the next day, writing the wrong year in the date – easily done in January. For once, thankfully, he wrote the whole date, including the day of the week, which is correct for 1944!

Fri 28th Jan 43. *[sic]*

Dear Kay,

Hallo, how goes it? I feel a lot better today. I've been eating the fat-free diet with gusto and occasionally the ordinary one as well. The Brownness still lingers on but I'm pretty certain I'll be getting out by next Thursday at the latest. There's also the rather useful point I've gleaned; that they let W.O.'s out of the hospital pretty frequently without passes. So if you do decide to come (and oh boy, I hope you do!) it looks as if we shall be able to make the best of my convalescence and then my week's leave.

Personally I'm not at all discouraged by this period of rest and reading: After all, 95% of the Regiment had no responsibility at all during the recent campaign, except for the short but severe trial of the operation. I had to think out ways of keeping the lads interested during the whole journey. It was an ever present problem.

After this period I shall be up and sniffing the air for activity (I hope). There's no doubt that the over-secretion of bile during the weeks preceding my going sick had a very deadening and depressing effect. The colossal emotional thrill of walking back into your arms kept the bad effects at bay for a few days, but I didn't feel as lively as I had hoped. I didn't want you to notice anything and I still hope you didn't.

One sign of returning health is perhaps the fact that one of the young nurses seems to be casting rather inexperienced eyes at me. Believe me I feel so mature and experienced now I sit back and suppress a smile at the rather obvious "passes" she makes. But I know you will not grudge me the slight change of colour in the sexual "aura" of the surrounding air when she chats to me. A woman of your experience will understand what I mean.

It's all right – no danger to the jolly old family institution! Vive la famille – avec une ferme base de copulation sur laquelle on édifie la surstructure culturelle!

As a matter of fact you may be surprised, but I honestly think you derive benefit from another woman smiling at me. Just before leaving Africa the bile had created a rather nasty feeling in me – general physical and mental inability to appeal to you, to <u>mate</u> with your slickness and scientifico-maternal efficiency. You yourself nearly dispelled that by the way that you received me back to your heart and bed. I shall never forget that. But the nasty undercurrent remained.

I don't know if you remember a passage in Vera Brittain's Testament of Youth[266] where she says that when she returned from V.A.D. [267]

---

266 Pub. Victor Gollancz 1933, acclaimed as a classic for its description of the impact of World War I on the lives of women and the middle-class civilian population of Great Britain. Vera Brittain's daughter was the politician Shirley Williams.

267 Voluntary Aid Detachment.

nursing in France she had a period of depression during which she wondered if her features were changing and if she were even growing an ugly growth of hair.

I must confess to you (and I do so because it's gone and done with) that I had a similar feeling. I felt (particularly with these Army glasses) that my chin had grown weak and my smile forced and childish. Now I know that it was general "fatigue of personality," and the jaundice.

I still need to be reassured a bit but I know you can do that.

The fact that someone else even finds me interesting enough to smile at me means that the jolly old human batteries are definitely recharging and I shall soon be "psychically" up to your standard.

And believe me, in spite of the cold, which I hope has gone, I found your psyche pretty radiant as a result of two years of motherhood. As I told you, your figure seemed to have altered, to be neater, more compact and slimmer at the waist. I think that's all connected with increased confidence in one's personality.

All we need to do in love, I suppose, is to be ourselves, to develop our own tendencies for the one we love and never to try and pass off on him or her other qualities or characteristics in place of the ones we possess.

I love you most when you are most yourself, when you are as you want to be – not so much as you think I like women to be (though I suppose that enters into it).

Dare I hope that you like me best when I am most myself?

Love
Ron

There follows a postcard dated (and postmarked) 31st January 1944, which was a Monday:

[Ward] M4, 31.1.44.

Dearest K,

Glad to hear from Ma you are coming on Thursday. If I can possibly get out of this place for the afternoon I will meet you but it's doubtful.

If the whole thing looks too strenuous at the last minute be sensible and don't tire yourself out doing it. But please phone me a telegram if you decide not to.

Don't bother about bringing anything for me unless you have room for Gordon Schaffe's (3d) recent pamphlet "Rule of the Trusts"[268] and that book I had out by Evan's "The British Empire" (R.I.I.A)

XXXXXX – Love Ron

The next letter is dated simply, "Thursday". Since Mum and I were due to arrive in Warrington on Thursday 3rd February, it was probably written on the 10th:

Ward M4,
Thursday.

Dearest K,

The new blood-test shows that there is still some derivative of bile in my blood and though the colour has faded it has not decreased as rapidly as last week. Consequently the doctor has only promoted me to the status of "half-up-patient." I am allowed up but am not allowed to leave the ward or do anything much.

This is rather disappointing but it can't be helped. I am casting around for some means of working in the ward, with the slender and (more baffling) unsystematic supply of reading material I get from the old folks, the hospital newspaper-man and the hospital library. Thank you, by the way, for the bundle of papers.

I suspect very much the Government's attitude towards the war at the moment. We are told that the Tehran Conference settled everything, including even the date, regarding the Second Front. But now both Britain and U.S. seem to be doing their best to pick a quarrel with U.S.S.R. over the Polish business.

Probably the extreme Right think that Germany (and Russia) have now received a suitable blood-letting, but that the advance

---

268 A misspelling of Gordon Schaffer, a left-wing political journalist who wrote a pamphlet with the title *Who Owns Britain?* pub. Co-operative Press, Manchester, 1944.

of Russia very much further will create a difficult problem for "civilisation."

I think likewise their attitude towards the organisation of UNRRA[269] has little of the Moscow Conference[270] in it – or even of the Atlantic Charter.[271] The Americans have suggested that since India is practically a battle-front their funds should be used for relief of the Bengal famine. The British angelically opposed on the grounds that "UNRRA funds were for the relief of the Axis-oppressed peoples only." War is indivisible! But apparently hunger is divisible, according to the gents.

We had a man of curious nationality in today, a Maltese from Tunis. (There are 90,000 French, 95,000 Italians and colonies of Maltese, Greeks and Jews as well as the Arabs.) The Doc wanted to question him on the history of his illness, so he did it through me. It was quite a good bit of fun, though hardly of the highest importance.

Incidentally, something struck me the other day about Michael, i.e. that I ought to be learning a bit about handling him and doing odd jobs. So when my leave comes I want you to initiate me. O.K?

I've been doing a little Russian today. It's jolly tough going but it certainly passes the time usefully. Also keeping up the French, German and Italian. I wish I could get that parcel of books you sent me which included the German military reader.[272] If you happen to see a copy of "Die Zeitung"[273] on sale perhaps you would bring it or send it.

I am also very interested in the book shown on the enclosed advert. If you think of it could you please have a look in some booksellers and tell me what you think its purpose is and its general interest, some of the Contents and anything else of importance. Don't buy it unless

---

269 The United Nations Relief and Rehabilitation Administration was an international relief agency, largely dominated by the United States but representing forty-four nations, and founded in 1943.

270 The Third Moscow Conference between the major Allies – 18th October to 11th November 1943.

271 A policy statement of 14th August 1941 setting out the Allies' goals for the post-war world.

272 Probably *Deutsches Soldatentum: A German Military Reader* by W B P Aspinall, pub. Harrap, 1943.

273 A German-language newspaper published in London during the war.

you want it yourself – but the news that it is a sequel to Maths for the Million[274] sounds interesting.

Hope you are both well and enjoying life. Don't see Frankie <u>too</u> much will you (or whatever his name was)?

Lots of love,

Ron

XXXXX

After the intensive letter-writing of January while Dad was in hospital, there was now a week's gap while he went home on leave, as confirmed by the next two letters (although the postcard had said Mum was going to Warrington on 3rd February). These two letters may have been posted in the same cream-coloured envelope, which matches the first letter but is postmarked "19 Feb 44", matching the second:

Ward M4

17.2.44.

Dear K,

I had a good journey here and got a meal at the British Restaurant. Then I went to see Father. Mother was by chance at the theatre, so she came with me to the bus.

The morning after, the A.E.C. Sergeant made a request to me to take a discussion for him. I did so well enough.

My cold got worse as the day went on. My nose today is not working well. (Ah ha, nearly got myself into a mess there!) The doctor I saw at 2 p.m. made me go to bed – so here I am.

I shall probably be in bed for two or three days and then go through the colours again.

A letter was here from the Staff Officer (Education) Airborne Div. He says that I will be put with the Airborne again so I have no cares on that point.

This cold makes me very tired, so I will not make this letter longer.

---

274 *Mathematics for the Million* by Lancelot Hogben, pub. George Allen & Unwin, 1936. The sequel was *Science for the Citizen*, pub. ibid., 1938.

I have one or two observations on our leave but I must put them in another letter.

Love

Ron

XXXXX

This is the second of the two letters, which may have been posted in the same envelope postmarked "19th February":

Ward M4

Sat.

Dearest K,

My leave is receding somewhat into the past, while the featureless Warrington sky and the brisk monotony of the ward have become the reality.

I suppose I shall be up again soon, but I wish I could have avoided this anti-climax. When I returned here at first my morale was high. It is difficult to wind it up again.

The week at home was quite an experiment and I think we had some success. You had to work too hard with the house and Michael. I should have helped more, but I will do so on the next occasion. I was too much of a book-worm.

This is a tendency that I have to fight in the next few months. What do you think causes anyone to run away into books?

Perhaps it is only a normally healthy tendency which has been made morbid by my stay in hospital. What do you think?

Sometimes I think that my job is not worthwhile, just a matter of gassing instead of getting down to practical details. However, I suppose I am definitely wrong in thinking that. So many people have their noses kept so close to the grindstone that they don't have the chance to delve into things. I have a position of trust because I can do that delving for others, on their behalf.

I have been having some interesting arguments with an R.C. corporal of the RA.F. in the next bed. He is very bitter about the deal which R.C.'s get in the new Education Bill. His complaint is that RC schools have never had the support in £.s.d. from the State that others have had. I must find out about this.

By the way, a welcome parcel arrived yesterday, via God-knows-where. In it were the German reader and the book on North Africa, for both of which many thanks.

(10 mins later)

I have just been told I can get up again. This is curious in view of the fact that my cold is not completely cured, but I suppose it's gone sufficiently to deprive me of the status of bed-patient, with all the little luxuries entailed therein.

I'm afraid this week-end will be rather quiet, but I shall go a little walk around the hospital if the sun comes out. The trees are rather peculiar here. They are blacker than any I've seen before, making a perfect ebony outline against the white sky and green grass.

Congratulations on the progress Michael is making. He seems perfectly happy and active. I think you are wise in not teaching him too much at once. Living or at least moving things seem to be the most attractive. He certainly reflects your moods. The only time I heard him scream and really cry was on that first day when you were out of sorts.

Please don't work too hard. You looked as though you were going it a bit hard for a married woman. (!!?%)

All my love, Ron

XX – for Michael

XXXXXXXXXXX

P.S.

Address from Monday (day after tomorrow)

Hefferston Grange

  Convalescent Home,

    Weaverham,

      Cheshire.

Dad writes again the following day, his last at Winwick Hospital:

as from Hefferston Grange Convalescent Home
Weaverham, Cheshire.
Sunday.

Dearest K,

I have just had the impulse to open a bundle of newspapers etc. forwarded by some unknown hand from the G.P.R. To my surprise I found 5/- from the M.C.C., letters from you, airgraphs from your Ma, all kinds of notes and postcards, making appointments, etc., etc. In the middle of the papers were 2 copies of "Our Time," for which many thanks.

It is sad-sweet looking through your letters of Nov-Dec. How I wanted them at that time! You were very enthusiastic about the School and set on doing the reading. I hope you do the same for the forthcoming one. The booklet by Dobb on "Economics of Capitalism"[275] looks particularly good, judging by the informative introduction. Dobb seems to have acquired great powers of simplification these days.

Talking of Schools, and therefore conferences I had rather a surprise at the single A.B.C.A. I took this week. The discussion got on to post-war planning and I found quite a large number of chaps interested in the idea of flats after the war!

So I may have to recant and hand the palm of knowledge to you on that point. Apparently people are not so biased.

I have been learning quite a lot about this Convalescent Home I am going to. It is at Weaverham, about ten miles from our house at Waverley Ave. and the Army seems determined to coddle me.

A man who was there for a week recently said he would give me £5 to change places with me. It is said to be a dream. Visitors are allowed any time. The house is perfect. There are about five patients there, and they send one or two from Winwick occasionally to keep it open. The staff have a very good reputation.

If I am well enough to get a 48-hours there would you like me to come home, or would you like to come up again. I hardly imagine you favour the latter. Of course I could try and find somewhere for you and Michael to stay in Weaverham for a week, but that is completely speculative.

---

275 Probably *Political Economy and Capitalism* by Maurice Dobb, pub. Routledge, 1937.

In any case I don't ask you to co-ordinate your activities with my trivial ones. You and M are the important part of our family at the moment. You are both doing something! I feel rather a drone, an unproductive drone rolling around from one institution to another. However I shall not always be that.

(Mon 1100 hrs)

I am sitting in the ward at Winwick waiting for the ambulance to cart me off. I feel much freer of cold and in general benefit by my two days in bed. They insist on sending me as a stretcher case to avoid draughts. I shall be able to jump down and give them a hand carrying myself if they find it heavy work.

Please don't worry if our love-life was not too perfect during leave. I'm afraid general physical condition affects that. In fact it must do. You will remember that on one occasion each one of us has been ready for the crisis too soon. I was beginning to feel quite confident about that problem just before I left England.

Wish I could go a nice walk with you this morning. It is cold but I believe there is not much wind. Spring will soon be here, and I, who am very "heliotropic" will welcome it more than ever.

Lots of the two l's

XXXXXXX Ron

P.S. I've sent M's red dog.

Chapter 13

Convalescence

The next day, Tuesday 22nd February 1944, finds Dad at Hefferston Grange, a sanatorium in the village of Weaverham, near Northwich in Cheshire:

E.M.S.Hefferston Grange,

Weaverham Grange,

Cheshire, Tues. Feb 44

Dearest,

Here I am at Weaverham. The sister at Winwick carried through the "stretcher-patient" farce to the end. I was up and fully dressed (including boots) during the day, then when the ambulance came they loaded me on under a blanket and wheeled me through the corridors, myself groaning realistically with pain. I carried the stretcher down the stairs. Then when we got to the ambulance I jumped in in front with the F.A.N.Y.[276] and showed her the best way to Weaverham.

It is a curious show they have here.

It is fitted out in a modern way. About a dozen bright huts around the old Grange form the wards. Then comes the anti-climax. In the whole hospital there are only two military patients, myself and another chap, together with half a dozen civilians. To look after us there are a doctor, a matron, two sisters, two staff-nurses and about a dozen nurses (of which have no fear!).

They seemed disappointed when I, the stretcher case, walked briskly in the reception room. The grub here is good and knocks

---

276 First Aid Nursing Yeomanry, a voluntary organisation.

W into a cocked-hat. When I had settled down I asked if there were somewhere I could do some work. They offered me the sister's office in the next (empty) ward block, complete with electric fire, table, black-out and everything.

The young doctor (24) came and visited me today (in my office). After a few remarks on my "complaint" (what exactly is it, by the way?) he seemed relieved to sit down and hear all about Inter-Glossa, A.B.C.A. and the work I do in the army. He said he was bored stiff by the place and wished he could take over a neighbouring sanatorium in addition. I can foresee quite a number of discussions with him, though I don't imagine he is of particular importance.

I am awaiting the result of some enquiries about digs in the village, which is ten minutes' walk away. Then if you should feel like coming up you can. I know you don't want to visit Waverley Ave[277] again.

Even though there seemed to be one or two slight (very slight) tensions during my leave, possibly due to my not doing enough with Michael, I do want to see you again. It may be based on the rising of the old sap again, but I don't care, I want to see you to be <u>with</u> you again, all of you, the mental, emotional and physical you.

However, perhaps you will prefer to wait till I can get a week-end. I don't know whether they grant leave from this place yet or whether I shall be fit to travel yet awhile.

Afraid all this sounds miles away from the Anzio beachhead and the 2nd Front – but I can't help it. I'm not quite fit so I'm damned if I'm going to flagellate myself. I'm going to laugh at my irresponsibility for once!

XXXXXXXXXXXX Love,
Ron

Dad followed this with another letter the following day, 23rd February:

---

277 Dad's parents' home in Warrington.

Heffersdon Grange E.M.S.
Weaverham, Cheshire.
Wed.

Dearest K,

I've done quite a bit of work while I've been here including an article on Bodmer[278] and Hogben's new language teaching methods. Some day I shall get an article accepted, but so far I am trying to improve my writing.

They are giving me at present two aspirins and T.C.P. inhalant four-hourly. The aspirins are making me feel a bit heated, especially as I am up. The chief doctor from Winwick visited us today. He is quite a decent bird, though he has a rather curious restless manner.

(RETIRES TO BED, THE
ASPIRINS HAVING PRODUCED
A BUZZING IN THE EARS).

Thurs.

This morning is sunnier, though the fields look sodden and cold. The doctor let me out for a few minutes, when Mother came. I felt shivery and weak when I returned, so I think I shall go very slowly. It's strange that I was able to stand that week's leave, because I don't feel as well now. Jaundice certainly lives up to its reputation.

I hope Michael is better. He probably caught my cold, poor little chap. Give him an extra listen to the "teetock" for me, please.

The doctor said he had found a place nearby where you and M. could come and stay if you would like to. He was keeping it for his own young lady, but doesn't bother too much about retaining it.

Are you fed up with travelling? I thought you might like a change. I could meet you. I would like to talk over with you the question of taking a commission. Or alternatively you can wait until I get a week-end leave and we'll try and go to Herbert Corke's or somewhere similar. I'm rather in favour of us changing surroundings, you know, if the third party can be worked in.

---

278 Frederick Bodmer, author of *The Loom of Language: An Approach to the Mastery of Many Languages*, ed. Lancelot Hogben, pub. unknown, 1944.

I haven't done anything very interesting today, though it was fairly pleasant chatting to my Ma. It takes her about twenty minutes to get here on the bus.

Of course you must decide yourself about travelling. Please don't get yourself all tired out if you think mere epidermal juxtaposition is the main problem in our minds.

Lots of love,

Ron

XXXXXXX

The next letter was dated "Mon." and found in a matching envelope with the postmark "warrington lancs. / 9 am / 29 feb / 1944", which was a Tuesday:

Weaverham,

Mon.

Dearest K,

Your letter of Friday reassured me about le petit singe. I suppose <u>some</u> such ailments are unavoidable and form part of the mother's burden. Hope yours isn't pressing down on you too much!

I applied today for 48-hrs. leave. The young doc said there was no reason why I shouldn't have more, so I shall probably be home on Friday for four or five days. There seems no prospect of my release for another two or three weeks. They don't seem very bothered what I do while I'm here, but discharge is regarded as a grave step, almost a thing it is impolite to refer to. Or reference to it is laughed at, as if it were a good joke. So I just can't do anything but follow my own devices.

There are now <u>three</u> Service patients and <u>two</u> civis (one of whom goes tomorrow)!

I have been considering this business of a commission dispassionately and I think now that other matters besides purely utilitarian ones <u>have</u> influenced me. Your future and that of M. weigh very heavily in the balance. It is easy to say that I should be insuring your future and his if I fought in the front ranks but it's harder to convince oneself of that. There is also the selfish side. You have <u>provided</u> me for six years with a basis for my life – which as a youth I didn't have previously. And it's a basis that expands continually.

The more I think how you have put a pattern and purpose into our joint life the more enthusiastic I am. If only we can take advantage of the joyous fact that we started family-building while we were children ourselves! The essence of all this rambling is that life has become potentially very sweet to me.

So the question is – have I had a conservative streak infiltrated into me?

The question would be much clearer if your future were better provided for. I should then have to fight only with my own selfish love – and yours.

I almost wish at times that we <u>could</u> make some practical insurance. The ideal but fantastic thing would be a couple of people (like Bernard or Brian[279]) one of whom you could marry straight away if I were bumped off and if he were still alive and unattached. But I can't quite see anybody in view who would lend himself to the idea. And it would be horrible if the scheme went wrong and you fastened your second string too firmly on the bow and I didn't get bumped off.

What do you think of the idea? Do you like Bernard enough to keep him soft-pedalling for a year or two. Or conversely does <u>he</u> like <u>you</u> enough?

However, think over the scheme in your inimitable level-headed manner and give me a scientific reply (you can give it to me in bed, however, if you prefer).

The point about the commission business is that I should put in for the Intelligence Corps (languages) but I might get put in the PBI[280], just like Gordon.

My cold still clings on, though it makes slight progress from week to week. But I feel fitter in myself as the days go by.

---

279 Bernard Stone, Dad's former teaching colleague, and possibly Brian O'Malley, Mum's boyfriend before she met Dad.
280 Apparently this acronym stood for Poor Bloody Infantry.

There is snow on the ground here and I have been on several quick walks in the whip-like air. Capt. Edge (S.O. Edn.) has written me a very nice note, enclosing pamphlets and telling me he has fixed up my return to A.D.[281]

Mit tiefster Liebe,

R

XXXXXXX
XXXXXX

pour le petit singe – XX

The next letter was simply dated "Sun." and the envelope was postmarked "Northwich, 13th March", which was a Monday. The opening lines about "having to come all up here again" presumably refer to his return from leave in Brighton up to the hospital near Warrington:

Heffersdon

Sun.

Dearest K,

Sorry I have not written before. I was in a black mood at having to come all up here again. But it has passed. This morning I set off for home and walked four or five miles before I got a lift in a Yank lorry.

Mother was very pleased to see me but I didn't stay too long and was back at the Grange for tea. I shall ask the Doc if he can discharge me next time I see him.

Today I have been talking quite a bit to the Canadian driver who is in here. He is about 31, looks 23, and comes from the real bush country of Winnipeg, where he had a small farm. I like the slow earthy confident way he speaks, and he never shoots a line, except a little, justifiably, when he speaks of his horses. He left home and school when he was eleven and has had no book-learning since but he is as intelligent as you or I. Tells a good joke – the one about the man who shouted himself hoarse at a race and went to see a doctor is one of his.

---

281 Airborne Division (I presume).

I'm a bit apprehensive about your position down there if any bombing starts. I suppose it is considered good political ethics to remain where one is. But if you ever consider that Michael should be put out of danger you could always come up to Warrington for a month or two (bad as that sounds!) They told me today that they would reshuffle the house and give you a couple of rooms if you wanted to do that and wouldn't charge us anything (since it's nearly their own place now).

I'm only giving you this as "information material" because you can judge the situation better than me, but if you <u>do</u> think of moving anywhere you don't want to leave it until you are a definite menace to an overloaded transport-system.

Sheridan has been on leave since I came back, so you will be pleased to know there have been no pinchings and slappings taking place. I am in any case much too concerned to live up to you and get out of this place au plus vite que possible.

There was a little concert given the other evening for the T.B. patients and the Cannuck and I went. It was a Woman's Choir from Warrington and they were so atrocious that they were really very funny. At the end of the concert I had the job of moving a vote of thanks and they had really tried so hard (though with such tragic-comic results) that I had to say something nice.

I thought I heard the Doc invite me to tea with his fiancée yesterday when he came round, but he hasn't been about today. Perhaps I misheard or maybe they got into a huddle somewhere and haven't got out of it yet. In any case I don't bother, She's a little bit silkily high-class, although pretty attractive.

This latest Russian breakthrough at Uman and Tarnopol[282] appears to be terrific, doesn't it? I hope the movement makes the greatest use of it. The recent apathy has manifested itself in a few people I have met with a complete blankness about the world of mud, flames, slaughter

---

282 These were Ukrainian cities which suffered pogroms under the Nazis. The Nazi occupation of Uman ended on 10th March 1944. The Russians completely destroyed Tarnopol on 7th and 8th March, but the city was not liberated until 15th April 1944. Dad could not have known in 1944 that the Russians would deport the Poles of Tarnopol en masse to Poland.

and triumph on the other side of the Germans. One woman who does part-time nursing here even said yesterday, "Well, they have an easier time of it, don't they, because the country is so flat and suits them." I wanted to vomit.

Still, I can say little enough until I begin to fight again.

XXXXXXXXXXXXXXXXXXXXXXXX Love, Ron

In his next letter, Dad starts by referring to his leave around 3rd to 8th March:

Heffersdon Grange,
16 Mar.

Dearest K,

Don't thank me for the leave. Surely it's something we enjoyed together, not a present made by one to the other.

Sorry le petit singe has had trouble with his eye-teeth again. Give him a big hug from me. I love him very much now I have got to know him better. He's sealed our bargain in living form. When I look at him I see you in him and vice-versa him in you.

The material for his trousers is very nice. I'm sure you will turn out something tasteful and artistic. The Doctor has taken me out to Ma's each morning, on his way to the Warrington clinic. So she has had quite a fill of me. If only I had managed to make that original train-journey on January 13/14 I should have been in and out of home instead of Waverley Ave., still,

"the moving Finger writes and having writ

Moves on, nor all thy piety nor wit

Can stop or cancel one small line of it."[283]

The Doc called for me at 5.30 p.m. each day, had tea with Ma and took me back, then he usually invites me up to his rooms for supper and

---

283 Not bad from memory, Dad! From The Rubáiyát of Omar Khayyam (trans. 1859, Edward FitzGerald):

The Moving Finger writes; and, having writ,
Moves on: nor all thy Piety nor Wit
Shall lure it back to cancel half a Line,
Nor all thy Tears wash out a Word of it.

we argue about the New Health Bill or his marriage until I am paralytic with lack of sleep. Then I come down and stoke up the fifteen fires and furnaces (sometimes with Sheri, sometimes with Bill the Canadian).

There is no further development in the scandalous "affaire Sheri" which I described to you. I have curfuffled once or twice with her, but don't please try and seek to be even with me, unless you want to very much. After all, the proximity of young women all day long, and all night for that matter, is a bit of an unusual temptation to philander. But I think they will finally pack me off on Monday and there the matter will rest.

Please write by return and tell me that you don't mind too much. You know that you and M are the centre of my universe. But we have promised to be honest with one another and so I tell you quickly so that you may know the grand total of microscopic damage.

If by any chance Dixon refuses to let me out for still one more week I suppose you wouldn't think of coming up to those digs I mentioned? I'm not pressing the point, but if you did you could see this Sheri person and assert your superiority over her by one glance at Michael. Or rather she would apologise to you.

(PAUSE WHILE INK IS STRENGTHENED)

When I went for the ink they gave me your letter of Tuesday; a real budget! I have noted the farm address and I guess if I ever lost it I could find one of the FIVE aunts.

I'm glad you've bought a summer frock and I'm sure if it's anything like your usual style I shall like it.

I have sent to the Glider Pilots saying I want all my stuff sent to Hangleton Road. Hope you don't mind. I can pick it up there. It consists of

1   Kit-bag, white (+contents)
1   do. , blue (+ contents , incl. specs I hope).
1   Haversack, small (+ ring, tied to a cord)
1   Set webbing equipment (cross-straps etc)
[1 Rifle and bayonet (perhaps)]
1   Type-writer (I hope)
About 15 books.

I've got quite interested in this new Medical Scheme.[284] The Doc is against it, which rather surprises me, as he was secretary of the Manchester Student Socialist Club when I was secretary of the Sheffield one.

Incidentally I now remember quite a lot of meetings we used to attend together and I even remember some letters we wrote to each other on the Youth Charter or Spanish Aid.

In the middle of all this I have done quite an amount of reading, especially of the Coates history. It is excellent, especially on the "Zinoviev letter" and the Arcos raid.[285] But the interesting part will really come with the League of Nations period and the William Strang fiasco in 1939. I think the main value is not the critical disclosures, but the tracing of the pro-Soviet and anti-Soviet groups, who have not altered (except for the Churchillites) for many years.

(I think the last sentence is thoroughly bad – what I mean is that muck-raking is not much good, but we want to know where the present opposition arose and how widespread it may be.)

Sorry I didn't report on my progress in my last letter. My cold went after two days here. I have asked the Doc definitely to recommend returning me to duty. I want to get back to the harness.

By the way, about the sentence in your letter "I think I need brightening up a bit." I believe that you are doing a bigger job than you realise. You are probably only just realising what the load of a young mother is, especially when her man can't help. You will feel brighter when you get M organised with the nursery school and step outside the shell of the home again. Not that you have ever become sealed up in it, but I have noticed how much work you have to do and I feel a lazy good-for-nothing parasite by comparison.

I shall probably have rung you up by the time this arrives, but please let me know by return that you still trust me.

Lots of love

Ron

XXXXXXXXXXXXX

---

284 The proposed National Health Service, about which a pamphlet containing an "official abridged version of the Government's proposals" was published in 1944.
285 *A History of Anglo-Soviet Relations*, William and Zelda Coates, pub. Lawrence & Wishart 1943.

Is this the last letter before getting out of hospital?

Heffersdon Grange,
19 Mar 44.

Dearest K,

The longest lounge in my life is coming to an end. I start from here tomorrow, though whether I go to Winwick to be discharged or straight back to duty I don't know.

I certainly feel in the pink now. My cheeks have even grown fatter, a thing that I don't think has happened for years. Yesterday I went a long walk away from the hospital towards Delamere, a little village which I used to know when I wandered around here in my mis-spent youth. On the way back I saw an aeroplane accident, but I'd better not say anything about it in case it's security.[286]

The Doc wheeled me off to the pub the other evening and stood me two 1/2-pints on an empty stomach. (I had been late for tea and only had a bit of bread). The beer made me pretty light-headed and he was practically the same. We went back to his room arguing about all kinds of irrelevant nonsense, befitting the state of two men isolated in the country from the greatest events that the world has ever witnessed.

Still, I feel I have been of some use to him, because he has been in a much worse state of mind than I have and I have probably caused him to leave this place and join the R.A.F. At least if all the influence is not mine, part of it probably is.

Sorry I can't help you about the house-problem. It certainly looks as though a tight hold on this present place would be better than a speculation on something uncertain.

The only feeling I have is that we must try and get a place of our own when I come back. I think that living with your people has been a useful phase in our existence, but we now feel the need for home-building on an independent basis. After all I could learn the job if I set

---

286 I have ascertained that the plane was a Handley Page Halifax which was on a test flight from Ringway Airport and not yet assigned to the RAF. The two occupants, a civilian test pilot and an engineer, were killed. The crash site was in Lob Slack field, Oakmere (near Delamere): David Huxley, *Handley Page Halifax Forum* website.

about it. While all house-problems are settled by you and your people it leaves me no chance to learn.

I'm well on past the Zinoviev Letter period in that "History of Anglo-Soviet Relations." It's really a terrific indictment of the Tories. If you can get it from the Library I should.

Also been re-reading a novel I did for Matric or H.S.C. called "La Terre qui Meurt," principally for the good vocabulary it has.[287]

I can't quite understand why the consistently steady interest in language-work which I had during my first weeks in hospital has flagged. Perhaps it's because the 2nd Front and the political problems of the moment now loom much closer whereas in the days when I was ill I felt less responsible and could indulge myself in the less-useful language work.

Can't understand that announcement in the papers about transport drivers needed for the 2nd Front. If it's time then it gives the Jerries the information that the thing is not starting for a month or two. If it's a bluff then I feel it will have a frustrating effect on men in the Forces.

Well, Kath, we have just finished dinner, and an even more complete silence has descended on the little ward. The nurses on duty are sitting around the fire reading the papers and the patients (all four of them) are respectively sleeping, reading the papers and in the wash-room washing.

I have borrowed a bike from a nurse and am going over to Warrington to see the folks for the last time – for many months. The person who will be most concerned at seeing me go is the old lady – Gran. She is absolutely disinterested in her pure affection.

It is a bit affecting to think I shall probably not see her again. People surely don't live long after 85. Yet when I was in the day before yesterday she had dressed herself in a smart black coat with an Astrakhan streak on it which added dignity to her height. She'd a smart black hat and looked 50 years younger. And she was off to the pictures in town by herself![288]

---

287 By René Bazin, pub. Calmann-Lévy, 1898.
288 "The old lady – Gran" was Dad's maternal grandmother Ann Retchford (née Watton). She was eighty-three when Dad wrote this. Dad must have seen her several times before she died eight years later. I remember meeting her in 1950 and 1951 when we stayed at their house.

So if ever we think we've wasted a few years and we've been getting apathetic or losing our youth, let's think of her, two generations ahead of us and as cheerful as a cricket.

I'm sorry our letters keep "crossing" but I thought you would like a line rather than have to wait for your letter.

Please take care of yourself and le petit for me, especially yourself. Work steadily at those things you can do without too much strain and don't fall into the vice I've had at times – reacting too strongly about things beyond my scope. It always leads to doing less about them than if one had considered them coolly and calmly and then done perhaps a little less but done it well.

I love you terribly – please wait for me.

Love Ron

P.S. Address as soon as possible.

On the following day Dad is still at Heffersdon:

Heffersdon
Mon 20th.
(waiting for posting)

Dearest K,

Touché! You know what is best calculated to make me see sense and I "can't take it." I love you terribly, but the threat in the form of the friend of Gwen's is terrible.

I don't mean that you have necessarily been using him as a threat, but that's how it works out.

Please, please don't do anything to endanger our little set-up. I promise I won't.

I'm waiting now for the letter from Winwick which will settle where I am to go to. If I could get away quicker I would, but now it's getting towards noon I think another day is unavoidable.

You say I haven't resisted temptation. Believe me I have, and am still. But what a position when the nurses sleep (or rather snatch a few hours sleep) in the same wards! The night staff come on duty at 8-9 o'clock, full of life (it's "morning" for them) and after weeks and weeks in the dullness of Weaverham they're looking for company. The five of us, on the other hand, are just thinking of bed (for sleeping purposes). So it's a continual struggle between us who want to get some sleep and they who want some fun.

I know, as you say, that "writing about these things always seems to put them out of focus." But I have done so because I know you wouldn't want me to keep anything back.

I'm thoroughly fed up, because I think you must be unhappy about what I've said. Any woman with a husband and family must be. But as soon as I've written this I'm going to tell Sheri (via a note sent down to the Nurses' Home) exactly what the mention of this friend of Gwen's means to me and that she must dismiss the whole thing as a wild flirtation. <u>And if only I can get away</u> I shall try to keep out of hospitals in future.

<u>Please</u> wait for me. I'll get to see you somehow soon if there's the slightest possible chance.

Even though my derangement has only been emotional I feel terrible about what has happened to my picture of our little home and family. It always stands for a clean shining centre in my life, symbolised in the little suits you make for Michael, your own personal spotlessness and efficiency. Now even this cuddling under blankets seems to have drawn an ugly streak across the picture.

Thank you for saying "your faith in me is effortless and automatic." I have taken it too much for granted. Don't think I am trying to cut you off from men friends but please tell me that the affair with this bloke won't be physical.

Love
Ron

Believe it or not, Dad is still at Heffersdon five days later and so has time to write a discursive, eight-page letter:

Hefferston, *[sic]* 25/3/44.

Dearest K,

Thanks for your note reassuring me. Somehow the illness has subsided, quite suddenly. I am still friendly with Sheri, but I think she is being quite sensible and sees that an affair without a future is like ashes in the mouth.

I am going on ~~Monday~~ *[deleted]* Wednesday it's ~~pretty~~ completely certain, and I suppose it will be back to G.P., in spite of the letter I had when on leave.

Today is the reductio ad absurdum of the whole hospital farce. The other two patients have gone on hospital pass and I am the only one left. So I shall dine in solemn state at noon with four or five nurses to look after me.

After about Tuesday the place will be empty till a new bunch come in, though I think something has broken down in the arrangements and they may continue in their stately emptiness.

I know my horizon is impossibly limited by this place at present, but perhaps a pen-picture of some of the people I have been mixing with may interest you.

First, the Doc; young for his 24 years, bespectacled, smart even when he wears old clothes, with eyes that can twinkle sardonically. The one weakness in his face is a certain unimaginative cast it takes on when he is speaking officially.

He has been completely upset by his six months or so here. Until he started taking week-ends off they wouldn't let him off the premises. If there were no patients here he was an absolute prisoner.

So it was no wonder he fell for a blonde nurse from North Wales who came for a month's training here. After one or two amazing little interludes he got engaged and since then he has been trying to get her out of the Warrington Borough Hospital. He finally succeeded by abducting her, after a dance there.

She has now gone back to Pwllheli (thus the leave) and he is going into the R.A.F. as soon as he can get a medical commission.

I have had supper with him a half-dozen times – arguing about the new Medical Scheme, the local health services, the war, politics, women (his fiancée particularly) and the local countryside.

Then there are the two Matrons, who live in the central building and don't come down to the Emergency section very often. The senior one is a year off retirement and is a rather nice old dear. The second, Mrs. Lee, is reputed to be a bit of a Tartar, and certainly she manages to put the fear of the Lord into the nurses, but there isn't really anything to be disciplinary about in the hospital and she doesn't do a ward round unless she has to.

The day-sister, Jackson, is a very plain proletarian girl who has worked hard for her position, is happily married to a civilian in the local town and therefore doesn't care as much about nursing. The Staff-Nurse, Shaw, is a very tall girl, with a good figure and quite a deal of Lancashire grace in her face, but somehow she hasn't an ounce of attraction. Of the other four or five on days there is Nurse Cross, good-natured and forgetful, religious, of farming stock, interested in politics and with a deal of intelligence but very apt to assume the worst about socialism. "Shorty" is a carrot-haired little woman of thirty-five or so, a good pianist, a famous boxer (with the patients) and the butt of everybody's jokes, which she takes with a curious twinkle in her eye. Robinson is a woman of forty-five or more, an old maid, who has lived in the country all her life, is credulous, prim in manner, and at first I thought she was disapproving of the antics of the young people here. In reality she has not been too embittered by her loveless life, but what rather shocks her is to discover that the majority of people no longer think in terms of the prejudices she imbibed thirty years ago. With a somewhat faltering resolution she has set out to pick up some of the new ideas and I have argued with her about the theory of evolution. "Religion teaches us that despite apparent changes things don't really change very much." Such is the defiance hurled against the wicked theory of that young man Mr. Darwin of whom she has heard.

On the night staff there is Sister Costeyn, whom we don't see much because she is also in charge of the Sanatorium. The effective chief is Staff-Nurse Sheridan. She is small, with an oval, rather foreign-looking face (French, Chinese, Turkish, Irish?) and dark hair. She has made a dive at every interesting patient who has come in, and freely admits her flirting propensities ("Which," says the Doc, "is all part of the technique.")

Sheri is a good sport with all the patients, however, and is liked by males, hated by females. She has very large bright eyes which she uses to good effect. The Doc says they remind him of a spaniel's eyes when they turn appealingly to someone who is giving her a telling off. Chief interest: to prevent herself falling for a man until she is about 28. Hopes to make a good screw by then and, above all, to get in to the nursing service abroad, either in the forces or the Dominions. Poses as very cynical, sophisticated and worldly but is actually rather too impulsively wide-hearted. Reads "Women's Book Club," E. Mannin[289], D. du Maurier.[290]

Nurse Burgess is an interesting type. She is probably 32 or thereabouts, a little too tough and scrawny-chested to be attractive, but has bags of energy and a considerable if sometimes cruel humour. She lives in a big house in the village next to the Nurses' Home where Sheri lives. Brothers are all R.A.F Group Captains, Assistant Colonial Secretaries etc. etc. Would probably turn out an arrant snob. Has waited rather long about the marriage business. Has probably had a cut off the joint with Tony, the amiable but brainless gunner who is a patient here.

Finally there is Enid, a young Welsh girl (from the same village as the Doc's girl). She is a recent arrival, good-looking in the rather tense sharp-eyed Welsh way, anxious to have all the experience of her elder colleagues in the hospital. I don't think she will make a good nurse, however, since she is too self-centred.

The comic relief of the place is Sissons, the porter-cum -stoker. He is the dirtiest man I have ever seen, and looks like some grimy Caliban in the spotless ward with its white-frocked nurses. But he is good to patients and nurses and brings newspapers, cigarettes and razor-blades for them.

You will notice that since I started this letter definite news of my departure has arrived. Why the devil it's postponed till then I don't

---

289 Ethel Mannin was a socialist and strongly anti-fascist writer and freethinker. She was an admirer of A S Neill and lover of W B Yeats and Bertrand Russell.

290 Daphne du Maurier, successful novelist and playwright, author of *Rebecca* (1938).

know. But there's no argument possible and I now have the satisfaction of being certain.

Well, Kath, it's been a very mixed experience being in hospital. On the whole I wish I hadn't been sick, in spite of the extra leave and lavish care I've received.

In a completely static environment one loses the ability to work hard. I have worked, but the results achieved have very little to do with any real job. When I get out I shall have to haul myself bit by bit back to the realities of the war. Luckily I have the resolution left to really desire that.

The question of what happens to one during rest and recuperation is not completely known. Perhaps I shall find myself performing prodigies of valorous effort because of this rest.

I shall have phoned you again by the time you have received this letter. Please look after yourself and M during the coming weeks. Go to Derbyshire if possible and "look at cows, gee-gees, birds and f'owers." As you say in your letter, the day is coming when we shall be able to rebuild, in mutual trust and affection. Then we shall forget these vacant staring days.

Love,

Ron

XXXXXXX

XXXXXXX

XXXXXXX

Chapter 14

4th Parachute Brigade

The next letter is dated 3rd April 1944, which is the Monday nine days after the last. Dad has written part of the letter using Speedwords[291] and provides a key at the start. In the interest of better understanding I have translated the Speedwords into English. He is now transferring from the Glider Pilot Regiment to the Parachute Brigade which was based in Somerby, Leicestershire, a few miles west of Oakham, Rutland:

Swindon,

3 Apr 44.

7.15 p.m.

Dear K,

I have not been accepted here completely. They think the squadrons are too far apart to benefit by my work.

I have asked to go to Airborne Division to see the S.O. to talk over the whole question of my posting. This means long journeys during the next few days but I think it will be worthwhile.

I've seen Fanny[292] and most of the other blokes. They are still quite determined and cheerful and the big things that are coming off will be very safe in their hands.

Feel a bit "post" today, but I've done quite a bit of work.

Mixing in the atmosphere of work is a good incentive to start you off again.

---

291 A form of international shorthand. *Teach Yourself: Dutton's Speedwords* by Reginald J G Dutton pub. EUP 1959.

292 Fanny Waldron – see Appendix 2.

[The letter ends abruptly here and is then continued the following day on the other side of the page, where a PS is inserted in the top left-hand corner. 5.4.44 must be the day he wrote the PS. "Next Tuesday" must refer to 11th April.]

P.S. Next Tues I shall start looking for digs in <u>Okeham</u>[293] – 5.4.44.

4.4.44 9.30 p.m.

Sgts' Mess H.Q. 1st. Airborne Div,

Home Forces

(till 11.4.44)

Been whipped away from GPR[294] today, travelling hundreds of miles by train. I have to stay here now for almost a week until the S.O. comes back. Then I shall be attached to HQ 4th Parachute Brigade, H.F. and that will be my address. The actual place will be where I was informed originally. So if you feel like going to the farm now is the time. (P.S. but see note above the page)

The only thing is that there may be precious little leave for some time. I shall inform you of the exact position when I can.

It was a rather riotous week-end, wasn't it, but I think we both needed to "go off the top a little." Please trust me as much as you can. I meant what I said about you being the absolute centre of things and about me not spending our money or trying to see Sheri unless by any chance we all three can meet.

More later.

Love,

Ron

After handwriting his letters for months, Dad now has his typewriter back. His next letter is not dated but "Thursday" suggests 6th April 1944 (and 8th April 1944 was a Saturday!):

---

293 Oakham, the county town of Rutland.
294 Glider Pilot Regiment.

(for letters written after Sun 8 Apr)
254248 WOII etc AEC
Sgts' Mess
H.Q. 4th Parachute Bde
Home Forces.
Thurs.

Dear K,

I was glad to be able to have four precious minutes with you the other evening, though conscience smote me about the important wires I might be monopolising.[295] You will see from this that I have got my typewriter back from abroad, hardly the worse for wear, so I am 'one up' on the S.O. here at Div, who hasn't yet received one. I also have my personal books, minus, I'm afraid Aldous Huxley's "Art of Seeing." But it's good to get the main batch back.

I haven't got my personal equipment back from Larkhill,[296] including my specs. but I have written off for them. I think those specs will alter my outlook on life, psychologically if not visually.

Work is going to 'pan me out' for a few days until I get back into the swing of it, but with the 4th Brigade I shall have a completely fresh field. They haven't had an instructor till now and maybe I was long enough with the other Regiment.

I am beginning to get glimpses of new horizons in the work, but there must have been something clouding my outlook pretty seriously around the time I went into hospital. I don't know whether it was the jaundice or something "deep in the mental jungle." Anyway I shall clear it off in the near future.

It is, of course, necessary to concentrate one's energies very much on the 2nd Front and the actions which will lead to its success, but I feel at present that I need some personal life as well as the grim sameness of HQs, Orderly Rooms, army stoves, blanco and jeeps. Why I should desire it so ardently just now I don't know. Before I went abroad I was very content to bury myself in work for a week or a month at a time, secure in the knowledge that I would

---

295 Four minutes was the standard length of a long-distance phone call.
296 Fargo Camp, the main Glider Pilot Regiment base, was at Larkhill near Bulford on Salisbury Plain and where Dad was stationed previously.

have a short leave with you at the end of it.

Now leave life doesn't satisfy me. I regard it as a compressed mockery (sometimes attaining the bitter-sweet) of what life with a mate should be. All one's suppressed sex instincts come to the surface and leave no time for anything else – and to suppress them still further would be impossible (at least for me). There have been moments when we have risen above the "rush" atmosphere, but they have not been enough to satisfy.

Please don't regard as serious what I said about ringing Sheri the other evening. It was only a passing temptation and I was amused to realise that my friendship for her was valued somewhere between 1/6 and 2/5 (thus the refusal to ring her when I found the price of the call). Honestly, I wasn't out to make a date or suggest any continuation of our sinful and wicked liaison. In any case she's probably been out with half-a-dozen American officers since I saw her. I believe she was writing to one on the ward the last night I was there! It would be gaily typical of her.

But I would like to continue even a pen-friendship with her, even if an infrequent one, and yet carry it on within limits which you would approve and which (if it were possible, and I know it's expecting a lot) you participated in.

Also I promise you that the time I have to spare will never be devoted to writing to her when I might be writing to you. I'll get <u>all</u> your letters done first and then if there's no time left she's had it!

In any case she will probably not write!

I shall presumably be with the 4th Brigade on exactly the same terms as with the others i.e. I shall go abroad with them but I don't suppose I shall be with the first wave of paratroops. Don't forget it's a Brigade HQ I shall be with (if you are at all worried) and a Brigade is a pretty big thing. As regards the "monkey-ladder" of the Army I shall have moved up half-way to Div.

Speaking of Div; WO Williams has jumped up to W.O. 1 while I have been in hospital. This is strictly correct, as he is a few weeks senior to me in the Div, but being at Div with the S.O. has made it all the more certain. What is rather galling is the fact that old Swyer recommended me for WO 1 when I was with him! So by volunteering for Airborne I have presumably lost the chance. However, it's not much to worry about.

I may have the chance to qualify for Parawings while I am with Brigade. If so I shall take it, since I know they don't exactly cotton on to "non-jumping members."

I shouldn't mind the experience. It must be a lot livelier than flying in a glider or aeroplane, which so far I have found boring (better perhaps that it should be so).

More later Lots of love

xxxxxxxxxxxxxxxxxxxxxxxxxxxxxxxxxx *[signed]* Ron

Dad was now stationed at Somerby, Leicestershire:

as from Sergeants' Mess
HQ 4th Parachute Bde
Home Forces. 7.4.44.

Dearest Kath,

I haven't moved to my "final" posting yet. Am still hanging about for the boss to come back from leave.

The Sgts here are quartered in a pleasant old country house, with big rooms and a terrific old-style garden. Food is excellent, the country around is peculiarly English in a way which I have not seen till now. In each village there are magnificent light brown-stone buildings, houses, churches, barns and pubs in a much better state of preservation than in other districts. Perhaps the basic stone is better than elsewhere.

In the middle of all this I do not feel really isolated, though the nearest towns are miles away. There is too much expectancy in everything one sees to warrant boredom.

I have not been able to get into the town where there may be some digs, but I am anxious for us to see a bit more of each other and shall try and get over on Sunday, my day off. The prospects are fairly good, according to some PT instructors who are quartered there.[297]

---

297 The stone is ironstone, and the description accurately fits the villages of Rutland and East Leicestershire. The town where he will try and find digs is Oakham.

I rather think we should have tried harder to go on a real jollification for a couple of days, say to London. We haven't had the chance to be wrapped up in each other (except in bed) since my return to England. That has been half the trouble. Of course I know the obstacles were pretty terrific.

(Sorry about the pencil. Ink gone.)

There is one thing I would like to ask you, however. Do you still feel really keen on me? In other words, is my theory of the "baby-interest" correct, or were you perhaps a little less enamoured? I suppose as a Man I expect the usual rapt attention hitherto paid to males by females – a relic of the Victorian days? But don't let me get away with it!

But if by any chance you were fundamentally less interested perhaps I was not quite so much to blame for straying.

––––––

Well, it <u>is</u> difficult to write now. Abroad I could at least describe where I was in veiled security terms. Here I am forced back to personal or political matters.

I have been doing twenty minutes a day on those "Speedwords." It is a jolly good system and may very well become international. The great thing about it is that it's as easy as pie from the very start.

Could I possibly persuade you to take it up? It's only like doing a crossword every day for about a fortnight. It makes a little interest to have in common and wouldn't put any strain on you (like learning Pitman's or German). Otherwise I wouldn't suggest it because I should not be justified in foisting my interests on you.

The practical advantages are that on the traditional four sides of paper we could pack about six times as much writing and short notes to each other could be tossed off in a trice.

Q v vo fa t, pl.

Will you do it, please?

V p stu l to odi I 14 des. C e mu fas.

You can study the whole system in 14 days. It is very easy.

You know the textbook, I believe, Dutton's "Speedwords" 2/6 People's Bookshop, Brighton.

Now the wireless in here is blaring away "Don't Give Me that Jive," by Fats Waller, which gives me a pain at the moment. So I shall have to finish this letter and retire to the cold bedroom to read. The office fire would probably still be in but it's just too far and the hour too late to warrant going there.

Still no letters, K, but I shall devour every word when they do come, I feel they will be the only connection with "normality" for quite a time.

There has been a laugh of derision and hate from the parachutists in the room as the radio announces, "The Yorkshire miners have mostly decided to return to work <u>after the holidays</u>." The only relief was the remark "If only Joe could see it!" Please write lots, o wise wife! XXXXXXX – Love Ron

The next day Dad wrote again, using some Speedwords in the first three paragraphs:

as from H.Q 4th Bde. H.F.
8.4.44.

Dearest K,

I'm just waiting a l telephone f some bus times z that j can get a the town tomorrow. J can then spend 4 or 5 hrs looking f digs. X j can get some fixed up j vo be able to buckle into lab with a good will. Ah! here's my call!

….. V can see how isolated w are by l fact that there is only 1 bus tomorrow & that gives me 2½ hrs in Xtown. To catch that bus j vo have to hitch 12 miles. Luckily j shan't have to hitch the same 12 coming ba.

About your fear that you might h schizophrenic tendencies – I shouldn't worry about that. Y e one of the least moody people I have ever met. I mean that quite honestly. J think (Speedword = pu) that v have become even more equable since Michael's arrival.

I'm glad you have a nice view as you write my letter, Yesterday I had the rather unusual Army duty of timing an Army cross-country race. It started from a ducal manor in what looked like 18C style (but brown stone, not white).

For a big building it was one of the neatest I have seen. The parkland nearby I have only seen equalled in Buckinghamshire. The trees against which the runners were picked out were ~~terrific~~ huge, like this:-

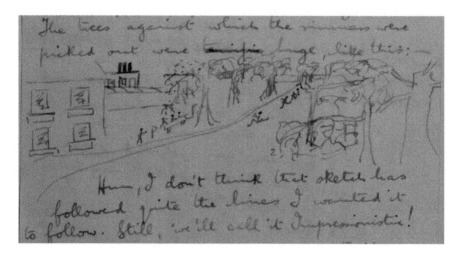

Hum, I don't think that sketch has followed quite the lines I wanted it to follow. Still, we'll call it Impressionistic! The park-land just outside my door now is also very majestic. The whole scene wants a bit of population to liven it up.

Your poem from Donne's work is very impressive. I feel the truth of the last bit particularly:

> Yet I would not have all yet,
> He that hath all can have no more
> And since thy love doth every day admit
> New growth, thou shouldst have new rewards in store.[298]

I'm sure I have new lots of 'rewards in store' as there are sides of you which I'm sure I've never plumbed. Who knows, there may even be sides of myself which like the other side of the moon, have been long out of sight! One hopes that there are, of course. If one had nothing

---

298 From Donne's *Lovers' Infiniteness*.

that was potential, everything important having been laid bare, it would be disastrous.

Re Vera Brittain. I may have told you I read her "Testament of Youth" in the ship's sick bay "coming back."[299] I thought she was very sincere but rather self-centred and uncooperative. I thought the part where she visited the graves of her boy-friends very masochistic. She seemed to get quite a kick out of the Italian visit. Perhaps I am being unkind, however, as regards a feeling that goes "way back" into history.

Money spent on such travel could be spent in better ways, I think.

Well, there's choice of three places from now (7.30 p.m.) till 10.30 p.m. – the Sgts' Mess (pleasant but where I know no-one), the bedroom (cold and somewhat the same as 100s of others) and the village pub. As I don't spend much time in pubs and will never make a drinker I think I'll sample the latter.

Lots of love,
Ron

On 9th April, Dad travelled to Oakham for the day to find accommodation for Mum and me, as he had said he would:

A.E.C attd *[=attached to]* HQ 4th etc
Sun. 1612 hrs

Dearest K,

Bused down to "X"ham today, though I have not officially moved. Expect to go myself tomorrow or Tuesday.

Called straight at the local WVS canteen and got a list of addresses from a very amiable dame. Struck lucky at about the 5th try. It is on the road out to where I shall be, though about 3½ miles away. I think buses run. I mean to check this before returning to H.Q. at 5.30 tonight.

The W.V.S. supervisor could probably fix something almost in the village itself but as I haven't the time to go there today and I want to fix <u>something</u> while I am here I have asked her to make enquiries and

---

299 See page 280.

left her a stamp with which to write me. If she found something good (and she looks a knowledgeable person) you could move nearer to my camp, either straight away or after a few days' rest.

In the meantime the address I have fixed up is

Mrs Wilford, 61 King's Rd.

I will send you the name of the town by separate means, <u>in case</u> you don't know. I believe, however, you said you passed it on the way to the farm and were surprised that it aspired to the honour of being a county town.[300]

I suggest you come up on Thursday. She has her mother with her till Wednesday. She is a pleasant young working-class wife (husband in Ipswich) with 2 well-behaved boys who look about 4 and 6. The house is in a "strip" but it is a reasonable strip and it is spotlessly clean, particularly the double bed-room you would have. She can let you have a big cot, in which a boy of 6 has slept when visiting the house.

The room is shaped like this. X marks an alcove screened by a large wardrobe. The cot can go in the alcove, she tells me. The wardrobe is so big that the alcove forms almost a little room in itself.

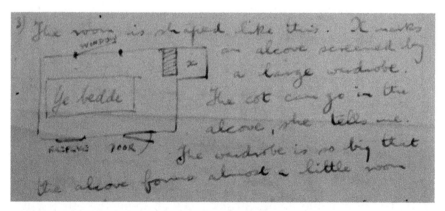

I didn't discuss the money side of it, but the woman was very honest, polite and dependable. She obviously belongs to the Co-op and knows a lot about its workings. I am sure there would be no quarrel over that side of it or over how you would obtain food – whether jointly with her or on your own separate account. She is not a "commercial," but

---

300 This confirms that Dad is referring to Oakham, the county town of Rutland. His directions to King's Road as the third road on the left are correct, except that he wrote "due E" when he meant "due W".

looked just a woman something like Ivy Powell, perhaps even a little glad to have someone in the house after living with just 2 boys.

I will now try and find the local Food Officer and slip a preliminary notice to him about an emergency food card for you. What about fuel? Is it possible to do a similar thing?

I may be able to meet you at the station or it may be impossible. If I fail it cannot be far from the station (though I have not seen the latter).

Ask for the railway crossing. It is then the third street or so on the left, off the road leading out due E. from the town. Ask in any case at the station. It is a small town and streets are well-known.

———

I do hope you <u>want</u> to come. I am aching to see you with every fibre in me. It may be the spring, possibly recent events, more likely a combination of these and a lot of other influences. I think I could work well if I could see you for a few hours every evening. Is that selfish, or do you feel the same? I'm afraid we shan't be together long enough to develop our own egos unduly.

If this letter arrives later that Tuesday you had better telegram instead of writing.

xxxxxxxxx With love & affection,

xxx ← Michael Ron

Chapter 15
History in the Making

The next letter is undated but, according to the letter following it, was written on 30th May 1944 ("3 days ago"). It is one of a group of letters which have been numbered 1 to 4, presumably by Mum. The gap of nearly eight weeks is because Mum and I spend most of April and May in Oakham. I remember Mum telling me many years later that we had moved to Oakham to be near Dad. One senses from the letters that something military is brewing, though I doubt if Dad was in on the secret. It was of course the lead-up to the D-Day landings in which the Parachute Brigade (though not Dad) was centrally and heroically involved. He moved with the brigade to Brize Norton RAF base, from where they (but not he) would take off:

W.O II – Instr. Spathaky 254248
attd. Camp H.Q.
No 2 A.F.T.C.
c/o R.A.F. Station
Brize Norton, Nr. Oxford.

Dear K,

Arrived safely, by truck, with Tom W. and "The Boy," as we call him. I hope you have had hot weather and that Apus[301] has got brown. Does he know "Daddy's gone?"

The country around here is very nice, though there is not so much luxuriance as where we have been.

---

301 From the context it is clear that Dad is referring to me. Maybe he thought that *apus* was the Latin for ape, as he had more than once called me *le petit singe*. If so, he was incorrect. *Apus* is a swift.

I'm afraid that I now have to reveal that there is no possibility at the moment of exploring the country to find somewhere for you. Temporarily I am very much of a disciplined cog in the huge machine. If conditions change however I shall certainly do my best.

Could you possibly ring Somerby 271 and ask for S/Sgt. Pearson, then give him my address and ask him if he would kindly tell the Post Corporal?

It was jolly nice seeing so much of you as I have done. I hope you didn't find me too engrossed in my official life. The evenings at home seemed to prime me nicely for the next day – except when the night was very rough!

The C.S.M. is quite a forthright pleasing old rogue, who accepts the Army's limitations and rackets with the cheerful smile of one who means well but believes that "life is just like that." I had a very interesting talk last night with him on the post-war world. He had lived in the States for 6 years and knew something of graft and corruption. He was also in the Shanghai Military Police.

Well, I must spend the first few days working hard to "dig in," but I'll keep you posted, to the best of my ability under the circumstances.

Lots of love

XXXX Ron

A couple of days later Dad is settling in at Brize Norton:

W.O II – Instr. Spathaky, A.E.C.

Transit Camp, Brize Norton,

Nr. Oxford. 2.6.44.

Dearest K,

Hope you got my letter of 3 days ago. You will be glad to know that I have good quarters here, although the restrictions are irksome; they are inevitable.

I managed to get all my stuff here, including the books. We came by truck instead of railway. Unfortunately the back of the truck was really stuffy and I was nearly sick but the railway would have been worse.

Worked a bit too hard yesterday, but have been taking it easier today. Hope I shall be able to see you in the not too distant future. I don't know how we can manage it, since railway travel is going to be reduced still more, but no doubt some way can be devised.

How is Michael? Does he still know his 16 letters? I can see him reading Einstein (or at least Haldane) before he's 14.

Lots of love

Ron

P.S. Please ring Somerby 271 and give S/Sgt. P. my address, if not already done.

RVS

Two days later:

W.O. II… A.E.C.

Transit Camp,

c/o R.A.F Station,

Brize Norton, nr. Oxford,

4.6.44.

Dear K,

Hope you got my other letters. I wasn't too sure about the address when I wrote them. Sorry I haven't much to say, in the shape of news. There just isn't a single thing one <u>can</u> discuss. I have been working fairly hard, though some of it has been pure study for later application.

Haven't had a word from you yet, but there is probably good reason for that. As soon as I can get a bit of leave I shall try to get to see you, but it won't be easy. If we can't make it I shall have to look round Oxford – "city of dreaming spires!" The part of it near the station looks to me like a city of wide awake commercial landladies, but I seem to remember visiting Magdalen in 1934.

I have sent off for some commission application forms once again. One of my periodic oscillations. Not a question of which is duty and which is self-interest, but which is the greater duty <u>or</u> self-interest. Both seem unclear.

Please tell me all about M's progress. Here are some letters for him:
SSSS MMMM AAAA

Tell him Daddy wrote them. By the way, he knows all the letters in both his names, doesn't he?

Life is horribly boring and limited at the moment, but my problems are such molehills compared with the mountain moving going on round about. Great about the advance in Italy isn't it?

Love

Ron

For a while Dad signed at the foot of each letter to signify that the letter had been self-censored. The next letter was written four days later, which was two days after D-Day, when the Allies invaded German-occupied France. It has a postscript inserted at its head:

P.S. If you get the chance to send me "W N & V" of May 20 I should be glad.[302] Also June monthlies (except the one I asked you not to send) and some "dailies." – Love, Ron.

Fri 8/6/44.

Brize Norton

(as before).

Dear K,

Just got the first letter (card) from you, written in Chesterfield. Bad luck to choose D-day for travelling. I had a queer feeling when you said you were waiting a week before travelling (pure intuition, of course, no-one knew anything). Naturally I couldn't even express misapprehension at <u>that</u> moment.

I suppose you realise from the address where I have been. It has been pretty deadly being unable to leave camp but the experiences I have had (releasable in due course, I imagine) have been unforgettable. In addition to the experience of history in the making I have had a few more jeep-driving lessons, so you see I am rapidly passing from the Medieval Scholastic right to the Industrial Revolution period in my culture epochs.

---

302 *World News and Views*, a Communist Party periodical.

Talking of revolutions, I spent 12/6 yesterday on Julian Huxley's "On Living in a Revolution".[303] It's quite good from the middle-class scientific point of view. Rather cosmic and long-range, however and in parts a bit disconnected.

I have seen my S.O. again and had a chat – it made quite a change after playing a lone hand. He is as cheerful as ever and looks even younger. Haven't seen anything of Tom W., who is in one of the other camps.

Latest news is that the bridge-heads are doing very well. The landing of our armour is going to make a hell of a difference. But it is inconceivable how many craft must be needed to transport one armoured division across the Channel. I have heard it said that the wheeled and tracked vehicles of one division, if spaced out with normal spacing along a straight road, would extend for 200 miles!

Of course the glory of the bridge-head undoubtedly goes to the Airborne Divisions. That operation will go down in history, and would no doubt do so even if the worst happened and we were unsuccessful.

Love,

Ron

S – for Michael.

The next letter was written nine days later, after two letters had become mixed up in some way. Is he blaming the censor?

P.S. Drawing £1.

W.O II – Instr. Spathaky, A.E.C.

c/o A.L.O., R.A.F. Station,

Brize Norton, Nr. Oxford,

17.6.44.

Dear K,

Sorry about the two letters of which the envelopes were changed. I'm pretty certain I put them in the correct ones, but one can never be certain.

---

303 *On Living in a Revolution* by Julian Huxley, pub. Chatto & Windus, 1944.

Just received yours of the 14/6/44, which means they are speeding up. In fact I have just got one from Ma dated the 16th., which is a real triumph for the A.P.O.

I received from you the various WNV's, for which many thanks, but <u>NO SOX OR HKCHFS</u> (to use laundry abbrevs.) I am about to give rise to an outbreak of bubonic plague having missed the laundry day, so they will be very welcome when they <u>do</u> arrive. No sign of the pen yet. If that's gone I shall ring up the Postmaster General and tell him a few things about his parents and ancestors.

Glad you've bobbed your hair I think I like it better that way. Don't try and look glamorous! That is only suitable for film stars (who only have to keep it up for the duration of "shots") and military nurses (who have to put in a lot of quick work in before their star patients are discharged.

Very sorry the prodigy has been diarrhoeic. Tell him his paterfamilias has been the opposite. I'm going out for the first mild spree in three weeks tonight. It may extend to the orgy of a dance nearby.

(cont. next day)

It did! The S.O. managed to lend a party of us his truck for recreational transport, which was pretty decent of him. We went to Swindon, where the dance was quite reasonable, but somewhat packed. Having thus let off steam for the first time since I left Oak. I returned back to work soberly today. More soon!

Love
Ron

SPA – for Michael

The next letter was stored in its envelope addressed to:

Mrs K. Spathaky,
4 Woodhouse Farm,
Bolsover,
nr Chesterfield
Derbyshire

Although I had only just turned two years old I remember staying at the farm where Auntie Aggie (one of the Mellor sisters) and Uncle Guy lived with their three sons, Max, Ron and Alan. I have a clear memory of standing at a doorway. It was a half-door, such as any farm might have, with the bottom half closed, so I must have been standing on a chair or box. I was watching an endless train of hoppers suspended from overhead cables carrying coal or pit waste over a landscape of coal or slag heaps. About fifty years later I visited the area and Mum confirmed that my memory must have been of Woodhouse Farm in 1944:

> W.O II Spathaky. A.E.C.
> A.L.O., RAF Station,
> Brize Norton,
> Nr Oxford.
> 21.6.44.

Dear K,

Thanks for yours of the 16th. You're right, comparative inactivity has made me put in an O.C.T.U. application for the Intelligence Corps. Maybe it won't get me far up the "monkey-ladder", but it'll do to fill up a file somewhere.

Sorry about the chemist's job you've missed through having our lively old Ball and Chain bound to you. The chance of something active <u>will</u> present itself sometime, you know.

I'm also disturbed about the old chap's diarrhoea. Perhaps it's something to do with the local water. Hope he doesn't get goitre – rather prevalent in those parts isn't it?

Yesterday I had my first day-pass since I last saw you. I went to Oxford. It was a lovely day, but I'm afraid I spent the morning in

Blackwells the famous publishers, without buying anything except the Government White Paper on "Employment Policy."

I had lunch in the British Restaurant and got a canoe out on the Cherwell, from Magdalen Bridge. The river is unbelievably dream-like and refreshing.

Apart from giving a ride in my canoe to a nurse from Oxford Hospital (I think the Nurses' Union must have drawn a bead on me!) I didn't indulge in any Oxford peccadilloes. Hope you don't object to me just being moderately human – or does the word "nurse" make you see red?

Lots of love
Ron

For Michael

  – AKYS

P.S. Received pen. Thanks. New nib which wasn't needed. Filler still US. – R.

The next letter contains a couple of otherwise rare deletions in the thick blue pencil or crayon of the censor. Again, Dad gets his dates wrong. 23rd June 1944 was a Friday:

W.O. II… 23.6.44
Sat. 6 p.m.

Dear K,

Not a very eventful week for me personally. I've had practically no-one to work with (though I've found a few *[word deleted by censor]* on the drome during the last 48 hours) and the local R.A.F. Regiment provides hopes.

Went to one dance at Witney, on Thursday. It was quite pleasant, though I didn't come across any partners who danced really well. That was the only comic relief in a week of fairly concentrated study. Been digesting the new White Paper on "Employment Policy." It's certainly a step in the direction of planning, though it has all the hall-marks of its hybrid parentage.

I enclose an Income Tax form for your amusement. You might fill in the parts I've ticked, will you? I leave to you, as Finance Minister, the interpretation of the words "amount paid for 1943-4" in the section on Superannuation charges. Does that mean <u>paid</u> in 1943-Apr '44 <u>or</u> <u>paid in respect of</u> that period? I suggest the latter, so I suppose it goes down on the return.

Better make certain, before putting down our small bank interest, that the Co-op Bank interest isn't taxed at source in some weird way.

Here is an account of my "poisonal" spending for the last month. It's a horrid picture, I agree, but now I've got details I can start buying more books or Savings stamps and less fags.

w.e.f. 30.5.44 to 23.6.44.

Smokes	18s-1d. *
Stamps	3s.-6d.
Lt drinks & suppers, beer	19s-10d. *
Books	20s-6d.
Fares	2s-3d.
Dances & Boat	13s-0d.
Personal sundries:	4s-2½
	£4-2-4½d.

I'm going to try and cut down the starred items, in that order. I'm sure they are expenditures born of monotony and frustration.

I hope you are enjoying this spell of weather, darling, though it seems to be ridiculous for us both to be marooned in the country, with little to do, yet 200 miles apart. I miss you ever so much and I'm sure we could have some marvellous times together in the country around here.

It's probably not worth looking round for digs, though I could do so. I think they will shift me soon, probably back to H.Q., possibly to 4th again though I may stick here until another *[word deleted by censor]* comes off (if there ever is one). I badly miss Michael as well, as he was just developing a sense of fun and of quaint humour, apart from his literary feats. I hope he doesn't forget me completely – what you tell me about his murmuring to himself seems to show that he doesn't.

I've got a fairly big pile of books in front of me at the moment. One was the "Loom of Languages,"[304] another "L'Orme du Mail" by Anatole France[305] which I haven't started yet. Then I have old K.M.'s chef d'oeuvre[306] and bags of "British Way and Porpoises."[307]

The Mess tent is a very cool little nook; the wireless is playing some violin concertos by Berliot, the Belgian player-composer.[308] The Sergeant-Cook (A.C.C) is the only other inhabitant this evening. He is deep in a fairly good adventure book – he is a decent middle-aged chap with a quick wit, an inflexible personality and a Leftish outlook, marred by an anti-Semitism derived (I imagine) from the catering trade. He was cooking for the Commandos before he came here!

You will see that the fountain-pen is working better now, after a bath of hot water. Also I have received the "People in Business" etc, for which many thanks.

L R T N – for Michael.

Stop Press. – Met Margaret's husband, in the GPR, this morning. Remember Margaret (A.T.S) in Bulford?

She got married about 6 months ago. Rose to full Lieutenant, now she's out of it with a baby coming in September.

Present address:

Mrs M H Apps,

140, Alexandra Rd.,

Maida Vale,

M.W.8.

Phone MAI 0148.

---

304 *The Loom of Language* by F Bodmer, one of the *Primers for the Age of Plenty* series edited by Lancelot Hogben, pub. George Allen & Unwin, London, 1944.

305 Pub. Calmann-Lévy, Paris, 1897. "An artistic translation of genuine news into fictional form", first published in the *Echo de Paris* in 1885-6.

306 Karl Marx – see page 114.

307 *The British Way and Purpose*, a series of pamphlets published by the Directorate of Army Education in 1942-43 and as a Consolidated Edition in 1944.

308 Charles-Auguste de Bériot (1802-1870), who wrote ten violin concertos.

She would be glad of a line from any of her old friends, as she says she is rather cut off at the moment.

He invited me to stay with them any time I was in London – but I never am. I may write, however, as we were pretty firm collaborators in Bulford.

Lots of love

Ron

[Dad then signs his full signature, and the censor has scrawled his in blue pencil.]

The following Thursday Dad writes:

Sick-Quarters,

R.A.F. Station,

Brize Norton,

29.6.44.

Dearest K,

Don't be perturbed by the above address. Camp conditions have been pretty bad for the past week (I believe I mentioned that we were under canvas) and the food, though plentiful; and even varied, has had a strong carbohydrate and fat basis. So when I began to feel a "fluey" feeling in the head, with lessening vigour and sluggish digestion, I went sick without delay.

They have admitted me just for a couple of days to the R.A.F. sick bay to see if it's the old jaundice recurring. So you see there is no danger. It's just that a period of most uncomfortable living has had its reaction. I don't feel too bad at the moment – just in need of a rest in bed and a little warmth. After that I shall be able to take up the job with zest again.

The life in the T.C. made me think back enviously to the job at 4th. It certainly was a good post. I had movement, a good number of discussions, and above all, you were there. Still one cannot always choose one's surroundings and occasionally it's necessary to fight them.

I'm glad Michael has taken to the animals at the farm. It's one of the most educative places he could be in. Wish I could see him!

Been to Oxford once or twice since I last wrote. The first time I saw "North Star," the film George Wint talked to us about.[309] It was very good indeed. Another time I had a look round the Colleges. They are certainly terrific as regards architecture. Went inside the Divinity Schools, where degrees are now presented. It has a marvellous roof with stone monograms and escutcheons. Also bought a couple of books at Blackwell's.

More as I "recover" (assuming the Doctor decides I'm ill).

Love

Ron

From the next letter, nearly a fortnight later, it's clear that Dad has spent some time with Mum and me at Woodhouse Farm in Bolsover:

HQ 4th. APO

12.7.44.

Dear K,

Thank you very much for the maps which I left at the farm. I'm afraid I left the other papers and pamphlets which I showed you didn't I? If I did, please send them on, especially that draft discussion document "Britain for the People."

Please don't worry about the little Oxfordised effort of mine which you found in the small note-book. It's really of no significance. Afraid I do get these outbreaks very occasionally. They seem quite fiery, when reduced to paper-form, but in about 4 days I'm thinking of my work or of getting to see you and Michael and forget such "glances" (eternised in verse in the best romantic manner).

It is true, on the other hand, that I am in a slightly chewed-up state

---

309 A 1943 US war film about the resistance of Ukrainian villagers, through guerrilla tactics, against the German invaders of the Ukrainian SSR. The film was unabashedly pro-Soviet propaganda and made at the height of the war.

emotionally. Not having any practical vent for emotional life I find my emotional attention wandering around all over the place, it becomes rather aimlessly attached to places, landscapes, books, occasionally a few people, then to memories of you or M. But all this is in a vague undefined way. Emotional attention, like visual attention, needs to be sharply defined. One needs to be doing something or seeing somebody. I'm <u>not</u> – usually.

I think you are knowledgeable enough about these things not to worry about my slight vagaries.

I'm afraid I'm not alone in experiencing them. I see them as a product of several years of war in thousands of chaps – who are often completely silent about them to their wives.

Meanwhile I'm jolly glad to get back to the old place. The few days I spent with S.O. and Tom Williams sickened me. I'm free to hawk my wares around again on the motor-cycle. The demand seems quite brisk at the moment.

At the moment I'm writing this in the lovely little garden of the old couple who allowed me the use of their room and garden before. In the intervals of writing I've been doing a few of old Aldous's eye-exercises.[310] The roses and other old English flowers make a good background for this "drill."

Last night I celebrated my arrival here by going with a few of the boys to a hop at the Victoria Hall in town (where we went). I had a jolly good time, dancing with various girls and making a damned good fool of myself in a "burlesque" dance that involved rolling up your trouser-legs and putting your blouse on your partner inside out. I danced the last dances with a nurse (stop me if you've heard that before!) from a local convalescent depot. She was quite pleasant – and deeply engaged to a R.A.F. sergeant in the A.D.G.B.[311]

Tonight I am doing reading and preparation, till the garden grows chilly, then off to the Sergeants' Mess to have a chat with the lads.

Having some time to spare at Lincoln the other evening when I was coming back, I hopped into a cinema and saw a film of Steinbeck's

---

310 *The Art of Seeing* by Aldous Huxley, pub. Harper and Row, 1942.
311 Air Defence of Great Britain, which became RAF Fighter Command.

Tortilla Flat.[312] You may remember me mentioning it as a book of his which I read in Italian. The film is excellent and does justice to the author more than the "Grapes of Wrath" did. Incidentally, it doesn't really take very long to get to Bolsover via Lincoln, does it? I was in quite early, even though I stayed at Lincoln for a few hours. As soon as they repeat the dose of leave I must pop up again.

That's all for now. Have you put me down as a plain case of "bad husband" by now? Or do I scrape by?

Love,
Ron

GO – for M.

Four days later, on 16th July 1944, Dad sends a telegram from Weybridge in Surrey addressed to "Spathaky Portslade", so presumably Mum and I have returned home from Derbyshire:

GOING FROM SOMERSET EDUCATION WORK WRITING.

He did get some leave however, at some time over the following two weeks, as the next letter shows. It is undated at the top but the last page was written on a Sunday. The next letter was probably written on about 5th and 6th August.

HQ 4th. APO (1½d. only).

Dearest K,

In spite of the bitter idiocy of part of the leave, I felt in love with you more than at any time for months. Perhaps it's because of your new independence and the confidence it has already brought with it. Pity we were so weak – so early.

Please let me know about the first fateful day. So many things occur all at once. M launches his scholastic career – you emerge from the domestic circle.

Done a fair amount of work since returning, though I've had

---

312 1942 film with Spencer Tracy and Hedy Lamarr, from John Steinbeck's 1935 book.

trouble with the bike and I don't quite see my way out of it at present.

Wish we could have had this last weekend together, but perhaps it'll be more interesting to hear your experiences next Saturday evening if I can get up there. I'm just hesitating as to whether I shall go along to the village hop at *[name deleted]* tonight. If I can get ready in time I shall, as it is a case of dancing or reading and I do too much of that already.

Just had a dip in a little lake near here. It was very cooling. Shall work most of tomorrow (Sunday), Hope everything goes well.

Lots of love,

Ron.

Sun 1800 hrs.

Just received your note and the note-book. Thank you very much. I always seem to leave something.

Good luck and courage for the job. Don't be discouraged if there are snags at first.

Love,

Ron.

We have no further communications until another telegram dated 14th August 1944 addressed to Mum in Chesterfield:

LEAVE CANCELLED SORRY WRITING = RON.

From service records we know that Dad was embarking for France on 14th August, although he probably didn't actually leave England until the 16th or 17th.[313]

---

313 Military service file, ref. D/APC/HD/39300.

Chapter 16

Normandy

The next letter is a surprise. Dad is in France, having arrived on 17th August. It must have been written on Monday 21st August 1944, as the following one was dated the 22nd. Mum and I are still in Derbyshire. It is in pencil, as Dad explains:

W.O II Spathaky, A.E.C.,
S.O. Edn
HQ 1st Airborne Division,
B.A.L.

Dearest,

Odd transformations and changes! Here we are in France. Just when I was getting ready to come home for week-end leave. However Europe, even Hitler-ridden, always sounds a bit more hospitable than the land of all stinks – Africa.

I'm peeved that I haven't been able to talk over with you the events of your début. Your last letter said Michael had cried in the morning but settled down in the afternoon. I don't suppose I shall get any letters which you may have posted since then, though I may do.

Please don't fall in love with too many people in your widened world. It must be pretty lonely for you and I expect the opportunity for fresh acquaintances will inevitably (and desirably so) present themselves from now on.

This first letter must be snappy, since there is nothing much we are allowed to say, but I will try as soon as possible to revive my epistolary powers and give you a pen-picture of the Festung Europa[314] – or the little bit of it I see, at least.

I have been with Tom Williams quite a bit recently. He is as cheery as ever, though I'm afraid he drinks like a fish when he gets the chance and smokes too much.

The night before we left the Sergeants' Mess they had a "do" till the early hours of the morning in true crude bawling Sergeants' style, some of us dancing with A.T.S. telephone operators, others just boozing. I spent my time jitter bugging with a girl I had never seen previously – and shall never see again!

Unfortunately I lost my fountain pen at 4th just before leaving there. This is a great blow.

I shall have to try and get one in France.

I've managed to bring quite a lot of books with me. Please send me as many newspapers as you have time to pack. I realise you will be quite a busy woman from now on of course!

I shall write to Warrington to tell them as soon as possible. Please send a card if you have time.

If I get into hospital with jaundice I shall have to try for the Chesterfield district next time! But so far I feel quite well, in spite of pretty stodgy grub.

Lots of love, Ron

The next letter is again in pencil and was posted in an 'Army Privilege Envelope' addressed to "MRS K SPATHAKY, 170 PARK ROAD, CHESTERFIELD, DERBYSH." and postmarked "23 AU 44." It was stamped: "PASSED BY CENSOR NO 15324":

B.A.L.
22.8.44.

Dearest,

Just a line to tell you I'm quite all right and thinking of you every day and of "notre fils." I suppose he's quite a social animal by now.

---

314 Fortress Europe, the German-occupied part of the continent.

I received by forwarded mail your letter describing how you plunged into the first day's work and how he took the first day at school. Now I am consciously awaiting the first B.A.L.[315] letter. Remember that only reduced postage rates are needed (I believe).

Am just going down the leafy lanes for half-an-hour's walk after a sweating day with 5 lectures and an hour on the paper. So this is just a note to show I haven't forgotten our solemn compact and oath.

Lots of love,

Ron

Dad typed his next letter and its envelope (which is postmarked "28 au 44."). A 'bite' has been taken out of the side of the letter; missing text is indicated by ellipses:

254248 W.O.II-Instr. Spathaky,

Army Educational Corps,

H.Q., L of C.

B.L.A. 26.8.44.

Dearest K,

Thanks very much for your letter which only took three days to arrive. Please note that it is B.L.A. and not B.A.L.[316] Also you will see other strange changes in my address. Although I have not actually left Tom Williams yet I shall be off soon and I don't think I shall see people wearing those hats for some time, if ever!

In other words I have been transferred to the more static local pool of instructors and I am now allowed to tell you that I shall be putting up W.O. I's badges within a few weeks unless something goes sadly wrong.

The new job is somewhat vague at the moment. I think I shall probably have to work but possibly in slightly more settled conditions than those we have been living under during the last week or so. Not

---

315 British Army of Liberation, later renamed British Liberation Army and then the British Army of the Rhine.

316 British Liberation Army – the official name given to the forces which fought on the Western Front after D-Day.

that these conditions have been unpleasant, the fields and orchards being at their best at the moment, but my hitherto-*[...]*des were never conspicuous for comfortable living, as you know. With luck my original qualifications, now refurbished, will come in handy for the new post.

I'm terribly glad you are taking to the new mode of existence and that it underworks you rather than the opposite, assuming that this is true by the time my letter arrives. You always had tendencies the opposite way, which may be a good thing in England in wartime, but intervals of change are necessary. As for "le petit chou," I can see from what you say that he has his feet firmly on the educational ladder, from which may he never look back (or downwards, or whatever one does on a ladder!). I can just see him now, rolling in the sunshine with the other kids.

I'm not so glad that you are unimpregnated. I think your old theory about the period of time between children is the correct one. However you have to do the blinkin' job, not me, so I think you should have the main say. Vive la permission en Angleterre, however! (Get out that dictionary!)

At the present time the Editorial offices here consist of a cart-shed, open on one side on to the yard of a typical French farm, which sells so much cider in the evenings that it takes on the appearance of an inn. Chaps lounge around the place drinking and singing or getting their washing done by Raymonde and Fernande, the two charming, but rather young, daughters of the house. People racking their brains as to what will be in tomorrow's *[...]* and around dinner-time the pace gets really hot and fevered as the copy is got ready for the rolling off.

I can really claim that until I found a good cartoonist, however, I carried the burden of the thing on my own, with articles, typing, map-drawing and other work as well.

I will send back "The Nature of Biblical Crisis" as soon as possible. Hope you don't have to pay too much for it! But as we shall once again be disgustingly rich for so-called members of the working-class I shan't have too much conscience about it.

I agree with you that we felt jolly glad that we had been loyal to each other when I arrived back from Timbuctoo last time. I mean to keep to the same compact this time and if I can avoid a spell in hospital upon arrival next time the reuniting should be all the happier.

There have been less incidents around here than in the London area for some time now. Naturally I can't say where I am but I can assure you that I am disgustingly safe at the moment and can't seem to keep away from headquarters of various kinds. They shift me around from one to another but always at safe distance from the smell of powder. I shall probably find myself woken up with a jerk at some time or other – still, tant pis!

The news you mention about Paris being in our hands seems a bit premature, though I believe we now have it after … German attempt to break the armistice conditions. I suppose there will be a big move-up of all kinds of troops to that area as soon as the lower Seine is cleared. Chaps going up there tell me that the roads to the Seine are three-deep with our stuff moving east and that there is never any possibility of aerial attack. Hope they get to the flying-bomb bases soon, however and that the Germans don't develop this new Me 163 jetless fighter in time to have any effect on the war. It seems to be highly effective, as regards speed anyway, though one hears nothing about its manoeuvrability or fire-power.

Well, I'm just going down to the well a hundred yards away to draw my evening bucket of water for a good wash and shave. One gets rather dusty living on a loose earth floor, though we have good typing tables, boxes to act as desks and all our normal books with us. Speaking of publications thanks a lot for the promise of books to come.

I wish I could be with you, now, darling, to talk with you and tell you how much I feel you are part of me. I can feel our little family union growing in strength as the months go by, even though I don't see much of you. I love you mentally, physically (I could certainly prove that at the moment, and then some!) and I want to come back and see you as soon as possible, so please expect great rapery and "frottement des lards" as Rabelais puts it so delicately, as soon as I get any Blighty leave.

Lots of love,
[signed in pencil] Ron

Dad wrote again the next day:

Education Office,
No 15 Convalescent Depot,
B.L.A. 29.8.44 Tues.

Dearest K,

You will see that I have been reposted from the static H.Q. of the A.E.C and am now completely "unairborne." This leaves me with rather mixed feelings, but it was an order, concerning which I had no choice, so I am adopting the policy of not worrying about a development which I cannot influence.

They have promised me W.O. I. within a few days, so you can ask Renée[317] to get her father working on plans for a set of superfine for my first Blighty leave! That's assuming they ever start any. I believe there has been a vague promise about it in the House already. I shall be in a mood to celebrate so make certain you get some time off, in accordance with the Essential Works Order.[318]

Of course at the rate things are moving they may decide to get into Germany first and leave all welfare considerations like Blighty passes for a more settled period.

I've proposed in my draft educational programme here a discussion class on "Letter-writing," so I suppose from now on I'd better seize opportunity by the horns and improve the form and content of my own letters. I think it's about time, since up to now I've followed the precept of old Montaigne "et en pensant j'écrit," which may be a good precept for essays but doesn't produce such good letters as the reverse motto "en écrivant je pense." I think the pondering should come first.

The people in the farm-house near here don't look so interesting as in the place where I was billeted. In the latter the youngest girl used to press my battle-dress and arrange flowers in the office, in return for a few English lessons – all under the watchful eye of Madame, of course. Here, on the other hand, the two girls look

---

317 Renée Shulman – see page 72.
318 The Essential Work (General Provisions) Order of March 1941.

rather older, 20 to 24 I should say, and are dourer and more ponderous, though one of the two physical training "ex-teachers" on the camp staff here tells me that the family as a whole is quite decent when one gets to know it. They are taking me around later on this evening.

Incidentally, there is one <u>possible</u> advantage I have thought of in connection with this new job. I imagine (although it is pure speculation without any practical basis) that my erstwhile colleagues will wander further over the waste spaces of the world than I shall. As I was prepared to accept the same fate as the others so, now, I envisage cheerfully a somewhat closer attachment to the U.K. and therefore to you and le petit singe.

One does not feel so cut off from England in this country as we were in B.N.A.F. The countryside is very much like Lincolnshire, and even the French here have a reminiscence of 1066 about them – as though they are just some of the invaders of that day who missed the draft, were left behind and didn't settle in Stratford or Arundel.

Some of the chaps don't like them, but they are mainly the insular type who do no thinking at all about foreigners, except to decry them. A peasant population suffers from similar limitations, and has similar virtues, the world over. Now I come to think of it, your Uncle Guy[319] would be absolutely in the right setting here, so would the boys, though your Aunt, like other female members of your family would be a little too strong a personality for a French farm-house. To make the parallel more complete, both Guy and Clarke are Anglo-French names!

Looks as though General Patton is all set for the "fly-bomb" sites now, doesn't it? V II and V III are going to be a little too late to alter the course of the war now, however much damage they may do to the S of England.[320]

---

319 Guy Clarke, husband of Agnes 'Aggie' Mellor, with whom Mum and I stayed at the farm at Bolsover. Aggie was one of the formidable Mellor sisters, who also included Mum's mother Annie.

320 This is a reference to the German V-1 and later flying bombs (also known as V-weapons or doodlebugs).

If you happen to come across one of those metal mirrors you once bought me I should be very glad of it. Also a book called "Hitler's Generals" by -- ? published late 1943 or early 1944.[321]

Lots of love,

Ron

XXXXXXX

The next letter followed two days later. Dad has altered the date from 30th to 31st, suggesting that it was started on the former date. It is handwritten in ink, so Dad has clearly acquired a replacement for his missing pen. It covers nine small (100 x 156 mm) pages. For some reason page 6 is followed by page 6A, and page 7 is missing:

15 (Br) Convalescent Depot,

B.L.A.,

31.8.44.

Dearest wife,

I still have only one letter from you, though I hear that certain others are being redirected from the other addresses I visited. However you were so cheerful and (apparently) happy when you wrote that I am reassured and can await the others.

In the meantime I am rapidly settling down in the new environment and when we really get going I hope to have a really full programme.

To-day I went to see the local school-teacher about a "hospitality" scheme for the convalescents and found a young spectacled chap who was very much a French version of myself. He and his wife take the two older age-groups of children in the school of this scattered village, while a young woman teacher takes the infants.

He gave me an interesting sketch of the French system of rural education. In this part it seems to have been very backward, and the young teacher who tries to introduce ordinary modern methods of instruction and administration is constantly viewed by the more backward peasants as a dangerous radical.

---

321 By W E Hart, pub. Cresset Press, 1944.

There is a lack of every kind of equipment which might make the child's school life interesting, from craft materials to gardening-tools. Therefore they are constantly forced back upon the classical methods – chalk and blackboard and book. Within such narrow limits French classroom technique has, I believe, been of a very high order indeed, but the tradition sets a premium upon experiment and does not produce really creative work.

I believe my French gained more from an hour's conversation with him than with three hours chat with a dour peasant. He was so much more like myself and (I had better say, in addition) so intelligent. And when a Frenchman is intelligent one just has to sit and listen – unless one has the same flow of vocabulary as him!

I didn't see Madame, les enfants, or the nursery-mistress, though a smart petite young thing crossed the yard of the house as I came in and she may have been the latter.

I think he will be of great help in the scheme I have in mind for the convalescents, since he is the Mayor's secretary and quite a power in the little commune.

I'm afraid all this seems very remote from the titanic destinies that are being decided near the Belgian border and at Annecy, but je n'y pense rien. I could not get nearer the seat of operations if I wanted to, I don't suppose.

Talking of becoming operational, you haven't said where Gordon is lately. If he comes over here please give me his address, as I may possibly run in to him.

Since I arrived here I made one rush visit to a famous French town. It was not too interesting, but perhaps that was because the S.O. was with Tom and myself. He is a bit fussy and speaks "less than no French." Still, we looked round a marvellous cathedral which was completely untouched by any air-raids.[322]

I spent a week's wages on a book called "Études Normandes"[323] which will help me in my work at some time.

---

322 Probably Bayeux, since Rouen was only liberated on 30th August 1944, the cathedral of Evreux was badly damaged and that of Caen destroyed by Allied bombing.

323 Possibly *Les études normandes: exposés et méthodes*, pub. Comité d'études régionales normandes, 1944.

I have not moved too far away from Tom and shall be able to see him for a chat occasionally until they move out of the district. Still, I have already begun to sort out the genuine coins from those with a spurious metallic rattle in this depot and the making of new friends should not be too hard.

If you see any interesting books, please buy them and send them off. The depot gets English papers [*word deleted by censor*] after the date of issue, but it's impossible for me to exist on a diet of Beaverbrook, Odham's Press[324] and the "Daily Mirror." I hope to get one of the Depot wireless-sets for educational purposes, but one must not ask for everything at once in this place.

(DON'T TURN OVER)[325]

… about it yet

Well, that's about all I have to say about my little doings. I haven't said much about you, but what can I do except tell you how much I long for the day when we shall be together again? Every victory that the Russians or Anglo-Americans have means that day is nearer, even if one is not altruistic enough to see the wider implications very clearly.

The light has almost completely faded in my tent now so very reluctantly (but no doubt to the censor's relief) I shall have to finish.

Speed the day!

Love,

Ron.

P.S. I don't think <u>your</u> letters are censored, so you can put in enough affection for us both.

P.P.S. Just received your 2nd. letter.

It's again just two days before Dad wrote again. On the first page (of nine!) the ink has been smudged in places by drops of water:

---

324 Lord Beaverbrook was the owner of the *Daily Express;* Odhams Press were publishers of the *Daily Herald.*

325 At this point Dad changes to writing on one side of each sheet only, as the ink was bleeding through. However, the next page is now missing.

No 15 (Br) Convalescent Depot,
B.L.A. 2.9.44.

Dearest K,

I've just received your voluminous letter and I hope you've got the rival effort which I sent off just before the receipt of yours. This must be shorter because I simply <u>have to</u> reply to one of Mother's.

We are now settling down in the depot and there seems to be the opportunity of some good work in my line. There is a good recreational tent (albeit somewhat leaky) which, I have been promised, will be replaced by a better one. You will probably see the effect of the leaks on this paper, but I hope it won't be too bad. (Letter abandoned due to increase of leaks)

5.9.44. 1.35 p. –

I must answer some of the questions in your welcome tome. First as to adequate postage on your parcels of papers. So far I have one set of five dailies, but with no "Lilliput." I devoured them immediately. <u>Please</u> repeat when you find time.

Secondly, there is a strong dialect in this district, but we don't notice it much because families use it amongst themselves and reserve their best French for strangers. Words like "mois" (mwa) sometimes become (mwai) here and they say "je sais cet homme" for the Parisian "je connais cet homme." Dialect is not so general as in the Midi, however, where "cette femme" becomes "sta femma" and "cette chambre" "sta chambra."

Since this is a peasant district it suffered probably less from the occupation than more urban areas. (Caen is apparently a horrible sight, though I have not managed to get there and haven't much desire to do so. The Nazis' plan was to make an agricultural France complementary to an industrial Germany. Consequently they even gave good prices for some food-stuffs to local farmers. A kilo of butter costing the French 80 francs in peacetime brought in 200 German francs. But this was only one side of the medal. On all the big railway lines could be seen truck after truck moving away to the Reich with requisitioned goods and manufactured articles. The French were allowed one suit a year and a pair of shoes every two years. Linen was very hard to get. Finally, on D-day and after came the open looting of farms by the departing "master-race."

2100

I have been fixing up our new Recreation Tent all afternoon. I am writing this surrounded by about 40 "trainees" (convalescents) who come from every possible kind of regiment and went to hospital for the most varied reasons. They are nearly all fit at the moment but some of them show, by their interest in the simple amenities of this room, that they feel somewhat strange in the atmosphere of the "rear," so different from the atmosphere of the front or of the hospitals.

They have been listening attentively to the news on the wireless of the liberation of Brussels.

But to return to the points of your letter: I can realise that it is difficult for you wives to bring fresh horizons within your vision, while husbands are away, but I'm sure it's not such a problem for you, with your talents and mental sharpness. Your letters themselves prove that.

Then as to the little homily, made palatable by quotation, on the subject of tidiness. I agree with you completely. I would even go so far as to agree with the old Army (and school) precept, that one reveals one's capacity for dealing with big things by one's technique in dealing with the small. In this respect I really think that my time with the Glider Pilots, with the 4th. and with HQ taught me a lot. I simply had to be more tidy or I shouldn't have kept up with the convoys.

I would even claim that I look like a W.O. these days – and that is claiming a lot, in the bullshitting British Army. The next thing is to cut out the reaction which occurs when I come on leave, when I simply want to place myself on a sofa or bed and loll, with my kit strewn in graceful festoons around me.

I'm most awe-stricken by your new position of Dispenser i/c Shops, as described in your latest letter, which has just arrived (thanks ever so much – if you <u>knew</u> what it <u>means</u>). My W.O I rank hasn't come through yet. I shall need that to "keep up sides" with you. But you wait......!

And as regards your latest letter – Condepots have <u>no</u> nurses in them, so I have no opportunity for practising austerity.

It's very flattering to be told, as you tell me, that I am missed. Vice versa to you, madame! But I never knew that I spent time on arid logic when there was love-making that should have been done. When was that? Please tell me.

Anyway, not much time was lost on conversation when I called in on Exercise Bones. Do you remember the very satisfactory mutual rape? Please have the bed placed next to the front door when I come home again, will you. And <u>try</u> not to have dear little M (bless his wisdom teeth) in the room.

Or perhaps we should wait for a few days? – perhaps?… I'm afraid I'm getting into the habit of going to sleep lately with the vivid mental image of you lying next to me (and often not even <u>next</u> to me) and I can almost turn and kiss your lips, your neck and shoulders and breasts and… all of you. I can feel us both gently growing warmer and touching with a thrilling communion of hips, a gentle joining of legs and a jolly little warming of bellies (vive le père Rabelais!). Then follows the height of comradeship, the symbol of friendship, the perfection of art, the ecstasy of drunken abandon, the complete searing thrill of sudden secrets shared, the evocation of radiant-heated bodies luxurious in their stretchings and twining, the establishment on a material phallic plane (like glove on hand) of woman's and man's destiny to complete each other, to <u>be</u> part of one another. You've said it – some fuck!

Yes, I think this letter will definitely go in a Green Envelope!

Now, as any other remarks will be an anti-climax, I will conclude. I hope you don't read the aforesaid just when you've had a bath and are going to bed. If so, avoid all carnal thoughts, or else……!

I must now arrange for an early call by the guard, as I have a class early in the morning. So I'll walk back under the impassive French moon, lighting up the little apples in the orchards, to my office tent with its stack of stationery and material which I carted away from an advanced Stationery Depot, "to sleep, perchance to dream" – of <u>you</u>.

– Love

Ron

The next letter we have is seven closely-written pages and dated nine days later. Someone has scribbled in pencil over pages 2 and 3 and then on the back of the last page, where there are also some large capitals, also in pencil. I have no memory of doing this!

W.O II Spathaky. A.E.C.

15 (Br) Convalesc. Depot

B.L.A.

14.9.44.

Dearest K,

I've just received your original bundle of 2 dailies and a Lilliput, for which many thanks. I should send them newspaper rate in future, as the postage is pretty heavy.

The work here is expanding rapidly. I now do ABCAs pretty continuously all day and have a librarian and a recreation-room orderly working for me. I expect a new Sgt. Instr. A.E.C. to arrive at any moment. The result is I get practically no time to look outside the camp but I hope to tear myself away for a morning or afternoon soon.

There has been quite an interesting Belgian lad in the camp during the last week, so I have polished up my French on him. He has been quite useful in the voluntary French classes in the evenings.

The weather is very pleasant at the moment, and the trainees seem correspondingly pleased with the P.T. and concerts and discussions which have been arranged for them. It is surprising how many chaps want to get back to their units in the front line. It seems to me as though they have missed the harrowing in-fighting which some infantry regiments experienced in Italy. Convalescents and people I saw there were not quite so keen to get back to the fray!

The food is good at the moment, due possibly to the work done by an enterprising Messing Officer. Therefore I feel quite fit, though I make slow progress in cutting down my smoking. In fact sometimes I am definitely marking time and slipping backwards. Of course the free distribution of 50 fags a week is not much of an incentive to abstention.

My washing is done by a cheerful old crone down the road, who charged me surprisingly little for it. Quite a number of the local peasantry have been making hay while the sun shone. I don't blame them really, because if about two thousand blokes suddenly ask for a cottager to do their washing the obvious way to cut down the number to manageable proportions is to raise the price.

I've been reading from time to time a rather sincere novel written by Alec Waugh, called "The Loom of Youth." It's about Public School life and he wrote it at the age of 17. I think it gives a good view of the aquarium-like isolation that afflicts the public-school boy – a divorce from reality.[326]

(Later)

My assistant has now arrived. He is Sgt. Instr. Foster, A.E.C. and coincidentally he was A.E.C. Instr. at Winwick Hospital, responsible for the E.M.S. hospitals! He never came to Heffersdon Grange because there were never any patients.

I occasionally get a letter addressed to W.O I Sp---, from HQ, but that must be a typist's error. The promotion has not actually reached this depot, in any case.

There has not been a letter from you for about 2 days now, though I have had two more letters with papers in them, for which many thanks. Since we were both spoiling each other with more letters than we have ever written the 2 days seem an age.

How I envy the people who are working with you, when I can't take you in my arms and kiss you, let alone be with you often! I still feel very strong physical desire for your presence, your touch. The presence of thousands of men is <u>sometimes</u> more annoying than country silence. You would make either the crowds or the solitude easy to support.

I begin to feel substantial hope for our future home these days, therefore I don't blame you at all for thinking of washing-machines, wringers, radios and all the gadgets. So far I have preferred not to

326 Pub. Methuen, 1917. Waugh was asked to leave Sherborne School a year early. The book, written the following year, caused some controversy as it dealt with homosexuality at a public school. His younger brother Evelyn went to Lancing College rather than Sherborne.

build up an ideal picture, but these days, with the German border crossed, one cannot help a bit of subdued castle-building. Is there any news of house-building plans in Brighton and district, or do we have to wait until hostilities have actually finished? If there <u>are</u> any schemes on hand we shall have to get our names in early, n'est-ce pas?

What did you do yesterday evening? I didn't finish work till about 8.15 p.m. Then I went across to the Mess, listened to the news about Rotgen, the first town across the German frontier, inspected some new steel shelves we have in the Library and went with Foster to our tent to read the news. I was still reading at 10.45 p.m. The result is I feel a little "rougher" than usual today, but so far we have got through the work pretty well.

It is now 2 p.m., and I must start thinking again of the old problem – how to distract, amuse, convince, interest hundreds of men of every temperament from the "barbary" Scotchman who wonders why the hell he's been shoved around by a set of Sassenachs, to spritely ambitious bespectacled clerks who will want more interesting jobs after this war, who in spite of their harrowing experiences have been shaken out of the rut, who will never fit completely into dull monotonous routine.

I think we can feel pretty confident in the "day-after-tomorrow" as we look at them, even if "tomorrow" is uncertain. I am glad to be helping them, anyway. There are crowds of them in front of our tent now, marching along, athletic young Tynesiders with hard-bitten but kindly faces, old men from cook-houses, frail clerks, R.A.F "family-men" from Air Force dumps, men with bags of intelligence and others who will have to grope their way around for years. All come within my scope.

Lots of love – Please wait for me.

Yours,

Ron

Dad's next letter is undated but must have been sent around 16th September as Dad later refers to Mum's reply to it as being dated the 18th:

Sgts' Mess

15 (Br) Conv. Depot,

B.L.A.

Dearest K,

Your letters are now arriving in a steady flow. This is just a note dashed off in the dinner-hour to prove I have not become dumb just because I have become busier.

The pace is becoming a bit hot, since I am doing quite a lot of entertainment work as well as education. The padre and I ran a whist-drive last night, we managed about 5 tables and the air rang to the priestly incantation, "Winning Lady moves UP. losing gent moves DOWN." I collected the money and distributed the prizes, generally acting as factotum and dry-nurse. I rolled into bed tired out but felt O.K this morning. It's a case of doing as much as possible as long as the educational work does not suffer.

I now have an educational clerk working for me, a Gil. Wilson. He is a trainee (convalescent) and seems pretty keen and practical.

I've been trying to find time to go to a farm a mile away and get my washing but for three days I've not succeeded. Tonight I mean to go coûte que coûte.

No word from Tom Williams since I came here. I imagine he must have shifted.

If you come across a good atlas I should be awfully glad to buy it from you. I'll get a batch of money shifted to your allowance as soon as my credits have mounted a bit.

Lots of love – Ron

The next letter is dated and helps to narrow down the date of the previous one, as Dad had clearly had a reply from Mum expressing concern about his washing:

W.O I – Instr. Spathaky
H.Q. (Br) Convalescent Depot,
B.L.A. 24.9.44.

Dearest,

I could tell from your letter of the 18th. that you must have been undergoing some kind of (I hope) temporary strain, either physical or psychic. If it is what you diagnose it to be, perhaps the recent news about demobilisation plans will cheer you up a bit. I see that I am in Group 30 and that a certain number of teachers will be released early from the Army.

In any case please don't worry. Make lots of friends if there are chances of doing so, but count a thousand before you let anyone kiss you!

In answer to your question; I have managed to get my washing, and there is <u>NO</u> water shortage during this campaign!

Sorry about Eileen.[327] I'm afraid she looks the physical type prone to such things.

Your mention of Doris brings to mind a small request to add to my numerous others. When you write to him, if you ever do, you might ask him to send me some A.B.C.A.[328] pamphlets.[329] We aren't getting any. Tell him it's only the new series since they changed the covers that I am concerned about.

As for the temptation to return to Brighton, please don't. You can never tell. Of course the campaign appears to be going swimmingly, but I am quite certain from the papers, that people in U.K. are getting are getting foolishly elated about what will be desperate and bloody battles. You have only to meet the hundreds of men coming back from the Front to see that all this selling of victory flags is badly out of place. The front-line men to whom I have talked about it are grimly ironical, if not blasphemous.

---

327 Eileen Ireland – see page 72.
328 See footnote 149 on page 139.
329 Doris is Mum's sister-in-law, so "him" must refer to Mum's brother Gordon Cree who is also in the Army – and a communist stalwart.

I have just packed up the Strachey book in order to post it.[330] Sorry to have caused trouble but there simply hasn't been a chance before.

Your last paragraph was a promise to write on Wednesday.[331] If you did I haven't had it yet! Still, I know you must be as busy as me – in your double profession.

I think my work is probably not secret enough to prevent me mentioning one or two things. Sgt. Foster and myself do about 11 ABCA's a week each. We have a Library of over 2,000 books, a recreation-tent with a wireless and games, a concert tent in which we have organised quite a few shows, both with ENSA[332] and "local" talent. I take two French classes every evening and we enrol people for correspondence-courses, answer a certain number of queries on vocational training and diffuse news-sheets and papers. We started a lively Discussion Group the other evening and we hope to launch out sooner or later with maths classes (Sgt F), handicrafts (an officer, plus trainee-help) and a Depot wall-newspaper.

Unfortunately the entertainment side takes more time than everything else put together. We are slowly getting more help from other sections of the depot, but of course they all have their own jobs and one cannot expect the impossible.

Ted Foster (who you remember I said was A.E.C. Sergeant at Winwick Hospital!) and I get on well together and the Corporal we have been allotted is one of the keenest youths I have found. He is called Wilson and he works like fury in our Library and News-Room. There is just a chance of him getting on to the permanent staff, since he is not eligible for front-line service any more. If we do get this concession it will be a great help and will make it possible to expand all sides of our work.

Sorry if this is badly written, but I am sitting on my bed writing on my lap, holding the note-pad near an ordinary hurricane-lantern. The light is quite good for ordinary domestic purposes, but one has to adopt queer acrobatic postures to get any close work done.

---

330 This could refer to one of several books by John Strachey (1901-1963), later a Labour MP, who had been a communist in the 1930s.
331 20th September.
332 The Entertainments National Service Association which provided entertainment for the British armed forces.

Outside our tent the wind is rising, and the damp hedge is rustling as the apple-trees stir it in the breeze. A watery moon is rising over the "vergers clos," the orchards surrounded with dense hedges, which are the big feature of this countryside. Along the dark muddy paths, shadowed deeply by foliage, the few trainees who have ventured out into the sparsely-populated hinterland are wandering back.

This is peasant-land, which not even the advent of thousands of town-bred allies can stir very deeply. From hereabouts came the Chouans, the retreating peasant movement of the 18th century, who fought Liberty, Fraternity and Equality because they were misled by the Lavals and Bonnets of their day. Yet even here changes do come and France will even now rise to greatness again through contributions to civilisation from this among her other provinces.

XXXXXX Lots of love, Ron

The next brief letter was in an 'Army Service Envelope' postmarked "Sep 44" (the exact date being illegible). It was addressed to Mum, still at 170 Park Road, Chesterfield:

W.O I – Instr. Spathaky, A.E.C.
HQ 15 (Br) Convalescent Depot,
B.L.A. 27.9.44.
22 hrs.

Dearest K,

Been working very hard during the last few days, so I have had very little time for writing. Since I have not had the letter which you said you would write last Wednesday, I suppose you have had a very busy time too.

I think of you and Michael very much, in whatever minutes I can snatch to think of anything besides ABCA and Entertainments.

<u>Please</u> write when the presence of work (or depression?) lifts.

What does everybody think of the Gov's new Social Insurance White Paper?

Much love,
Ron

P.S. Any chance of
White Paper on Social Insurance
"   " " Demobilisation?
<u>No</u> means of getting them out here.

The next letter was written five days later on a page torn out of an exercise book, then torn in half and turned sideways:

W.O I Instr. Spathaky,
HQ 15 Br Convalesc. Depot,
B.L.A. 2.10.44.

Dearest K,

Thanks very much for the letter of 29.9.44. Sorry you have such responsibilities saddled on you. I know you'll organise these affairs successfully, however.

I seem to be film-manager, theatre-manager, ticket printer, vocational guidance wallah, and (very occasionally) A.E.C. instructor, rolled into one.

The W.O I-ship (or is it W.O I-ness?) has come through. I shall have to see what the next step in the ladder is now.

About the job, Monsieur M and Bridlington: I hope very much that you will weigh the pros and cons. I can't see personally what great burden your aunt Gertie has to bear when you are out all day and M is at school. She ought to have half a dozen evacuees (preferably "white" Poles[333]) planted on her for a short time. But if she is not co-operating that obviously cannot lead to happiness for you or M.

The only doubt in my mind is about this aunt K now looming into the foreground. Is she quite the pleasantest company for somebody with intelligent ideas and ideals like yourself? And is Bridlington safer than Brighton?[334]

---

333 This is a reference to the members of the much demonised Polish Home Army (the *Armia Krajowa*) of the Polish Resistance, many of whom fled Poland after the Soviets took over the country from the Nazis in the summer of 1944.

334 Monsieur M refers to me. Bridlington is on the east coast and was thus presumably vulnerable to German bombing. Gertie and K (Kitty) are Mum's aunts, two of the five formidable Mellor sisters.

I don't know your aunts like you do, but I hope she's the right sort. Perhaps boarding-houses recall to me unpleasant memories of seedy gentlemen with unpleasant habits (especially towards the opposite sex). It must be your own choice but frankly it sounds horrible to me. One is so impotent as regards advice, at a distance of 500 miles.

However, these little problems are meant to be tackled, and I hope to goodness we can tackle our domestic problems together before many years are out. I am not easily depressed now, but the bucolic idiocy of this part of France does not lead to terrifically high morale (even among the "morale-merchants!") If you could see some of these "battle exhaustion" cases, however, you would realise it is worthwhile. More tomorrow!

Love Ron

"Tomorrow's" letter is undated:

W.O II-Instr. Spathaky,
15 (Br) Convalescent Depot,
B.L.A.

Dearest K,

Just a line written, without time to refer to your last letter.

I've had rather a lot of extra duties, though I'm beginning to break the back of the educational side of them at the moment. For instance we have a library of about 2,500 books in this depot. That alone gives quite a few problems to solve, before we start ABCA and other little fol-de-rols.

My S.O. told me today that my W.O I-ship, having gone all the way up the Army ladder to be approved, has been accepted and is now half way down the monkey-ladder – so when it reaches this Depot I am "Wog I" as Tom Williams used to call it.

My only personal difficulties apart from lack of you and M are having enough time to go out of camp and collect my washing and getting to the Q.M. stores on the particular day required in order to get a new pair of braces.

I accept the work of this place as a challenge. It requires more skill than the work with my former unit, which was nearly all interesting. I mean to break the back of it, however and I feel the knowledge gained will be invaluable in later life.

But nothing will make me <u>very</u> happy out here – I want to see YOU and feel that we are going forward to rebuild our future and contribute <u>together</u> to rebuilding the community's future.

Lots of love to M. Don't run after the manager <u>too</u> much, will you? XXXXXXX Love & deep lust, Ron

The next letter is in pencil:

W.O.I Spathaky. A.E.C
HQ 15 (Br) Convalescent Depot,
B.L.A. 9.10.44.

Dearest K,

Just received yours of the 27th, somewhat delayed. Great changes are afoot, forsooth. I don't blame you for having another period with Michael now, if the job is getting a bit irksome.

Please excuse the appearance of this letter. Two days ago I had my injection of Tet Tox and T.A.B. for this year.[335] It seems I am very allergic to the sera, since it produces all the symptoms of typhoid in me. Last night at 10.30 p.m. I felt as if my head would roll off my shoulders. My teeth chattered and alternately I sweated like a soul roasting in Hades. Just now it is passing off, though I still have an extremely depressed feeling. It is all very well to comfort oneself with the thought that it will be gone tomorrow. In the meantime I have wasted 24 hours working time at least.

Talking of work we have quite a good AEC instructor here at the moment, Foster, whom I mentioned to you. A third fellow has been added for the purpose of handicrafts. He is rather a curious man. Admittedly he has not had the chance to do any handicrafts while he has been here but he shows the blandest lack of intention to co-operate with any other work that I have come across. Possibly he has

---

335 Tet Tox is tetanus toxoid vaccine; TAB is typhoid, paratyphoid A and paratyphoid B triple vaccine.

the excuse that he has been ill for a long time but I feel I shall have to prod him pretty hard soon if he doesn't get going. By comparison, Cpl. Wilson (a former engineering apprentice) who is attached to me as trainee Education Clerk, performs prodigies of work. He built a complete set of book-shelves for the Library out of scrap-wood, to say nothing of a book-case for my ABCA books and a board for the wall-newspaper.

The Private-Librarian works quite hard, so does a little tough Scottish corporal who does a lot of Entertainment work for me. Then there are two privates, office-clerks, one of whom works hard and the other only when he is pushed.

Such is our "mighty" department. We get through a pretty wide variety of activities in course of a week, from enrolling people for Conference Courses to holding Brains Trusts, with the C.O. participating.

Nevertheless the depression caused by the injections makes me wish the whole ruddy thing were over.

I have made no alteration in my pay yet, but I will get a lump sum transferred to you in the near future. I have been drawing £1 per week for the last couple of months and my full rate is 16/- (I believe) plus field allowance (6d. or 1/- a day?)

You seem awfully far away at the moment, dear, but I am sure we shall be able to build up a better life than ever, with the experience we have had. Think how dumb we would be if we were just getting married! Or perhaps you think I am dumb, do you?

Well, the depression is passing off now, and I can begin to think of work. Please keep on planning, won't you! Lots of love,

XXXXXX Ron

Dad wrote again the next day reversing his plea of only a fortnight or so earlier for Mum and me not to move back to Brighton. For some reason Bridlington seems far worse in his mind:

W.O. I SPATHAKY   15 (Br) Convalesc. Depot,
                                          B.L.A. 10.10.44.

Dearest K,

Just time for a quick note. I imagine Brighton would be better than Bridlington. After all it hasn't been officially scheduled as a danger area for some time, has it?

Bags of work on now. I've had letters from Percy and your Ma recently. Not had time to answer the former but I mean to do so in the next couple of days. Not had much opportunity to polish up my French for the last fortnight. I haven't seen a Frenchman, except a local farm-boy working on the other side of a fence.

I don't see any prospect of leave at the moment, but presumably they will have to bring in some system within the next six months or year so really we should be quite cheerful!

I see that I come in Group 30 for Demob purposes. But there is bound to be a terrific tug between B of Ed authorities and the Army Education Directorate over our release so I am just awaiting my fate and not hoping too much. After all, the sternest battles against Germany may still have to come!

Did you see in Reynolds[336] that AEC 1st Airborne Div jumped into Holland? Personally I don't believe it. I believe they glided, but even so it's almost incredible that Tom and the S.O., who always fought my application for "air-training" have gone into the thick of it.[337] Hope they get out of it.

Love, Ron

W.O I Spathaky, A.E.C.
15 (Br), Convalescent Depot,
B.L.A. 14.10.44.

Dearest K,

I am writing this after dinner on Sunday afternoon, the freest time during the week. I am lying flat on my bed in the tent, with my

---

336 *Reynold's News* was a Sunday newspaper owned by the Co-operative Press.
337 This was the Battle of Arnhem. In fact, they jumped *and* glided – the 1st Airborne Division was reinforced by the addition of 1,200 men of the Glider Pilot Regiment.

head towards the open leeward side, while rain pours down like a permanent shower bath outside. The two Sgts. A.E.C. are browned off to the back teeth with the squelching mass of mud that constitutes the camp but curiously enough I feel quite cheerful, apart from the fact that I can't be with you (which is <u>the</u> hateful factor). I don't seem to get any colds, in spite of the permanent damp and it's not half as bad as Texas Transit Camp, Bizerta, or Blidah Transit Camp, Algeria. At least our beds are wooden ones raised from the damp ground and even if the ground is flooded to a depth of four or five inches we shall sleep in the dry.

I am somewhat reassured by your letter outlining your future movements. Brighton should be reasonably safe now. It hasn't had many doodle-bugs has it? On the other hand I hope you will delay your departure for as many weeks (or even days) as possible. I have a good reason for asking that, though I cannot explain it at the moment. I will be able to explain after a week or two.

I'm still ever so much in love with you. I think of you as the young "garçonne-mère," smart and efficient, living your own life and making your own plans, and keeping a bit of a place in the plans for me if and when I ever do get out of this khaki horror.

As for the passionate side of it! Please keep yourself for the great meeting, as much as you can, at least. Even as I write, "le petit dieu qu'adorent les femmes lève la tête impatiemment."[338] I only hope I shan't be too violent and tear you to pieces. Or vice-versa!

Have there been any minor encounters this time? Not even with the cousins?

There would be no chance for me to be naughty, even if I did not want to be faithful. I never go out of the camp, unfortunately, except for a few hours on duty. But if you, living nearer to the other sex, have had more temptation, please tell me about it. You know, as usual, that I shouldn't be mad, as long as it was purely physical (but the danger is that it so rarely is – and if it is, it is unsatisfactory!)

Work has been going well lately, in spite of the dreadful environment. We have been trying to build a thing called a Contact Bureau, to provide

---

338 "The little god whom women adore lifts his head impatiently."

local papers and general contacts from the U.K. Many newspaper firms have written sympathetically. We are also trying to put people from the same towns and jobs in touch with one another.

Bother is, I want some blasted "contact" myself. As professional morale merchant I can <u>never</u> be down-hearted. Still, I fancy it has bred a good kind of psychology. If the camp were to be blown away by shells at this minute or flooded completely my first words would automatically be "Right, now to organise the reconstruction of a better camp..." Is it awful to be married to a professional ray of sunshine? Or does it make me take refuge in you too much, as my only confidante?

Lots of love and bare-limbed lust – Ron

XXXXXXXXXXXXXXXXXXXXXX

W.O I Spathaky, A.E.C.

15 (Br) Convalescent Depot,

B.L.A. 18.10.44.

My dearest Kath,

For a few moments I have complete quiet in the tent. The gale is raging outside across the soggy meadows, but the violent gusts, hail-laden, which threatened to tear several of my big tents off the ground this afternoon, have abated for a time. As I write the rain comes again.

I still find that if I can dry my feet several times a day I can keep colds more or less at bay. The morale of the other two is rather low at the moment. In the case of Ted because he hasn't been abroad before (I think, certainly not with the Army) and he doesn't know how much worse it may get in this camp before something is done about it. In Eric Deemer's case I believe it's because he has been ill for a few months and cannot get adequate food in the Army. So it is necessary to try and bolster their morale so that they can bolster others, since that is part of our job.

(There is a noise like thunder outside. I can't quite make out what it is. I hope it isn't the weakest of the tents, the lecture-tent, being blown down. I must go out and see when this latest squall of rain has passed by.)

I am jolly glad I have a fair selection of books with me, so that I can go on studying, otherwise the conditions would be very bad. While one can dig into old Huberman[339], or your very interesting "Eastern Europe"! by Hanč[340] the conditions can be withstood.

I pointed out to a group of chaps this morning that we "infect" each other by useless groaning and grumbling and we give each other better power of resistance by making a mental fight against the mud and wetness. I don't think the cold is really much of a problem by itself. Certainly I always found the coke-stoves of English barrack-rooms much more unhealthy. Of course cold is probably much more undesirable for chaps who have been in hospital recently.

(Sounds as though the rain is not coming down quite so straight at the moment… Fortunately the lecture tent is <u>not</u> down. I thought the fatigue party had made a good job of the stakes and pegs this afternoon.)

Well, how are you and the young man now? The mail has brought me nothing except your very welcome papers for the last few days, so I am looking forward to the next letter, very anxiously. Is Michael's bout of colds over yet? I hope they look after him at the school. It would be pretty hard to bear if anything went wrong with him or you at present. I can get along if I can feel that somehow this is helping our common future. It wouldn't be enough just to have my own 30s, 40s and 50s to look forward to (or however long one had on average!) So please don't take him or yourself for granted just because you see him (and yourself in a mirror – I hope) every day.

Your mother has been very kind recently and has sent a number of Lilliputs and other magazines "for the boys." So has the M.C.C. When you write you might tell her how very much they are appreciated. She's a good old warhorse, you know.

I've written to Percy and I believe I owe Renée a letter from when we were in U.K.[341] I will pay the debt as soon as possible.

A few days ago I went to the local town on duty and found that the Paris papers were on sale again. This was a very pleasant surprise. They had Le Populaire, Le Front National, Le Franc-Tireur and L'Humanité. If it is possible I mean to open a subscription for some of them. We get

---

339 Possibly *Aus der Werkstatt des Virtuosen* (From the workshop of the virtuoso) by Bronislaw Huberman, pub. 1912.
340 Pub. Museum Press, London, 1943.
341 Percy Ireland and Renée Shulman – see page 72.

the English papers only a day late but it would be a double source of information to have the French journalists as well. Percy asked me to send him some copies of L'Huma but unfortunately there is a law against sending out any magazines, papers or other printed matter. I will try and bring him back some copies if it is possible by the time we return.

I have just received your epistle of the 16th. Thanks a lot for the nice things you say in it. One can only make a rather pale reply when all is subject to the censor's delectation but it is an interesting example of how much a part of the common "warp and woof" of humanity we all are when we read with such encouragement the age-old assurances and words of affection.

As regards the prospect of leave I very much doubt whether there will be a scheme. I suppose the problem was simplified in the old days of trench-warfare. Except in the days of a big offensive, when all leave was cancelled, a man would find his way back to his unit automatically. Nowadays a man who left his regiment on the Somme might wander into Holland before he saw them again. In any case if they do start a scheme before Germany is beaten the front-line troops will quite rightly have priority and our priority will be X.

I think your idea of taking over "49" at some time is a good one.[342] Are your Ma and Pa thinking of moving elsewhere, then? I rather like the S. Coast to live on. I think the mixture of town and country facilities take a bit of beating. Or perhaps that's mere nostalgia.

Incidentally – a curious development. The Old Man at Warrington,[343] who has rarely written to me all the years I've been away from home, has taken to writing me cheery notes, which are quite surprising in their friendliness. He seems to have made good in his "old age" with this proffered job in Huddersfield. It seems strange that after the very serious period of '26-'30 that he should have started climbing the ladder afresh. À propos of nothing – did you see A.E.C. went into Holland by air with 1st A/B (Reynold's News)?

Lots of love,

Ron

---

342 Mum's parents' house, 49 Hangleton Road, Hove, which was also our home, although we were in Chesterfield in October 1944.

343 My 'Grandad Spathaky', who lived with Grandma and her mother.

Suddenly Dad and Mum have an opportunity to be together for a few days! An envelope arrives, addressed to Mum in Chesterfield and postmarked "23 Oct 44":

> W.O. I Spathaky, A.E.C.
> 15 Brit. Convalesc. Depot,
> 22.10.44.

Dearest K,

This means <u>YOU</u>. Unless I send to you cancelling this letter get digs in Preston (Lancs) as near to CUERDON HALL, as possible, 31 Oct – 3 Nov inclusive.[344] Bring M or leave him at home, or with relations, as you decide.

If you get into touch with Warrington, please write or cable and let me know, otherwise I shall not tell them about the whole affair.

Can't say more, unfortunately,

> Love,
> Ron

P.S. If necessary get Mrs. C. Spathaky to go to Preston and book the digs for you, but if you do this she will probably stay as well.

> In transit.
> W.O I Spathaky, A.E.C.
> B.L.A. 26.10.44

Dearest K,

As I explained in my first letter, I shall be at a short course at CUERDON HALL near Preston, from Oct 31 – Nov 3 (inclusive), after which I shall have 48 hours leave.

If you have managed to get digs anywhere near the place we shall be thumbs up.

If not, please leave a message with R.T.O. Preston as to where you are and how I can contact you.

---

344 Cuerden Hall (sic), a former stately home that became an Army Education Centre during World War II.

I shall probably land and re-embark at the port 8 miles from our home[345] (security – movement of 1 man involved!)

Love, etc!!

Ron

P.S. I shall probably be able to sleep out.

Dad's military service record showed that he "embarked BLA" (that is, from BLA) on 28th October for his course near Preston. So Mum and Dad clearly had their time together. He arrived back in France on 10th November but the journey was not straightforward, as he described in his next letter:

In transit

11.11.44.

Dearest K,

It may amuse you to know that we dithered in the camp for another day before setting sail. The boat stood on end all the way and I had a bunk in the bows which swung over an arc of about 70° when the full force of the waves hit her. We arrived outside the harbour and could not enter because it was too rough so we went all the way back. They gave us a meal of salmon (!!!) and Russian salad in the transit camp and later piled us back on the floating toast-rack.

The second crossing was smooth as could be and I found my unit had moved, as I expected. I am sitting in the fairly warm office of the transit camp writing this. They have made me moderately comfortable here (allowing for the fact that the place is a sewage farm!), while some other part of the Army is racking its brains over my problem.

I have a complete big pack of books and bags of French and English newspapers, so I have been doing quite a lot of reading. It is quite comfortable to be doing this while the others, who didn't carry out as much work as I did, move the unit and solve the problems. It will give them a chance to develop a sense of responsibility.

---

345 Newhaven, Sussex, is eight miles from Brighton.

If the truck doesn't arrive soon I shall hook off down to the town for the evening; not that there is much to do there but I manage to practise my French on innocent defenceless Frenchmen.

Must drop a line to Mother now explaining that I've been travelling.

XXXXXXXXXX Yours with love,
Ron

P.S. Thanks for the nice leave. 'Fraid I was lazy!

Chapter 17
Calais – Winter

At some time in November 1944 Mum and I must have moved from Derbyshire back home to Mum's parents' house in Hove. Having no envelopes for this period we cannot say exactly when this took place:

W.O I – Instr. Spathaky,
15 Br Convalescent Depot,
B.L.A. 15.11.44.

Dearest K,

Got back here with practically no difficulty at all. I am not where I thought I would be; naturally I cannot say <u>where</u> I am but I can say that I am nearer to you than I imagined and probably as near as I shall ever be during the war.

I look back on the short period spent with you with very great pleasure and with no great concern about the problem we discussed several times. I do not believe that we are provided with a buckshee pleasure-apparatus by evolution. There has to be some inhibitory mechanism to prevent couples from spending too much time and energy in fucking.

It just happens that the inhibitions are different in the two sexes. You <u>completely</u> lose interest once the act is over. Very often I don't and could repeat it during the night. But then the inhibition operates the next day with me.

Michael seems to be progressing very well indeed and I am very proud of him. I hope you will take some <u>definite</u> time every day or two in which to engage him in conversation – apart from the continuous treatment involved in the day's routine.

There are considerably more people near us in this part of France and they are much more friendly. My French is improving considerably and a number of school-teachers now tell me that my vocabulary is well in advance of the average Frenchman's.

We are still engaged in reorganisation work, with very few staff to help, but when the real work commences I can see there will be little time to spare. But I mean to retain rigorously a few nights a week for contact with the local population.

I have written to Warrington merely saying that I have been away on special work and not had the chance to write. For goodness sake don't breathe a word in your letters.

Must be off to work for the afternoon now. There is a mist among the tall trees of the park and I leave the centrally-heated room with its B.B.C gas-pipe furniture (by courtesy of the Luftwaffe HQ) with some regret.

Keep going!
XXXXX Love, Ron

On his thirtieth birthday Dad seems a little confused about his rank, reverting to Warrant Officer II in this letter:

W.O II Spathaky, A.E.C.
15 (Br) Convalescent Depot.
B.L.A.
22.11.44

Dearest K,

Some of the questions you asked in your letter of the 13th are answered in my last Green Envelope. This is just a scribble in between jobs.

First, re finance. I am now drawing (theoretically) 16/6 p.d. From 26 Nov 44 you will receive a V.A. + C.A. of 11/-. I shall have 5/5 net rate left, but I shall go on drawing £1 a week if I can. I have vouchered over to you £10 from my credits and will send more as soon as the Pay wallah finds out my credit balance.

We have moved up country and the nearest place is a country town of more than 5,000 pop., half-ruined by the blitz (ours <u>and</u> Jerry's) but with quite a lot of life left in the unbattered end. Two of the P.T. Sergeants (ex-N.U.T.) have chummed up with a bloke called Vasseur who is a local school-teacher. His wife Berthe was a nurse and they have been married a year. She has a baby of about three months, who was born prematurely (7½ months) in the only filthy shelter of the town. It looks fairly sturdy now but does not seem to sleep very much during the day.

We have been to their house several times. Next door but one to them is their friend Vérité, a railwayman. He was one of the four leaders of the F.F.I. and has given me a lot of griff *[=accurate information (slang)]* about the situation, which I propose to work up into an article.[346] His wife has a baby girl of about 2½.

Yesterday evening we had supper in Vérité's house and then put the wireless on and danced. It's a very small house and much less pretentious than any skilled worker's in England but we had a bit of fun teaching them English steps. The two chaps wouldn't dance. They just sat and applauded our efforts.

They are a sterling set of people and it was the first evening's relaxation I've <u>really</u> enjoyed either in N.A., Italy or France. We are near the real heart of France here and the heartless damp "verger clos" of Normandy seem far away.

Some time I would like you to send me "Fils du Peuple" by Maurice T.[347] It would be a valuable guide (from the political point of view) to this part of the world though he deals actually with the region from Béthune to Lens if I remember rightly.

Thanks very much for the promise of Snow's "People on our Side." [348] I miss the supply of daily papers very much but I know you will realise how much I depend on you for material to supplement the "yellow press" which we get here fairly regularly.

---

346 Forces Françaises de l'Intérieur, formal title of the French Resistance in the liberation stages of WWII. From October 1944 to March 1945 they were progressively amalgamated with the Free French Army.

347 *Le Fils du Peuple* by Maurice Thorez, pub. Éditions Sociales Internationales, Paris, 1937. Thorez was Secretary-General of the French Communist Party.

348 Pub. Random House, 1944. An account of American journalist Edgar Snow's coverage of India, Russia and China during WWII.

I'm glad to hear that Nesbit is around again.[349] I remember her very well, dark, vivacious and quite intellectual. In fact (as our friends here say "Elle a du singe, comment donc!" Oh, boy, has she got oomph!) Or perhaps she's all maternal now instead.

Branson's book[350] is certainly a worthy complement to Dutt's.[351] Aren't the quotations on famine-deaths in Bengal terrible?

Sorry I've got to stop now.

Tout à toi! R

For once, Dad's birthday has not gone unrecognised – it was his thirtieth:

W.O I Spathaky, A.E.C.
15 (Br) Convalescent Depot, B.L.A.
30.11.44.

Dearest K,

Thank you very much for your congratulations on my entry into the third decade. Here's to the sixth and seventh – with you![352]

We are busier and busier as the days go by, therefore your letter was like a sparkling oasis in a desert of routine, a pool of water in a burning wilderness. It was one of the nicest you've written me for quite a time. The time-table of daily activities was especially interesting. I think my activities are of a sufficiently non-military matter for me to reciprocate. Here goes:-

0715

Woken up by the RSM with whom I share a room.

0725-740

Wash & shave in the washing place, waking up the while.

---

349 I have been unable to trace Nesbit. The writer E Nesbit was a socialist and had lived in her later life at Friston, Sussex, but she died in 1924.

350 *British Soldier In India: The Letters of Clive Branson*, pub. Communist Party, London, 1944.

351 Probably *Fascism and Social Revolution* by Rajani Palme Dutt, International Publishers, 1935.

352 Dad's birthday was on 22nd November. They celebrated their seventy-fifth wedding anniversary in 2012.

740-750

Tidy up and collect my papers and books, glance at the day's programme.

0830

Several hundred men arrive on parade for Education. I share them out into various small rooms around the ex-German lecture theatre, allocating one of my convalescent A.B.C.A. instructors to each room.

0840-930

Wander round the rooms checking up on the work of the instructors, (My 2 Sgts AEC. are on the Preston Course).

This activity is varied by peeps at the Light Handicrafts Room, where a Guards Sergeant is teaching 5 men Perspex modelling and a glimpse of the Heavy Handicrafts shed, where I have set four convalescents on to building heavy wooden benches ready for the Handicrafts A.E.C. Instructor's return.

Often I am interrupted in the middle of this by a query such as the following from the C.O., "Here are a Czeck, a Pole and a French Canadian, who are in difficulties in the Depot because they can't understand English. Can you teach them some?

0930

I grab one of my instructors as the classes dismiss and ascertain that he knows a little German. The Pole & the Czech also know a little, so they get going. "Where is the Quarter-Master's stores?" "What time must we come in from the town?" etc.

The Adjutant then sends to say that a wooden step leading up to the entrance to the canteen hut has broken. One of the men who is building benches must go and mend it, because the Pioneer Sergeant (who is the normal bloke for the job) is too busy.

I get this started and go in for a brief post-mortem with my instructors' class on their efforts.

1015

Into the Education Office to ask the two Corporal Clerks to do some posters in red-pencil for a concert which is to be held on Friday. Get involved by the Adjutant in a scheme for persuading men to fill in AFB2626, the form which puts them on the list of voters at General Elections.

1030

Go to the mess for a cup of tea.

1100

Instruct the clerks how to indent to higher headquarters for perspex, book-binding material, rug-wool, embroidery material and dozens of other things needed. Answer three or four letters.

1145

Visit the Library; discuss with the convalescent librarians the problem of safeguarding the books. The Germans took the key of the door away with them. We decide to take the handle off the door when the Library is closed.

1200

Am stopped in a corner of the building by Fusilier Roberts, who was posted to the unit as a bandsman, but who is on general muck-sweeping duties. "Why aren't we having any concerts or entertainments?" I arrange with him to advertise a "Go as You Please" Concert on Friday. Adverts to be done by Education Clerks.

1220

Go for dinner and a short read of the papers (sent by you) and a shorter rest on the bed.

1.30

Off with my notes to give a lesson to my instructors on "Class-Room Technique." Considerable discussion with them as to how to deal with various types of people in the groups. One of the instructors, McRobbie, is an art teacher and a knowledgeable man. I feel I have at least half the class thoroughly on my side.

3.30.

Two hundred men arrive and are shared out as before, but as there are 40 over when we have squeezed them into the small rooms I take them myself in the body of the lecture-theatre on the subject of "How we are governed." Much discussion on advisability of political parties.

4.30

Tea.

6.0.

Elementary French class and inspection of voluntary handicraft activities.

7.30

Supper.

After that, preparation of next day's work or down to the local town with two of the P.T. instructors to chat with the two friends I mentioned and their wives.

Thanks a lot for the promise of Snow's new book and the one on Psychiatry.

Please "go on doing what you are doing." You and M are all I work for, apart from the common good – but working for the latter is my job. I love you ever so ever so much and want to hold you in my arms again.

Lots of love, Ron

(as you say – not forgetting "t'other")

The next letter was dated 3rd December, which was a Sunday:

W.O I Spathaky,
15 (Br) Convalescent Depot, B.L.A.
3.12.44.

Dearest K,

Quite a flood of letters from you! Is December so exhilarating in Sussex? I have also had your bundles of papers – for which many thanks. The young mothers' organisation (God forbid it should be matronly) sounds a sound step forward in the solving of your and their problems.

I have just heard that Sgt. Foster, one of my two instructors. is nearly back here from the Preston course. He is about 50 miles from here and trying to get transport. When they both get back things will be a bit easier and I shall be able to turn my energies to matters that I have had to drop while I have been away; a spot of reading for example.

This afternoon (Sat) and tomorrow afternoon I am taking off in any case, both to clear up my correspondence and prepare some A.B.C.A. There is a dance on tonight at a place not far from here to which a few of us are going. I have no idea what it will be like but I fear that our band will not be up to much. However, I'm going to press the old slacks and let my hair down (not too far, however!)

I was landed in a bit of a mess when our unit moved from the last location. My laundry was at a house quite a distance from the camp. It looks as if I have lost the whole bundle but there is just a chance that I may get it back.

Haven't been out very much here, but the countryside is quite pleasant, even in winter, probably because it's very much like England. There is a difference, however. I can't quite describe it, but one feels a hint of Flanders in the air and the number of Flemish-speaking people one meets is fairly large. The ground is dry compared with Normandy and the air is very crisp after a frost. If I were to see a band of young skaters on a pond I should be very much reminded of those old dark-coloured Flemish prints by Riezdyck, with village churches, frozen streams and urchins skimming over the hard surface.

The French dialect, while quite easy to understand, is quite different from Norman French. Here they say, "esch trottoir" for "le trottoir" and "elle table" for "la table." Vasseur, the local school-teacher, maintains that the "elle" is Spanish influence – the influence if not the rule of the Spanish Netherlands reached as far as this. They also say "fu" for "feu."

The operations are taking place in some pretty bad country, that's obvious isn't it? The weather doesn't help and the Siegfried line is not to be pushed over in a day. What deeds our blokes are performing and what they are putting up with, a Press-fed England cannot imagine and it's difficult even for us in the back areas to do so.

Lots of love,

Ron

For M – XXXX

XXXXXXXXX

P.S. I believe I read that the telephone service is going between France and England again. Some day I'll arrange with you to ring, if it's time!

The next letter was dated on the Thursday eleven days later.

W.O I Spathaky, A.E.C.

as before. 14.12.44

Dearest K,

Yours of 6.12.44 just received. Sorry you feel rather less settled emotionally then hitherto. Since you say, "I want so much to be faithful to you <u>but</u>…" you obviously feel certain strong tendencies elsewhere. Or am I exaggerating?

I sympathise very much, I hope. Winter has settled down rather grimly on the Northern Plain and as France is still a battered place with little transport facilities or community life one's emotional outlets are limited. The local town, with a few lights and French civilians, is just far enough away for it to be a nuisance to walk there. I suppose it's good exercise however.

Very often, when I have no evening classes, I go down with a couple of PT Sgts. both ex-schoolteachers. I believe I've described the Vasseurs and Vérités, neighbouring families whom we visit.

At the Vasseurs we occasionally see Mrs. Vasseur's younger sister Marie, who comes in from a village about 15 miles away, and her young man Fred who is from Arras. He is a struggling young motor-driver.

Last night there was another schoolteacher from the town, an "English specialist" by the name of Contel. He is quite interested in English literature and his command of the language is excellent.

Then when we went to an Army dance one week-end we met a couple of girls who lived in Paris until just before D-Day; Monique and Jacqueline Bisquet. Two of us have been to their parents' place. The old man is the manager of a state-owned distillery in the town.

Occasionally we have a dance to the wireless. The girls are rather petty-bourgeoise in outlook, but they are interested in the fact that they have the vote soon – for the first time in French history. Monique, the younger one, who is 19, seems to be making some attempt to discover how politics work.

Their old man is frankly Pétainist[353] and a Laval supporter.[354] I think he's a nasty piece of work but the Vasseurs and the Vérités give the other side of the picture – they are sterling through and through. Vérité was a leader of the F.F.I. He has given me a report on sabotage carried out by his group, which I am translating and sending to suitable quarters. Or on second thoughts I may send it to you for disposal as you think fit.

You can see there is little chance of straying in this community. The great complaint is being so far away from you. Monique is moderately interesting to see occasionally, but I wouldn't walk 5 miles to see her very often. Also I have learned a little sense from previous experiences and I know, apart from my undertaking with you, that if I became thick with her (in the worst sense) then I should no longer be friends. Also my work would suffer.

You are the only one with whom I want to be personally intimate and friendly as well. I PROMISE.

Lots of love,

xxxxxxxxx Ron

---

353 A supporter of collaboration with the Germans.
354 Pierre Laval, leader of the Vichy government, executed for treason in 1945.

The next letter was written in bright bluish-green ink:

W.O I Spathaky, A.E.C.
(as before),
18.12.44.

Dearest K,

Please excuse this terrible writing. It's not mental decay setting in (I hope) but the bad ink I have been forced to use in my pen.

I have not had a line from you for about a week now. I put this down to the congested mail services around Xmas. So I am not unduly worried, yet!

I have not bought you anything for Christmas but will make another block transference of funds. My impression is that there is much less in the few shops open here than in Italy, so I don't feel justified in competing with the local population for some miserable memento which you can buy much more easily in England. The Press pictures one sees of Tommies flooding into shops for purchases must apply to a few leave centres, probably mainly Brussels. Belgium seems better off for luxury goods, though worse off for food.

Have just been pulling myself out of an unwonted period of browned-offness, due to some administrative difficulties. I haven't had such a feeling since I was in Italy and had a quarrel with Fanny.[355]

Also this Greek set-back is an awful smack in the teeth for us as supporters of the Government war-effort. What <u>can</u> one say to the blokes? All I have tried to do so far is to point out our successes in other spheres, the French administration, support for Marshall Tito and our friendship with Russia and leave them to draw their own conclusions about the Greek situation – after an exposition of whatever facts we know.

It must be nice for Churchill to have the support of the Hearst Press in the States. Blast the pen, I can't stand it any longer.[356] Though this pencil seems too hard to make a better job of it.

---

355 Alec Waldron - see Appendix 2.
356 Here, Dad changed mid-paragraph from the bright blue ink to pencil.

Please write again as soon as possible. I may not be a model husband as regards my correspondence but I hope to prove myself really worthwhile when I come home again.

The French around here are trying to arrange Christmas trees for those kids whose families are bombed out or missing. It's pitiful to see what they are putting on the "trees," bits of silver paper and bars of chocolate from the Allied troops cut into a hundred pieces and wrapped in cellophane papers. I'm trying to think of some way of organising a collection for them – I am giving my Christmas ration of chocolate for a start. Hope you don't mind. We're debarred from sending it home in any case.

Well here's an end to the worst letter I've ever written, solely due to technical reasons. Courage, Love R

XXXXXX

Dad wrote again the next day, a Tuesday:

W.O. I Spathaky, A.E.C.
(as above) 19.12.44.

Dearest,

I hope you have forgiven me for the horrible letter I wrote yesterday. My pen seems to have recovered a little and my bad mood has also disappeared.

I am sitting here in my narrow little room, the discomfort of which is softened by the radiator, the hot and cold water-basin and the decent bed. Through the thinnest of partitions I can hear my A.E.C. colleagues and an R.A.M.C. W.O arguing blithely about bridge tactics (cards, I mean, not bridging the Meuse or Rhine).

Outside my window a chill mist drips from the trees of the estate, and I feel glad of the guessed presence of the homely haystacks and ploughed fields on the crest stretching away to the north.

At present I am trying to solve some of the material difficulties of the education in this place. Advertising is the worst thing and the elements lacking are paint which will take chalk and brushes to put the paint on with. All our efforts to popularise languages-classes and discussions stumble unless we can get over this.

England seems a vague dream again now. Are you really there and does the S.R. train still give that half-musical hoot as it goes over the crossing at Portslade?[357] Does Cissbury Ring still dream calmly against a light laughing sky? I should like to be certain and the only way to be certain is to see a bit of it again – then the certainty of the whole is with one in a flash.

I yearn for your comradeship and love. An Army can hardly become a community under the present system, because men cannot choose whom they live with. Yet it is strange that among the throngs of men who pass through this "Quai de Brumes" of a depot one sometimes sees someone who is obviously a figure of the future – a leader in the making.

There is a Scottish sergeant here now who is one of the most balanced types I have seen, a man who has obviously led his men in action, chased them away from the brothels, gone and seen HQ to find why the hell their rations haven't come, joined in their games of cards and led their A.B.C.A. discussions.

Without consultation he took up our education scheme in a disciplined way and started plugging away at it in his tenacious Highland manner, allowing no difficulties to blunt his endeavour and no foggy abstractions to influence him.

Hope Michael and the family are well. Tell your Ma I keep trying to write and can't. I'll post this off now in the hope that you'll get it before Xmas.

Yours with lots of rather grim resolution – love, Ron

XXXXXXXXXX

The following letter is undated but, from its contents, seems to have been written before Christmas, though not long before:

---

357 Wow! I too remember the green Southern Railway electric trains at Portslade level crossing. A number 1 on the front indicated a Worthing train.

W.O I Spathaky, A.E.C.

(as before)

Dearest K,

Today has been a day of minor successes, discussions going well, voluntary classes well-attended and a debate in the evening which held definite promise. So I feel that things are not so bad, after all. Even if the number of blokes one really influences is small, something is done to make the army a mental community – a place with intellectual institutions – instead of an agglomeration, a mere addition of units.

The Xmas rush of mail has still prevented me hearing from you at all, except that I have the Thorez book and the Penguins, for which many thanks

The country around is dripping and foggy though still much better than the unrelieved mud of our last site.

As you know, the news from certain sectors of the front is a bit disquieting, but no doubt it is a temporary setback which will be retrieved by a big offensive. A wag in the mess the other day suggested it might be the German Army running hard from their enemies on the Hungarian front.

It's much more serious than that but it shows you a little of how the usually undemonstrative British soldier looks at events on the Russo-German side.

I haven't been going out lately. The last time was on Sunday when Reg and I were invited over to dinner to the distillery near the local town. He couldn't come finally but since I had put in for a day pass and received it I went and spent a rather glum day with M. and Mme. Bisquet and their two daughters Monique and Jacqueline, whom I mentioned to you. The liveliest episode was a series of arguments with the old boy, who is a staunch follower of Pétain and uses arguments against me which you would have thought he would conceal – as things are at present. Several times, however, I have hit him one in the 'teeth' (verbally), much to the satisfaction of the rest of the family. I tried to teach the girls a bit of English, but it is extraordinarily difficult to teach one's own language to foreigners. If I ever do it again I shall have to prepare it – and that's a bit of an effort when one is always preparing things for somebody or other.

Are you doing (or should I say "will you have done") anything special at Christmas? I suppose Christmas trees and witch balls are either unobtainable or much too old-fashioned for le petit singe? I should rather like to buy him a tree. For some perverse reason I was bored stiff at an early age by the ponderous sentimentality of Christmas at home but if one could enjoy them without taking them too seriously it would be splendid.

How shall we plan our Christmases when I get out of this horrible brown jacket? A house-party with a few friends (preferably somewhere like Cork's place on the outskirts of Horsham) would be ideal?

Talking of Sussex, have you been out that way at all lately? I should love to see Worth Church again, with its colours blending with the trunks of the trees around it and even its eighteenth (or 17th?) century font with the Frisian inscription.[358]

Do you remember the old boy who showed us the parish registers, with enough old handwriting of various periods to satisfy any calligraphist?

Please tell me about all your doings, your thoughts and plans, your occupations and amusements. I will try and write better and longer letters, as I get this job better organised.

Lots of love,

XXXXXXXXX Ron

P.S. Thanks a lot for the card

Dad wrote again on Boxing Day:

W.O. I Spathaky, A.E.C.

as before 26.12.44.

Dearest,

I'm sorry you also have had your mail delayed by the Christmas rush. I have just received yours of the 13th! Thank you very much for

---

358 See his poem *Forest of Worth* (page 187).

the book on Tito. It's very good indeed. The parcels of papers arrive regularly. I really don't need English daily papers except the one we agreed upon, because I see most of them in the mess.

Christmas has been quite gay here, in spite of the German counter-offensive. I spent an evening carousing with Mr. & Mrs. Vasseur and their friends. One afternoon I spent at the distillery with one of our P.T. staff helping the two girls I mentioned to you to decorate a Christmas tree for the kids of the district.

The news tonight was that the German thrust has got to within 4 miles of DINAN, on the Meuse. This gives them a 50 mile penetration, but their total movement seems to be slowing down. The R.A.F. is certainly giving them a pasting.

It's marvellous to hear of M's new progress. I wish with all my heart that I could see him, and also that there were someone else to keep him company (subject to the High Contracting Parties being in agreement). Still, I suppose they will re-open the leave question even for us "static b--s" when the present crisis has been overcome. At the present moment we have the least right of anyone to think of leave.

I'm rapidly falling asleep as I write, so I'll get this note into the Postbox and write a better letter tomorrow.

There is a deep frost over the whole area, which makes me feel twice as energetic, but <u>not</u> late at night.

Love,

Ron xxxxxxxxxx

Dad wrote on New Year's Eve, in the bright blue ink:

W.O. I R. Spathaky, A.E.C.
as before 31.12.44.

Dearest K,

Still no letter since the 13th! The Christmas mails seem to be a disaster instead of a blessing. However I have the copies of "Gen" and the paper up to Dec 24th, so I know you have not been "V-2'd" up till then.

I think I have made a little progress since I last wrote. There are several excellent fellows among the convalescents who are helping wholeheartedly with the Education Scheme.

We have had a period of marvellous frosty sunny weather. Now it has turned slightly warmer, and correspondingly damper, but I still like this part of France, apart from the horrors of military life, chiefly the isolation from most institutions which go to make mental life possible.

Went down to the Bisquets with a friend of mine and spent most of the evening chatting in front of the kitchen fire while my friend, whose French is rudimentary though vigorous, cooked waffles on a special gadget called a "waffler." The three previous evenings I had had evening classes so I was glad of a break. The Bisquet girls are a bit inane but fairly pleasant to talk to, as they are quick-witted.

Excuse the blooming pen again. I dropped it yesterday, which didn't do it a lot of good. I shall have to treat myself to a new one. Then I shall feel like writing a decent long letter.

Hope I hear from you soon.

XXXXXXXXX Lots of love and desire,

Ron

Dad's first letter of 1945 was in an 'Active Service – Army Privilege Envelope' which, as it is printed in green, is perhaps the "Green Envelope" Dad has referred to. It was addressed to Mum at our home address, 49 Hangleton Rd., Hove 4, Sx.:

W.O I Spathaky,
as before 3.1.45.

Dearest K,

Happy New Year! – in case my other letter hasn't reached you. Mail seems to be all over the shop and I can't be certain when you are getting my rather poor literary efforts.

Luckily I have your two letters of Christmas Day and of the 27th. I have in addition the parcel of books including Marshall Tito[359], the

---

359 Probably *Marshall Tito* by Michael Padev, pub. Frederick Muller Ltd, London, 1944.

one with Fils du Peuple[360] and the White Paper on the War Effort.[361] Thanks very much indeed. I must write Renée[362] immediately about the post-card she sent. It is a grand reminder of Sussex.

Michael's photo is top-notch. I've added it to my little collection. I don't mind you getting my letter typed for "Wheatsheaf,"[363] as long as it says "A Military Convalescent Depot" and not "15 (Br) Condepot."

They are now starting leave for the staff of this Depot. As I have not yet done 6 months I am not eligible at the moment, but I shall get over some time. Probably in 4 or 5 months, time. Anyway, I'll put it thus pessimistically unless something unforeseen and pleasant happens.

I've been doing quite a lot more reading lately, Kath, and probably more thinking. I take less classes but do more training of instructors, convalescent and other. We have some grand fellows in at the moment, very anxious to help and quite good at putting the stuff over. In the morning, when I divide the 200 odd men out, the big black board generally looks something like this:-

Room	1.	"The Social Insurance Act."
"	2.	"State Control After the War."
"	3.	"The Arnhem Operation."
"	4.	"Are you a One-Woman Man?"
"	5.	Elementary Electricity. Lesson 4.
"	6.	Shorthand. Lesson 1.

The people doing Light or Heavy Handicrafts are a separate section but you see we are giving them as much choice as possible.

We have a library, separate from our general library, of trade and technical magazines (including B.P.J.![364]) and I have written to Citrine[365] to ask for trade-union journals.

I have recovered from my browned-offness now and feel more

---

360 See page 367.

361 *Statistics relating to the war effort of the United Kingdom*, White Paper (Cmd. 6564), HMSO, 1944.

362 Renée Shulman – see page 72.

363 Monthly publication for members of co-operative societies, pub. the Co-operative Wholesale Society.

364 British Pharmaceutical Journal.

365 Walter Citrine, TUC General Secretary and, incidentally, an opponent of the Communist Party.

calm about the whole job we have to do. In the near future I should be able to get down to planning my time as accurately as I did when I was P.O., but with the additional organising experience which will prevent me going up too many by-paths.

Meanwhile I love you and love you and love you! Please go on building our home. Some day it'll be an institution, even if it's a bit late. After all we did get glimmerings of what a home might be, didn't we? I am now sure it can be a little mirror of progress, not so much an oasis in a desert of social disruption, but a place where people are good and kind to each other and create beauty – a basis for the deeds which they do outside the home.

I never saw this picture vividly when I was in England before, but your letters and your descriptions of Michael have taught me a lot.

Well, it's nearly ten o'clock and I haven't prepared a couple of classes I have tomorrow, so I must send this off just as it is. I'm getting a Credit Statement as soon as poss so that I can see how much money can safely be shifted over to you.

So, keep planning, acting and checking.

Love
Ron

Next is a brief letter pencilled on the back of a printed form:

W.O. Spathaky
as before
5.1.45.

Dear Kath,

Some French people near here have asked me whether anyone in England could send a pair of baby's light shoes (felt, etc.) for a kid in the village (2½ years) whose father is a prisoner.

Do you know anyone in the Co-op? Or have you an old pair you could send?

In haste.
Love,
Ron

The next letter is mis-dated 1944 (when Dad was only a WO II). It was surely written on 9th January 1945:

W.O. I Spathaky A.E.C.

9 Jan 44

Dearest K,

I've just reread your letter of the 2nd. I'm glad you feel I'm making a certain amount of progress with my letters.

I'm doing some revision of my thinking as a whole, and if I am successful it will surely show itself in my letters.

Firstly, I want to suggest we become more friendly in our letters, if you agree. Can we reveal ourselves to each other a little more? Up till now I have been writing under the nose of the censor, but Army Group have just conceded that W.O. Is can censor their own letters.

You see, I feel that in a correspondence the style adopted by one partner influences that of the other. My letters have been flat, often mixed and incoherent and very often banal. You are a good correspondent, you describe what you do and see vigorously and without literary effort, but I feel sometimes that your letters have replied in the same tone as my pitiful scribbles.

If we are going to write as man and wife (and it's our only contact apart from the Paymaster) I'm going to tell you more completely what I feel. Will you do the same? Let's even be a bit adventurous about it – because every human being is so complicated that to reveal his or her mind to another is always rather adventurous – and therefore interesting.

Now as to my revision, my replanning. I've just realised that since Normandy, where I worked abominably hard, I've been getting a bit slack. I've not had a clear idea of what I was getting at in this camp, though I have built up a fairly large organisation, with an educational staff (instructors and administrators) of about 20.

I mean to hold regular conferences with myself as I did when P.O. in Sussex and revise my aims and check progress and regular staff conferences to spread my "line" outwards. Also I want to solve certain difficulties between my Sergeants and myself by being more social.

The difficulty has been that they spend most of their spare time playing cards. I hate cards and therefore appear rude. I like going to the local town and seeing either the people at the Distillery or the school-teacher and his friends. I'm going to cut down the visits to town, for several reasons. First of all, it's rather too far to the Distillery and I think it wastes too much time. Secondly (and I want you to understand me clearly) although the lieutenant and myself are perfectly correct in our attitude towards the girls there you know what it is. The proximity of young people of the opposite sex is in itself a sexual stimulant, even when Maman is there. I was really first conscious of this when one evening the girls invited some young fellows from the town and made quite a lot of fuss of them. I felt an emotion which was something between annoyance, pique and jealousy. There wasn't much of the last in it, but the fact that it entered into my mind is a warning note.

I can't stop going there altogether, since they have been very hospitable. They lack company altogether and it would be ungracious, but I shall go down less and devote more time to preparation, to getting among the blokes here and to developing a few contacts in the mining district just north of here, where the real people live. The local town is petty-bourgeois to the extreme and I have been very remiss in not exploring the towns to the north, which are industrial.

The situation of some of the "foreigners" around here is interesting and rather tragic. Even before the war, the declining French birth-rate made it necessary for the French to allow lots of Poles, Belgians, Dutch and Italians to settle down. There is a young boy, Ennio, with whom I speak Italian when he does odd electrical jobs in my room. He has never seen Italy. He complains that the French near this town treat the foreigners like dirt and give them the rough end of the stick – then vilify them and speak of them "taking the bread out of French mouths." I have explained the reason for the whole thing to him and he is so intelligent he grasps the social significance of the whole matter.

He is about 18 or 19 and so good-looking that I wouldn't trust even you near him too much – and I trust you a lot.

So you see what I am doing (to return to the main theme of this letter) is to give myself a good mental shaking in this misty fifth year of war and remind myself that I have very little to complain of in health, food, clothing, quarters, pay or work and I must GET ON WITH THE JOB.

How about you? Will you draw aside the veil a little in return? Not that your letters aren't already miles better than mine.

Does Michael absorb your full energy? Do you have lots of sexual desire? Do you do anything about it, either yourself or with anyone? Do you still think you are attractive – if so, what do you do to accentuate your most attractive features? Who are your real friends as distinct from acquaintances – Renée,[366] Nesbitt or who? Tell me about some of the intimate conversations you have with them.

What do you think of when you're favourably inclined towards me? What comes into your mind when, no doubt, you have one of those moments when you say, "He's a slack bastard and not worth bothering about much – but I'll write him a couple of pages." How is the Mothers' Meeting? What do you do when you're a bad girl, as distinct from a good girl who organises militant meetings? Do you stay in bed in the morning and neglect Michael ever?

What's it like to be a woman? When I come home on leave will you want a fuck with me as badly as I want one with you? Or shall we have forgotten how?

Shall we delay for a day or two and sleep apart until we've broken the emotional ice?

How do the Americans and other allies get on in England now? Is there a danger that we shall be the lost generation and that people will "absorb" our women – either foreigners or young men?

Finally, if I manage to get that block sum made over to you will you send me the new Edgar Snow book, <u>please</u>, and the Manual of Psychiatry (if it's not too impossibly technical in the medical sense – if it is, send it back). Is there any chance of the enclosed Harrap book, as a special present?

Five people have already read the Tito book. Thanks a lot.

---

366 Renée Shulman – see page 72.

If only I had you here, in this little room, with its bright lights, its gleaming white wash-bowl, its cheery white-wood German furniture and its modest bed! Why can't you be here? If they ever allow civilians on the Continent will you come? I want you with all my love and affection. / Ron

He wrote again the following day:

> W.O I Spathaky,
> as before 10.1.45.

Dearest Kath,

As part of my new "regime" I resisted the feeling of dismay at staying in camp tonight and did <u>not</u> go down to the town. This week-end I mean to explore the mining region, if I can spare the time.

One of my sergeants is taking an Army correspondence course in History and I am reading his main text-book on "19th & 20th Century History of Europe." It has interested me to the point of applying for one of their short courses, entitled "General Economics." Please don't think I am returning into academic seclusion, but I am conscious, now living conditions are (temporarily?) more comfortable, that my reading has recently been a bit too catholic. Have you ever thought of taking a single subject for a correspondence course? It has the advantage that it doesn't commit you too much and yet it gives a bit of pattern to your reading. Needless to say I shall bitterly contest anything phoney which I find in the stuff they serve out.

The battle of the Ardennes[367] is still raging and it must be one of terrific endurance. Sometimes I still feel the desire to do something more active than teach, in this war. Then I tell myself I have been trained for just such a job as this and it would be folly to make myself into just an infantry number – and one of doubtful efficiency at that.

Generally I finish by flattering myself that I am thinking of you and M, which is probably sheer egotism – or partly so. The fact is, I suppose, that I love life so much and want to live with you so

---

367 The Battle of the Bulge, the last major German offensive on the Western Front.

passionately that I build all kinds of noble motives around it. But on the whole I think my job lies here.

I have just written a short note to Renée.

The Mess is moderately noisy tonight. From this room I can hear a party of Czechs playing cards, shouting some strange words like "Čzeste Slovo." I believe it's the name of a Czech newspaper so I suppose they are discussing politics.

Last night I experienced an unusual occurrence, a "night emission." Not having experienced any sexual manifestations for weeks and months on end I have wondered vaguely at the cause of it. Perhaps the room is too hot, or perhaps it was an overdose of cheese for supper.

It has delayed my new personal campaign a little today by making me feel a bit flat but "haec sunt lacrimae rerum" (these are the tears of things) as the Latins said.

Hope you're getting my new outburst of letters. Thanks for yours of the 3rd and 4th.

Lots of love
Ron

There follows a brief letter, written on 13th January:

W.O. I Spathaky A.E.C.
as before 13.1.45.

Dear K,

Rotten cold, otherwise everything O.K. Snow about 3 ft. deep, but it is dry snow so far!

Still thinking of you a lot. Not many letters coming in at the moment.

Have not been down to our petty-bourgeois friends for a week. Tomorrow thinking of going into big town some miles away to get newspapers and make some contacts.

Longer letter soon. This is just to remind you I am still here.

Love, Ron

XXXXXX

For M – XXXX

The next letter we have is dated almost a fortnight later:

W.O I Spathaky, A.E.C.

(as before) 26.1.45.

Dearest,

It's 10.20 p.m. I've just put some socks in boiling water in my wash-bowl to soak, so I have time to dash off a short note between the washing and bed-time.

Thanks a lot for packing off the shoes. I can guarantee that the parents who want them have no other means of getting any at the moment.

The job is still growing here, and I expect to have a couple more educational instructors attached to my Department within the next few weeks. I cannot say more about them for security reasons, but the interesting thing is that they will not be English.

They will give me staff as per the following diagram:-

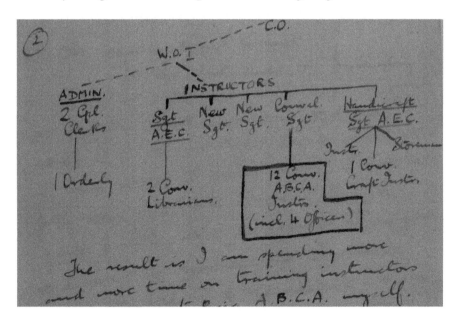

The result is I am spending more and more time on training instructors and less on taking A.B.C.A. myself. This is inevitable, I think. A big change I am contemplating this week is the conversion of one of the Cpl. clerks into an "Educational Quartermaster," i.e. someone who can keep tags on accommodation, keys and turning-up of classes at the right time.

I also take French classes in the evening and one class with an outside unit who send a truck for me.

All this gives me enough work to keep me occupied, but I am beginning to see light at the end of the organisational tunnel.

At the week-ends, on Saturday and Sunday afternoons, I get out as much as possible. Last week-end but one I went to a dance held by a unit at a town about 10 miles away. I met a jolly nice girl, with whom I danced quite a lot, but as regards whom you need have no apprehensions whatsoever. She is the wife of a Frenchman who has been a P.O.W. in Germany since <u>1939</u>! Anyone who indulged in anything but friendship with someone like her would be a pretty bad kind of skunk.

I must admit I feel the need for a bit of non-masculine company, since this beehive is so far from home, but <u>I promise</u>…!

You see if one does nothing but work one becomes completely dehumanised and my French makes it so easy to get on with any of these people. Please give your opinion on this little point.

I have seen the list of leave passes for Blighty. Afraid my name is way down at the bottom of the list, but I shall get it some time. Unless the war finished soon in Europe (and the Russians seem to be smashing towards Berlin – Breslau just gone!) I suppose I shall get it around August.

Well, I must hop off to one of the wirelesses in the camp now to get the last news bulletin.

Please write a long letter and tell me all that you are thinking. The last few have been frequent and cheery, but a bit short.

Lots of love,
Ron

XXXXXX For M

P.S. Thanks for papers and good book on Army!

Chapter 18
Falling from Grace

Three days later, Dad dates a letter 26th January, altered to 29th – or it could be the other way round but unlikely since the previous letter was dated 26th. It appears that some two-year-old has scribbled in pencil on the first page:

W.O I Spathaky A.E.C.
as before 29.1.45.

Dearest K,

When I get you to spend so much on books for me Lord forbid that I should kick at you buying as many as you want. Your decision re Michael seems impeccable – to base your action on his and your actual health and energy.

Bloody annoying about the other business. I do it myself, but only about once in four or five months. When I was at school and even as a student before I met you I used to worry about it a lot because I seemed to do it regularly about twice a week. It exhausted me terrifically and I still think that a lot of our very early troubles were due to it. The problem and its solution probably lie deep in psychology somewhere, but it's extraordinarily difficult to psycho-analyse oneself. Ever thought of seeing a woman doctor about it? Not that I think it's a disease, or even very important, but I know too well how it knocks the glitter off everything.

The extreme psychological pressure of this 5th year of war affects all our emotional and psychical reactions. I suppose we should exhort ourselves with the notion that the war is moving so fast that in Europe it <u>can't</u> last very much longer than 6 months – if we work hard, put everything in to the last lap. Then for those of us who plump for Burma or China it will be a case of super-hardening of the will.

My bother in the above connection is similar, due to the different environment. Quite frankly I have had terrific gusts of physical desire for bed-companionship with a woman recently – it may be the weather as well as the war! It's also partly due to the comparatively thick population around here compared with N. Africa, Italy, Lincolnshire and Normandy.

It's something to which I shall have to work out a progressive solution myself, but if we can consult each other on these things it will help both of us. The obvious solution <u>would</u> be to make friends with a girl of intellectual and progressive tendencies in order to have a little company occasionally and try and build a rational friendship based on my obligations to you and M and myself. But among the fair number of women in the little town north of here the only ones I have spoken to seem to be typical examples of ordinary French girls – but under war-time conditions, with very few men in the district. Many of them have been married for five years and have not seen their husbands for four.

What do you suggest? Of course the biggest thing of all is the necessity not to get V.D.[368] but the emotional questions are probably just as important in the long run.

I know you won't give me an answer which is just based on fear of unfaithfulness. You know I want to be faithful and not do anything to besmirch our family relationship. But what are the things that you dislike most in the idea of unfaithfulness. Should I try to keep away from women altogether and not go to dances such as they hold around here?

I haven't thought of that idea very much. Perhaps that's the only real solution. With women I'm forced reluctantly to the old-fashioned conclusion that <u>unless</u> you have a lucky meeting with an outstanding one whose friendship is cultivable without physical relations then it's a case of avoiding the thin end of the wedge.

---

368 Venereal disease, now called sexually transmitted infection. Gonorrhoea and syphilis were the main infections. AIDS was unknown in 1945.

There's an old Scottish sergeant-major opposite my "bunk" who is a model of rectitude and wisdom on these things. I mean to cultivate him. He enjoys a bit of feminine company with the best but he has apparently always been able to introduce his friends to his wife with a clear conscience. He has a daughter 23!

In the meanwhile bags of work is a useful palliative.

Love to you & the little Spathacus Ron

Four days later Dad still craves the company of women:

W.O I Spath
(as before) 2.2.45.

Dearest K,

Sorry if a sex-inflamed imagination spoke in the last letter. I think I've begun to resolve the mental conflict in a way of which you would approve. If I must go out of camp and mix with a few of the females around here, I <u>must</u> at all costs establish a comradely attitude towards them, and one which is in line with the chivalry required by our position in this country.

Otherwise I should be a sad degenerate. It's not an easy thing to do, but I have the example of the old Sergeant-Major of whom I spoke, to help me.

Thank you, darling, for the dailies[369] which continue to arrive. They remind me continually that you are with me in spirit. You are my central axis, from whom I may occasionally take a wobble, but only when I get boxed in and mad and ask myself <u>how long</u>, <u>how long</u>?

Recently I read a marvellous novel by a Chinese girl of seventeen, "Dark Tide," by Lih Shinh-Lih (I think), which, by showing the spirit of many Chinese under circumstances compared with which ours are an orgy of luxury, brought me back to earth with a bump.[370] It's nearly

---

369 The *Daily Worker* was the newspaper of the Communist Party.

370 I wonder if Dad has confused the title with that of a 1923 novel by Vera Brittain, as he had already mentioned her twice in his letters.

all about women and I thoroughly recommend it. It's published by Faber, but I'm not <u>certain</u> about the author's name.

Lots of love to you & little imp.

Ron

Dad writes again on a Wednesday, five days later:

W.O I Spath

(as before) 7.2.45.

Dearest K,

I hope I'm forgiven for the two miserable letters you received. Really I didn't carry out my promise to "get in touch" with you, made a few weeks ago. It was a miserable outburst about a passing problem and relates to the fact that a neighbouring unit had asked some of us over to a couple of dances and I cast languorous glances at some of the females. I'm now fully in possession of my faculties again.

Meanwhile I don't hear from you! Last letter was 28.1.45 (dated). The snow here was quite pleasant and melted suddenly under pressure from a high warm wind in a matter of four hours. The rain that followed a burst of sunshine was not so pleasant.

I agree with you that one must look ahead and plan some future, otherwise one sticks one's nose to the moving arrows on the maps and to the job on hand and becomes a hopeless automaton.

Also I very much share your view that we should have a couple of days together when I get my "Churchill leave" – whenever that is (I'm very low on the list in this Depot!). If we are able to achieve this I am quite willing to go to Netherwood, though I must confess that somewhere alone with you would appeal more, coupled with a few trips round to other people, during the "domestic period" at no. 49.[371]

Thanks ever so much for the regular stream of pamphlets and WN&V's.[372] You've no idea what a help these are. They get passed around and well-worn.

---

371 Mum's parents' house, 49 Hangleton Road, Hove, this being "home".
372 *World News and Views*, a Communist Party periodical.

You surprised me with your account of Michael's (I nearly said "Mike's"!) linguistic progress, in a recent letter. Can he really say "Daddy come back some day"? I suppose it's something he's learnt from you and doesn't really understand? Suppose we shall have to be very careful with our conversation from now on – making it fit for the pure ears of a 3-year old and not larded with the Rabelaisian touches we sometimes employ.

The education work continues to expand. You didn't tell me whether you had received my little account of it and what you thought of it.

My Educational cadre-course is perhaps the most important thing I do. The eight blokes I train for A.B.C.A. work each fortnight provide the Depot with a solid intellectual leavening, which is a great help in our educational work here.

But of course the big development of activity is in the Occupational Therapy department; to think that I should ever become responsible for a big handicraft department! However I seem to be weathering the storm pretty well and the organisational details fall into place as time goes on. Some day we shall be able to dismiss the experience I have had in these long hurried days and I shall look back on them as at least a period of great experiments, even if bitter.

over --   Lots of love & t'other, Ron.

The word "over" does not make sense. As it's below the last line of the text and alongside "Lots of love…" it seems to indicate further content over the page. But there is none.

I found Dad's next letter slightly confusing, but my understanding of the second paragraph is that Mum had started a sexual relationship with a "lad", which is a real surprise to me, and that Dad had only flirted with the woman whose husband is away:

W.O. I Spathaky
(same) 11.2.45.

Dearest wife,

Just a short note (on the same theory as your letters) about one or two points that strike me.

As you will see from letters that cross-posted with yours, I have only been guilty of a little "adolescent-Xmas-party" passion up till now. I will not make the love-making with the lad an excuse for going any further, if I can help it. It's sheer lust on both sides, I'm afraid, plus the fact of both being healthy, unused to such things for a long time and me enjoying brushing up my French!

But I do happen to know that since the girl's husband has been away, she's only been out with one man, a doctor from Lille, and that only on three occasions. That's in 5 years! Her father is very strict.

I agree very much about avoiding a "negative attitude" to our marriage. I haven't one, I hope, but I don't feel that this sort of thing has anything to do with OUR relations. which are already something so vastly important because of M and because of what we have taught each other in the past.

I promise you to hold myself in check, if I can. Are you careful over this disease business? And over contraception? If you are I think I can accept the chap with an ill grace as a substitute – but please not as a permanent replacement! And don't make any mistakes. Tell him from me that I expect him to be straight with you and myself and not go philandering with anyone else at the same time as with you.

I went to Brussels yesterday on business. It hasn't changed much since 1939 when we were there last, except that it has become a den of "leave-vice." Don't let's sink too far ourselves in this general upset of morality, K. Let's stick to each other if we can and if we can't, avoid promiscuity. I'm sure that way lie insanity and degradation.

The work continues to grow and I am certain we can make a success of the Release Education Scheme if we put our backs into it. I'm hoping to be able to write to you soon and tell you that I am doing nothing except work. Is there any hope that you may aim for the same thing?

More love than ever. Take care of little Spathacus.

Yours, Ron

Three days later Dad wrote on a Wednesday, St Valentine's Day, but Dad would not have realised the significance of the date. The envelope was postmarked "17 FE 45":

W.O I Spathaky
(as before) 14.2.45.

Dear K,

Just feeling a bit worn after a hard day's work. Should like to escape somewhere for an hour or two from the sight of the bunk, the Sergeants' Mess, the wet woods and fields that start outside my door – though they have a fresh appealing smell – but there is nowhere to escape to for a couple of hours. I may go along to the house of Ennio Durini, the little Italian I know, if my resolution holds, though I long for a complete invigorating change, a day's tramp within Sussex woods, a plunge into the sea at Brighton, an evening with George's records of Peter and the Wolf or just an evening by the fire, with the red backs of our books reflecting the glow and a talk over "possible worlds."

I haven't had time to study the Gratuity Scheme you mention yet. Most of the blokes who mention it seem to accept it like most other things – with a grain of salt. "The proof of the pudding is in the eating."

I've sent you £50 on a transfer form. I haven't drawn any pay for a few weeks so there'll be a bit more mounting up already.

I'm not surprised at all at what you call the intensity of your sexual feelings during my absence. I don't believe they're any stronger or weaker than anyone's should be – though there's no doubt that there's a general lassitude prevailing which turns very large numbers of people towards increased sex-activity.

You didn't tell me much about your "incident." You might describe the business a bit dramatically for me. I have a certain interest in what you experience, you know. Did you discuss it with him beforehand? Was it in bed or elsewhere? Did you use contraceptives? Was he confident, shy, domineering, athletic, or just a "cheerful beginner?" Did you keep the light on, or was it one of those Dreadful Deeds in the Dark? Did he kiss you all over?

And has it happened again?

Personally I'll have to think over this "fatigue" business again. I think possibly it's what I said – that I need to exert myself more than once at a time and when I don't I am sort of half-satisfied. But I couldn't swear to that being the reason.

(later)

I think the idea of twin beds is a good one. I always used to believe in the sugary romantic stories of people lying "asleep in each other's arms." Personally I don't think I could sleep properly like that, because it can't be a completely relaxed position though it is a very pleasant one.

By the way, talking of your "young lad," it would be pretty awful if you <u>did</u> have a kid by him, particularly from the point of view of your parents, who have the common-sense to count up to nine. Is that side completely ensured against?

Needless to say, if you did, I would stand by you, as you have stood by me, emotionally and spiritually, for seven years. I haven't so much belief in heredity that I think my own genes and chromosomes are essential to make a fine kid. As long as <u>you</u> didn't part from me!

Incidentally I have just discovered the R.L. with your new photograph, on the mess-table. It's very thoughtful of you, K, to send it me and if I can do the same for you I will. It's far and away the best you've had done in years – though the Polyphotos have been a source of delight to me. But in this your hair looks lovely, your forehead high, your eyes soft and affectionate but intelligent, your smile gentle and comradely and your chin firm.

All for now – a longer letter soon,

Ron

XXXXXXXXX
XXXXXXXXX
XXXXXXXXX

Dad wrote again on 18th February, the day after his last was posted:

W.O I Spathaky
(as before) 18.2.45.

Dearest,

We have had a fine day today, perhaps a harbinger of spring, though I believe there are still frosty days ahead of us. The news is terrific, isn't it? The Crimea Conference[373] seems to have struck a good deal of horror into the hearts of the Nazi leaders. The joint announcement of punitive measures against the chiefs and "no mass revenge against the German people" seems obviously the correct approach.

I have just received a correspondence course (through the Army) from Ruskin College, Oxford, on "elementary economics." I think it will sharpen my wits doing some disciplined study and preparing the written work. The text-book is Henry Clay "Economics for the General Reader," a thoroughly respectable one, but not too right-wing in trend.[374]

Also I have rooted out quite a posh German desk from an underground building and transported it (or <u>had</u> it transported) to my bunk, and the presence of it in the room is a much greater incentive to study.

Your last letter, darling, was that of 7th Feb. I am anxiously awaiting the next one. There was nothing about Michael in the last. I suppose he is all right, still? Are you still patient with him and will he be a good fighter for a better young life than we're having?

What I am wondering at the moment is whether they will ever allow civilians over to Europe while troops are on garrison duties. They did during the last Occupation. I know the existence of Michael would be a great barrier to such a visit on your part (assuming I had the good luck to be kept in Europe) but the Army even organised schools for children just after the last war. It's worth keeping in mind, I think.

I definitely need to see you again, K. I feel exasperated that this ink on this paper will be in your hands in four or five days, hardly the time for it to dry, and I, at the end of the pen, cannot follow it.

---

373 Now generally known as the Yalta Conference.
374 *Economics: An Introduction for the General Reader* by Henry Clay, pub. Macmillan, 1919.

I'm afraid I <u>have</u> followed you in falling from grace, but please don't think there's any comparison between the two of you. Her name is Jacqueline Lemaire. She's 23 and quite attractive, though on political matters I imagine I should weep if I really sorted out what she thinks – a mixture of racial prejudice and anti-Red emotion seems to be the basis. But she is intelligent and <u>completely healthy</u>. There's no danger in that direction. I used the means the Army provides and it was a moderate success, though I still think the things are a ruddy drawback.

She knows I am married (as she is herself) and that you are my basis of emotional existence. In fact one of the things I needed to go to a woman for was to have someone to talk to about you and M. She thinks you look incredibly smart, but "not at all English, rather more Polish or Russian."

I suppose it was the natty little "throat-piece" that you were wearing that gives you that look.

And now please let's both try to work our way back to faithfulness. I know it'll be difficult and I'll probably fall again, but the bother is that I do so like to get away from the camp <u>once</u> a week (Saturday night) and after the dance there's a house there awaiting me, with a bed just asking to be slept in. As <u>you</u> remarked, "opportunity unexpectedly presented itself."

But please don't make any comparison between this lust for an attractive intelligent woman and my love for you, who are attractive, intelligent and "my mate."

Work is going pretty well, but our teaching accommodation is a big problem at the moment. One or two of the particular medical grades (who all come together to us) have swollen in numbers compared with the others and it's a real head-ache packing them in. Also the N.C.O. who helped me very much with the Educational Cadre has been posted away. He was a real treasure and "one of our people" into the bargain. The new one is taking his time to find his feet.

Most nights in the week I spend in preparation on A.B.C.A. I mean to spend a little more time in the convalescents' messes and canteens in the next week or two. Their canteen accommodation has improved enormously just lately and it opens up a big field of work.

Please let's keep on loving each other – Yours

Ron XXXXXXXX

A week later, again on a Sunday:

W.O. I Spathaky, A.E.C.

(as before) 25.2.45.

Dearest,

Your last letter showed a very down-in-the-dumps mood. I'm afraid my recent ones, crossing post with yours, will have done nothing to alleviate that feeling. I don't think you were whining, as you suggest. After all, human relations are very tangled at the moment, aren't they? But back of the whole mess I don't feel so far out of touch as when I was in North Africa. There one doubted often if it would ever be possible to get back. Here we are in neighbouring counties (so to speak) with only that irritating little strip of water between. I should only have to hitch-hike for a few hours and I should be looking on waves that were exact replicas of those you see at the bottom of the street.

Sorry your Ma has been so ill. Please convey my sympathies to her.

Thanks very much for the Bevan book. It looks very interesting if somewhat "Leftish"[375] Your supplies of literature are still terrifically helpful and I appreciate them enormously.

Michael looks as though he's developing quite a will of his own. He's obviously not quite the little obeying silent soul he was before, but he will be even more interesting, I hope, as he becomes independent. I wish I were there to help with him, though I think you have been magnificent as father and mother rolled into one.

Afraid my little "affaire" continues, though I only leave the camp at weekends. I have made love to her twice now. I'm a damned fool and I want to break off the acquaintanceship if I can but I find it difficult. You

---

375 Probably *Why Not Trust The Tories?* by Aneurin Bevan, an MP on the left of the Labour Party, pub. Victor Gollancz, 1944.

need have no fear as regards my heart, however. It seems paradoxical to say it, but I'm completely faithful to you emotionally. But I realise the risk of giving her a child and that's the reason I want to stop.

She is interested in you and Michael and asks all kinds of questions about you both. I praise you up to the skies and have made it clear how precious you both are to me. She is very smart and clean and like a lot of Frenchwomen sports a remarkable coiffure. How they've managed to maintain their allure after the war I don't know.

But I <u>love</u> you. I rather admire her and am physically interested in her, but she has some of the most <u>curious</u> ideas, coupled with a generous and intelligent temperament. But admiration and lust don't make love. IF ONLY I COULD BREAK AWAY – <u>NOW</u>!

Lots of love,

Ron

Again, it's a week before Dad writes:

W.O I Spathaky, A.E.C.

(as before) 4.3.45.

Dearest wife,

Thanks a lot for yours of Fri last. This week-end I'm really going to try and bring myself to suggest to Jacqueline, the girl "in the case," that we remain "bons copains," good pals, and cut out the love-stuff. If we don't I can see disaster looming ahead, not emotional disaster because I would never be drawn away from you, but something might go wrong some time and I don't know what I should do if it did.

I never thought that both you and I would be affected by the wave of irregular living which has swept over the British people, but we have, especially me because I have sunk deeper than you. I feel tainted and unable to give a clear lead to the men at the present time.

There is one phrase I hang on to, at the moment, as though it were a religious utterance, the last one of your letter "I love you, don't <u>ever</u> forget that." I take your letter out again and again to look at it and imprint it on my mind.

All this has happened when I should be preparing myself for the greatest opportunity democratic educationalists have ever had. The men are eager for news, eager to discuss, and, thank goodness, the Cadre chaps I set going on the discussions are responding to the increased interest and working. It is lucky for the men that I have built up a machine that will function for some time while I am wrestling with this problem of mine. But it won't function for ever without a strong lead and my two sergeants need leadership in addition which I can give when I haven't something on my conscience.

Next week we are starting a four-page newspaper in the Depot, called the "Château." This is a big camp and it should be an important educational force in the place, as well as a forum of opinion.

The economics course is going moderately well. I keep at it in order to shut out distracting thoughts if nothing else, which is not an adequate motive for this but better than not working at all.

This is the most miserable letter I have ever written, K, but I still have a hard core of resistance within me, resistance to circumstances.

If you will stand by me I will rebuild our lives, however difficult it may seem at the moment. Eight years is a long time for two people to cleave together through various difficulties, and I cannot believe that what has been built up can be easily destroyed. Please reassure me that you mean to struggle with me and I shall get through the "reefs and shallows" I have got into. Please!

Upon the red-bound books the fire gleams still;
Dark hangs the print of Shoreham Harbour there.
Across the water, by a feat of will,
My mind moves on, burdened with narrow care,
To talk with you.

Chill blows the wind from Worth, from Horsham through the air
Still brings the faintest scent of Sussex pines.
Back springs my soul to tortured Europe where
Nowhere the spirit of man to fate resigns.
Nor yet shall I.

Your lovely descriptions of Michael keep me in touch with both of you as nothing else could do. Why it hasn't been enough to inspire me to work and nothing else I cannot imagine. It should have been. Your correspondence for four years has been detailed and unfaltering, a true comradeship.

I shall always love you for what has gone between us in the past.

Yours, Ron

I find that short poem very moving. Dad is evoking scenes from the early years of their marriage before he was called up. I remember that print of Shoreham Harbour from my childhood. It was indeed dark – a charcoal drawing perhaps – just areas of black on a white background, dockyard cranes, the chimney of Shoreham power station looming. I wonder what happened to it. The "wind from Worth" recalls a visit there in February 1943 to which he had referred twice before.[376] *The "red-bound books" are the monthly hardback volumes of the Left Book Club, probably some of the books shown in this photograph taken in 1940 in their first home in Old Shoreham Road, Brighton.*

Dad reading among "the red-bound books" at home in 1940.

The next letter is dated on the Saturday six days later, but postmarked on the Sunday:

---

376 See pages 187, 242 and 379.

W.O. I Spathaky, A.E.C.

15 (Br) Convalescent Depot,

B.L.A. 9.3.45.

Dearest,

Just a wee note to tell you I'm thinking of you a terrible lot, and longing to be back out of this tortured land, even if only for a time.

Just starting some preparation for tomorrow.

Love,

Ron

XXXXXX

On the Sunday he wrote a longer letter:

W.O. I Spathaky, R.V. A.E.C.

as before 10.3.45.

Dearest K,

How cheery you were on the 3rd when you wrote! It bucked me up in turn. I have been worrying a little lately as to whether you were being turned into the household organiser for your Ma and Pa. They aren't exploiting you, are they?

I suppose you don't consider the question of moving, placed as you are? It would provide a fresh crop of problems, might land you in a far worse district and in any case I imagine houses or flats are very difficult to find still? If your Pa and Ma are guilty of that, however, it would be the only solution, wouldn't it?

The letter from Fanny really surprised me. I'm awfully glad he's still alive. Thought he'd probably "gone for a six" at Arnhem.[377]

---

377 Battle of Arnhem, 17–26th September 1944. Troops were parachuted in and landed by glider. Two members of the Parachute Brigade were awarded posthumous VCs. Dad's friend, Sergeant Instructor Alec 'Fanny' Waldron of the Glider Pilot Regiment (see Appendix 2), played a heroic part, piloting a glider to land near Arnhem and, when all the officers and the RSM had been killed, taking command of 2 Wing HQ of the GPR. He was wounded again but made it back to Britain. He was mentioned in despatches and awarded a commission. The 4th Parachute Brigade's total casualties in the Battle amounted to seventy-eight per cent, and it was disbanded soon afterwards.

As I've just written letters to my Ma and Pa I don't know whether I can keep my eyes open to finish this one. I nearly always start the other way round and don't even start their letters but I had to alter the procedure for once.

Work here is increasing at the present time, for reasons which I can't explain. The handicrafts sergeant got a curious bee in his bonnet about three months ago and started working furiously. Since then he has almost worked himself to death. There is no analyzing the deep motives beneath some of these chaps' minds. The other one has been working less recently.

I have had some very useful men from among the convalescents. The Scottish sergeant got posted away suddenly but I found a Staff-Sergeant of the military Provost Staff Corps, a man who had been in charge of a military prison. He has been very helpful indeed. With the A.E.C. instructor at his prison he has been attempting modern psychological treatment of the men, including quite a lot of A.B.C.A.

When the next batch of your books arrives (I have the Cobbett for which many thanks) I shall have to suggest reluctantly that you don't bother with any more, though I hope it will be possible to keep up the pamphlets etc. If I have any more books I shan't be able to move them, which would be a devil of a pity.

I hope we <u>do</u> more. We have been getting too "base"-minded in this place and it would shake us up a bit.

The hells that open are within the mind;
Uncrushable, the flowers sprout upward near the Pit.
On winds of spring a flower from you I find;
Now I must keep and treasure it.

I wish I could have made you as happy as you have made me, during these long years that have floated past.

I love you
Ron

XXXXXXX
XXXXXXX

The next letter we have is dated 2nd April, over three weeks later. The reason may be related to the "scrape" referred to in the next letter, notwithstanding that there is clearly a letter missing:

W.O I Spathaky, A.E.C.

as before 2.4.45.

Dear K,

By now I hope you will have got my letter saying that I have come somewhat ingloriously out of the scrape I was in, for the loss of £15 (I suppose) and a month during which my work suffered badly and a burden of worry was passed on to you. Though curiously enough the machine I had set going functioned to some extent and even produced a few surprises in the shape of a printed Depot newspaper which the convalescents edited. Apart from a guiding hand concluding negotiations with the French printers and an article on the Army Release scheme I did very little – and got a fair amount of credit.

Still, I have now started to work very hard indeed and even in a week made up a deal of leeway.

Jacqueline must have a constitution like a horse. She hardly looks affected at all. You needn't worry from now on, however, (if you do worry!?%) – I believe I've learned not to play with fire. In any case there is a good reason why you need not fear Jacqueline's influence on me, something which I cannot explain to you.

I believe I told you in my last letter that my leave will probably come in June or July. Of course something may happen to hasten it, although I rather doubt it.

I'm preparing another application for a commission in the A.E.C. If you have a birth-certificate handy would you please send it. If not could you send to Somerset House for one, please? Or on second thoughts you could let me know and I will send. There is an ACI which looks as if it will help me to a few pips.

(P.S. My date of birth: 22.11.14 at Canton, Cardiff – father Albert, mother Clara née Retchford).

I haven't said anything which might make Mother worry.

I feel justified in saying "Yes" to your offer of the "Geographical Survey." Please don't bother with the Arnhem book, as I know the story of the op inside out, including the part played by GPR. As for Hansard on the Crimea, I'll have them perhaps when you've digested them.

Our forward columns are well into central Germany now, so we surely can't stay this side of the Channel too long. I'm a bit nervous about my release number (30). It's got a bit of a Burma smell about it but I think I should certainly be able to see you before I went and then there's always a) the chance of teachers being Class B or b) use being made of my German or c) A.E.C. being retained in Europe, to work the Release Scheme. In fact the situation is really quite bright.

I think we shall be a bit blushful with each other when we meet, what do you say? But don't be afraid that I shall take anything for granted. You belong to yourself and I shall fit into any scheme of common living you suggest, with or without single beds (or rooms)!

Lots of love, Ron

Three days later:

W.O I Spathaky, A.E.C.
as before 5.4.45.

Dearest,

Tanks at Erfurt! Surely this is <u>near</u> the end. I know that there may be difficulties ahead for all of us on the Continent, especially when the question of who is to move back to the U.K. and who is to garrison Germany arises, but it looks as though the worst nightmare, the war without end, has disappeared.

This is just a note to let you know I am more bound to you than ever for the way you stood by me when I was in the soup. It will take a lot of forgetting, that incident, but I don't think I have any "psychological scar" as a result of it. I didn't express my feelings at first when I wrote, because they were mainly those of sheer relief and relaxation of tension, but I realise now that if a woman can stick to a man through <u>that</u> she can stick to him through anything.

I'm having a bit of reaction at the moment, but am moving slowly to the attack.

Lots more later,

Love,
Ron

Three days later again:

284245 W.O I Spathaky, R. A.E.C.
HQ 15(Br) Convalescent Depot,
B.L.A. 8.4.45

Dearest K,

I feel a wee bit disconcerted, not having seen a line from you for 9 days. One hears vague stories of occasional grave damage by the V2s, though I believe they are really shooting their last bolts now. Or perhaps, like me, you are feeling badly the reaction of the mess I got us into a few weeks ago.

Still, the mail is being sorted at present in the P.O. and we are all stalking about pretending not to be waiting. Maybe there's une petite lettre de ma très chère compagne. The last letter I had told me of your interest in the women's hospital and its dispensing department. Jolly good idea as far as I can see. (No other reason for wanting to be near the women's hospital is there? – There, you see, my own lamentable exploits have made me think everyone's like myself!)

Work is going pretty well at the moment. The C.O. signed my application for a pip, saying "A keen and excellent instructor. Would probably not make a good infantry officer but should do well as an education officer."

(YOUR LETTER OF 3/4/45 JUST IN HOORAY!)

It is a restrained but pleasant little letter. Merci beaucoup Madame Spathaky! Répétez aussi vite que possible.

I have just finished Snow's book.[378] Parts of it were very good. I was more interested in the part on India than that on Russia. For me the latter seemed much more of a rehash of what has been written very well before, but he has an astounding news sense. I shall certainly try and bring all these books with me, though it's going to be difficult.

As for my leave. You see the difficulty is this; men ballot in groups according to the month of their arrival. Most people here came in June, about 25% in July and only 6 of us in August. The result is that if the numbers allocated in say, April, happen to be low, then a lot of June or July people are put back into the hat in the next month's ballot. It is only when all of the June and July people have gone, perhaps at the rate of 10 a month, that we 6 go into the hat. It seems unjust but any method is unjust. The saving grace is that the next allotment to this Depot may be much later, possibly even 65% of our strength. Guessing all round, I should say June or July, unless the war ends or I get shifted to an O.C.T.U. in England before then.

For the holiday with you a Sussex village sounds nice, though I would rather you chose where you would like to go this time. It will really be you who need the change of scenery. Don't choose for me a place with too much regimentation, please, otherwise I shall black the landlord's eye or otherwise assert my reaction to Army discipline.

Don't mention the leave business to Ma. I agree.

By the way, with regard to your newspaper articles on "Absent Husbands." I really don't feel very "psychological" about returning to you. For one thing I haven't been away really any time compared with these blokes mentioned. Secondly, your letters and books have kept me closely in touch with home and you.

Thirdly, there is no doubt as to whether I love you, when you have made such a job of our lad and stood by me. But I remember what you once said about men taking too much for granted when they come back after an absence. I won't!

Fit in your twin beds – if you want to! Make one of them a bit bigger than the other, however. After all, even if you decided I'd changed for the worse and wanted a divorce you'd want the beds some

---

378 Presumably *People on our Side* – see page 367.

time or other. I'm merely giving advice on a technical problem, in a purely theoretical way. Purely!

Now I must go out of the sun and do a bit of economics. I'm a bit browned off with Henry Clay, but it's interesting sometimes to see how the liberal professor's mind works.

Incidentally, I shall not be able to see J again, for military reasons which I cannot tell you but which anyone could probably guess.

Yours with lots of love,

Ron

It is six days before Dad writes again, which is a Saturday:

254248 W.O. I R.V.Spathaky A.E.C.

HQ 15 (Br) Convalescent Depot, B.L.A.

14.4.45.

Dearest K,

I hope and believe (knowing you) that you have reassured yourself about the anxieties you mentioned in your letter of 5/4/45. You represent home and duty all right, but it's the kind of duty I would give my ears to exchange for the present one! As for the other business, please let's consider it a thing of the past until I come home, then you can get out the traditional rolling-pin. Agreed? The essence of the matter is that I love you only and I have now realised the old truth that one cannot play with fire. Work is going better and apart from a certain physical malaise due to rapid changes of weather I hope to forge ahead with it.

It will perhaps be a certain guarantee if I reserve my contacts with the local populations to men.

I only talked about separate beds etc. because I thought you might like some time to find out whether I am now a sex-stained monster or pretty much the same as before.

Let's meet in London by all means. I think I shall be able to tell you when I am due to arrive. It will give us a nice new slant on each other to meet in a new environment. I hope we can make it a good hotel. We've met in too many drab joints!

As for the sex-love side, it isn't a snare and a delusion, when one is doing something natural and not trying to perform something which doesn't and cannot lead anywhere i.e. with another woman. That's the act that leads to ashes and corruption. That's why I shall resist the Spring-time rising of the sap from now on, difficult as it may be when you're pretty vigorous and full-blooded as I am.

By the way Spring has definitely started around here. There is a wood I can see from my window which has primulae, daffodils, anemones, hawthorns, violets and an attractive pale blue flower like an anemone. I've been doing a bit of French botany recently. The above are des coucous, des narcisses sauvages, des anémonies, de l'aubépines et des violettes.

Incidentally, the civilian rationing problem around here doesn't seem to get any better, particularly as regards soap, cooking fats and meat. There will be a terrible legacy as regards these French and Polish children one day. Can <u>nothing</u> be done in the U.K.?

Lots of love,

Ron

The 'scrape' that Dad said he had been in, the 'the mess I got us into', is still a mystery to me. I know no more about it than is contained in these letters, as neither Mum nor he ever mentioned the incident. But then they almost never talked about the war at all.

A loss of £15, a month in which his work 'suffered badly', something about a printing machine – it seems that Jacqueline was central to the business and Dad writes a couple of times about having learned his lesson about 'playing with fire'. And then: "I shall not be able to see J again, for military reasons which I cannot tell you but which anyone could probably guess."

When he writes on the Sunday of the following weekend Dad says it's only been "a day or two" so a letter may be missing, but more likely he's lost count of the days:

254248 W.O. I Spathaky A.E.C.

HQ 15 (Br) Convalescent Depot,

B.L.A. 22.4.45.

Dearest K,

Sorry you haven't heard from me for a day or two. I've been travelling rather a lot and even now I haven't settled down and organised pen and ink and the other necessities.

The place I am in is less friendly if anything than the others I have been in lately, but it is more of a built-up area so that there is something besides cows and hedges to look at, though those are becoming very pleasant at this time of year. The foliage covers up the traces of destruction a little.

At the present moment I am sitting up in bed in a big old barracks, writing by a poor electric light. There are five other chaps in the room, which is an unusual thing after having my own room for quite a time.

Regarding your pre-pre-natal problem, I think all the former arguments hold, especially the one about having children who are not too far apart in ages. In fact I have wished many times that artificial insemination existed (for married but separated couples).

As soon as I get settled down I'll write a long letter about all this, but the conditions are not too good for writing at the moment. Someone is telling a story about Americans and the others are in various stages of undress. So I'll close.

Love, Ron

Talk about losing count of the days – Dad writes just the next day and says, "Excuse silence":

254248 W.O I Spathaky, A.E.C.

HQ 15 (Br) Convalescent Depot,

B.L.A. 23.4.45.

Dearest K,

Excuse silence. Considerable changes in the offing. Writing soon. In meantime could you do me a great favour. There is a chap in a town

I once stopped in who lent me a bike on several occasions and I ruined the tires completely. I am told that they are fairly easily available at the moment in Blighty. Be a darling and buy him a pair, with a puncture outfit, pack with all your expert knowledge without markings on the outside & send to him. His address is:-

M. ROUANET,

COIFFEUR

BRUAY

808 RUE VICTOR HUGO

PAS-DE-CALAIS

The size of the tires is: 650B cm. balloon-type. This is a continental measure, by circumference. If you ask in a shop like Curry's etc. they will say what measure this corresponds to.

Lots of love, Ron

| For M | XXXXX
P.S. It's a lady's bike.

Chapter 19
Belgium

A week later Dad is based in a new location, and a couple of snippets in his next letter suggest the Netherlands, although it later appears that he is in Hasselt, Belgium:

> 254248 W.O I Spathaky, A.E.C.
> 15 (Br) Convalescent Depot, B.L.A.
> 29.4.45.

Dearest wife,

I think I can now say with confidence that I shall get my leave in July, unless anything unforeseen (either favourable or unfavourable) happens.

There is lots of work to do in this new place. At present I wish there were 28 hours to the day. By the way, how do you like the new string I have added to my bow. "Ik kan nu ein bitje nederlandsche spraken." You see I've been making good use of the Teach Yourself series which I bought.

The town where I am is very clean and the houses are relatively untouched by the war. You could still eat off the floors and domestic architecture is of a very high level, rising superior to that of England in a number of cases. They have a technique of employing thin overlapping bricks or tiles on the outside of the house which gives the whole thing a very delicate appearance, like the ruling of a number of very thin and accurate lines on a piece of good paper.

The people are better off than others I have seen, though no doubt they have had their troubles.

My convalescent helpers are working marvellously at the moment, though they have very little prospect of self-advancement at this place. It's a sheer case of men who have been through bitter experiences finding joy in work which is creative. The man who does all my quartermastering, Pte. Fincham, R.A.M.C. is a London bus-driver, a proper cockney, who has a real flair for educational organising and leading discussion, but who will just as willingly lead a discussion, chair a committee on Reconstruction and Employment, or draw a poster for a language-class.

This evening I slipped into the local cinema to see "Pride and Prejudice," with Greer Garson (somewhat hidden behind French <u>and</u> Dutch subtitles). It seemed to be excellent in spite of its restricted local background.

We haven't had any mail for five or six days so I can't answer the points you will have no doubt raised in your letters to me. I hope the war ends soon. The crust of sanity which forces people full-tilt through their day's work in all sorts of circumstances wears very thin indeed sometimes.

I want so much to see you, to tell you of the strange things I have seen and to hold you so close to me.

Love,

Ron

Dad writes again on the Friday, five days later:

> 254248 W.O I Spathaky, A.E.C.
> HQ 15 (Br) Convalescent Depot, B.L.A.
> 4.5.45.

Dearest K,

Very sorry to send another letter in pencil, but I have just mislaid my pen. Last night about 30 nurses were billeted on one floor of our Sergeants' Mess, turning us out of all our rooms at short notice very inconveniently. We have now moved back but I can't lay my hands on anything at the moment.

Just got in from the first discussion we've run in the local town. The subject was "Is Europe Doomed?", the place the local YMCA Canteen. Attendance was 28, the two speakers privates from the Condepot, the chairman Sgt Foster, A.E.C.[379] and the YM sold us tea and cakes. The level of discussion was excellent. Speaker after speaker, including a couple of Czechs, a Walloon (Belgian) and an American on pass from the front line reiterated that Europe is not doomed, if the forces of the Resistance that have united during the Liberation reunite against poverty, disease and exploitation.

On Friday evening I have a French and a Dutch class organised at the same place, taken by local girl students. I don't quite know how they will go, but I have considerable hopes about them. The Army is going to pay civilian teachers in this theatre of war.

This is on top of a vast network of ABCA and other activities which we are undertaking at the present time; employment information committees, two newspapers (including one printed by a local firm), 4 handicraft workshops and two libraries. This afternoon I paraded 350 of the men, pinched 3 of the P.T. Instructors and marched them out to a couple of fields on the edge of the town. We started off with a brief discussion of the news and then split up into groups and played football, soft-ball, rounders and generally enjoyed ourselves. Though the blokes were Grades I and II (i.e. convalescents who have not been out of hospital long) they seemed to stand the march very well and joined in uncommon well.

My Staff-Officer visited me this morning and seemed very pleased with everything that is going on. I'm afraid there has been a heck of delay over the application for a commission, since I have had to get evidence of date of birth. It should be going off any moment now.

Well, K darling, I'm longing to see you and tell you all the gentle things I've longed to tell you for such a time. The gap in mail occasioned by our movements has been disturbing, but I am hoping we shall be together at least for one glorious week, in June or July. Perhaps it won't be too long then before we are reunited permanently. Please try and keep the old demon lust at bay until it can turn itself loose on me! I can tame it! On my part I'm taking part in more interesting work than I have ever done and you need have less fears than at any time since I have been abroad. If any woman presents herself to me

---

379 Ted Foster – see pages 348, 351, 355 and 372.

on a golden platter (which is vastly unlikely in this country) I shall require medical certificates from her, evidence of good character, financial documents proving complete ability to sustain a family by herself, and then I'll take out all your letters and read them and tell myself I'm the lowest basket that ever walked. In other words I'll try my very best – and I think I'll succeed. I know you try and succeed (often ?*!%) as well.

All my love,

Ron

Four days later Dad writes again. It was VE Day, the day the Allies officially accepted the Germans' unconditional surrender and celebrated the end of the war in Europe. It seems strange that Dad did not mention the "great news" until the last two paragraphs of his letter, and even then he can only say, "The end of the European war may come at any hour." Perhaps he was writing on the previous evening and dated the letter in anticipation of posting it in the morning.:

254248 W.O I Spathaky, A.E.C.

HQ 15 Br Convalescent Depot, B.L.A.

8.5.45.

Dearest K,

I haven't ignored you for 10 days, honestly. The one dated 26.4.45 has only recently arrived. I have written at least every 4 days. It makes me wonder if some of the mail got lost during the move.

I haven't seen Butler's statement on teachers and Class B[380] – hope it's true! I have quite a large organisation here but it's very much at

---

380 "The essential details of Bevin's demob plan had been announced back in September 1944… One in ten servicemen were known as the Class B 'key men'. They had been in pre-war civilian occupations – coal mining, building and civil engineering, teaching, the police service – which were considered so vital to reconstruction that it was justifiable on grounds of national interest to discharge them ahead of the rest of their Release Group… Butler's two months in office [in Churchill's caretaker government that followed the break-up of the wartime coalition] were almost exclusively concerned with holding to the target figures for demobilisation against demands for acceleration from MPs eager to impress the service voters." (*Demobbed: Coming Home After World War Two* by Alan Allport, pub. Yale University Press, 2009.)

the whim of a set of blockheads who don't know what they want. The A.E.C. higher up certainly do know and they gave us a lot of support but it's regarded as a convenient but rather risky way of filling in the training programme by the powers that be.

The photos have arrived and they are lovely. How thoughtful of you to include a whole stretch of the coastline from the Undercliff out towards Seaford. It has come out quite clearly hasn't it? Michael looks a big chap but rather subdued in all of them. What or who was he browned off with?

I've just heard that my leave is likely to be in June and not July which is a good thing. I fancy it will be about the middle of the month, something like the 17th-24th, though I don't know for certain.

Reference the tyres. In view of the export difficulties, is there any chance of you sending some to me and me posting them to the bloke concerned? If you could do this it would be a very great service to a bloke who was extremely nice to me all the time I was in France. They would need inner tubes with them, but if that particular measurement of tyres is not available than I shall have to get him something else.

I should also be very grateful if you could get my brown shoes mended and sent to me, or buy me another pair to send. We are returning to peace-time dress here and you've no idea what a swell I've had to become. I go about the Depot in collar and tie and I have a battle-dress at the tailor's being bespoke. A pair of brown kid gloves would go down well and an A.E.C. dress side-hat, but I imagine you would have great difficulty in finding those. Sorry to mention all these things but I've never bothered with them all the rest of the time I've been in the Army – now smartness is beginning to count again in my eyes.

You see we are actually in the town here – once again for the first time since I've been on foreign service. There is an allied training-unit not far away with British instructors and we dare not let them down.

The news is wonderful, isn't it? The end of the European war may come at any hour. I haven't moved from El Alamein to Berlin, but I've moved from El Djem to here, even if it was via Lincolnshire, and I'm fed up with it all. I've seen enough to know that human beings are marvellous in their similarity and their diversity. Anyone who doesn't realise to the full how both of these apply doesn't know the human race. Now I'd like to study a few people a lot instead of a lot superficially – two or three would be best, you and two or three more, preferably small people.

And I'd like to spend quite a lot of time preventing another war – or delaying it.

Lots of love,

Ron

XXXXXXXX

Dad is clearly keeping closely to the routine that he mentioned, of writing at least one letter every four days:

254248 W.O I Spathaky, R.V.

HQ 15 (Br) Convalescent Depot, B.L.A.

12.5.45.

Dearest K,

Letters from you are rather sparse; even a bit short. I forgive you in view of the heat. Or is it having too many lovers to write to? If it's the latter I excuse you also.

It's funny to look out from the large window of the terrific apartment where I live and see the wisterias on the town car-park, the half-Flemish, half-French buildings, and "see" them really for the first time. Everything I have looked at, human and inanimate, has had the big black letters WAR written on it, for so long. Now the gnats in the sunshine seem to be waltzing to a different tune, a hint of peace to come and even some prosperity.

I've given 300 odd blokes an afternoon off this afternoon, to go to the Belgium versus England football match. I'm even going myself, for the first time since the war began. I've been criticized for not attending up to now, but as these few days are obviously not meant for hard work I'm breaking the rule.

The night before last this little town celebrated in the streets with bands, processions, banners and a ceremonial appearance of "de Langeman" (the long man) a huge armoured figure of legend who represents the spirit of the town. Everyone, Belgian, French, Dutch, British, American and Czech, celebrated by dancing round-dances in the streets. I also drank innumerable red lemonades at Les Trois Pistolets (De Drie Pistolen) and felt quite vicariously drunk.

I know there will be much work to do before Japan is defeated but one can't help feeling much better about things.

Suppose we shall switch over to the Educational Release Scheme in the near future. This should provide much more satisfying work. I am slowly learning how to balance educational administration with teaching work. We have enormous offices in this place, so different from the tents and cellars where I've worked before. In the office alone the desks are marked thus as you come in the door:

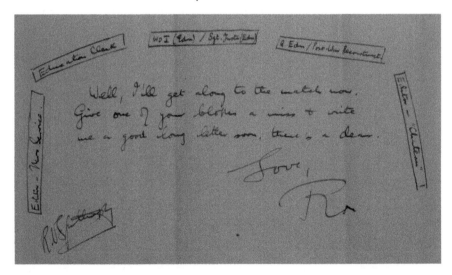

Well, I'll get along to the match now. Give one of your blokes a miss and write me a good long letter soon, there's a dear.

Love,
Ron

The next day he wrote again:

254248 W.O I Spathaky, A.E.C.
HQ 15 (Br) Convalescent Depot,
B.L.A. 13.5.45.

Dearest K,

I am hoping that when I get back to camp with this letter there will be one awaiting me from you. I have not had one now for 4 days, as I don't know yet your reactions to the end of the war. How did Hove and Brighton celebrate? I hope you didn't get tight and led away into "bad company" – most company seemed pretty free on the Continent during those days.

During the last couple of days there has been a heat-wave here. I have been in Hasselt and luckily the Albert Canal runs quite near. Yesterday afternoon Sgt. Demer A.E.C., myself and the P.T. staff walked half undressed as far as some locks which make a big basin or artificial lake. The Belgian landscape is very flat but well-wooded with young trees and the farms look quite prosperous. What with electric train rails, long lines of firs, the geometric dock installations and the straight motor-road, there is a futurist air about the place, completed by a swarm of low-flying Forts[381] bringing prisoners back from Germany. We added to it still further by clearing V's with our bodies in the still, clean and sunlit waters of the Canal.

Later on in the evening, having provided myself with a 24-hours pass, I took my tooth-brush and shaving kit and hitch-hiked (sorry I'm getting mixed up what with Flemish, French, English, Italian, German and the heat!) along the main autobahn in the direction of Eindhoven. About ten kilometres south of the border, however, I remembered that I hadn't got any Dutch money, so my passing whim of passing the night on Netherlands soil was ruled out of order. So seven kilometres from the border I got down near a pleasant little township called Groot Barrier (Grande Barrière) which has an enormous zinc-works nearby. I put up in a spotlessly clean café for the night, danced a few steps with the stupid-looking daughter of the house to the wireless, talked to her a bit in French, Flemish and English, in none of which we got on very well, her French and English

---

381 American Flying Fortress planes.

being lousy and then I went to bed and slept till 10 a.m. Breakfast consisted of two eggs, bacon, bread and butter, coffee and rhubarb jam – the cost 35 fr. Belgian, which as far as I can make out is 4/6 (175 to the £1). This was my end of war celebration – not bad. I set out at 1030, having read the study pamphlet on The New Education Act and a bit of a Flemish history of Hasselt I had given me. Now I'm a few miles down the tree-lined heat-laden road going back to Hasselt.

I'm writing this in a marvellous corner-house inn, of the type in which Belgium seems to abound, with shining beer engines, polished tables and cool tiled floor.

I don't feel like going further, since it's so cool in here and so hot outside. But I think I ought to push on a little and see a little more of this pleasant if somewhat rectangular countryside.

I'm told an order has just come out saying that all men who came out in August <u>must</u> go on leave in June, so the situation improves. I thought of letting Sgt. Foster go first of the three of us, as he is going to get married, but he has been a bit rude occasionally lately, so I've a good mind to let him roast a fortnight or so longer, as I'm due first of the three.

So it looks as though I may be giving you a big kiss some time between the 4th and 10th June.

Lots of love,

Ron

XXXXXXXXXXXX

The next letter we have is dated on the Monday, eight days later, and postmarked another two days after that:

W.O I Spathaky, A.E.C.

HQ 15 (Br) Convalescent Depot, B.L.A.

21.5.45.

Dearest wife,

Thanks very much for your two letters posted on the 10th.

You will be glad to know that I <u>may</u> come on leave any time now, though I think it will be put off until the 8th or 9th of June. A few people have been taken off the roster because they are due for release in a few weeks in any case. This has brought me a bit further up the list. If I am sent on leave suddenly I will write a letter straightway, but I am afraid I shall almost certainly arrive before it.

Work has been extraordinarily hard during the last month or so, chiefly because the C.O. has been extraordinarily formal and autocratic towards my department, exacting punctilious observance of all details of regulations but taking very little account (in my opinion) of the administrative difficulties of a unit that is constantly changing size and even physical shape. But I have gained certain points, at the expense of much preparatory work for interview.

This week-end, like last one which I described to you, I have fled the barracks and the town to see a few fresh places, and faces. I am writing this in a place called Winterslag, a mining town not far from the bulge of Dutch territory in which Maastricht stands.

It is a revelation in Belgian life. In France the mining districts are grim and poverty-stricken. One sees often a miner going off to a full day's work with a "thumb-piece" of bread and mustard.

Here they seem superficially to have suffered very little from the occupation, though of course there are deep injuries beneath the surface. The town is a garden-city, unlike the "corons," the endless strips of blind-houses, of the Pas-de-Calais. I have not been here long enough to see the inside of a typical miner's house, but I searched about yesterday to see if there was a poor quarter and couldn't find anything but fine houses and apartments, in a setting very much like Patcham but with much more space and four or five times as many trees and shrubs.

The young people who cycle about these boulevards are well-dressed in smart summer clothes, though some miners I saw coming out of work looked pale and ragged, like all others I have seen.

I believe many of them are on strike at the moment, due to a fresh wage-scale which the companies tried to force on them suddenly. It's not so easy to find out things in Flemish country because apart from the language the people are more dour on first meeting than the French. They soften out later in most cases.

———

Yesterday the three of us in the A.E.C. received a note from the Corps asking whether we wanted to serve:

a) a year, b) two years, or c) indefinitely after the date of our release group.

We all replied by return saying we did not propose serving beyond normal date of release at all, though I added a rider that if my wife and child could be brought to live with me I should not mind considering serving one year beyond my release date. This letter was not binding in any way, but I thought I might consult you about the idea. If it were anywhere around here or in Holland it would be a real change, the army would have responsibility for housing us at W.O. I's scale (which is pretty high) and probably for feeding us. Personally I don't feel that putting a young boy among foreigners is bad for him. The evidence I have seen suggests that they settle down better than adults. And of course the A.E.C. is responsible for the education of married soldiers' children! You wouldn't like me to train you as a teacher, would you?

All this is pure speculation of course and I'm not particularly keen on the idea, but I must admit that I like adult educational work much better than the teaching of children. Children rely on so many stories and fantasies for their progress and I am not too hot at making up stories.

Incidentally I should still have reinstatement rights if I did another year.

The great disadvantage is that the Army, with the best will in the world, has to move you around occasionally, though they would have to provide the transport.

On the whole I think it would be better for me to get out as soon as possible, because I still think the Army environment cramps (and even tries to crush) its intellectual workers. I feel somewhat less inclined to read now than ever before, though that is partly due to the lack of authoritative reference books on the things I am interested in at the moment. Though your papers and pamphlets are of terrific use to me in my work I should like to get to grips with some piece of original work, involving continuous study and research over a period of years. It is only in civilian life that I could do that.

A crowd of little boys from the big commercial hotel have now come and settled on the garden table where I am writing, so I can't concentrate very well, but I'll do me best!

They are now telling me in excited Flemish about the English and the Americans, especially the negroes, whom they have seen around here, ending up with "De Engelsche zijn beter," "The English are better."

The hotel-woman is preparing an open-air dance-floor for this evening, under the laburnum-trees, but I expect I shall have to catch the train back before they start dancing. If you were here I should stay until the last minute and then walk back through the night!

Lots of love to both, Ron

The next letter we have is dated eight days later, on 29th May, and postmarked the 30th:

254248 W.O I Spathaky, A.E.C.
HQ 15 (Br) Convalescent Depot, B.L.A.
29.5.45.

My dearest K,

I hope my mother's visit went down alright. I have been very lax about writing to her for months now and she is justly annoyed, not knowing how busy I am at present.

My leave date is definitely fixed now, for the 25 June. That means I shall arrive home about 10 (p.m.) o'clock on the 26th. Please tell me by return how that affects the begetting business. If, as you say, the 4th is the vital day, then presumably the 2nd is as well? As I shall still be at home then we ought to be able to get <u>something</u> moving, even if we break a bedstead or two in the attempt.

I'm afraid my gross lascivious ideas of leave at the moment, if "untouched by gentle civilised influence," would involve a couple of days in bed to start with. But don't be alarmed, I'm still amenable to reason – somewhat! However, I have faint hopes that you may feel like that too. I gather, incidentally, that roughly the 16th to the 20th is the time <u>NOT</u> to come on leave. Right?

But I am talking glibly about arriving home, and forgetting our arrangement about the hotel. If you will book at the Kingsley for the 26th (night of) and the 27th (night of) I will come straight there. It's no use me telling you what time I shall arrive at the station because I don't know. Any last minute information I can pick up I will send on, but don't be too alarmed if I am 24 hours late because it has been known for that to happen through bad weather. One party was even delayed for 3 days, but that was while ops were still on and would not happen now.

I have sent off two birthday cards to the children.[382] If I can find anything suitable as a present for Michael I will bring it with me. Has he got a good lorry? I imagine he has.

I should explain that I have offered to put my leave off from the 15th to the 25th because Sgt. Foster, A.E.C. is getting married on his leave and had been calculating on the 15th. Then he was put on the 25th so I swopped. His only brother will be on POW leave till the 21st after being in an Austrian POW camp, so I couldn't very well do anything else, could I?

On Saturday I was invited to a Belgian wedding in our town of Hasselt. The church is quite near our barracks so I slipped out for a brief time in the morning to see the ceremonial blessing at the big parish church. Then in the evening I went to a posh reception. The Belgian Minister of Supply, a member of the family, was there and a set of as merry bourgeoisie as could be found. The Belgian bourgeoisie is not so snobbish as the British, however, at least in local circles, and I got on very well with everyone, being considerably petted as the only Englishman there.

The family, which includes 3 girls from 15-21, extremely devout, healthy, cultured and rather lacking in oomph, lives in the same street as the barracks. That is how I know them. No danger! In any case you'd

---

382 The children must be my cousin Helen and me. My birthday is 26th May, so he was a bit late; Helen is ten days younger than I am.

be amazed and possibly relieved at the religion and respectability of all Belgian families that I've met. They have a highly developed chaperonage system and girls are never left alone with a male stranger for one minute. Madame or big brother is always unobtrusively but steadfastly there.

Now I must get some preparation done for tomorrow. Lots of love,

– Ron

XXXXXXXXX

To Mich :- XXXXX

DADDY

[Then in red crayon with very large letters:]

DADDY

The next letter is dated six days later:

254248 W.O I Spathaky, A.E.C.

HQ 15 (Br) Convalescent Depot,

B.L.A.

4.6.45

My dear K,

I can now confirm that my leave will be starting on the 25th i.e. I shall leave here on the 24th and arrive in London some time on the evening of the 25th. I do hope you can manage to come up to London, if it's only for that one night and we have to return the next day. I would love to meet you where I can see you as <u>you</u> and not as part of the Cree-Spathaky household. However I will abide by what you say in the last of your letters that I receive before the date I start off from here. If I don't receive any precise indications I shall go up to town in any case and phone home from there. We come in to Dover or Folkestone so in any case it'll be much quicker than coming along the coast line.

The day before yesterday I started two days' leave and took the 7.15. a.m. train from Hasselt to Brussels. Arriving there at 9.30. I went to the Officers' Shop to try and persuade them to sell me a beret and a soft shirt. I failed in both, but met inside the shop Colonel White, V.C., Chief Education Officer 21st Army Group. He is our A.E.C. boss in all the district ranging from Oslo to Munich, by way of Copenhagen and the Ruhr.

He asked me if I was in for a commission seeing I was in an Officers' Shop. I said, "No Sir, I applied for one two and a half months ago and the application is still in the Depot, because of a technical hitch in connection with confirmation of my date of birth."

He said, "Nip into my car outside and I'll take you to 21 A Gp and set the thing in motion."

The result was that four hours later I had passed a board of officers and was recommended for an interview with a Brigadier half-way down the monkey-ladder. The only thing is, the application for me to have the interview came <u>from above</u> not from <u>below</u>. So perhaps I shall be walking about with suspiciously new pips on my shoulder before long. If Gordon has any useful hints about buying of kit I shall be pleased to hear them. I presume we have enough money to live on during any period intervening between my last pay-day as an O.R. and my first cheque as an officer. If not please let me know immediately so that I can take measures. You know of course that one doesn't <u>lose</u> pay on the deal. The only hitch is in the arrangement for payment of your money through an agent or some ruddy thing. You might ask Gordon how he's paid, when you see him, and if my present banking account is a "recognised instrument."

I fancy that as a W.O. I, I go up to full Lieut. straightway but I couldn't be certain on that point. In any case I shall be an S.O. Edn. so presumably I shall have staff-pay over and above my ordinary officer's*[383] money. Anyway I've been assured by the Colonel that it doesn't make any W.O I's position ~~work~~ worse financially (sorry – that <u>was</u> a bad slip of the pen – hope it wasn't Freudian!)

I've just written to Ma and told her I shall be home on the 25th. Afraid there was nothing else to it since you had already taken the first step. In any case, as you say, we could hardly hide this trip if our grapplings and heavings lead to anything. (Oh boy, don't I just

---

383 This asterisk suggests Dad intended a footnote, but there is none.

think of those grapplings and heavings! Please be good from now on, whatever you've been like before!)

I'm assuming you'll tell me in your next letter what the chances are of begetting. I shall be very glad if we do, although what I want to do <u>urgently</u> is to make love to you and know you again, but I'm afraid this is one of those occasions when I want to do my loving as quickly and as deeply as you'll let me and lie back and have a long talk afterwards – but we'll <u>take your speed</u>!

The election business is a bit disconcerting after the class-collaboration of war-time but we are doing our part here. I frankly disbelieve the story of 90% of Service-men having registered, either for a proxy vote or for postal ballot-papers.

I <u>know</u> only 40 to 50% have got on the register because I have the figures.

It's a pity this isn't more widely known. Why the heck they didn't do it by compiling it on the basis of O. i/c Records' next-of-kin addresses I cannot imagine, unless someone was keen to sabotage the thing by arguing that a few Jamaicans or Canadians might slip on to the Register.

We have large posters out in the Depot, marked:-

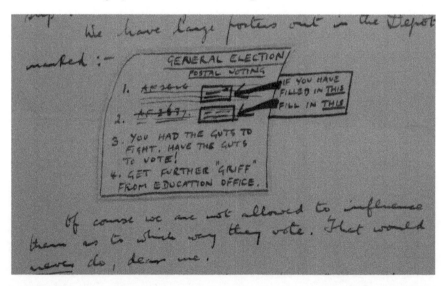

Of course we are not allowed to influence them as to which way they vote. That would <u>never</u> do, dear me.

Well, if you have any other "affairs" to confess to me, better compile your confessions now. I shall be home soon – though you're forgiven from the start, as I hope I shall be, as long as you've now cast off all other tow-ropes. If you haven't, well, I've got a big hand and you've got enough space to smack.

XXXXXXX – Love – Ron

The next letter, dated eleven days later on Saturday 16th June, is headed by a rather cryptic postscript, as 16th June was a Sunday:

(Next day, Thursday – a bit better – RVS)

254248 W.O I Spathaky, A.E.C.
HQ 15 (Br) Convalescent Depot, B.L.A.
16.6.45.

Dearest K,

Please don't be disturbed if this letter is badly written. I am coming to the end of a day in bed with a slight attack of something like 'flu. As several of the staff are down with it and I have had no signs of a cold I think it is more likely to be something we have eaten. It's nothing to bother about, anyway, and I have rather welcomed the change. Naturally the numbers of patients in the Depot is pretty low these days and there is not a great deal of work.

Two days ago I crossed the border into Helmond in Holland, where I had an interview with the Brigadier commanding this area concerning my commission. He agreed to recommend me. I still have one interview, the usual three-day affair called a "Wozbee" (War Office Selection Board).

Looks as though I have another year to serve in the Army, unless I get out in Class "B." They may be in such a mess that they speed up Class "B" releases but so far they have only talked about putting Groups 1-26 into Class B.

Incidentally an order from 21 A.G. came around last week saying there is a shortage of German-speaking personnel in Germany, so I dashed my name in for that. If that takes precedence it means that I shall stay in Europe, which is something.

You explain about the house very clearly. Nothing to be done, as far as I can see, except keep an eye open for something for one of the two parts of our family. I'll write to the Chairman of the Brighton Housing Committee soon and ask what they are going to do about it… or else.

Sorry Michael has been ill. If ever anything serious happens to him you can telegram the War Office (Compassionate leave Branch, I think, but I'll confirm that) and they'll send me home. It counts as a privilege leave.

Afraid I feel a bit weak in the fingers now! (If you ever get the chance read some funny stories by Damon Runyan. They're damned funny.)

Love to both
Ron

The next letter is undated, but a mention of Friday 13th points to a date some time before that. The long gap is, of course, explained by the long leave from 25th June (a Monday) for about twelve days. The letter implies that Dad arrived back on a Saturday, was given the Sunday to recover, and then set out for his War Office Selection Board (WOSB) on the following day, when the letter was written, Monday 9th July 1945:

254248 W.O I-Instr. Spathaky, A.E.C.,
W.O.S.B. c/o 49 R.H.U.
B.L.A. (for a letter posted up to
Fri 13th incl.) Thereafter old address.

Meine hochliebste Frau,

I arrived back in quick time, allowing even for a tea at Emiel's. The Depot had closed down and moved to a little place called Sonnis, near the village of Helchteren, north of Hasselt. Various odds and ends of staffs were collected together in a former S.S. barracks in pleasant sandy pine-wooded country. Nobody was doing a thing except sun-bathing.

They gave me the Sunday to recover from my leave, which I hardly needed to do (I have put on weight in England and filled in the hollows in my cheeks). Then I set off (with a Dutch driver) on a long ride to the W.O.S.B., first to Brussels where I had a good lunch in the W.O.'s Club, then to Termonde (Dendermonde), a small town 20 miles east of the capital. This is the collecting point for candidates. There are very few here at the moment, except a rather gloomy sergeant of the Desert Rats and a dozen Corporals and O.R.'s

There is some talk of us having to sign on for another year if we want a commission. I shall only do so if I am booked for Germany and married quarters are available.

The actual interview doesn't start until the day after tomorrow, so once again I am sitting and waiting, which is fairly pleasant in this hot weather, I must admit.

———

The leave was the best ever. I enjoyed rediscovering and discovering interests with you and Michael. I also enjoyed the physical side of it, enormously.[384] Remembering how full of pent-up desires I was when I left Hasselt I can compare the present state of my mind very favourably with the former. I am calm, confident, full of interest in everything I see and hopeful for the future. You did everything that could be done to make me happy, in every sphere, and I am very grateful.

Do you know you are <u>very</u> attractive "in the altogether" nowadays? Don't go to the other extreme from plumpness and get thin, will you?

———

Sid Morris sends his comradely regards to you. He recommends me another excellent book for when I have finished "Rainbow," by Vassieliewska.[385]

---

384 I calculate that the day Dad returned from leave was exactly forty weeks before my sister Jean's date of birth.

385 *Rainbow* was the title of the English translation of Wanda Wasilewska's novel *Tęcza*, pub. Foreign Languages Publishing House, Moscow, 1943.

It is "The Road to Calvary" by Alexei Tolstoy.[386] He says it is a work of genius, whereas "Rainbow" is a work of high talent and enthusiasm. I shall try and get a French translation of it.

How is the German going? I must write you a few sentences now. This will spur you to buy a good dictionary (preferably a Duden or Harrap's) in order to understand it.

Gestern bin ich zu einer Befreiungsfeierabend in Dorf Helchteren gegangen. Es war sehr interessante. Viele Dorfeinwohner trugen bunte Kleider. Nach alle den Leuten die zu Fuss oder auf Wagen fahrten kamen ein "Jeep" mit britischen R.A.F.-flieger und Unteroffizieren gefüllt. An dem Rück des Jeeps halten sie mit Kreide geschrieben "Stimmt für den Arbeiterpartei" in grossen Buchstaben![387]

––––––

The C.O. of the 15 Condepot is being demobbed on Friday next, so I shan't see him again, thank goodness. If only I could say the same of the R.S.M. I should be very pleased. However, I cannot spend more than a couple of days in his company so things look pretty bright.

Incidentally as I moved along the main road today I believe I passed the whole of Jaap van Cleef's unit moving eastward. The letters on that address he gave are evidently P.H.Q. If you reply I should put

Cpl. J van Cleef,

    Police Headquarters,

        R.A.F. Security Police etc.

As he has lost all relatives he ever had he would probably be quite bucked to have even a couple of lines from an Englishwoman. I don't think he has ever met one – certainly not for long.

Goodbye now; do lots for the cause. Draw Mrs. Huzinga into your Wives' Circle and thus help to solve the child problem. That's the only way.

––––––––––

386 An English translation of the trilogy Khozhdeniye po mukam (1935), pub. Boni & Liveright, New York, 1923 (sic).

387 Yesterday I went to a liberation evening in village of Helchteren. It was very interesting. Many of the villagers wore colourful clothes. After the people who arrived on foot or by car came a "jeep" filled with British airmen and NCOs. They chalked "Vote for the Workers' Party" in big letters on the back of the jeep!

Lots of love,

Ron

XXXX

XXXX

No doubt because of the WOSB, Dad did not write again until he was back at the Convalescent Depot at Helchteren eleven days later. This letter is one that was kept in its envelope, and Mum used the back of the envelope to make some notes, which are shown here after the letter:

W.O I Spathaky, A.E.C.
HQ 36 Beach BRICK,
B.L.A. 19.7.45.

Dearest,

Thanks for your <u>very</u> nice letter, which I found today at 15 Condepot on my return.

When I last wrote I think I was still at Termonde. The transport from there only managed to take me to Eindhoven in Holland, where I spent 52 hours hanging around A.E.C. HQ and looking at the local town which is certainly the nicest I have seen from the point of view of domestic architecture.

The women in the town are extraordinarily good-looking and well-dressed. They remind me of you.

Today a truck came for me and whipped me back to the isolated S.S. Barracks in Belgium where 15th is dying on its feet. This is a mere formality, because I have been posted to Calais (oh agony!) but I suppose I shall only be there for a couple of days before my commission comes through. Then they will have to post me elsewhere, possibly to Germany, since it wouldn't warrant a high personage like a 2/Lt in Calais!?

I am very anxious to get my new job now and all this travelling is most annoying – it's a pure waste of time, pay, public money, petrol and transport.

I hear release of teachers under Class B started yesterday, but I'm told they are only releasing initially 3,000 altogether, those whom the authorities ask for. Another aspect of it however, is that a lot of teachers are refusing Class "B." This may cause them to extend the Release Groups which they send out. If they do I think I shall take the Class "B" and risk it, but am afraid it won't affect me for some time.

As to professional prospects, I suggest we put an advert in the Times Educational Supplement, with the wording enclosed, as an experiment. I can't find a copy of the T.E.S. here, so perhaps you wouldn't mind looking it out in the Library and sending it in – if you agree with the idea, that is?

All for now. Lots of love and more desire than ever,

XXXXXX Ron
for M XXXX
M for . . . .
H for . . . .
D for . . . .

On a separate slip of paper, Dad has written the advertisement:

Army Education officer, expecting release May 1946 seeks interesting post in adult education. Hons. B.A. (French & English) 2nd class. Diploma M of E. Secretary of University Union 1936. 5 Yrs. teaching in Central School (French, English, History). Considerable experience in teaching Current Affairs, vocational information, administration of large Edn. Centre (incl. Handicrafts). Education under difficulties with combat division in N. Africa & Italy. Practical knowledge German, Italian, Dutch. Willing to go abroad. Age 30. Box No.....

Mum has clearly been to the library, as Dad asked, and has noted on the back of the envelope, in her recognisable handwriting:

Times Pub. Co. Ltd.
Printing House Sq.
Blackfriars,
London E C 4
15/2 per annum

After a little cogitation I worked out that 15 shillings and tuppence was exactly fifty-two times 3½d., so almost certainly she was working out how much it would cost to take the Times Educational Supplement for a year – typical of her eagle-eyed budgetary management.

Chapter 20

2nd Lieutenant

The next letter is also undated, but from the address and the existence of an envelope postmarked 22nd July 1945 it would appear to have been written on that date.

254248 W.O I Spathaky, A.E.C.,

15 (Br) Convalescent Depot, B.L.A.

[BOTTOM
RIGHT]

| IF NOT DELIVERED FORWARD TO
| 2/Lieut. Spathaky, A.E.C.
| c/o H.Q. (Edn.) 21 L of C[388] Sub-Area
| B.L.A.

Dearest K,

You will see by the above address that I have got through the W.O.S.B. successfully. It was a pleasant three-day interview, made a little more gruelling by the heat. I was surprised to find that on agility and strength I was well up to the standard of the infantry candidates. I did very well in the boxing, wielding a murderous left on a young L/Cpl for whom I felt sorry. He had never touched gloves before. I fancy I was below infantry candidates on judgement of spatial differences, weights and times in the solving of combat problems, but that is hardly to be wondered at. When it came to discussions it was a busman's holiday.

I have scrounged the information from a regular W.O. I that I shall probably have to wear the hated one pip for a couple of months, possibly as long as four. On the other hand, thanks to a certain A.C.I.,

---

388 Normally 'Line of Communication'.

I can squeeze my pay up to about 19/- a day plus Staff-Pay. The new regulation says that I can choose to draw W.O. I's rate of pay plus Officer's W.S. Increment (1/- instead of 6d.a day). Thus it will still be an advantage to draw this scale even when I am full Lieutenant. I don't think you will have to make any special application concerning your allowance, though it may be as well to ask. In any case I shall not be 2/Lt. till about 18 July 1945, unless it's backdated to the last day of W.O.S.B.

I shall settle all kit questions this end, so I shan't need to bother you, I hope. I'm in the lucky position of having two fairly good battle-dresses, one of which I think I can keep. If I get my overcoat cleaned and altered I think it will pass muster.

Unfortunately for our conjugal bliss, rights, pleasures and duties I shall not be coming to England for an O.C.T.U. since my commission is Immediate Emergency. But we have the next leave at the end of 3 months to look forward to.

Der Wetter[389] ist hier furchtbar heiss, deshalb müssten wir noch mehr Energie an der W.O.S.B. ausgeben. Ich kann nicht vier Seiten schreiben, so heiss ist es. Kein Brief ist von dir an Termonde (48 R.H.U.) angekommen. Ich hoffe einen bald zu erholen. Schreib schnell, Liebling!

Ich habe den Roman "Regenbogen," von Wasilievska[390] in Brüssel gekaufen. Wunderbar realistisch! Jetzt halb gelesen.[391]

I shall probably be wandering about for four or five days, trying to find someone to report to, so please don't worry if my letters don't refer to any points you raise. I shall get your letters in due course – maybe immediately.

Don't worry about the signing-on business; they didn't even raise the point with me at W.O.S.B. A number of other candidates up to Group 26 were asked, however. So I shan't have to commit myself at all. This will give us a chance to study this matter of quarters in Germany.

---

389 An unusual mistake for Dad – it should read "Das Wetter…"
390 *Regenbogen über dem Dnjepr*, by Wanda Wasilewska, pub. Steinberg, 1945
391 "The weather here is terribly hot, so we need more energy at the W.O.S.B. It's so hot that I cannot write four pages. No letter has arrived from you at Termonde (48 R.H.U.). I hope to recover soon. Write quickly, darling! I bought the novel 'Rainbow' by Wasilievska in Brussels. Wonderfully realistic! Now read half."

You certainly re-captivated me, dear, during the leave. I think of you with considerable warmth and admiration. The snooty little walking-out kit is "just the job," including the pill-box hat, though I'm afraid I should be there to give it the <u>perfect</u> tilt – i.e. slightly forward and a bit to your right. Kolossal! There are some damn smart women on the continent, and I'm afraid Englishwomen compare unfavourably with them on the whole, but you compare very favourably with the smartest and were the smartest I saw in England.

Love Ron

Dad wrote again four days later:

W.O I-Instr Spathaky, A.E.C.,

HQ 36 Brick, B.L.A. 26.7.45.

Dearest K,

I've just received your last three letters all in one bunch, coinciding with the terrific news of the Labour victory in the election. It shows how one can underestimate the political sagacity of the British people. I hoped in a vague kind of way for a simple majority, but never dared to hope for the complete majority they now have. It will alter the world situation in every country. We can get to work with the feeling that our efforts during the past years have not been wasted and planning now becomes a real possibility. I haven't heard the complete results of how the Party has done yet – not too well the rumour says.

Very sorry to hear about the fall from the bike and the consequences. You must be very careful in your double capacity as wife and chief producer of man-power of the family!

A great deal of Calais here is very depressing. The north of the town is completely destroyed, but where we work and live there is no destruction, only dinginess and dirt.

The job is a thousand times more interesting than a Condepot, but the area I cover is colossal, stretching right over beyond Lille to unit locations it will take me days to reach. I am going out to them soon by motor-bike.

On Sunday afternoon, the only time they take off at this HQ, the Sergeants' Mess took me by truck to the famous pleasure resort of Le Touquet. Unfortunately there was a very high wind there, but I couldn't easily imagine that it had been anything else but a sort of third-rate Eastbourne. Unfortunately also in playing rugby on the beach I completely smashed my civilian glasses, so I am now wearing one of the two horrible pairs which the Army provides. I am trying to get the other army pair fitted with shell frames, but so far I haven't managed to get around the town for even ten minutes during the day when the shops are open.

There is no confirmation of my promotion from the C-in-C yet, but it may come any day. I'm acquiring a few staff here and there, not too satisfactorily so far. The main job is to open a study centre in Calais during the next fortnight. Naturally I have to indent to different authorities for everything; labour, furniture, fittings, stationery, telephone, fire-points, locks and keys, timber, tools, etc. etc. When I have actually set it going the position may be a bit easier and I shall be able to leave the rather elderly, French crippled clerk in charge, but at the moment I have to do nearly everything connected with the opening, then find the instructors and persuade the men to come.

Of course a considerable part of the new scheme is compulsory, but units in this area are so regularly engaged in technical work that I fail to see how many of them can implement the thing in working hours. But I now begin to get a bit of authority behind me and shall stick out for some of them to do it.

We live in a small house in the main street, which forms the Sergeants' Mess. I have a room to myself with a rather grandiose civilian bed (double) which would cost £30 at present prices. The collection of junk and boxes in the rest of the room is rather at variance with the bed and rather fine futuristic light shade. I'm working up the courage, after nearly a week here, to give it its first clean-out. Luckily it was fairly clean when I came and doesn't seem to catch the dust very much.

I haven't heard any more from Bernard,[392] except a letter when I got back to 15 Condepot at the end of my round-tour of Flanders. He

---

392 Bernard Stone, Dad's pre-war teaching colleague.

apologised for losing sight of me at Brussels on our way back from leave. I replied immediately and I hope we are going to keep in touch from now on a bit better than we used to. One letter in about four years is not very good, is it? I find myself drawn towards him much more than in the old days, when I think I hadn't enough time to appreciate his ~~whistful~~ wistful qualities (bad error, there, what?)

Any news of the great production race? Lots of love to both

Ron

Three days later Dad writes again:

> W.O I-Instr Spathaky, A.E.C.,
> HQ 36 Brick.
> 29.7.45.

Dearest wife,

The above address is quite permanent (so far as Army addresses go!). It is the name of the sub-area HQ at Calais and actually much more usable for correspondence purposes than the Condepot, where things were likely to go astray. I believe I described the town a little to you in my last letter.

Congratulations to both of us on "hitting the gong" as the Army crudely and expressively puts it. I shall await confirmation with bated breath. The first experiment was so successful I think you need have little fear about a second one! Have you solved your other minor sexual problems, in any degree? I'm almost too busy to have any sex urge at the present time.

I've got my new Study Centre fixed up (almost single-handed) and hope to open next Monday 6th. It will comprise handicrafts as well as the usual embellishments, so staffing is going to be the big problem, but the units in the Area are co-operative in spite of the highly technical nature of their work. I doubt if we can run the full Education Scheme in this Area within even six months, but we can get a modified scheme going within 2 months and if the higher authority live up to even a part of their promises as regards equipment books and material I can forge something that will be of use to the men.

I shall have to use quite a lot of paid French staff, male and female. That is a bit of a nuisance, because they haven't the same incentive of promotion as soldiers but luckily I can control them from the linguistic side.

In reply to your "Financial Column" I believe I dealt with the points in a letter which has crossed post with yours, but in case I didn't make my point clear re the opting for WO's pay, here is an idea of the principle.

<u>Pay</u> and <u>Allowances</u> are two separate things altogether. If I opted for W.O. I's pay (16/6 p.d. compared with 11/- p.d. – an obvious choice) I should receive 2/Lt's allowances and other perquisites. I believe I should go on receiving WO's field allowance, but the difference between that and an officer's is so small that it doesn't level up the balance.

A job in Bristol I applied for has already been filled. I'm just going to fill in the forms for another one at London University. I don't suppose I have much of a chance of it, but they may be looking for young blood and it's good to aim high!

I now hear that I may get my leave quicker than I imagined. I am certainly in the right place for it – the leave port for the whole of B.L.A. The Transit Camp which takes the leave allocations is one of "my" units. Our HQ controls it from the Admin point of view. But I mustn't raise your hopes too unduly about that because I don't feel justified in applying for leave when I am just expanding a new job. The time for that will be when I have built up my organization and stabilized it a bit in the hands of a capable staff.

Write me lots – and please send the papers!

Love –

Ron

In case it is not clear, the second paragraph in the above letter refers to Mum's confirmation that she was pregnant again. We can now place my sister Jean's conception to the period of his leave from 25th June to 7th July.

They probably spent the first night or two in a hotel in London (though that was never confirmed in Dad's letters) and the rest of the time at home – that is Mum's parents' home – at 49 Hangleton Road, Hove. Jean was born on 13th April 1946, exactly forty weeks after 7th July 1945.

The next letter we have was dated ten days after the last one and written in pencil:

2/Lt Spathaky, A.E.C.

HQ 36 Brick. B.L.A.

5.8.45.

Dearest K,

Congratulations on the presumed event once again!

Just a scribble to tell you my promotion has come through. I am also a wearer of –

1. The 1939-45 Star

2. The Africa Star

3. The Italian Star

4. The France/Germany Star

I look like a ruddy field-marshal! What a joke isn't it? I'll tell you the story of how I captured the Algiers Palace Hotel one day. Single-handed!

Lots of love

Ron

P.S. Please send pyjamas, brushes & papers!

– Love R

A week later Dad wrote enclosing a cheque and a memo to their bank in Brighton authorising her to cash it:

2/Lt Spathaky, A.E.C.

HQ 36 Brick. B.L.A. 13.8.45.

Dearest wife,

Today I'm having my first spell of leisure since I came here about three weeks ago. I'm spending the day alternatively in the Officers'

Mess and in the HQ building as Duty Officer. Yesterday I had a long journey to Ghent for a rather surprising interview. You may remember that while I was still at the Condepot a compulsory return was asked for of all German-speaking personnel, in connection with Intelligence duties in German. I was called at 12 hours' notice and asked if I would transfer to the Intelligence Corps, with a prospect of considerable promotion. There was still no question of signing on for another year, so don't worry. The only thing that was asked me was what my possible attitude might be later to a job (possible a civilian one) on the Control Commission for Germany, in the section for re-education of the population. I said that I would only consider signing on for another year at a later date if families were allowed to come out. The answer was that they certainly would be, probably next year. Of course that wasn't an authoritative answer, but as I haven't taken any binding action it was quite interesting. Anyway, I signed the forms for this new job, so I expect the Education Corps has seen the last of me when I've wound up my affairs in Calais. I'm afraid the prospect of tackling a practical problem instead of always teaching others tipped the balance against the notion that I should stay in my own job. And with the speed-up of the demob scheme I've got the feeling that the Release Education Scheme isn't going to be the thing it was cracked up to be, unless they work damned quickly. Do you approve? How'd you like me as the Grand-Duke of Oschenleben-Oberstein or A.M.G. Commission for Bomberg-Pfinkelstadt?

Of course it's now up to the A.E.C. and I.C. to fight for my body, but I'm in a position to not bother much which happens.

———

Even if you've been feeling a bit lethargic about letter-writing, yours of the 3rd was very bright and energetic. You needn't be afraid of lethargy, my darling, you've too much vitality in you at bottom. Perhaps it's just a temporary transference of intent from the Plough to the dormant Seed. Your periods of dullness, I believe, have similar origins to mine. I suspect that we are both a bit uneconomical in our planning of relaxation and don't choose some form of recreation which will be really a release. It's probably connected with the fact that we delight in sexual activity. That <u>does</u> bring complete relaxation.

I am full of desire again, like you, and the old memory-files more regularly bring to the surface images of ourselves – in the act; sitting with you astride me on the bed in London, or you lying on your back on me (a particularly enticing posture, because of the possibilities for caresses), or, slightly more on the subdued and emotional plane, seeing you slip off your dressing-gown at the bedside in Brighton and realising that you were not tired of loving me but were thus proposing more bouts of love.

I revel in making love with you, because I think we understand, however imperfectly, the basic relationship between the sex act and the other things we want to do. The fact that we haven't been able to do many of those other things is no reason for not enjoying the love. Also, however frantic we both become, there is none of that artificiality which Aldous Huxley describes in his new novel "Time Must Have a Stop,"[393] as of "two cannibals in Bedlam." The self-exaltation is always fairly well related to the other person and it doesn't degenerate into masturbation. Though I'm inclined to think (and condone the fact that) a certain large percentage of the sex-act is just solo pleasure in one's own body.

But even when you're doing your famous "ride" upon me, which I like you to do so much, you do it <u>very</u> gracefully and don't cut me out of consideration. You face is lovely to see, with the pleasure and friendliness of it.

Hope I'm able to see you again before I go to Germany. It's such a way to travel back.

———

I've got together a small staff here. I may even be able to work things so that they can carry on if there is a gap when I am shifted. One is Andreé Zénard (29) a girl clerk and typist, who also does a little teaching for me. She is (or claims to be) a leading member of the Resistance in the Pas-de-Calais. I say "claims to be" because there <u>are</u>

---

393 Pub. Chatto & Windus, 1944.

such things as "double traitors" over here and one has to be 100% certain. She's quite good looking in rather a heavily cosmetized way, engaged to an officer who works in Boulogne and seems to be home more than at his post. She speaks excellent German.

The second is an elderly man, a M. Guerlin, a cripple in both legs, whom I can't fit in with the work much at the present time because he can't nip about in the way that educational organising demands. The other is the janitor, a plain elderly good-natured man from the centre of France (from Moulins, near Vichy), whose honesty is only equalled by his anxiousness to make himself useful.

I'm getting an English Lance-Corporal as a clerk tomorrow. I don't know what he'll be like but at least he'll provide the military touch – the knowledge of Army staff-work and "the monkey-ladder."

———

In answer to some of your points. I've had a pair of shell frames made for some Army spectacle-lenses, so I feel quite presentable again. They were quite cheap too.

I should delay the ad. to the Times Edn. Supp. for a short time.

The business of becoming an officer is certainly still a bit ticklish. This HQ hasn't a supply of the various forms to get an allowance paid to you, but I'm getting them from another unit. If your allowance dries up suddenly send an S.O.S. and I can send you some of my advance of pay (£18-15-0) which I have an Advance of Pay-Book to draw. I believe Grigg[394] once said in a reply in the House, however, that arrangements had been made to go on paying new officers' wives whatever happened. Try and bully them a bit by quoting that. I shall make arrangements if possible for you to draw exactly the same amount as before, until I have practical proof that I need more.

Thanks a lot for the papers. They've just come. No letter from my Mother since I came back from leave.

You should see me with my 4 medal-ribbons up. Disgusting! I've got to have passport photos done so I'll send you a couple. *Vanitas vanitatum.*

---

394 Sir Edward Grigg, MP, who had been Under-Secretary of State for War.

Look after the little bear, won't you? Tell him Daddy will take him to Holland and Germany one day, and we'll have boats and oars and paddle in the sea at Stumpfberg-Westochterplatz (or thereabouts).

XXXXXXXX – Love and lust

Ron

The following note was written in pencil and clearly in a hurry:

2/Lt Spathaky, A.E.C.

HQ 11 L of C

B.L.A.

22.8.45.

Dearest,

Dead-tired with travelling once again. Shifted to Malines, leaving my lovely Education Centre at Calais in the hands of a Corporal and the three French.

Had any difficulty re allowances? If so I can now send you something, though I have not settled the whole thing.

How's the work, and M?

Love,

R.

A longer letter followed three days later:

2/Lt Spathaky, A.E.C

HQ 11 L of C, <u>B.A.O.R.</u>[395]

25.8.45

Dearest wife,

I'm very glad your spell of work turned out well, at least up to when you wrote. Has the G-I Joe shown any signs of interest or had he definitely dug himself in?

---

[395] It was actually on this date that British Army of the Rhine replaced British Liberation Army as the name of the British forces which were to run the military government of the British zone of occupied Germany.

For goodness sake soft-pedal on all this "getting old" business, you little chump. If you feel you're getting *[old]* in the mid-twenties, what do you think I feel in the first year of the thirties? The answer is, I feel experienced enough to tackle the problem of living moderately correctly for the first time and <u>when you get to my age</u> (!?X%) you'll feel the same. You goose! We'll solve the problem of the house somehow when I get back.

You'll note I've suddenly been moved from Calais, this time to Malines.[396] It was a bit of a blow because I'd just got the machinery ticking over for the first time, though I hadn't had the time to build up much second-string leadership. I had actually to leave a Corporal in charge, a university student without really the necessary background. But as my new HQ is in charge of the 36 Brick, with about 20 other places, I can still keep a potential eye on it – at a distance of about 250 miles!

It is all rather distressing because having visited France again I realise there is something about it that I love. Poor France! Bomb-scarred, without transport, its streets ill-swept and its houses unhygienic, it's the country of a wonderful people. The French are a nation of wits and philosophers, laughing somewhat darkly at their own sorrows, full of personal independence and capable of romantic depths of personal feeling. When I talk to some of them I think of some beautiful girl (imaginary) who was given a marvellous education, including an education of the tastes, and at the age of 25 was set to work at some numbskull occupation like carting brushwood. "Intelligence chained to the wheel," that's the French.

By contrast the Belgians are prosperous, well-fed and somewhat placid. One feels that their conversation in a town like this, only 30 miles from Brussels, is one series of complaints that things have not returned completely to normal. But perhaps I do them an injustice here, because obviously Belgium has its problems, as a little fellow living in a world of giants.

Unfortunately the A.E.C. Major for whom I work here has brought me up to HQ so that he can get out to the sub-formation HQs like 36

---

396 Malines/Mechelen is in the Flemish part of Belgium, between Brussels and Antwerp and about 20 km from each.

Brick and L of C[397] Sub-Areas and give advice on the spot. This means I sit in the middle of a large building and work out fairly complicated but fairly remote organisational problems, receiving callers and answering enquiries from HQ L of C and from "down below." But I've had my period of joyous organising at Calais and I shan't kick for a time at doing this desk job. I have a reasonable staff, which is something.

When I have reduced the thing to manageable proportions I shall teach the Sgt. A.E.C. (ex-Winwick Hospital!!) the job and persuade the Major, who seems a reasonable sort but a bit of a bureaucrat, to let me out to have a crack at problems on the spot. I picked up my motor-bike riding again while I was with Brick, so I feel potentially more mobile than when I was in that static limbo, the Condepot. (I hoped I would never get into a Condepot again when I was at 114 and now I repeat that vow! What a "shower"!)

This HQ works very long hours, but the Mess in which I live is palatial and the food excellent. I am tasting comfort for the first time since I have been in the Army (apart from one or two brief experiences when I was with you). It is in a suburban chateau, with marvellous gilded rooms and huge grounds. The company however, is much less formal than in Sergeants' Messes, so far. I find much less pressure on me to drink when I don't want to.

At Brisk living conditions were extraordinarily haphazard and carefree, because of the lack of requisitionable accommodation in Calais. I was without a batman and couldn't even get a bed in the proper mess. In fact it was France all over. Here things are calm and stately and I can do with it for a bit. It will give me time to think. Then I can plunge into the organising battle again – on the spot.

Well, K, you haven't written to me much while you've been away, but I suppose that's because of the new-found professional responsibilities. I hope you get over them quickly enough to put me together a really long letter.

I don't know why you should have bad dreams about me. Have you any suggestion as to why? Is it the prospect of my return or what?

---

397 Lines of communication.

It may take time for a couple of your letters to catch me up, but meanwhile love the Little Bear a lot for me and take three big kisses for yourself. See you when 4 months from my last leave has elapsed. Love –

XXXXXXXX Ron

Four days on, Dad writes again:

> 2/Lt Spathaky, A.E.C.
> HQ 11 L of C, (Education)
> B.A.O.R. 29.8.45

My darling Kath,

There are one of two phrases in your last letter "of which I would hear more." No doubt they refer very logically to something in my last letter but one, but taken by themselves they seem to indicate something deep travailling in that practical little head of yours. For instance you say, concerning "settling down,"

"I began last week to wonder if that was what I wanted."

Quite a common war-time feeling, but what exactly would be the "unsettled" alternative? Presumably you had something in your mind, even if it was a vague glimpse. Then

"I know you can help me fight the dangers of domesticity <u>but I don't want to take any risks yet</u>."

What does the underlined part mean? What do you therefore consider is the best way to avoid dangers of undue domesticity?

Or did you mean that by venturing out and working you are combating the shut-in feeling? Finally

"I want to see a bit more of the world."

I can understand that feeling. The world is "colossal big" and living in just a few towns one forgets most of the others, but do you mean you want to see a bit more of the world now, or when?

However, these feelings are perfectly normal in all of us, Now I've got into commissioned [*sic*] I see the sham and triviality of much that goes under the name of staff-work. Majors never seem to be a good investment for me. Quite honestly I am afraid after a few weeks that he will begin to become annoyed with me because I could honestly do all the work he does and my own in a morning and spend the afternoon and evening doing some real organising. So far I've not found out how to get away from this desk environment in the "third rung" of the five- or six-rung monkey-ladder but in a week or two I shall break out and start moving things.

Old Frances Armstrong (mariée Moore)[398] certainly has turned out some good stuff, if the bits you mentioned to me are anything to go by. Strictly between me and you, she and I were quite fond of each other in a sentimental adolescent way at one time but Dave Moore came to the University and so captivated her with his pathetic slav eyes and gorgeous Bohemian manner and gentle voice that the friendship never developed very far.[399] He was one of the most genuine men I've met and I didn't remember till yesterday that I'd been told months before that they were married. I believe Chang Ashford told me when we once visited him in London. Do you remember – the big dark-haired sailor bloke who had come sixth in the Civil Service exams in the whole country?

But I've digressed badly from what I was saying about staff-work. The difficulty is this. I've begun to get a bit of an obsession about this Army Education Scheme. I feel that I've acquired a particular technique for getting people to work with me. Maybe I'm "line-shooting" but when I left Calais the old crippled Frenchman who kept my records blessed me, the decent old janitor saluted me and said he was sorry, the girl typist cried and the Corporal I had kidnapped from another unit swore he'd found some pleasure in work for the first time since he'd entered the Army. And what's more they've kept the place going since I left, which is extraordinary for a Corporal and three foreigners!

---

398 Frances Armstrong (1913-1984), a Sheffield teacher, poet and activist in the National Union of Teachers, was a life-long Communist Party member, having joined the Party in Sheffield on May Day 1935. (Graham Stevenson's *Compendium of Communist Biographies*, with thanks.)

399 Presumably *Bill* Moore, who was described at his death, aged ninety-seven in 2008, as a Sheffield local historian and peace campaigner and a member of the Communist Party for more than thirty years. He and Frances married in 1937. He served in the Army between 1940 and 1946 (Ibid.).

Now I believe the big shots in the Corps are going out like ninepins due to the Release scheme. Ergo I may get some rapid promotion if I'm careful and don't overplay. I know you wouldn't suspect me of undue ambition, but if I could land a Major's job before my "A" Release I could alter the face of things. Even as a 2nd Lieutenant in Calais I was responsible for the Education of all British troops left in France, admittedly not more than about 5,000 but you can see what an amount one can do.

Have you thought at all about this possibility of coming out to see me, and in fact living somewhere out here? If you did I would then raise with you, much later, the question of signing on for another year, and trying for bigger fish still! But perhaps I'm counting my chickens before they're hatched! I may get a push down the ladder in a short time.

Well, so much for this evening. I must do a bit of reading and meditating for tomorrow.

Please write me lots and don't hesitate to tell me about any troubles in which I can help, even if you don't think they would interest a mere man – and a mere husband at that. We'll sort 'em out. Lots of love, Ron.

P.S. If your allowance dries up you will find money is being paid into our Bank. More re this!

The next letter we have is dated over a week later. Mum and I had clearly been visiting one of her aunts, probably Kitty:

> 2/Lieut. Spathaky, A.E.C.,
> HQ (Education) 11 L of C,
> B.A.O.R. 6.9.45

Dearest K,

Just received your two Bridlington letters together, full of the light and sea-air of the Yorkshire coast. How I wish I could be there to see you revel in it. Michael will be quite a traveller by the time he's ten.

When I was down at Calais I went down to the beach on the few occasions, but there is a narrow strip for the whole population, not even completely cleared of mines and bathing in the sea is not really a comfortable experience because one might run into a piece of wire or steel from one of the obstacles which line the beach still in their grotesque thousands. Here at Malines (Mechelen) there is only an indoor baths, but I had the misfortune to choose ladies' day on the only occasion on which I went there so I haven't solved the exercise problem yet. Still I mean to go again as soon as possible.

This job is very interesting but there are two points which rather overcloud the prospect at the moment:-

1. I begin to doubt very much whether the Scheme will get under way in time to meet the needs of the release classes 23-29, which are the big ones. Therefore we may be reduced to catering for the permanent cadres of the expanded peace-time army.

2. I gather that I may still be whipped away for that Intelligence Job I mentioned to you. If it were Political Intelligence in Germany, however, I should probably welcome the last-minute change.

About my leave, I believe it will start on the 2nd November. They've really played a dirty trick on me in connection with that. Most people managed to get in a second leave within the first year of landing, *[but]* I didn't. Then they suddenly made a rule that 4 months should elapse between leaves – after so many had had their second. Still I'm used to these injustices by now. It's the kind of thing a soldier's wife might get a question asked about in the House, but naturally if one's name were dragged in one would suffer in some other petty way. You see the first leave was drawn by ballot, those who landed in June balloting together, those in July the same and so on. Then vacancies were allotted to units according to their strengths. By this system I was nearly the last man to go on leave in 15 Condepot. Already people were going on their second.

The system adopted for the second was a bit hazy. Units were given to understand that two leaves in one year were permissible, as long as "reasonable time" elapsed between the two. Quite a lot of personnel took a fortnight or three weeks as being reasonable. If I had stayed at Calais I should probably have gone on the 5th Sep. Then they brought in the 4 months rule!

So in short the promise has not been kept of 2 leaves a year! I am most browned off about it because there are so many things I want to discuss with you, including those remarks I re-quoted to you from your own letter. They rather surprised me in a way, not so much by their sentiment, which is natural enough after a couple of years of absence, but by the way they were put. We must put them to the test of a good argybargyment and find out what underlies them.

I have gained a lot of new insight into things during the last few months and I shall want to take a hand in replanning our future, which I have selfishly left to you in the past, like most practical problems connected with our joint affairs.

How's the old tummy these days? Any signs of "things to come" yet?

I still think Belgium is a bit stuffy and complacent after the hungry heroism of the poor old French. You know, Kath, I love France with an affection which was kindled in my school-days and which has been revived by everything I have seen during this journey.

The Resistance Movement is something of which one will hear when the story of the war is really told. At the moment, as I believe I have told you, the people who did great things in the localities are often brushed aside (temporarily) by the stop-gap administrations. An example was the young woman who worked in the Study Centre at Calais. She was 29 and has been an accredited "section-leader" of the secret army. She spent the vital years of her life, from what I could gather, gathering information about V1-sites in a little isolated country district to which she had been assigned. Those were the very years when she should have been marrying herself off. Now France has very few young men available, and she works as a typist for the British Army, in which most of the men of her age are married. She suffers badly from malnutrition, like all the French. Yet she speaks two or three languages fluently, has the French "baccalauréat" (Higher School Certificate) and could tackle a responsible job. Her parents are old and are still in the evaluation area because their home in Boulogne was blasted to bits.

I felt really sorry for her but couldn't do much to help except take her a few odd rations occasionally. Britain owes her a big debt yet Englishmen don't seem to be able to do anything. What she really needs is a chance to get over her experiences, which included interrogation by the Gestapo and even suspicion by her own people who at the time of the Liberation were not in the know as to who was in the Resistance.

Still, I left before anything could be done for her, though I would still like to help.

Incidentally don't be alarmed by my talk of a Frenchwoman. She is from another world compared with the girl I got mixed up with in Bruay. This one is genuine Resistance, whereas the other had the queerest political ideas.

In any case a complete country now separates me from Calais. And I've too much interest in what we've manufactured between us and in your mental welfare to have anything but rather admiring memories. I just wish I had been able to help.

Well, now for a read of the "Daily Worker" and other papers I have just received. Thanks a lot.

Lots of love,
Ron.

XXXXXXXXX
XXXXXXXX

We resume the sequence of Dad's letters eleven days after the last one:

As before,
17.9.45.

Dearest wife,

I hope you haven't worked yourself up into <u>too</u> much of a stew about where to have the new "x" (the unknown quantity!) It's difficult to know what to advise, at this distance, but it is news to me that you felt uncomfortable at the nursing-home the last time. If you really did then surely your mother could spare some time to help you on this occasion. We know from long experience that political and social goes on and on. No-one is so important that they can't give a hand to important family affairs now and again. After all, though the war is over, I am still forcibly separated from you and can't be there to help, so I expect someone on the spot to help as a social duty.

A release for me by next March seems a little problematical, but I may be able to get my leave around that time. I am coming on leave, all things being equal, on October 6th, i.e. in just over three weeks' time. I have had to create a bit of a rumpus to get my leave then, but I have succeeded.

That will bring my next leave at about the right time, either just before, to encourage you, or just afterwards, to congratulate you. Which would you prefer?

I have received several letters from the Paymaster and from the Organisation Department, saying that my documents in respect of pay are in order, so I think you can take it that money is now flowing into our joint banking account. I signed a request that the allowance should be paid direct to you, so I presume you still go on using the Allowance Book. Perhaps the fact that the rest of my pay will be going into our joint account will encourage me to save a bit more, since drawing any pay now will involve the physical effort of a visit to the cash office on my part.

About the Army as a temporary career, I am not involved in any way whatsoever, and should do nothing without consulting you, but as you say, the danger might possibly arise of reservations in A.E.C. or the I.C. But according to Release Regs. such reservations can only be temporary, so don't worry about that. I agree that Germany doesn't present a very pretty picture at the present time, and I doubt whether there is a just argument for bringing wives and children to the Continent. Luckily we are not called upon to take an irrevocable decision either way. If there is a chance of renting a house, however, I shouldn't hesitate to do so. It looks to me as if the housing position is so grim that any opportunity in that direction should be seized. <u>I don't want to live with other people when I do come home.</u>

Afraid I have had a slack week as regards letters, but you must admit that it has been unusual since my last leave.

The reason is that I have been out travelling with the Major. Between us we are responsible for Army Education in the whole of France and Belgium so you can imagine that travelling takes a bit of time. I have been to Bruges, Antwerp, Ostende, Ghent, Knocke, Furnes and Calais.

Incidentally while I was in Calais I had a tea in the Y.M.C.A. with Andrée Zénard, the girl who was my secretary at Calais Study Centre. Please don't imagine that I am mixed up with her or in love with her. I have always told you everything about my private affairs and shall continue to do so. But really, K, it makes me feel sick to see such a fine character being starved and crushed, physically and mentally. I think she will go under from sheer despair at her surroundings and the lack of gratitude on the part of the noble allies for what she did during the vital years of her life – for democracy.

She has a small flat in Boulogne, which she dare not give up because she would never get it again. So she lives in a room somewhere in blitzed Calais, in which she cannot do any preparation of meals or any washing. Week-ends she returns to Boulogne to have what sounds like the only <u>meal</u> of the week, with her sister-in-law.

Civilian employees of the British Army get 4.000 frs a month (about £15) and a very poor mid-day meal and what she eats the rest of the day I shudder to think. French ration cards procure a little butter, fats, tea and sugar and sometimes a piece of meat per week about as big as a cake of toilet soap. For one person it amounts to nothing and when one is working in a strange town one can't get out to queue for vegetables, fruit and bread. The result is she is starving and there is just no-one who apparently can help. In fact she is in such a bad psychological state that she no longer cares consciously. But it is taking its toll and she has started to get white hairs in patches, since I knew her. She confessed to me on this brief visit that she has stopped sleeping at nights and has started to take double sleeping-draughts, without success. You know where <u>that</u> leads.

I know that you will think that I have some ulterior interest in her, but I can solemnly assure you that apart from a certain romantic admiration and gratitude there is nothing for you to bother about, otherwise I would say, in spite of your being pregnant, so that I shouldn't have to tell you later.

The C.S.M. (A.E.C.) who has taken my place at Calais has his hands full with his new job but has promised to do what he can (re the ration business I mentioned) but I feel very gloomy about the whole business and feel that I am going to see the agonizing break-up of a fine character, capable of an altruism and self-sacrifice which neither you nor I, Kath, would be quite capable of.

It is very worrying and I wonder if you, at a distance, might be able to suggest something. You see, being in Belgium myself I can do practically nothing as regards her employment. A highly placed man in the Resistance who was going to give her a lift-up and find her a semi-military job has apparently let her down and there are just no authorities in France who can deal with such individual problems. So she just goes typing away and will collapse suddenly.

Sorry to bother you with such things but you are capable of estimating whether a story rings genuine or not and I won't conceal that I do think about it a fair amount in Malines

XXXXXXXXX Love, Ron

The next letter is dated nine days later:

2/Lt Spathaky, A.E.C.
Edn. HQ 11 L of C,
B.A.O.R. 26.9.45

Dearest K,

I am feeling temporarily under the weather myself, but that doesn't prevent me rejoicing in your success in your recent job and the methodical way you are going about the confinement business.

Last week I had to go on a long tour down to Bayeux, hundreds of miles away. The car journey was so exhausting that I relieved the driver for a short time (I have learned to drive a little). Unfortunately I was involved in a bloodless accident near Rouen, as a result of which the truck was damaged, apparently not severely, but just enough to be "beyond local repair." The usual Court of Enquiry has not been held yet, but it is just possible I may have to stump up some money, how much I don't know. They tell me there has never been a case of an officer having to pay at this HQ but I'm hoping I'm not the first. It would put our joint finances back badly to have to stump up £20-0-0, though needless to say I should have it stopped from my part of the pay.

The money for my pay and your allowances should now be going into the joint a/c though the latest thing I am told is that as I have signed for the allowance to be paid direct to you, you will draw it from the P.O. on a book the same or similar to the O.R.'s one. Anyway, the main thing is to go on drawing it from somewhere, either the bank or the P.O. and I shall check up as time goes on. A letter had just come into the office as I was leaving saying something about it but I was too tired to read it.

As my leave starts on the 6th I shall probably get home on the 7th starting from this distance, since the train journey is not quite so convenient as before. I suggest we go up to Warrington for a couple of days in the middle of the leave, but I'm open to conviction as regards any other arrangement. I certainly shan't want to stay there more than 2 days.

It's marvellous about Fanny's kid, isn't it?[400] I must stir myself to send them a note.

Thank you very much for the papers once again. I should miss them terrifically if you didn't send them, because I'm afraid I'm beginning to feel a real European these days, reading the French and Belgian Press and (like many French and Belgians) wondering what those fog-bound people on the little island over the way really are like!

Thank you for not being alarmed at the genuine feeling of horror I have at the fate overtaking another woman. I can see no way out for her and if ever I see her, when I have come out of some well-stocked officers' club after lunch, when she has probably half-hitched a few biscuits and a cup of tea at the YMCA I am silent with confusion, especially as she says "No, you can't help practically. If you'll just help me keep my morale up a bit that'll be good."

---

400 Alec 'Fanny' Waldron – see Appendix 2.

She has given everything in life for a cause and now she's getting the rough edge, in a country where everything is confused.

The Education work is going quite well, but the question of speeding up demobilisation seems to be the prime thing in everybody's mind.

Lots of love
Ron

Love to M
from
DADDY
P.S. Just found out they can't soak me for more than £5. Hurrah!

– RVS

If Dad's leave started on 6th October he must have had barely a week, as the next letter is dated 14th October and written at an airfield while waiting to board a plane to a new posting in the Middle East!

Belgium
as from: HQ Edn 3 Brit. Inf. Div.
M.E.F.[401]
14.10.45.

Dearest,

Please forgive me for the anguish I must have caused you. It must have been the worst leave ever. I do love you and I'll try and make amends for my beastly attitude when I come back.

Andrée asked me to thank you sincerely for the parcel, especially the Nescafé. Like ourselves she is very sceptical of possibilities.

In order to help me forget please write to her and be as nice as you can. I'll never forget it if you do.

Michael is more wonderful than ever. You must have been very patient with him. Remember he's very tiny if you ever feel hasty or like shouting at home.

When I come home I'll take up my share of him with a good heart.

---

401 Middle East Forces.

Waiting near the airfield now. If you hear of a plane crashing don't worry. It wasn't ours. There are less accidents than on the London buses! – Love, Ron

Chapter 21
Egypt

It is two days before Dad is airborne (on 16th October 1945). He writes about the flight that evening:

HQ 3 Brit. Inf. Div.
16.x.45. 2100 hrs.

Dearest wife,

This morning we set off by Liberator transport plane from Brussels. I sat with two huge observation panels at either side and had a splendid view as we flew at great height over the Ardennes, above Dijon in France and down the River Rhone with the castle-like crests of the Alps on our left.

Crossing the Mediterranean, we passed over Sicily, cut across the edge of Tunisia and made a perfect landing at the impressive clean airport of Castel Benito, twenty miles from Tripoli.

Most of the chaps are now seeing an outdoor performance of "Lady Hamilton," but I don't like seeing a film in bits so I am having a good wash and writing this.

I suppose I should feel impressed at being in Africa again, but we did the trip so casually I can't believe we are. Only the familiar voices of the Italian mess-waiters strike a nostalgic familiar note in the mind.

Thank you once again for being so patient with me on leave. I have just written a note (shorter than this) to Andrée to keep her courage up.

We are now waiting for another plane to take us on to Egypt. A night trip will not be half so interesting.

Please be cheerful and don't worry about the squall upon our domestic horizon. You know I love you.

If you will do what you can in the other matter it will help me to forget.

Give a big kiss to Michael for me.

Yours with love, Ron

Two days later Dad is still waiting for his onward flight to Egypt:

HQ Edn 3 Brit. Inf. Div.
M.E.F.
2200 hrs 18.10.1945

Dearest K,

We are still lounging in this fairly comfortable but exceedingly restricted transit camp at Castel Benito. The Naafi is a very well-furnished and supplied building. A large number of the men are playing "housey" in their room. The officers are playing monopoly, reading, eating or drawing up chairs on the "piazza" outside to see an open-air film-show.

I spend my time talking to the young lieutenant, the acting Camp Commandant of Div HQ, who is travelling with me, or, more often, studying Arabic and reading Coates' "Anglo-Soviet Relations" which is one of the four books I managed to carry with me.[402] Occasionally I brush up my Italian with the mess-waiters.

I have surprised myself with the progress I am making with Arabic. In token of this I write you herewith the first sentence I have made up: –

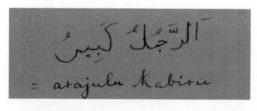 which means "Great is Man!" I suppose in view of my behaviour you will think this is an exaggeration, but I don't

---

402 *A History of Anglo-Soviet Relations* by W P and Z K Coates, Vol. I, pub. Lawrence and Wishart, 1943. William Coates was an Irish labour activist and was involved in the founding of the CPGB in 1920.

know how feminine nouns work yet, so I can't write "Great is Woman" to balance it up.

The plane journey upset my digestion a bit but it was only a temporary inhibition and is already righting itself. The food here is good and plentiful because of the 24-hour Naafi canteen.

Quite a few of the troops in transit here are S.E.A.C. veterans being flown home. They look very tired and very keen to see England again.

I hope you have cheered up since my departure. You are really very admirable, K. In spite of my ingratitude for all you have done for me you didn't raise hell with me when I was on leave – and you would have been very justified in doing so.

I managed to see Andrée in passing through Calais and as I promised you I told her of your new family expectations. Such is man's (or my) deceit however, K, that I told her that you had only just told me. Don't be angry with me. The important thing was to tell her, wasn't it? When I got to Malines there was a letter there which she had written during my leave.

In it she says, "she had realised I had become very devoted to her" and then goes on to say that you have nothing to fear.

"Je n'accepterais jamais de jouer le rôle méprisable et méprisé de la femme qui désunit. Peut-on même envisager un bonheur à ce prix? Les dieux de la morale l'empêcheraient…"[403]

I think you can translate this and you will see what a fine character she is, just as you are. It is a matter of chance and bad luck that I have developed such a strong feeling for her, but she goes to suggest what I have suggested to myself in a slightly different way, that friendship can sublimate love.

She quotes a rather charming saying from La Bruyère:

"Absence or separation, which weaken love, strengthen friendship."[404]

So you see there will be a happy ending to this typical war-time tangle, if you will still be as courageous as you have been.

---

403 "I would never accept to play the despicable and despised role of marriage wrecker. Can one even consider happiness at that price? The gods of morality would prevent it…"
404 Jean de La Bruyère (1645-1696), French satiric moralist.

If in addition you can persuade her to take the steps necessary for her to come to visit you, now when she needs it so much, you will enable me to discharge in one act of affection for her (albeit done by you) what I should bottle-up dangerously inside myself. I should be released emotionally – and you would meet a friend more marvellous than you can imagine.

Love –

XXXXXXXX Ron

The following evening Dad has arrived in Egypt:

HQ Edn 3 Brit Inf Div.

M.E.F.

2245 hrs 19.10.1945

Dearest,

Landed at Cairo-West aerodrome an hour ago and were whisked by truck to a big transit-camp twenty minutes' walk from the Sphinx and the two famous great Pyramids. We shall be off at 5 o/clock in the morning so I shall have to content myself with the view of the latter from my tent.

The white-robed red-fezzed Egyptian waiters are quite impressive. Pity I'm not in a more receptive mood but rather sick at the emotional upheavals I've been the cause of in Europe, so near by plane, so far by boat.

More later,

Love,

XXXXXXXX Ron

Three days later Dad has travelled through Cairo, where the Egyptians were quite hostile, and out to a huge camp which is the British Army's headquarters for the Middle East:

HQ 3 Brit Inf Div.
M.E.F.
2245 hrs 22.x.45

Dear K,

After landing at Cairo-West, we were transported by truck across the seventy miles of Egypt's delta to our present semi-permanent location. The route lay for the first few miles through semi-desert, with the Sphinx and the two pyramids on our right, then through the more opulent boulevards of Cairo.

There is the usual background of striking modernity, a double lane autobahn with trams in a separate channel in the centre, huge private houses and flats decked out in yellows, light greens and browns, vile hoardings advertising Bingo's Pills, beauty products and films indiscriminately in English, French and Arabic and a motley horde of impoverished Egyptians looking like tramps who have invaded the stately precincts of their capital city. Some are in European dress, apart from the red fez or skull-cap. Others, in the miserable thousands, in an oriental motley that defies description. An Army overcoat half covers an old sheet and a pair of ragged pants. Or old military P.T. shorts vie in decrepitude with the faded glory of a blue velvet jacket in the Turkish style.

Ninety per cent of Egyptians suffer from ophthalmic complaints and 75% from bilharzia, a blood disease caused by contaminated water.

The great impression left by Cairo is much more massive than that left by Algiers, with its plastered façades. It must be five or six times as big and is really the capital of the Arab world, as well as the metropolis of Egypt.

I must mention that our reception, as we drove slowly through in big trucks and trailers was a mixed one. Quite a number of men standing here and there at odd points shouted obscenities at us in English. I heard "Fucking bastard pigs," "Get out, you bastards," and "Swine" from three or four of these. There were some, however, who gave us the thumbs up sign and the universal Arab greeting "Saïda" (Peace be with you).

Soon we were out on the long military road which follows the Ismaïlia canal, forming with it the double vertebrae of the characteristic long narrow stretch of peasant gardens and estates probing the desert between Ismaïlia and the north-east.

I cannot describe the dirty, straw-laden, smoky hovels that go by the name of villages, nor the lethargy and despair writ large upon the faces of the people. It is obvious that a positive attitude is found among the more developed wafdists (nationalists) of the middle-classes and presumably among the workers in what few industries Egypt possesses, but one comes into contact first with the teeming millions, with whom there is no means of communication for a European, at least at first.

After a short stretch of pure desert road we arrived at the immense British military camp at Qassasin,[405] about twenty miles from Ismaïlia. This is behind barbed-wire entanglements and patrolled by smart Basutos (S. African negro guards) with fixed bayonets.

We soon unloaded in the middle of this "Buller barracks in the desert" and were issued on free loan with a complete outfit of khaki-drill, stockings, underclothes, camp-bed, chair, washing bowl, bucket and mosquito-net. So I have lost nothing and may even gain by the failure to purchase kit in the U.K. or B.A.O.R.

The environment of the camp itself appears monotonous in the extreme, but the brilliant late autumn sunshine undisturbed by the slightest cloud makes me feel on top of the world physically. Our officers' tents and quarters are excellent, the food light, varied and so far plentiful and insofar as I have met them the A.E.C. officers are reasonable.

I am told that the English and French bookshops in Cairo have among the widest selections in the world so I want to get in at the earliest opportunity.

A number of O.R.s in the Corps are coming out under Class B; in fact some have gone. I shall write to Mr. Cooper[406] and ask what the chances are, and if you get the chance to bump into him or Percy perhaps you could ask.

---

405 Al Qassasin al Qadimah.
406 See page 23.

In the meantime, torn away from my normal interests and from my problems alike I am prepared to sink myself in the work, which should offer more scope than 11 L of C, though I fear it will involve a similar mass of administrative junk.

During the last few months my emotional aberrations have tended to make me more introvert than before, but I can feel myself recovering, even though my emotional life is still disturbed to the very foundations, a condition which will endure for a very long time. I know yours must be as well, so please tell me about how you feel and we'll éclairer la lanterne l'un à l'autre.[407]

I mean to turn my attention to the great events occurring on all sides. That should help, and if I can learn a bit of Arabic into the bargain I should be able to return to you and Michael a wiser, even if a much sadder man.

XXXXXXXXXX Much love, as always

– Ron

Two days later again, Dad seems to be settling in to his new environment:

HQ Edn 3 Brit Inf Div.
M.E.F. 24.10.45

Dearest K,

Thank you very much for the air-letter, which as you see took no time. I hope you have some of my letters. This must be the fourth or fifth I have written since Castel Benito.

We have now started work at this military camp of Qassasin, in the desert not far from Ismaïlia. My present A.E.C. colleagues are two captains who are both very pleasant, one of them being about 34 and the other a very idealistic "pukka" student of the Politics, Philosophy and Economics tripos at Oxford.[408] I preen myself that I can hold my own with them very well as a 2/Lieut. and it is possible that I know the men's reactions to education better. However, I am rather humbled

---

407 "Light each other's lamps."
408 The latter was Norman Scarfe – see next letter.

lately by a knowledge of the mistakes I have made in the past. For instance I feel I shall never make a good spontaneous mixer with the predominantly "haw-hawy" type that rule the roost in messes.

We are also due to have a Major A.E.C. posted to us. I await him with much more apprehension. You know my experience with Majors A.E.C. so far!

The large "other ranks" staff has possibilities. There is a W.O. II who was a Sergeant under old Major Swyer of unhappy memory. A Sergeant whom I don't know and who looks fair, a second one with a B.Econ or B.Commerce degree who looks a bit "unmilitary" (bow-wow!) but may be good at his own instructional work, and a W.O. II who, I understand, is a bit of an old rogue, complete the instructional staff. The Corporal Clerk appears to be a gem and the two other assistant clerks very reasonable.

The brigades in the Division have similar but much smaller A.E.C. staffs of officers and O.R.s and the battalions (regiments) have unit education officers and instructors (non-A.E.C.).

The day before yesterday I went into Cairo by truck to do some business there. The centre of the city is even more like Paris than I imagined. It is huge and the traffic circulation is rapid, dangerous and strident.

I dined at the Officers' Club (run by N.A.A.F.I., not the notorious and fashionable Shepheard's) and found to my annoyance that the bill was about 4/-. The setting of the club, in a resplendent French-style building on the Nile embankment, was luxurious in the extreme and my conscience was very heavy once again when I thought of the French and the starving, scrofulous and benighted millions in the Egyptian villages a few miles away.

When I had finished my official business I visited the bookshops, which give the best selection of English and French books I have seen outside the U.K. I bought a novel by Saint-Exupéry, Terre des Hommes.[409] He is the author of "Night Flight," from which the film was made, and a famous pilot of this war until he was killed.

---

409 Antoine de Saint-Exupéry (1900-1944), aviator and writer. *Terre des hommes* was a memoir of his time as a pilot in North Africa; pub. Gallimard, 1939.

I wanted to get for Andrée a copy of Vercors' Silence de la Mer, the classic of the resistance movement, but it was much too dear.

Renée Shulmann[410] had a cheap MacMillan edition (2/- I believe) which she borrowed from her school. If you could get one from her or from Wards to send to Andrée I think it would be a good eye-opener. It's very hard to get hold of in Pas de Calais and it's awful that someone who led a Resistance group in exactly the same spirit as the heroine of Vercors' book should not have read <u>the</u> book of the Resistance.[411]

I hope Michael and you are not getting on each other's nerves and are building up an atmosphere of family goodwill and tolerance for the future. I know it seems easy for me at a distance, but the people I live with, closer than one lives to any family, are young would-be aristocrats, teachers, clerks, Camp Commandants and the young soldiers of this new division. Still I should be able to regenerate myself by work after the emotional furnace I have gone through, a good deal through my own fault.

– Love, Ron

Dad's next letter is equally long and interesting, as he meets Norman Scarfe, who later became a well-known writer:

HQ Edn 3 Brit. Inf. Div.
M.E.F. 28.10.45

Dear wife,

Yesterday I received your letter posted shortly after my return from leave, well after your first Air-Mail Letter but very welcome. Once again mail becomes extraordinarily important because of the artificiality of life out here inside the edge of the desert. So if you don't hate me too much because of recent experiences please write a lot.

I think you will agree I have sent quite a few letters off. I am not inundated with work so far, so I bear in mind the time in the near

---

410 Renée Shulman – see page 72.
411 *Le Silence de la Mer* by Jean Bruller (using the pseudonym Vercors), pub. Éditions de Minuit, 1942. Mum made a note of this title so may have bought it in Brighton.

future when I undoubtedly shall be, before we move once again and I can sit back and watch the scenery while the "mobiles" work.

We work here from 0800 to 1300, then we rest until 6 p.m. and work till 8 p.m. This afternoon I got out my motor-bike and took Norman Scarfe, the young captain A.E.C., on the pillion to Ismaïlia.[412] The Arab town is the usual slum, but the European part, designed mainly for the large British garrison, is very modern and a little like the French Riviera, with flower-beds in the streets and lots of palm-trees. The town is on the shores of Shalt-el-Tisma, a very large salt lake, like a young sea.[413]

There are several bathing beaches and sun-bathing on them were quite a number of officers' wives. You know, I suppose, that Regulars have been able to have their wives here for years past. The water didn't seem too clean where we were but it was very invigorating and I have had several refreshing conversations with Scarfe, who is an acute observer of affairs and whom I think I can persuade in time to enter into Army Education with a swing. Since he read Philosophy, Politics and Economics at Oxford he is no fool, though as I now see, as a man of 30, that a student of 21 must lack real experience of the political world.

He is in charge, among other things, of A.B.C.A. and "British Way and Purpose" in the Division, so that although I have taken on the more prosaic matters of equipment, materials, tools, books, libraries and finance I shall be able to keep an eye on A.B.C.A. by using my persuasion with him. Incidentally there's no longer any need to worry about me being in charge of the above. I've had such a grounding at 15 Condepot, Calais and Malines, that I think I could run a department store. I think I've found out the Army knack of running these things. First you acquire a big staff, of various ranks, then you ensure that all stores etc. are locked up in all regiments except when they are being used. You see that every piece of wood or metal which is used has a beastly piece of paper corresponding to it in a file somewhere and then you go round jipping up the work of your staff.

---

412 Norman Scarfe MBE (1923-2014), historian, journalist and writer on all things Suffolk.
413 Timsah Lake.

So that I, who could never remember whether I had three pairs of socks or four and a half, don't seem to have much bother in accounting for:

Bits, triangular, spoon, 3¼" (Mark 7218) – 471.

<u>or</u>

Attachments, leather, hammers, soldering, (Mark 3124*) – 92.

Perhaps the strain will increase when the units start indenting in large quantities however. There are many thousands of men in a division, as you know.

There has still been practically no chance of getting in touch with the Egyptians. We seem more hermetically sealed off from them than ever we were from the populations of Europe, and that was bad enough. However, I am punching up my Arabic and will soon know enough to say, "Hello, how are you?"

(Suspended due to intense heat – Sat. night 2230 hrs.)

(next afternoon)

I have had further talks with Norman Scarfe today and foresee great possibilities.

We have had a half-promise that the Division will be allowed to implement the full Army Release scheme and we are now grouping our Brigades for the "take-off."

I am starting an officers' French class at Div HQ during afternoons, three times a week. This will help me to mix with them a bit better, I think. It must be more valuable than standing around in a bar boozing.

Incidentally, we had better try the old system of numbering letters again, in the order in which they are written. I'll call this Letter I (though it obviously isn't).

Please tell me as soon as possible about that worrying little medical problem that frightened us so much. I don't think it <u>can</u> be anything serious but it puts the wind up anyone. Naturally such things can be pretty rapidly cured nowadays, but they are still horrible and subject to all kinds of uncertainty.

I haven't heard from Andrée yet. Perhaps she's decided not to risk troubling our domestic felicity by keeping in touch.

The climate here has a queer effect on me. It both spurs me on to fresh work and ensures that I am very tired when I finish. When I get up in the morning I feel ghastly and I feel pretty bad after dinner at night. In the heat of the afternoon sun I feel jolly fine.

Our AEC Sergeants and WO's are pretty browned off, since the planning stage has not yet been passed and action has not been relayed to them, but we hope to remedy that very soon.

Lots of love,

XXXXXX Ron

Dad's next letter has a postscript inserted at the top:

P.S. Don't bother to use Air-Mail letters. All letters come <u>to this theatre</u> by the same planes. – Ron.

HQ Edn 3 Brit. Inf. Div.

M.E.F. 2.11.45 8.30 p.m.

Dearest K,

Your double Air-Mail letter to hand. I've had one letter from my Mother, but apart from that nothing. Thank you also for your sympathy in connection with my emotional "sickness." You must feel I have precious little to bother about compared with you, though I can say that my responsibilities are now growing.

The aforementioned "sickness" is not really sickness caused by longing or desire but I still feel, perhaps like you, that I have had too little time for a private life of my own, spent among people that I really like. You have given me what opportunity for a "personal life" I have had and it was considerable. Then I was deprived of it and when I met Andrée, who possessed qualities I had not met before, qualities which are different from yours (and from any I may have) I could not help liking her. When I had to leave her in Calais I was genuinely appalled by the situation she was in and I know that whereas I shall come back to you (if you want me) I shall probably never see again a person whom I regard with genuine admiration as having probably the most simple, intelligent and persistent character I have met in my life. She will either have "gone to the wall" under the pressure of the difficulties that face her or she will be married to some odious bloke for the sake of security. So there is the kernel of the matter. <u>You</u> I love and have reasonable hope of having with me; <u>she</u> was probably going out of my life for good at the moment when I came on leave.

You are perhaps right when you accuse me of deceiving myself or quieting my conscience by suggesting there might be someone else you could care for.

About your political strivings – I should no doubt feel at variance with certain methods of presentation of propaganda if I were at home, but I suppose we must bear in mind that the movement we are in is a proletarian movement and will work out its destiny in its own way and using its own language. Both of us, especially myself lately, have been drawn into a petty-bourgeois atmosphere, where cultivated phrases and considerable technical efficiency may often cover shallowness of heart and selfishness.

Or perhaps it is the glib petty-bourgeois talkers in the movement itself that you object to.

The problem of "organising" J.M. while you enter on the last lap with the new baby must be a considerable one. I suppose you couldn't get two or three of the women together who are in a similar position and take turns living with one another or in each other's houses for certain periods? I think the only solution is in some novel and bold form of co-operation, since domestic help is so rare nowadays.

How about an Expectant Mothers' Mutual Help Society, or does that sound flippant?

Talking of the forthcoming event, I will make enquiries about the ante-natal allowance. And while on the subject of filthy lucre I have had a slight increase in pay. Field Allowance, which I drew to the tune of 2/6 or thereabouts a day, is replaced by a Mediterranean Allowance of 4/6 a day here. I have had to arrange to draw it out here, but that merely means I shall be able to leave a bit more in my account.

The blokes at the same table in the mess are talking too much for me to go on with this letter, but I will continue tomorrow as soon as I can.

Lots of love,

XXXXXXX Ron

The following day Dad writes mostly about the minutiae of camp life:

2/Lt. Spathaky A.E.C.

HQ Edn 3 Brit. Inf. Div. M.E.F.

3.11.45.

Dear K,

Thank you very much for your long letter of the 23rd. I had better answer some of the matters therein before I write anything else. First, as to names for the new babe, I don't like Ruth Ann. I think Ruth is too biblical. Anne would be very nice if it weren't for "Annie," which has been done to death in too many comic songs. Incidentally is there any reason why the infant should have two names? We had such trouble with Michael's two names and finally made a sad mess of it (which I think should be withheld from him until he is old enough to need to read his birth certificate).

If it is a boy I prefer Brian to all others you have mentioned. For a girl I like Hazel, Mary, Joyce, if Andrée makes the whole thing too foreign ! (?%!)

I have not had any parcels at all here. I hope to goodness my pyjamas have not been lost in the Med.

There is a general slackening off in our work here at the moment, for reasons which I cannot mention. It is very annoying because work is the only immediate and apparent justification for living.

A couple of days ago I had forty-eight hours leave as a result of all my inoculations being renewed. The weather was not too grand but I went down to a rather pleasant rest camp at Lake Timsah, near Ismaïlia. It reminded me a bit of Hammamet, up in Tunisia, of which you may possibly remember the description I wrote to you when I was at a rest-camp there. The main difference, of course, is that this is on a largish lake instead of the sea. But there were lots of welcome greenery after the maddening sand. I did little but read part of Tolstoy's War and Peace while I was there, but I felt refreshed afterwards.

The weather having turned very cold here we have taken sharpish like to battle-dress, in place of the khaki-drill we were wearing.

A menace has suddenly appeared in our tent, in the form of a wireless set owned by the elder of my two A.E.C. colleagues. The younger one and myself are seriously alarmed at the way it is turned on at odd moments when one is writing letters or reading. This letter, I am sure, will be disjointed as a result of it.

Incidentally, if you had sent me the measurement of your foot, I should have been able to get you a pair of suede half-shoes (or half-boots?) made. Now it's too late to do it at this particular place, but please send them and I'll try and get them done at the next place. The measurements are needed in centimetres as follows:

1. Across the place where the toe-cap comes on toe-cap type shoes.
2. Across the foot similarly from floor to floor, further back on the thick part where the foot turns up to become leg.
3. (An outline of the foot on paper.)

If you will send Michael's measurements as well I will try and get him some. I should allow a cm. or two in his case. The measuring should be done on the stockinged feet.

The Lieutenant who is Officers' Mess Secretary is now making it even more difficult to write because he's having the whole of the accounts read out to him by Pearson, the owner of the wireless.

I'm doing my best to find out something about the tangled problem of Palestine, but it's difficult because the Government seems to be pursuing a "wobbly" line. If they would only say straight out that they are in favour of Arab aspirations in all these Arab countries but are willing to let genuine refugees in, it would be better than nothing. Personally I think they ought to persuade the latter to go to some other part of the world, and indicate some reasonable place, but as it is they are laying themselves wide open to charges of vagueness from both sides.

I sent a 5/- postal order some three weeks ago to Collet's, to try and get something on the Middle East and Palestine in particular. I haven't had any reply yet, but that may be due to difficulties with the surface-mail.

Well, Kathie, I'm feeling a bit overcome by the wireless at the moment, so I'll give up the attempt and try and write my letters from now on in the Mess or the Camp Library.

By the way, do you agree that my writing is improving a little? It had gone to pot a short time ago. Now I feel the letters are acquiring a little more shape again, even if it's not all it should be. I must be recovering from my psychological upsets and flurries.

Please write lots and soon.

Your badly-behaved

R

The next letter we have is dated ten days later. Dad has a trip outside the camp and gives vent to some fine descriptive writing:

Letter 8 (about)

2/Lt. Spathaky A.E.C.

HQ Edn 3 Brit. Inf. Div.

M.E.F. 13.11.45.

Dearest K,

Thank you for the letter written on the 2nd Nov. The daily routine continues, with bright sunshine to cheer it, but the sensation persists of being in a highly artificial community miles from any soil in which one has natural roots. Your warning about the officers' wives and their predatory practices strikes a queer note in a camp which has probably 6,000 men in it and ne'er a female that I have seen up to now. And Cairo is 70 miles away.

In any case I've had enough to do with women to last me for a long time, that is to say with unattached women as distinct from you. I hope I've had enough for ever as regards the troubles associated therewith.

Yesterday I had to go by truck to a place called Fayed, about 50 miles from here. I haven't any maps handy, but as far as I know the lay-out is as shown on this sketch. The x shows where our camp is and the arrow the place I visited. The black line represents the road.

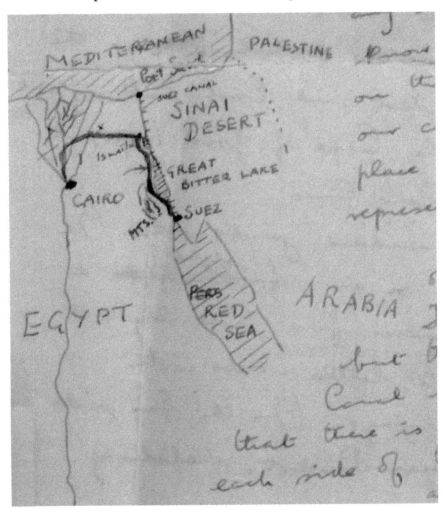

First we came out of our piece of desert on to the Ismailia road. The desert is never far away but the fact that the Sweetwater Canal lies alongside the road means that there is a strip of cultivated land each side of the water, in places as wide as three or four miles either side.

As I may have told you, Ismailia lies alongside Lake Timsa. Yesterday it looked very fairy-like, with its modern hotels and clubs towering up from among palm-trees, with triangular-sailed Arab feluccas on the lake, and a huge modern luxury yacht belonging to some Egyptian or Greek millionaire reflected in the calm water. I have seen a little of the dense squalor of the native town, however.

We skirted the west shore of the lake and at its southern tip found ourselves on the very edge of the Suez canal. The prospect was magnificent and I felt more interested and moved than I have been on account of any other sight in Egypt. Everywhere else I feel my natural friendliness towards foreigners rebuffed by the constant hatred that envelopes us, the derisory glances that follow our trucks everywhere. But here was an engineering feat, an epic in stone, metal and water, which must be finally of benefit to all mankind. Nations may still juggle and squabble over its control, but as the slender sea-link between West and East, cutting out the long journey around the Cape of Good Hope, it will stand supreme for a long time.

It is three or four hundred yards wide. On our side was the road and on our right a double or triple row of evergreen firs, widening out occasionally into respectable little woods with peasant fields in the clearings. On the far side was the Sinai Desert, stretching limitless to Palestine, Transjordan and Arabia, according to which way you look. The sand-hills are whorled into sharp ridges by some wind which blew perhaps five years ago. The long wide expanse of the canal gleams pastel-blue in the light. So the panorama is sharply divided from left to right – yellowy-brown (the desert), light blue (the Canal), then the dark metallic blue of the road and finally the restful green of the trees.

There is no general change in the scene this side of the Great Bitter Lake. The changes are in details, the sand-hills, the trees, and different kinds of floating buoys on the canal, but all the time the impression is one of vastness and of a giant change wrought by man, a fertilisation of what would have been desert, a closeness to the element which, however indirectly, washes to the shore of the English Channel.

Suddenly the jeep comes out of the shady green tunnel and another wonder is upon us, the vast inland sea called the Great Bitter Lake. It is so big that one can only just see the far desert shore. On its calm surface are quite a lot of cargo vessels sailing along at speed in this strange sand-locked world, heading for the next stretch of the Canal.

But this is no longer a flat world, like the Nile Delta. To our half-right (see map) are high rugged ochre, brown and red mountains, reminding me of Tunisia. Desert mountains always seem to be sleeping in the sun, expectant and slightly menacing, but they are welcome after a flat one-dimensional world.

So we ran down to Fayed and the dust, noise and uniformity of a big military camp. On the shore of the lake stood the gleaming columns of a palatial officers' club. We had lunch there after our business was finished. A German P.W. dance-band played American (and perhaps some German) jazz. German and Austrian P.W. waiters moved in white coats among the tables. On the shore a few score men bathed or lay in the sun. Half a dozen women chatted with them, probably Wrens from a nearby naval stores depot.

And delighted as I had been by the day's experience I felt anxious to give up my wanderer's experience, always moving among sights and scenes with which I can have nothing to do, except very indirectly, and to take my place in normal community life once again.

Hope things are going all right – Ron
XXXXXXX

1) No need for Air-Mail Letters. All letters come by air. Same delay.
2) For a birthday present I should like above everything a long letter of 12 pages. What would you like? There are some leather bags here and brooches.
3) Love to Michael from DADDY.

We first hear of Mum's expressions of negative feelings in Dad's letter of 25.8.45, but he seems rather dismissive of them.

It is clear that she has laid out a number of issues, which he summarises in his letter of 29.8.45 as "something deep travailling in that practical little head of yours".

So, there are signs that Mum is suffering from stress. He addresses these a little more but then says, "However, these feelings are perfectly normal in all of us." He then moves on to his concerns about his army situation.

Then, in his letter of 6.9.45, he mentions his interest in "your mental welfare".

It is hardly surprising that Mum is suffering from depression, as Dad has been away for five years, she has effectively been a single parent living with her parents for over three of those years and is now expecting a second child.

I am pretty sure that Nan and Grandpop, as I knew them, would have been supportive. I certainly formed a strong bond with them through this period, but the war would have been a stressful time for them too. Grandpop would have been working long hours "building railway engines" (as his job was described to me) at the Southern Railway engineering works. It was also producing components for tanks and anti-aircraft guns. Nan was active in the Co-operative movement. While Dad was abroad, the balance of options for Mum seems to have stayed in favour of living at 49 Hangleton Road, with occasional periods with her aunts in Derbyshire and Yorkshire.

An idea of the true depth of Mum's feelings of despair can be gleaned from some rough pencilled notes she made, which she kept with Dad's letters. Each comprised a list of things to do, written in Mum's (to me) unmistakable hand.

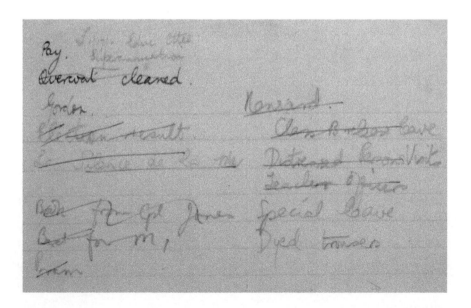

Page 1:
Left-hand list:

    Pay, £1/17/- Educ Cttee, Superannuation
    Overcoat cleaned
    Gordon
    Election result.
    Le Silence de la Mer
    Book from Cpl Jones
    Bed for M
    Pram

Right-hand list:

    Hansard
    Class B release leave
    Distressed Persons Visits
    Teacher Officers
    Special leave
    Dyed trousers

Page 2:

    Book de Schweinitz
    Oram
    Shoes   Michael
    School – easy return –   private schools
                     interim period – useful

    Pram
    Grandma's visit
    Weather – gale
    Dayella
    Circle of acquaintances
    Sylvia's problem
    Hilda
    Scooter (Gordon) Slide at school
    Citizen Tom Paine
    Parcels sent
    Ante-natal allowance

The listing of the book "Le Silence de la Mer" which Dad had mentioned in his letter of 24th October 1945 places the notes at some date soon after that.

The reverse side of page 2 has some more revealing notes in which Mum appears to be trying to sort out her most basic feelings about herself and her relationship to Dad. Clearly the notes were not written with any intention of sending them to Dad.

Role of Mother taken on.
 Looking after clothes food etc
 Always sympathetic & forgiving e.g. Expected
 forgiveness re Jacqueline
 + Physical side
Your reaction mainly one of gratitude
No reciprocation when I needed it
 Pregnancy always emotional
 Specially after reconciliation
Don't try to reassure me
I have touched bottom and stand alone
Still love you but do not hope for much
Alternative?
Do not underestimate your sense of responsibility & loyalty
Does not affect my promise to do all I can to help Andrée.
She is only part or a symptom of our problem.

There seems to be a gap of a couple of weeks now. Then Mum receives a letter from Andrée, the former French Resistance worker, who seems to have been the unwitting cause of much of the trouble in Mum and Dad's relationship at this period. She was still working as a civilian employee of the British Army in Calais. Her handwriting is typically French, but the envelope was addressed to Mum as from a "W.O II Brown AEC at HQ 25 Garrison BAOR". Perhaps he was her boss at the Calais office. The postmark is "6 Nov 1945". The date on the letter has been altered and is not at all clear. It may be 1st November. Dad would have forwarded the letter to Mum, which is why it has survived:

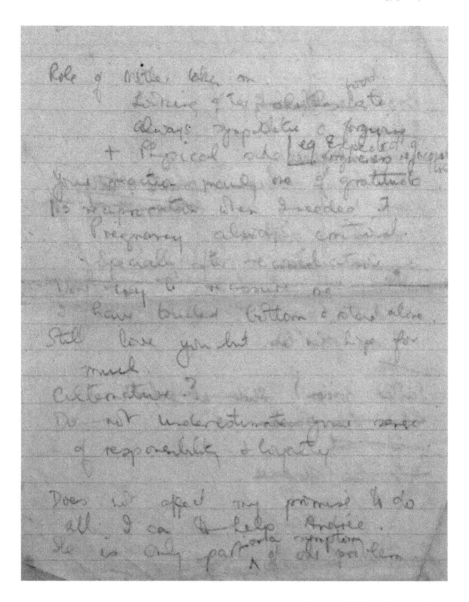

Calais, *[?]*1st November

Dear Mrs. Spathaky,

I must apologise for not having answered your letter before. I thank you very much for it and for your kind invitation. I have enquired about possibilities of going to England but find that at the present it is impossible to obtain permission unless there is an official or a strong compassionate reason. I hope that, little by little, they will relax these regulations and that I shall be able to visit you next summer.

I am very grateful to you for your thoughtfulness in trying to send me parcels, but even if you could have done so I would rather you did not, as I appreciate the difficulty you have in obtaining food in England now.

I am really sorry not to be able to visit you yet because I am sure, from what your husband told me of you, that we should have been good friends and enjoyed each other's company. I feel rather depressed having to spend the winter in Calais. Life is not very bright here, the town has been badly damaged and the climate is awfully rainy and windy. Fortunately the people working at my office are all very nice, the place itself is not too uncomfortable, and we spend most of our evenings there reading and studying or teasing each other.

Dear Mrs Spathaky, I am indeed very sensible of your kind offer – I hope to hear from you again and remain,

Yours sincerely
Andrée

Next comes a letter that was annotated years later by Dad as "The first hint of being sent home from the Middle East". Unfortunately, only the first page survives:

HQ 3 Brit Inf Div M.E.F.
8 Nov 45 1730 hrs

Dear Kath,

No letters since your double-paged air letter. The mail seems to be much worse out here than in Tunisia. For that reason and because of the discomfort of sitting in a desert 5,000 miles from home the Army can jolly well demobilise me as soon as it likes.

Apart from the trips into Cairo on duty I haven't been outside this artificial tenement stockade. The first time was on the day of Arab demonstrations against the Balfour Declaration. Our open jeep got a few half-bricks thrown at it, but none of us were hurt. This morning I went in again and all seemed quiet. Troops, and civilian European women, were walking the Americanized streets and there was obviously no danger. I visited GHQ, Middle East, which occupies a whole little quarter of the city's most modern buildings.

The truck ride there and back is still just moderately interesting but in a few weeks it will be deadly monotonous. The road runs straight as a die beside the "Sweetwater" Canal the whole way. Still, the men hauling boats, building barges, working in the very un-European fields, and sitting in the village streets are a rest for the eyes after the straightness and organised amorphousness of Qassasin.

Work is going quite well. I dropped a bit of a bloomer over the wording of an order yesterday,

The letter ends abruptly here at the end of a page, the remaining pages having gone missing.

Dad's next letter is dated six days later. The poem that follows it may or may not be the one he refers to. It was written around that period:

HQ 3 Brit. Inf. Div.
M.E.F. 14.11.45. 2015 hrs.

Dearest K,

The inspiration for the poem on the electric train has not been forthcoming until this evening. There is literally nothing to do so I have been trying my 'prentice hand. Please tell me what he thinks of it.

Last night I went with a fellow A.E.C. officer from a nearby part of the Div to see Lauren Bacall in "To Have and to Hold." [414] I just forget if this is the film you said you saw her in recently. The book was written by Ernest Hemingway and I thought the producers made a very good job of it. You know she may have a very obvious technique but she does it very well and you don't get the impression of over-acting as you sometimes did with Garbo and Dietrich. Anyway I think she's bloody attractive, because she's human, not the "poured-in-the-mould" type. The story is full of interesting character studies, though

---

414 This is the title of a silent film of the 1920s. The film with Lauren Bacall was *To Have and Have Not*, based on Hemingway's 1937 book of the same title.

as with "For Whom the Bell Tolls" the total impression given is that Hemingway is a visitor to the struggle, half in it but half distrusting it.

This is just a note to accompany the poem. <u>Please</u> write. This desert affair we're in is awfully big. I'm a bit browned off with it. I shall probably cheer up with the morning sunlight, however.

Lots of love

Ron.

NEXT YEAR.

Daddy and Mummy and Michael
(That's me)
Are going next summer to play by
the sea.
We'll all take our buckets and
spades on the sand
And Michael will paddle and
hold Daddy's hand.

Then when we've had ices and
eaten a snack
The train will be waiting and
clickety-clack
The gates and the bridges will
go speeding by
And the moon will look down
from her home in the sky.

Three days later Dad writes some interesting comments about the situation in Palestine:

Approx (No 8) HQ 3 Brit. Inf. Div.
M.E.F. 17.11.45.

Dear K,

Your letters are coming a bit more regularly now, though I have whacked you hollow with correspondence so far on this trip!

Work is increasing, so it will be a bit difficult to keep it up. I am duty officer today and I am writing this in the office without your letters to hand but I thought I would not waste time while I am forced to be here.

I fancy, K, that my moral fibre and quality of work are improving a little, after the setback of recent months. I am tackling the beastly smoking habit which had gripped me, by the realistic method of smoking less as time goes on, not hoping for any apocalyptic solution. In addition I am taking more exercise, by swimming when I can in the Bitter Lake and by an occasional game of tennis at the local Y.M.C.A.

There is no reasonable social life available, but the roster of short leaves to places like Ismailia, Cairo and Alexandria appears fairly adequate.

The educational work is fair, though I am not satisfied because I rather doubt whether the Div is serious enough about the scheme. Its semi-operational basis makes it difficult for the higher officers to back us up, but the Tommy of course doesn't see it like that. Not being in action he is only conscious of the fact that he is miles away from home and in a country where he is not well received by the inhabitants.

The situation is really very serious indeed in Palestine and I wonder if the world knows the truth about it. Jewish Zionist violence is increasing and I cannot think that the Zionists have a good case. The Arabs have been the dwellers on the soil for 1300 years and the fact that the Jews from ex-occupied Europe are in a sad state doesn't excuse their fellow-religionists in Palestine from claiming control and waiving all claims of the Arabs. I rather feel that British military and police action against the Jews who infiltrate is justified, though it seems strange to be against the Jews after so many years of being with them.

The fact that the Republicans of the USA support the Zionist policy seems to be one of the strongest points against them.

The C.P. Palestine and the Ichod, a union of left-wing intellectuals, are for co-operation between Jews and Arabs but I doubt whether they will prevent bloodshed in the near future.

Please tell me what people think of the problem out here and send out any interesting stuff you see in the shops about Palestine and/or Egypt.

Hope you don't feel <u>too</u> full yet, or is it a nice feeling?

I've just had the only letter so far from Andrée. She bewails the fact that she can't write well enough in English to tell you how grateful she is for the invitation.[415] She says that "she considers you as a close friend and she would never do anything to cause trouble to anyone so kind as yourself." That was not meant to be passed on but I thought I would tell you.

Please let's start to knit together again our affection. I do so want to see you happy when I come home again.

I suppose that slight medical scare that took place while we were together on leave <u>was</u> just a scare, was it? You haven't said anything else about it.

I must go on with my studies on Palestine, now. I want to master the situation out here. I think left-wing movements in England may have a need in years to come of people who have knocked around a bit.

Meanwhile lots of love. Hope Michael liked the poem.

Love, Ron. XXXXXXXXX

Dad wrote again a few days later. Let's hope the business with Andrée is at last dead and buried:

---

415 But she had written – and in excellent English.

Lieut. R. Spathaky, A.E.C.
3 Br. Inf. Div. School,
M.E.F.

Dearest K,

I have answered Toyne's letter about release, suggesting that I go in for a fortnight at the end of term to revive my knowledge of school routine and start seriously at the beginning of the new school year. When do they break up for the holidays, I wonder? Perhaps you would ask Percy or any of the others you may see.[416]

It sounds to me as though lodging arrangements for my parents in Brighton would be far too complicated. I imagine a week in Warrington would be far simpler. Perhaps I could take Michael along with me, when he's got used to me again, three weeks or so after my return.

Sorry you feel so full and heavy at this stage. I imagine you will decide it's worth it when the first year or two has passed. One lonely little boy would always be a problem.

I've just finished Howard Spring's book "Fame is the Spur,"[417] as I think I told you. It contains so many lessons concerning the raising of children that I feel much enlightened about the whole business of parenthood. In the story he tells of two complete generations; one sees the minor vices (and qualities) of the parents reflected in the children. The relation between the parents affects them, tragically in the case of some.

Norman Scarfe and I have been passing several evenings recently by reading history to one another. We have got through quite a lot of H.A.L. Fisher's History of Europe[418] – solid liberal stuff with a radical tinge but with some conclusions which the war has made laughable. There is little else one can do in the evenings here. I have been to see quite a few of our friends in Palestine but there is little one can do about them. The people on courses at the School are such temporary birds that the organisation of discussions does not seem very fruitful. We have tried one or two just recently.

---

416 Toyne and Percy Ireland were teachers at Brighton Intermediate School, then in York Place, Brighton, where Dad was teaching when called up.
417 Pub. Collins, 1940.
418 Pub. Edward Arnold & Co., 1935.

The scribble from Michael was very interesting. I didn't realise he'd got to the stage of writing words. We shall have to see that he has some mechanical interests to balance his serious studies. Perhaps I can find him some fairly large unusable clock.

Well, I'm going to write for a few jobs now. I haven't heard your opinion on applying for a new job yet, but it does no harm to write. One can always say it is not possible to accept a job, on many grounds.

I should think with favour of a purely French-teaching job these days, with the possibility of taking chaps for Higher Schools and University Scholarships.

Lots of love,

Ron

Dad wrote next on the day after his thirty-first birthday:

2/Lt Spathaky, A.E.C.

HQ Edn 3 Br. Inf. Div.

23.11.45 1545 hrs.

Dearest K (& M & "x"),

Sorry you've had several bad days with Michael and I hope very much that he is better by the time this reaches you.

Thanks very much for the financial estimate, Mrs. Chancellor. I don't know where the money goes but I have a rough idea that everything you buy in U.K. costs about twice as much as it used to do. Does the reduction of our joint account to £50 take into consideration the £50 kit-allowance which must have been paid in at some time or other, and of which I spent comparatively little at the time?

Incidentally the Paymaster at M/c has sent me a note to say that the £21.19.2 will be deducted at the rate of £3-15-0 a month.

About my expenditure – I have drawn from the Field Cashier:

£18-6-0	since 21 Aug. (incl.)[419]
5-0-0	left in cash
£13-6-0	expenditure

---

419 A pencilled note at the side breaks this into 6-0-0, 8-4-0 and 4-2-0.

Our weekly mess subscription was 7 piastres (about 1/6) for the first three weeks here. It has now gone down to 5 piastres (1/-). In addition I have a small monthly mess bill of about 10/- and ½ a day's pay a month for maintenance charges. Washing costs about 12/- a month. I spend about 30 piastres (6/-) a week on NAAFI cigarettes and other sundries and the rest on meals when I'm out, a book or two or a day in Cairo, which can be catastrophic.

I feel extraordinarily tired at the moment, because yesterday the General Staff Officer (Intelligence) who was going to give a lecture to representatives of units on "Egypt," had to cancel it and I volunteered to do it instead. It meant about 10-12 hours solid reading, and I got up at 5.45 this morning to finish it. It went over fairly well. But as I'm dropping now I'll send off this letter as it is and cap it with another as soon as possible.

Love,

Ron

P.S. Thanks for the birthday greetings. I feel younger than ever. Too young!

A trip out is again a stimulus to Dad's descriptive writing:

2/Lt R. Spathaky, A.E.C.,
HQ Edn 3 Br. Inf. Div. M.E.F.,
27.11.45

Dearest K,

I was reminded by some passages from your latest letter that there are sometimes bits of official information that I have and forget to pass on to you; occasionally I imagine you know them already. First as regards Release; the ruling we have been given up to now is that

i. A.E.C. teachers cannot be spared for "B" release

ii. They will not be deferred beyond their normal "A" release date.

The picture changes as the weeks go by, but I imagine that is pretty well the legitimate forecast.

I'm looking forward to more news about the possible tenancy at No. 53 Hangleton (or No. 49). It must be jolly nice to have a roof-tree of one's own. I've never felt <u>really</u> attracted by the thought till recently. Now I definitely am.

(Letter suspended because falling asleep.)

NEXT DAY. About the above. I have just got a letter from the Brighton Education Committee saying they cannot allow me to volunteer for a further period of service in the Forces. It doesn't apply to me in the slightest, but it is interesting as the first indication that they place even "circular value" upon my services.

I know it's rather unfeeling to tell you about the new experiences I have in this strange and terrible land, but I expect it's better to experience things <u>through</u> someone else than not at all so I'll risk boring you by telling you of a journey I made the day before yesterday.

Norman Scarfe and myself took a few blokes from HQ office staffs by truck to Sakkhara[420] and Memphis. The former was the burying ground of most of ancient Egyptian royalty, while Memphis was the capital of Egypt.

I felt duly inspired by the idea of this visit, since my reading of Clive Bell's Penguin "The Idea of Civilisation"[421] had fairly convinced me that the Nile valley was the original birth-place of civilisation, from which influences spread out to all other civilising centres such as Crete, Babylon, India and China. You may remember that International Brigader[422] whom we put up at the flat in Brighton telling us about the theory.

We pushed through the rows of night-clubs and worse *[that]* form the fringes of Cairo to the south and turned off towards a range of high sand mountains. The first sign of Sakkhara was the "Step Pyramid," which shone imposingly over some foothills while we were still six or seven miles away. Then our truck was engulfed in a maze of dunes and old diggings until we drew up at a barrier manned by three or four Egyptians in native dress.

---

420 Now generally spelt *Saqqara*.
421 *Civilisation,* (not *The Idea of*), originally pub. Chatto & Windus, 1928.
422 Not 'Brigadier', so a member of the International Brigades in Spain.

One, who offered his services as a guide, seemed a cultivated and clean-featured individual, with a freshly washed robe and a neat turban. He spent a matter of three hours explaining the various carvings and tombs to us, in reasonable English, as good as any I've heard from an Egyptian here, anyway.

Sometimes the opening would be a rough crevice in the hillside, then a sloping passage lit by little native lamps we carried, opening into vast halls and vestibules beyond. The carvings really surprised me, since I have looked upon quite a number of the world's marvels with a jaundiced eye by now.

They were astounding by their variety, their developed technique, their design, their quality of depicting movement and their realism. It was evidently the aim of the ancient kings to impress the celestial beings with the diversity of human activity conducted in their earthly kingdoms. Here were marriages, battles, ships being built, oxen ploughing, bulls copulating with cows, boat-parties upon the Nile, sacrificial offerings, men snaring wild ducks, shepherds guarding flocks of sheep and goats and through it all the heroic figure of the Great King, shown five or six times human size, with perhaps a wife or son half his size, moving through the varied scenes as he probably flattered himself he did in his life-time.

In one system of great underground pits covered with slabs of granite weighing over fifty tons each were the tombs of the holy bulls who assumed deity on living to the age of 15 years. They opened off a large central chamber which imparted to the necropolis the atmosphere of an underground cathedral. In spite of the weight of the slabs covering the pits, they had been moved aside (five hundred, a thousand, two thousand years ago?) and rifled by robbers attracted by the gold and silver buried there.

When we had seen the tombs the truck took us and the guide some four miles away to a vastly different place, the site of Memphis. This was a flat marshy plain, thickly forested with sturdy date palms, the location of a decrepit Arab village whose ragged inhabitants went about their daily tasks unmindful of the fact that they lived at the earth's starting point, where all the trouble and all the splendour began.

Crowds of sturdy Arabs round the village "green" assailed us with baskets of fake statues, scarabs (sacred beetles) and other junk. I bought one or two, always having had a sneaking regard for persistent rogues of that kind.

In a covered-in gallery erected by the Egyptian government (I assume) lay the massive remains of a vast statue of Rameses II, smiling in a very life-like fashion. It was twenty-nine feet long. When I say "remains" I should add that part of the legs of the statue had been broken off, but the rest of it was as clean and fresh as if it had been carved yesterday. Such is the preservative effect of the desert air and the lack of corrosive dirt. When upright he must have made an imposing figure, in the act of making one enormous pace forward. his hand gripping tightly small ritual scrolls and as big as three men's heads.

Thanks a lot for telling me about Michael. I hope you're not too tired of the struggle with the "children." I'll train myself to help you as much as I can when I come back.

Lots of love, XXXXXXX Ron

Chapter 22

Palestine

A full sixteen days elapse before Dad writes again. As he explains, he has now moved to the British Mandate Territory of Palestine. The Mandate from the League of Nations dated from 1923 and gave Britain responsibility for administering this part of the former Ottoman Empire. The letters he wrote during his service there throw interesting light on the developing situation. Most of Palestine was destined to become the State of Israel in 1948:

HQ 3 Br Inf. Div

M.E.F. 13.12.45

Dearest K,

My literary efforts and delivery of your letters have both been suspended by our removal to Haifa in Palestine. Before I tell you about the country let me see if I need to answer anything in your interesting letter of the 28th.

Thank you very much for writing to Andrée. I think both addresses are all right, although I haven't written to or heard from her for some time.

About finance: your explanation about the £105 in the Co-op reassures me a little. I couldn't believe that either of us had been spending so much more than at other periods during the war. You ask whether the amount I have drawn includes Mediterranean allowance. I'm rather puzzled at your question. Can it be that the quick-witted Financial Member for Hangleton doesn't understand the system? There is no question of what <u>part</u> of my pay I draw from the Field

Cashier. It is all paid by the Army into our Joint Account at W. Hove, including the Mediterranean allowance. What I draw from the Field Cashier is deducted from the Hove account. Or perhaps you mean to ask whether the Med allowance is effectively being paid. I should have to see the Bank statement to know that. Perhaps you would get them to send me a complete detailed Statement of Account next time you go in. I imagine it's being paid.

It's perhaps a good thing that Gordon is going abroad for a short time before his release. If he's never been outside U.K. before he's got a big surprise coming to him, but it won't be like setting off for a period of years (I hope – D.O.V. willing!).

Our journey overland from Qassasin to Haifa was most interesting; one of those infrequent compensations for this rootless life. I had a minor job on the convoy, but it only became effective when we halted and the rest of the time I rode a motor-bike, for three days, covering about 480 miles.

The first day we didn't go very far but just crossed a pontoon bridge over the Suez Canal, went a few miles across the Sinai Desert

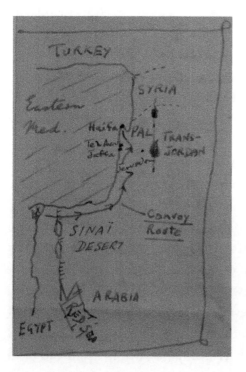

road and lagered for the night, sleeping in and around the vehicles. Wrapped in my issue valise with plenty of blankets I was fairly warm, but the chaps must have been freezing cold with a groundsheet and three blankets. There was no spare water for washing or shaving in the morning and we set off over the marvellous road, with fantastic dunes on left and right. Occasionally ranges of high sand or earth mountains appeared in the far heart of the desert with cliffs and silent crevasses which I shouldn't imagine anyone has ever explored – at least I shouldn't imagine it would profit even the most curious to do so.

There was no vegetation except a few tough clumps of spring grass from time to time. About ten o'clock we saw four camels grazing on the slopes to our left. I fancy they were hobbled, in which case their Bedouin owner must have been about, but he was invisible in the universe of sand and sky.

The sun was bright, but it was not unpleasantly hot in spite of our ordinary battle-dress. Riding along at a steady 25 m.p.h. I thought of all the other vast spaces which man has penetrated, of how very much bigger the Sahara is than this empty land of Sinai and of how the Children of Israel had wandered for forty years, as one bloke expressed it "with no N.A.A.F.I. and only one E.N.S.A. show" (the orgy and leg-show organised by the priests of Baal).

I was also reminded more seriously of a passage in Terre des Hommes by Saint-Exupéry,[423] in which he says that when one journeys in deserts one realises how small the favoured and settled regions of the earth are and how restless man has been in his probings into the great spaces in between. But however bold he is he is always bound by his bodily needs to the "garden of the earth," to which he must return right speedily, as though he were linked to them by some invisible umbilical cord.

Meanwhile we climbed higher and higher over undulating crests of road on to the sandy roof of Sinai. Once or twice, bored by the speed of the convoy, I speeded on ahead for ten miles or so, to put my bike on its stand and savour the strange charm of complete silence. On one such occasion I crossed a little ridge near the road and immediately was away from all civilisation in a way I had never been before. I sat on the dune and fingered the sand, running my hands through its coarse grains. I was struck by a thought I had before when in the tamer desert near the Nile. As I moved this handful of sand I was probably shifting it for the first time in decades. Possibly twenty years would go by before a wind would blow strong enough to shift these grains in the lee of the dune. In the trough of the sand-wave near

---

423 See page 470.

the road, however, there were signs of life. Quite a number of camel-tracks led off in various uncharted directions, while there were also the small three-pronged footmarks of some desert rodent, stretching away out of sight. But here was the convoy again, with a rumble and a roar, led by my A.E.C. colleague Capt. Pearson in the commander's truck.

Now we wound down to an immense plain, with dark-coloured mountains on our right, evidently of basalt or some ancient material, so blue were they. The sand on the verge of the road was noted on the maps as being hard enough to support the lorries, so we had our ten-minute halt, then up and up again around a series of tortuous curves with perilous drops for unwary drivers and finally down into the completely artificial camp, complete with NAAFI, where we filled up with petrol and settled down for the night.

Next day we crossed the Palestine border at a site of a large wadi (stream) with no water in it and from that point onwards the desert became speckled with Arab fields, then occasional villages, and somewhere just north of Beersheba we passed the modern buildings of a Jewish farm settlement, heralding the most-discussed social experiment since the Soviets, TVA[424] and Red China. Young boys passed us in European costume and handsome biblical faces surpassing the best types of English boyhood.

All the vaunted modernism of the settlements was there, clean outbuildings, vegetable forcing-frames, men and women with intellectual faces working in vegetable gardens and sturdy young girls in brief working-shorts hoeing and pruning fruit plants.

The country became more and more populous and attractive, occasionally buses and pavements and little villas made their appearance. A group of women in smart suburban costumes waiting at a bus stop with their shopping baskets completed the illusion of Patcham or Rottingdean. Yet a bare hundred miles away was the pitiless bare desert and even now, on a high ridge beyond the villas, I could see a rugged medievally-clad Arab ploughing a hopeless patch of ground with a donkey and a wooden plough. Two worlds touched.

---

424 The Tennessee Valley Authority.

Though the convoy was spending one more night at a transit camp I pushed on at speed with a couple of truck-loads of cooks to report our arrival at Haifa. We crossed the flat plain of Esdralon and came to the high-road about two miles from the sea. There was the Mediterranean, as far as I know the loveliest of all seas, blue as if hundreds of bags of the most regal dye had been poured into it, with white breakers on shore but hardly a ripple on its further expanses.

Lulled in the coils of crystalline streams.[425]

Soon we were in the straggling southern fringes of Haifa, with the vast terraces of Mount Carmel looming over us on our right. This was the mountain on which, according to Hebrew mythology, the prophet Elija was fed by the ravens.

Turning off to the right we wound up steep slopes, giving us a grander and grander view of the great Haifa bay and the thronged city, the ancient crusaders' walled city of Accre[426] further around the bay, then the long sweep of mountains towards the French-controlled Lebanon.

On the top of the mountain, above opulent Jewish mansions in remarkable modern styles, with their cypress and olive settings, was our new home, the big Carmelite monastery, with the monks still in residence and the lighthouse starting already to probe with its revolving finger across the bay, the city and the mountain slopes. The lighthouse is called Stella Maris, the Star of the Sea.

High over the building the HQ wireless aerials sent out their rays, as our people sent out their messages and received reports from the brigades and battalions now arriving at various spots throughout the country. In some Jewish collective farm the Haganah or the Palmach, the two Jewish secret armies, had their interceptor wireless working, tapping our messages and working out their plans accordingly for the next uprising or illegal settlement plan in the cause of אֶרֶץ יִשְׂרָאֵל (Eretz Israel), the land of the Jews.

More when I have time. Please write lots.

---

425 "Thou who didst waken from his summer dreams / The blue Mediterranean, where he lay, / Lulled by the coil of his crystalline streams", from Shelley's *Ode to the West Wind*.
426 Normally Acre in English and now Akko in Hebrew.

Love to Michael from

DAD

FROM

PALESTINE

XXXXXXXXXXXXXXXX

The next letter was written ten days later on Mum's birthday, but with no mention of it, nor of their eighth wedding anniversary on 21st December.

23.12.45

(as before)

Dearest K,

Sorry I haven't written for a few days, but work has been terrific and I have not been helped by a lousy cold acquired during the last few weeks. It is abating a little now.

Also the man in the next bunk to me has a bloody wireless which he uses to make the three-ply walls rattle on all possible leisure occasions. It's going now!

Queries from your letters: a) I am definitely banking on arrival in England by July, at the latest. b) It was promised that the freezing of officers in groups 21-23 would not interfere with the release of later groups.

I've no notion of where we could go for a holiday when I return. Surely you won't feel like travelling far or being very far from home with young Ebenezer? We'd better spend the holiday learning family management, or the difficult art of managing two young children. That will be difficult enough at home without going somewhere else I think.

As I shall feel very much better tomorrow I'll wait till then to write something worthwhile to you. Glad you feel so well. Haifa is fairly interesting.

Love,

Ron

Dad ends 1945 with a brief letter (but no special greeting):

HQ 3 Inf Div M.E.F.

31.12.45.

Dearest,

This, once again, is not a real letter, but just a line to reassure you in view of the recent bombing incidents in Palestine.

They sound horrible because it is peace-time, but don't worry about my safety.

Our boys still go about Haifa at night unarmed, visit all the cafés and take out the girls.

Work is still colossal here. We have had 3 surprise "releases" at HQ AEC and we are working three sessions to get through the job.

I'll write you a long letter as soon as I see daylight a little.

Lots of love,

XXXXXXXXX Ron

To Michael:

HALLO!

The next letter is dated 3rd January 1946 and the envelope was postmarked with the same date. Mum has used the back of the envelope for a short shopping list:

M's tabs

Fabric ?Hall

2nd hand furn.

Brassières

There is also a drawing of mine, apparently an abstract one. The letter indicates that Dad is still having to work hard:

HQ 3 Br Inf Div M.E.F.

3.1.46.

Dearest,

I am still a bit bleary after working for three sessions a day for about a week, but my cold has gone and I don't feel miserable as I did a week ago.

There is rather an interruption in my local studies at the moment. All of us are teaching in a course for the new Forces Preliminary Examination at a Divisional School at Natania,[427] further south. It should be an interesting experience after the pure administration job I've been doing for weeks now. It involves quite a bit of preparation, since we are a bit short on instructors and I am doing all the General Knowledge instruction and a little of the French and History.

One afternoon last week, however, I got the opportunity to visit by truck the forgotten remains of Montfort, a crusader castle of the 12th or 13th century, tucked away in a basin formed by the hills to the east of the famous walled city of Accre, also notable for its part played in the Crusades. However, I won't serve you up a scenistic eulogy as I did before, since I think I have dabbled a bit too much in scenery and not enough in people lately. But really it is rather difficult for me, stuck in a large military camp on the Mount Carmel, to get among any civilians. Incidentally the Education Office is in the part of the Carmelite Monastery used as a light-house. My office window is just below the revolving lantern which throws its beam 20 miles out to sea and over Haifa Bay. The monks are still in residence but once again our life is so governed by daily routine that I haven't been able to go and see them – though they are French-speaking! I believe they are the original Carmelite Fathers, who are famous the world over among Roman Catholics.

This Mount Carmel, as I believe I mentioned to you, is the mountain on which the Prophet Elijah was supposed to have been fed by ravens and on which he confounded the 450 prophets of Baal by some fire-raising jiggery-pokery he fixed up.

The view over Haifa is the most impressive I've ever seen, and I saw some wonderful sights around Taranto. The mountains of Lebanon

---

427 The usual spelling is Netanya. It is 35 miles (56km) south of Haifa.

and Syria, 40 or more miles away, can be seen quite clearly with the snow on their peaks.

————

I <u>have</u> received my pyjamas thank you. I'm afraid I forgot to thank you for them in my last two letters, though you will be used to that now!

I've also received and started to study, the book by Levy[428]. It should be quite useful for the course.

How would you like "The Arts of Mankind" by Hendrik van Loon? He is a great democratic populariser of history, geography and artistic history. I've read the last bit of it recently in our unit library and found it very interesting. I will send a cheque to Foyle's for it if you would like it, or to Ward's Book Shop in East Street. It is not a war-time publication but was written around 1937.[429]

About the housing problem. I feel with you at the moment that almost anywhere on our own would be better than living in somebody else's house, though whenever I have been at no. 49 your people have been quite self-effacing. But I don't have to stand them all the time.

I should seriously think of grabbing the flat, though you wouldn't be able to move in till I came back, would you? Perhaps that would be our first job. Is it likely to remain vacant all that time?

Don't worry about our future together. I told you when I was at home that I needed time to wrestle with demons. I have done so quite often. I love you very much indeed, while still keeping a very warm spot in my heart for poor Andrée.

I have had very few letters from her since I came away. The last one was too dispirited for words. She had been suffering from a bout of 'flu and bronchitis. *[This is a translation of what]* she said,

"I only sleep for a few hours at night and in the mornings. I'm like a dish-cloth. Forgive me for not writing more. I do not feel well and I cannot put my thoughts together.

"I received a nice letter from Kathleen a week or so ago."

So you see the inevitable effects of a Calais winter are in evidence.

---

428 This is probably *Aspects of Dialectical Materialism* by Hyman Levy, et al., pub. Watts, London, 1935, which Dad mentioned in his first letter to Mum in 1937 – see page 30).

429 Pub. Harrap, 1938.

You are very good to have written to her and tried to do something. I'm afraid it's of no avail, at the moment anyway. And that's 90 miles away!

Lots of love (not just
"letter-love"!)

– Ron

It appears to be ten days before Dad writes again:

Lieut. R.V. Spathaky, A.E.C.
3 Br. Inf. Div. Training School
M.E.F. 13.1.46.

Dearest K,

Just a line to assure you I am thinking of you a lot. It must be brief because I am trying to digest the whole of European history 1760-1919 in a week, in order to teach on a course for the Forces Preliminary Exam. How are you? – full of life?!

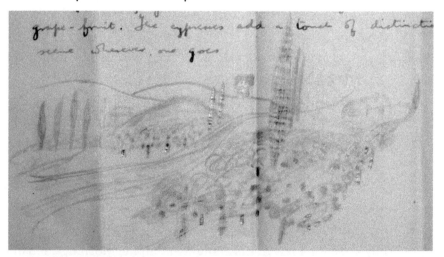

This School is at Natanya, about half way down the coast of Palestine and towards Tel-Aviv and Jaffa. It is on the sand cliffs, surrounded by Jewish collective and communal farms. One can walk for miles in entrancing colourful countryside, among groves laden with oranges, lemons and grape-fruit. The cypresses add a touch of distinction to the scene wherever one goes.

I am awfully glad the housing prospects have taken a turn for the better. Presumably your Pa and Ma will not move until the baby is born and organised a bit, will they?

Please tell Renée I will try and write to her in the near future. My opinions on Zionism haven't been worth much till recently, but I am making a few acquaintances among the Jews who organise Hospitality Committees for the forces, with superb propaganda results for their cause.

The broad masses of the people are as impenetrable as usual in a country where people speak different languages like Hebrew, Arabic, Polish, Bulgarian, Yemenite and so on.

Personally I think there is a lot to be said for the Jewish side, though the Arabs in all Arabic countries are suffering at least as much as the miserable Jews of the persecution areas in Europe.

The whole thing smells of petrol and strategic gateways to the East, though it's not enough to dismiss the matter by saying that. If the Labour Government just walked out of the various parts of the world where Tory governments have created privilege and corruption I can't think that the thing would be solved. For one thing I am sufficiently "administratively minded" to think that the 46 million people of England would be in a serious situation. Of this more anon.

Love,

Ron

XXXXXXXX

P.S. My cold has gone and I'm revelling in the sunshine here.

The next letter is four days later:

Lieut. R. Spathaky, A.E.C.
3 Br. Inf. Div. Training School
M.E.F. 17.1.46.

Dear K,

My browned-offness was only due to the cold which I caught. I feel quite fit now and I think the pleasant country surroundings of the School here will dissipate the last feelings of catarrhal depression.

As I believe I told you, we are at Natanya, down towards Jaffa. I have had to work extraordinarily hard on the Forces Prelim Course, but it is interesting work.

The other evening I went to the little house of a Jewish chap called Zimri, who used to live in the USA and after serving in the British Army in the last war settled in Palestine. He is fairly elderly now but quite a fund of information on the problems of the Middle East. Naturally he tried to pump me full of Zionism but I managed to preserve a certain amount of equilibrium. I feel however that there is more in the present situation than meets the eye. I rather wonder if the Arabs <u>would</u> object so strongly to Jewish emigration, seeing that the Arab League was so strongly influenced in its inception by us and since the Arabs in Palestine seem to have done reasonably well out of the Jewish development of the country.

It was very pleasant to hear about the Christmas festivities and their effect on the children. I am anxious to get home now and take seriously the job of earning a living and helping to raise a family. If I can do some extra work in politics in the educational field I shall do it enthusiastically but I must first remedy the obvious errors of our first "romantic-revolutionary" years.

I have quite a lot of good experience, linguistic and geographic, which should make me a reasonable prospect for most secondary schools, but to do a good week's teaching requires quite a good deal of concentrated preparation.

You know I don't want to isolate myself and live an "ivory tower" academic existence, but I don't propose to serve on branch committees and live in a whirl of meetings, at least for a time. At the same time I realise fully that the coming years present all those problems which we expected "in the first red mist of war." (Who wrote that phrase? Some great poet wasn't it? Oh, of course, I wrote it myself !?%½!)

Your letters are arriving very irregularly due to the move from Div HQ. Please write to me at the School until about 12th Feb. For letters posted after that use the Div HQ address.

Are all the confinement arrangements taped now? If there are any difficulties please tell me. I may possibly be able to offer some suggestions.

The hills just behind this camp on the inland side remind me of the Downs towards Washington. There are some little woods on the top which are delightful and further inland still one looks over the bright Palestinian plain with its white settlements. In the distance however, instead of the North Downs, there are the Palestine mountains which form a barrier between the coast and the Dead Sea-Jordan valley. In the passes are Arab towns and villages, built on slopes higgledy-piggledy. Nablus alone is a well-ordered dignified Arab town. None of them compares with the Jewish towns like Tel-Aviv or modern Haifa.

Percy Ireland has just written me a very pleasant letter which I mean to answer soon. Do you see him nowadays? If so please thank him very much for me. If I weren't so confoundedly busy I would write to all the people I knew so well, including Bernard for whom I have a special measure of affection.[430]

Your loving black sheep,

Ron

TO MICHAEL – HELLO – DADDY

The next letter is a week later:

Lieut. R. Spathaky, A.E.C.

3 Br. Inf. Div. Training School

M.E.F. 24.1.46.

Dearest wife,

I shall certainly try and keep the garden productive and reasonably pleasant to see, though I've done very little gardening. It will be a case of going to it with a manual in one hand and a trowel in the other.

My LM[431] is now arriving direct and it was a terrific change to have it so near the date of publication. Please don't bother to send "Picture Post" from now on, since they can be bought here at any bookshop.

I'm afraid I haven't kept an account of my spending, but my messing at the Div School here has gone up to 2/- a day, which is a bit steep.

---

430 Percy Ireland and Bernard Stone were Dad's former teaching colleagues at Brighton Intermediate School.

431 Labour Monthly.

My Advance of Pay Book shows I have drawn the following amounts:

    £17-8-6 in Egypt

    £ 6-0-0 since being commissioned (in English money)

    £<u>15-0-0</u> in Palestine

     38-8-6

add <u>18-0-0</u> joining advance

    <u>56-8-6</u> in about 6 months

This is £9-8-0 a month or £2-7-0 a week.

Qu'est-ce que tu en pense?[432]

The change to a full day's teaching down here has taken some getting used to but I am slowly taking up the load. The history is the main bother, since I have had no experience of teaching European history.

The blowing up of the coast-guard station at Givat Olga a couple of days ago has alienated all sympathy for the Zionist cause among soldiers here. There were over a dozen casualties, some serious, and two chaps were killed. The Jews one talks to say they don't sympathise with the Stern Group, an extremist political section who carry out these activities,[433] but we think that the Jewish community are giving no help in the arresting of the guilty parties and in the settlements they find many hiding places.

Feeling runs pretty high at the moment, as you may imagine. The chaps who were killed were Groups 27 and 32.

This afternoon was down on the programme here as Recreational Training. Only a few were down for football, so Norman Scarfe, the captain who is writing a history of 3 Div here, and I took them for a short cross-country run. I find myself quite good at this these days, which is curious because I went in for many cross-country runs at school with inglorious results. I seem to have more stamina now. Perhaps it is my enforced chastity – which is complete, but not very irksome at the moment because of the amount of work I have to do.

The military training staff of this school are a set of very decent fellows, though they spend rather a lot of time and money boozing.

---

432 What do you think of it?

433 The Stern Group's aim was to evict the British authorities from Palestine by resort to force. It repeatedly attacked British personnel.

It's astounding how much pleasure chaps seem to get out of nightly tipplings in each other's company. I have always wanted to learn too much and possibly spent too much time with books as a consequence. Still, I've probably learned a bit more about life than if I'd stayed in the U.K. during the whole war.

In the rather rare moments I have had free from duty here I have been writing a short story, more for distraction than anything else. When it is finished I will send it to you.

Please don't worry about the unsettled country I'm in. I doubt if the lid will blow off by March. After that we shall be a little further away I hope.

But in any case roll on May-June-July, or whenever it is the 30s come out.

Look after yourself, my dear.

Love Ron

Three days later Dad writes:

Lieut. R. Spathaky, A.E.C.
3 Div. Trng School
M.E.F. 27.1.46.

Dearest K,

I am writing to you tonight not just because I haven't written for some time, but because I really feel like expressing my thoughts to you. It is Saturday night, most people have gone out of the School for an evening's entertainment at Tel-Aviv, but I have so many things I want to think about that I prefer to sit here in the cold, in a little library-cum-class-room building isolated from the other buildings on the coast road and think on paper.

This morning I had only one lesson to collaborate in with one of our instructors, so I spent the rest of the time preparing some A.B.C.A. periods for the General Knowledge paper our chaps are taking in the Forces Preliminary examination.

Half-way through the morning I had a call from old Zamri the chairman of the collective village at Alchoeen near the camp.

He is always offering to conduct tours around various parts of the countryside, bring football teams to play our lads and always leaves me an invitation to go and argue with him at his pleasant little house, together with a bundle of Zionist propaganda pamphlets.

This afternoon I had to accompany Captain Scarfe, the former A.E.C. officer here who is writing the history of the Division, upon a journey to a military camp about 25 miles north of here, through the collective orangeries with their cypresses, in order to help clear up a muddle that has occurred in connection with accommodation stores.

This was a very boring business, in which I was only involved to the extent of identifying a letter which finally we could not discover in the files. However, the journey was a pleasant one.

Returning at five o'clock, I nipped along to Alchoeen and listened to old Zamri, who told me once again the story of the Jews' desire to have their own country and to constitute a majority in Palestine. He repeated the old story of how the Arab opposition was something created as a bogeyman by British imperialism and (very recently) espoused by American oil-interests, that the Arabs in Palestine don't really object to the Jews coming in again, on the contrary.

I asked him if the stoning of some of our chaps by Arab-Egyptians in Cairo a couple of months ago on the day of a demonstration against Jewish immigration was something fostered by the British. This rather stumped him, since he could only say lamely that the "Gippo's" would be much better advised to turn their wrath against their own rulers who keep them in festering poverty. He thought they were merely being used as tools of the Arab League, protesting in a paradoxical manner against the Jews, at the instigation of Britain finally.

Leaving him at seven o'clock I ran back to the officers' mess and had my dinner (quite a good one) and then had a brief chat at the bar in Italian with the waiter, an ex-P.O.W., one of the Italian Co-operators' Company attached to this camp. They are all very nice chaps, very browned off with their long imprisonment. He has been a prisoner for 3 years. They get their mail from home pretty regularly, however and their conditions in the company, as far as I can see, approximate roughly to ours, except that they get 2½d. a day pay!

I then sat in the Mess for an hour, listening to Schubert's "Unfinished Symphony" on the wireless and reading a Gollancz book on "Jewish Labour Economy in Palestine."[434] When the noise became too bad I retired here to my bunk and here I am, with the sound of the Mediterranean in my ears (it is 200 yards away) and my thoughts flying across the sea, through the Straits of Gibraltar, up the coast of France and Spain, to you in Brighton.

I'm working up my energy for an attack on an administrative problem which has accumulated while I have been teaching on this course. I am in charge of a unit library at Div HQ and one which we hold down here at the Battle School, as well as a number of text-books. We have signatures for practically all books issued, but they are in a bit of a mess, in various note-books and ledgers. I suppose there will be an accounting day in March some time, so I want to get the thing ship-shape and start a new system from scratch. The difficulty is that we are desperately short of clerks, and carrying out one's own admin work as well as instructing is a formidable burden. However, if I have to fork up £4 or so for books lost when I go out of the Army I shall regard it as a cheap career. I was lucky I didn't get stung for that truck I knocked sideways in Rouen.

If even the £4 can be avoided by a bit of hard work so much the better.

Well, here's hoping to see you in June.

Oh, talking of money, they have found an odd £5 due to me from my O.R.'s account[435] and have struck it off the over-issue of allowance "to make recovery quicker."

It's getting a bit too chilly to sit up any longer, so I think I'll retire to bed and read.

Tomorrow I'm taking a day off and going with our three instructors and a couple of other chaps in our educational truck to Tiberius on the Sea of Galilee. It'll brush the old cob-webs away.

I replied yesterday to the very pleasant letter I had from Percy.

Yours with love,

XXXXXXXXXXX Ron

P.S. No mail for 3 or 4 days!

---

434 By Gershon Meron, pub. Gollancz, 1945.
435 Other ranks (i.e. not officers).

Well, it was six days before Dad wrote again. It seems he waited this time to receive one from Mum. The backs of all the pages were used for a draft of a letter by a certain correspondent aged three:

Lieut. R. Spathaky,
A.E.C.,
3 Br. Inf. Div. School,
M.E.F. 2.2.46.

Dearest K,

Thank you for your customary cheerful letter. You have helped very much to maintain my spirits during the recent bout of rather intensive work. I'm glad you're doing some sensible reading ("Job in the North"[436] sounded very promising). I have read Priestley's "Three Men in New Suits," which I thought quite a feat on the author's part. He must have mixed with service or ex-servicemen quite a bit to be able to analyse their feelings so accurately.[437]

In answer to your questions, my cold disappeared quite a time ago, and I have been in quite a number of cross-country runs here, feeling much fitter and better at that kind of thing than when I was at school.

Unfortunately I have had occasional, even though rare, tendencies to masturbation lately, which was something that hadn't happened much in years. But I don't regard that as particularly serious. (A doctor in B.A.O.R. told me that practically all women experienced in sexual matters feel bound to practise it while their husbands are away in the Army, with varying frequency.)

I think it's partly through not building sufficient mental resolution to acquire varied interests and therefore becoming too self-centred.

I want to try and get out next week-end and visit the leaders of various political parties in Tel-Aviv and Jaffa and dig deeper into the question of Zionism and the Arabs.

Speaking of the Zionist claims, I managed to write a brief letter to

---

436 By Gordon Jeffery, pub. Gollancz, London, 1944.
437 By J B Priestly, pub. Heinemann, London, 1945. Dad seems unaware that Priestley served in the trenches during the First World War.

Renée, and also replied to the kind letter Percy J. sent me. In my reply to Percy I forgot to accept his offer to send me the "Times Ed."[438] When you are next in touch with him you might thank him and accept.

I also mean to write to a number of Education Authorities and schools and apply for a job. Have you the address of the Co-op College (the new one)? I shouldn't mind applying for a job there if they have anyone teaching Current Affairs, Civics and/or Languages. I had half-finished a stencilled circular for this purpose when I left Div HQ.

About names; I like Brian very much. I think Alison is too "olde Englishe" and a bit difficult to curtail in familiar speech. I am definitely against two Christian names. What's the use of two? What about Joan or Marjorie, preferably the former. Mary is a bit played out.

It may interest you to know that Norman Scarfe, who was my A.E.C. colleague till he started to write a "History of 3 Div" recently, and who still bunks next to me at the School, is coming to England, starting from here on 14th Feb. He doesn't yet know if he'll be coming by air or by ship and overland through France, but if any time a very boyish, cheerful and Public School accent is heard over the 'phone you'll know who it is. I'll let you know when he's coming. I may even be able to persuade him to call, especially if he comes via Newhaven.

Keep well; tell comrade Michael I'm dying to see him. Courage as regards the newcomer!

Love, Ron

It was five days before Dad wrote again:

Lieut. R. Spathaky, A.E.C.,
3 Div. Training School,
M.E.F. 7.2.46.

Dearest,

It must be a great nuisance to have your Mother and Doris ill at the same time. You will have to tackle things slowly and systematically,

---

438 The *Times Educational Supplement*, a weekly newspaper in which practically all teaching jobs in Britain were, and still are, advertised.

leaving aside the inessentials for a time. Please keep a good heart. I'm sure that when I come back we shall be able to share our problems more equitably than during my "lyrical revolutionary" period.

Next Tuesday the Forces Preliminary Exam starts for the chaps we have been teaching. I'm afraid some of them will come a cropper, but we have done what we can for them. It was advertised as a revision course but unfortunately some of them had not done very much beforehand. What makes things worse was the non-arrival of numbers of mathematical instruments for chaps taking Geometrical and Mechanical Drawing. Still, half of them ought to get through Part I of the Exam, the compulsory subjects English, Mathematics and General Knowledge.

Both the N.C.O. instructors and myself are a bit chilled by the number of things outside our control which have gone wrong but when the four days of the actual exam have passed we shall have three or four days off. It will be the first real break for a month.

I am struggling hard to renew my interest in the scheme and I think I am doing so. It's curious how from time to time one has to force oneself to undergo a sort of mental rebirth, isn't it? I think the main reason for lack of interest during some weeks has been the enormous piles of paper matter I've had to handle, with resultant loss of contact between myself and the men. There is a drive to rebuild interest in A.B.C.A. at the moment, however, and I imagine I can fit myself into that somehow.

I have gained some inspiration during the last week by the fact that the local town, Nataniya, has a good bookshop which sells a lot of French newspapers, including Les Lettres Françaises which I used to study carefully in France.[439]

Last Sunday I visited Haifa and got the secretary of the General Federation of Jewish Labour to give me some of the names of the different political parties. I visited one of them called

---

439 *Les Lettres Françaises* was a French literary publication, founded in 1941 as a clandestine magazine of the French Resistance in German-occupied territory. After the liberation it was financially supported by the French Communist Party.

Shomer Hatzonair (the Young Guard)[440] and found out about its programme. It claims to be a Marxist party, and works for a joint Jewish-Arab government within the framework of the United Nations Trusteeship scheme. "The idea of an independent small nation is anachronistic today in the age of the Atom Bomb," the secretary told me.

They wanted me to visit a settlement with them there and then but I hadn't time to stay in Haifa.

As I write I am trying to get in touch with Philip Locke, whom you may remember as a W.O. II, A.E.C. when he visited our digs at Preston. He is still with 6th Airborne, at Sarafand[441] near here. Between us we ought to work out some decent conception of the complicated position. I suppose it is despicable lethargy that has stopped me getting in touch with him before since I knew he was not more than fifty miles away.

(My call just came through from 6th Airborne. He is not in the office yet and will ring me back.)

Norman Scarfe and myself have been continuing our short sharp runs in the country round about. The orange-groves certainly are a golden sight during the season.

I still get your bundle of papers regularly. I have just had L.R.[442] for January and the book by Coombes. They are a great help, as is the earlier delivery of L.M.[443]

Now I must get down to the awful job of totting up my monthly Imprest Account. This is something I hate doing, but it just has to be done. Wish your mathematical talents were here to help me.

All my love, Ron

The next letter we have is dated two weeks later.

---

440 The Hashomer Hatzair Workers Party of Palestine was founded in 1946 as a Marxist-Zionist political party advocating a bi-national state.

441 Al-Sarafand, a small Arab village from which the inhabitants fled in 1948 – not to be confused with the larger village, Sarafand al-Amar, further south, deserted and destroyed in 1948.

442 Labour Review

443 Labour Monthly

Lieut. R. Spathaky, A.E.C.,
3 Br. Inf. Div. School,
M.E.F. 21.2.46.
(address still to be used)

Dearest K,

Afraid I haven't written for several days. I've been recovering from the effects of a course we ran and some temporary trouble with my eyes resulting from overstrain and incorrect lenses. As well as tackling it by the orthodox method of going sick I am taking up Huxley's nature-cure again, not because I have complete faith in it but because I believe it did my eyes good when I practised it before and because it cannot have bad effects.

I'm glad your Ma is up and about again. It is certainly the wrong time for you to have any extra strain or responsibility.

Thank you for arranging about the C.N. telegram. I should like you to impress upon your Mother the correct procedure in case of emergency involving compassionate leave (not that I imagine you will provide it!). There has to be a definite doctor's certificate and a S.S.A.F.A.[444] report that no other responsible male of the family is there to give help. Both these can be cabled. A telegram saying your wife is dangerously ill, sent by another member of the family, means nothing to the heartless old Army!

You will be glad to know that I have been in touch with the P [445] people both in Tel-Aviv and in Nathania and really feel I know a little more about the situation in Palestine. The local P is fully in agreement with what Palme Dutt[446] and Jack Gaster[447] have recently written on the subject.[448]

Tonight I am going with Norman Scarfe to rather an expensive Jewish orchestral concert in the local town. I hope you don't mind. It is very seldom that one gets the chance to listen to some good music. When a good orchestra <u>does</u> come to a small town like this the local

---

444 Soldiers, Sailors, Airmen and Families Association.
445 Party, i.e. The Communist Party.
446 Rajani Palme Dutt, leading theorist of the Communist Party of Great Britain.
447 Jacob Gaster, 1907-2007, human rights lawyer and CPGB activist.
448 Presumably foreshadowing R Palme Dutt's *Declaration on Palestine* of 1947.

Zionists take care to soak the British officers pretty thoroughly for their seats.

I have just had the office typewriter repaired so that I can get on with the oft-threatened letter to various councils and organisations for a better job. I shall do that in the morning. We are a bit slacker now that we have only the Basic Educational Course to do.

Lots of love, Ron

Two days later, on a Monday:

Lieut. R. Spathaky, A.E.C.,
3 Br. Inf. Div. Training School,
M.E.F. 23.2.46.

Dearest K,

Don't worry too much, darling, about Michael's trouble. After all it's nothing in the same category as permanent splints. I'm sure both boys and young dogs are subject to bandiness and knock-knees at certain points in their growth. He will grow out of it within a few months if he has correct treatment. If you can deal with this additional problem cheerfully it will help him; on the contrary if he sees you worrying about it when you are putting on the splints he will attach more importance to them than is necessary.[449]

When I was his age my ears started to grow out straight from my head like those of an elephant. They had to be strapped back every night, but they soon righted themselves.

My reason, or excuse, for not writing so regularly is general apathy for a few days at the conclusion of this month's course we have been running. I have been trying to wind up my enthusiasm again this week. It has been made easier by the announcement of Demob dates, June 6-16th. I think this presupposes arrival in England <u>by</u> these dates. So I shall leave Palestine (or Egypt) some time in May. I shall be at the Div School for another 3 weeks at least, so please go on using that address.

---

449 I can remember doing some exercises with my legs and feet, including one where I would make my feet crawl along the floor by alternately stretching and closing my toes. I don't remember any splints – Ed.

We have had some terrible storms recently, with great winds blowing in from the sea and lifting whole roofs from buildings. Today, however, the typical calm Mediterranean weather and, as I write, the last sun-rays are mellowing the little houses of Jewish settlements on the sandy hills. The horizon is marked by a delicate blue glow, merging into shell-pink higher up.

Next week's course is on the teaching of English. It should be quite interesting, since most of the work is done in syndicates of half-a-dozen.

The difficulty now is that staffs are disappearing on all sides and the administrative side of each course becomes more and more difficult. Every little bit of duplication and typing is harder to get done in Orderly rooms and offices. I shall be very glad to get home and help you, and put in some real work teaching.

Once again I hope you won't worry over Michael. I'm sure it's not your fault.

Love,
Ron

The next letter was probably sent on about 27th February 1946 – the postmark is ambiguous and the letter undated but the first sentence suggests it is very soon after the last one. Dad included a set of eight photographs he had bought, showing scenes in and around Haifa:

Lieut. R. Spathaky, A.E.C.,
3 Br. Inf. Div. Training School,
M.E.F.

Dearest wife,

Just an extra line or two to ask you to grit your teeth for the last lap of the difficult struggle you have been putting up. I'm sure things will take a turn for the better when we are together again and can take common council.

Did Michael submit with good grace to the remedial measure taken for his legs?

Are you still managing to carry the new burden around without too much strain? If your mother is seriously ill I should have no compunction in getting S.S.A,F.A. and doctor's reports and I'm sure they would send me home on compassionate leave or even <u>give me a compassionate home posting for the last few months of my Army career</u>. The grounds would be that you are unable to get adequate help for your confinement and for Michael. Please think about this seriously, please, and if you think there is a case send the documents

off straight away. They would probably fly me home.

We have just started a week's course for instructors of English. It is fairly interesting but I'm afraid the scheme doesn't hold the interest it did for me during the operational period. Perhaps I had become too A.B.C.A.-minded! It is probably useful for me to turn my thoughts to another type of activity, but it comes as a wrench.

The weather has been very stormy here, but it is still not very cold and occasionally we have days of spring-like charm with blue seas and gleaming surf to remind me of the South Coast of England.

How is the monetary and food situation at present? I know the latter is reported to be rather grim but is it grim in terms of real deficiencies of vital foods?

What do you think of this question of my applying for jobs elsewhere than in Brighton and district? Would it upset our plans very much if I got a job in London or even further north and had to go up there for the autumn term or would you prefer me to settle down in Brighton for a time?

Please do try and project your mind through the period or present problems and look forward to when we shall regain the basis of home life which we have lacked up to now. I do so want to be a reasonably good husband and father and if you can hang on for just these few months I'll do everything I can to prove it.

Love, Ron

The next letter was dated 2nd March and the envelope postmarked 4th March:

Div. School,
Sat. 1730 hrs
2.3.46.

Dearest K,

We have just finished our English instructors' course. It was a fair effort, but one or two organisational matters need to be improved in time for the next one.

Sorry my last letter but one took such a long time. There is a scarcity of mail this end at the present time, due no doubt to the bad weather in the Mediterranean.

Afraid I don't like the name Megan. It is too Welsh to go with Spathaky etc and I think it is a harsh name, reminiscent of nutmegs, though I confess I like Maureen, which is equally Celtic. (What about Atoma!). I also like Jean, Mavis, Doreen (special commendation).

But it's all a question of personal prejudice and as long as a name is phonetically pleasant and not too strange I rather feel with the poet "What's in a name?" On looking over the list I think I prefer Jean and Doreen.

Yesterday I succeeded in contacting Philip Locke, whom you may remember from Bamber Bridge. I set out to see him about a fortnight previously but landed up in a badly signposted region of Arab villages south of Sarafand. He has just got his commission and was only able to do so by signing on for another year. I'm very glad they didn't raise that point in my case.

I have just been awarded a certificate called the Commander-in-Chief's Certificate of Good Service for work done in B.A.O.R. Don't tell too many people until I find out how many people are getting it. It may be worthwhile having, on the other hand it may be a general kind of award for WO Is who served in the Rhine Army.

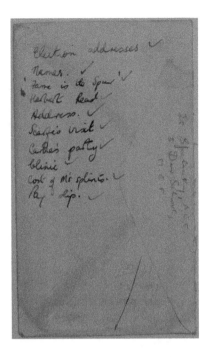

I am still in the middle of Howard Spring's Fame is the Spur.[450] I have not read such an interesting book for many a long day. I fancy you may have read it, but if you haven't I can thoroughly recommend it, as a study of the kind of life we know fairly well, of people who live in poverty or semi-poverty in the Midlands and then rise to more comfortable positions, either abandoning, modifying or sticking to various causes which they took up when they were young.

Norman Scarfe, who is a very good friend of mine, is now leaving here on 6th March and should be in UK by about the 20th. He is not at all sensitive to seeing women in "'t family way," so he will either 'phone or call, wherever you are when he arrives.

Lots of love,
Ron

Mum used the envelope of that letter to compile a shopping list – or more likely a to-do list. Every item is ticked!

The next letter we have is dated eleven days later:

---

450 Dad claimed to have finished it the previous November!

Lieut. R. Spathaky,
A.E.C. School,
M.E.F.
13.3.46.

Dearest K,

Just a line to tell you that Norman Scarfe, my very good friend, has started from here, and after a few days in Cairo will return by air to England. He will certainly call on you, and you needn't be afraid he'll be self-conscious. He's very natural in everything he does – in fact the perfectly educated golden boy, by liberal standards.

I have just had a letter from Renée,[451] in which she doesn't say very much about Zionism. It was quite pleasant.

I realise each letter I am sending may be the last one before you enter upon a very painful (though not in your case dangerous, I hope) experience. It doesn't help very much to hear that someone understands, I suppose. In any case men don't understand very clearly, since they don't undergo birth-pangs. But here's wishing you an easy delivery.

Lots of love, –
Ron

It does seem that Mum expects to go into labour any day now, which is rather surprising to me. Dad's long leave was from 25th June to 5th July 1945 so they should not have expected a birth before the very end of March. Dad wrote two days later, on a Friday:

Lieut. R.V. Spathaky, A.E.C.,
3 Br. Inf. Div. Training School,
M.E.F. 15.3.46.

Dearest K,

Today we come to the end of the five courses we have held down here at the School, and I have only to organise an exam called the Army Special Certificate examination before I finish for a week. It's a pity I can't spend that week with you, but I mean to use it as usefully as

---

451 Renée Shulman – see page 72.

possible studying the country and seeing a few famous places before I go away with the Div back to Egypt.

During the few days I am away I shall ring up the School every day to find out any news from you.

There has been a classical concert in the Naafi tonight. It was quite pleasant; a girl played several Schubert and Schumann sonatas on the violin and a Norwegian and what seemed to be an English girl sang several duets from Mozart's Barber of Seville and Marriage of Figaro.

The girl also played Debussy's En Bateau, which you may remember from our little collection of records at the flat.

When I have my few days off I rather fail to see what I can do to be useful, because we move off to Egypt on the 1st. I suppose that apart from packing up I shall have to read and sun bathe.

The chap who went through my A.B.C.A. course at 15 Condepot in Hasselt (Belgium) and applied for transfer to the A.E.C. has been posted to the School. So when my W.O. II goes in about a fortnight's time and I follow him in June we shall have at least one capable pair of Marxist hands to leave the place in.[452]

There was also a very good Sergeant on this last weekly instructors' course who could probably be borrowed from his unit in the Division for the benefit of the Army Education Scheme.

The post has been a little bit disorganised again; I am writing with confident expectation of news of yourself and Michael. I hope his legs are not too bad and that you have absolved yourself from any feeling of blame you may have had.

You will be relieved to know that I wrote a long letter to my Mother recently, enclosing a note for my Grandmother.[453]

Norman having moved to the U.K., I have moved into a luxurious big room which he occupied, with windows facing the bushes and spring flowers and then the blue Mediterranean stretching away to infinity and (finally) the Straits of Gibraltar. So perhaps you can picture me looking out of my window at the very "end of the

---

452 This is a surprisingly open admission (even in the more relaxed post-war censorship regime) of the nature of the propaganda which Marxists were able to undertake under the aegis of the ABCA.

453 Ann Elizabeth Retchford (née Watton), then aged eighty-five.

Mediterranean" and thinking of the boat which will bring me back, past Tunisia and Sicily (with all their memories), then up through France, whose unhappiness I feel so strongly myself, to Dieppe and across to Newhaven and up to the release camp, which I believe is near Guildford somewhere, though I can't remember exactly.

There is still no suggestion of any deferment for A.E.C. and my W.O. I went last Saturday.

So here's looking forward to "Der Tag."

Love, Ron

On the reverse of the last page, Dad wrote:

TO MICHAEL.
HALLO. DADDY'S
COMING HOME.

The next Wednesday he wrote:

Lieut. Spathaky, A.E.C.,
3 Br. Inf. Div. Trng School,
M.E.F. 20.3.46.

Dearest K,

I have had no letters for about five days, but I assume that everything is all right. Your Ma would presumably let me know if you were in any difficulties. I hope so, anyway.

It must be an amazing feeling to be "trembling on the brink." You know that you won't have much longer to wait, however. You will soon be back to normal size and activities.

I suppose the idea of love-making has been in the far background for three or four months now. How soon do you begin to take an interest in such things once again? Or shouldn't I ask in case I seem to be selfishly interested at a time when such an epoch-making event is due.

Last night I went sixty miles over fascinating moon-lit roads to Sarafand, to open a discussion for Phil Locke (of Bamber Bridge fame) on "Does Socialism Mean Less Freedom." It was a very good discussion and I enjoyed getting back into the old A.B.C.A. basis of our work. Most of the chaps were progressive but a number of them have recently been inoculated by the wave of anti-Russian propaganda which has been apparent here. The Middle-East is a real centre for that kind of thing.

After the discussion they took me to the last hour of a dance organised by the Jewish A.T.S. at Sarafand. This was the first social function (apart from horrible "mess" nights) which I have been to in M.E.F. But I hurried away in my draughty jeep as soon as it was over and there were no entanglements. But talk about concentrated indiscriminate boiling lust! I must be a real bagful of sin, in the old Catholic sense. However, it is pretty easy to keep away from women when the nearest eligible ones are about fifty miles away.

Perhaps you will accord me a little merit, however, when I say that I have kept away from women out here – in the sense of never going out to see whom I could encounter. I think my affection and love for you is winning battles over my vagabond nature.

Percy sent me a copy of the "Times Edn" (I believe I told you). Unfortunately I have not had time to answer him yet but I shall do now that my local leave is starting.

I have made my arrangements for instantaneous telephone communication on and around the 25th. Good luck et courage.

– Love – Ron

XXXXXXXXXXX

So it appears that the baby was expected just five days later on 25th March. The next letter was written on the 24th:

Lt. Spathaky, A.E.C.,
3 Br. Inf. Div. School,
M.E.F. 24.3.46.

Dearest wife,

I suppose that this letter will reach you after the event, though one never can tell and I remember that Michael was delayed for a few days. I am risking sending it to the hospital all the same.

What can I say that will be of help to you, my dear? You have all the ordeal and responsibility, unfortunately, and words are but feeble aids. Yet these are all I have, and I am grateful for what you have done. It's no easy thing to keep a home together, especially when your husband does his best on some occasions to break it up.

But we do learn, Kathie, and I'm sure our next try at home-building will be better than our previous ones were.

I'm writing this in the middle of Ashdoth Jacob, one of the largest collective farms in Palestine. I told you that I should be travelling around during this week, but I have decided to stay here because the life of the settlers is so interesting. There are 1200 souls on the farm and apart from personal belongings they have no private property. The farming, jam-making, building, political and social activity are led by a committee of 30 people who are elected annually.

The "mikhtar" or chairman is also elected by general election. All costings and calculations are carried out in "hours of work."

I visited lessons in English, Arithmetic and Music at the school and I found the standard very good.

All feeding is done in the huge communal restaurant, though babies, young children and teen-age kids have their own communal dining-halls, close to their communal houses. Parents see their children for a few hours after work each day, but the naturalness of parental affection doesn't seem to be affected by that fact.

Yesterday was the feast Yom ha Yeled (the Day of the Child) and a big exhibition of toys made by the various departments in their spare time was laid out in one of the houses. At a special ceremony they give them out to the children.

I am pretty well convinced this is real collective farming. If there is a snag it is in the overweening national feeling that they have. I have heard many Jews say, "Where would you find a nation able to do these things, in the whole world? Only the Jews can do it." In other words they have a "race-theory" which is something like the Nazis. Zionism, moreover, is no solution for the problem of Jewry, though it may be the only solution for a certain number.

In the meantime, however, they are very kind and overwhelm me with friendship. Tomorrow I have asked to do some work to repay them for my week's stay. They won't take any money and I can hardly eat myself into a hole in their rations for a week without doing something in return.

It will perhaps seem strange, Kathie, that I should go off for a week while you are due for your big event, but I was allotted these dates for leave without any choice and I preferred not to hang about the military camp (which is almost empty) and await my cablegram. It would have driven me batty.

Well, I hope to goodness everything goes as per program, though I am sure it will. This is definitely the last letter to be written before my cable comes and my heart will be with you all the while.

So, courage,

All my best love

Ron

XXXXXXXXXXXX

Chapter 23

Waiting

We have seen that the baby was expected around 25th March, but Dad writes four more letters and a telegram before he receives the news he has been waiting for:

as before.

4.4.46.

Dearest,

I have now received two letters from Norman Scarfe, which have reassured me mightily. When one hears from someone on the spot, whom one has seen recently, that things are not going badly, then it is very reassuring. It is like a personal link with home.

The letter system has always seemed queer and magical to me. Letters are delivered in quite a short time, but to me the distance always seems to have detracted from them. If I were in Southampton receiving

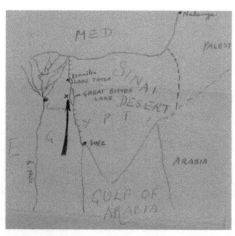

exactly the same screed they would seem much more real. Yet the paradox is that they are more precious, though less real. Silly idea, isn't it?

I don't quite know which address to write to, but I'm plumping for the Hospital again, because I gather that you <u>must</u> have got there by now.

Hope it wasn't too horribly painful. You'll probably forget the pain fairly soon. I remember asking you a few months after the last achievement and you said it was the kind of intense pain that disappeared quickly into the back of one's mind. Hope it does – and soon.

We are back in Egypt now and on the shores of the Great Bitter Lake (through which the Suez Canal passes).

It is rather depressingly military, but we have the blue of the lake in sight and a high range of typical North African hills behind us, reminding me somewhat of Tunisia.

I'm writing for numbers of jobs, but more for practice than anything else. I've had a few replies inviting me to fill in forms and offering to put me on the list of vacancies. So I've filled in the forms.

It is extraordinarily difficult to find any work to do, but in a fortnight or so we shall probably be up to our necks in some course or other.

I'm now going to write to Norman thanking him for going so far when he had so many other things to do in Britain.

Hope the cable comes tomorrow. It may be upset by our move.

Love,

Ron

Five days later Dad still had no news of the arrival of the baby and in fact it still hadn't been born!

Lt. Spathaky, A.E.C.,
HQ 3 Br. Inf. Div.
M.E.F.
9.4.46.

Dearest K,

You're right. I haven't known what to do this week to keep from thinking about you all the time. Unfortunately there has been practically no work to do so it has been all the harder. I've written once or twice to the hospital and I hope you have those letters by now.

It was most intriguing to hear about Michael's journey back from Doris's. It was probably just that he wanted to see you, but didn't like to say so. It is certainly very curious that he should take an adventurous decision like that, when there has been little in his activities previous which indicate adventurous tendencies.[454]

Egypt is hot, fly-ridden and enervating. I shall be back at Div by the time I get my next letter from you.

This will be even worse than working at Fanara, where we at least have the Great Bitter Lake to cool us.

I got replies from most of the forty local authorities I wrote to about a job. Unfortunately I neglected to put my demob date on a lot of them, but in a number of cases they asked me to contact them again as soon as I returned to the U.K.

Last night I went with the two A.E.C. Instructors here to a P.O.W. concert given by an Austrian string-orchestra. After the perfect music we have heard in Palestine it sounded a very ragged effort. One felt obliged to applaud, however, since there is obviously a certain amount of goodwill behind the P.O.W.s' playing.

Tonight I haven't quite decided what to do. I shall probably have a go at writing a short story. One cannot read, argue politics and sit in the mess all day and night, and I shan't be here long enough to get anything going in the way of discussion groups.

I've been reading a French novel I bought at Ismailia, "Katherine" by Hans Habe,[455] who wrote "A Thousand Shall Fall."[456] I cannot believe that the same man wrote the two. The second is an acute satire of the adventuress type of woman who "gets on" among the bourgeoisie, but compared with "A Thousand Shall Fall" I find it putrid.

---

454 I had been taken to stay with Doris and my cousin Helen in Kingston Close, Shoreham, for the period covering Mum's confinement. I decided to walk the three miles (5 km) or so back home, crossing Upper Shoreham Road, then re-crossing it to take a detour via Portslade Station to watch the trains by the level crossing. Mum was still at home with Nan and Grandpop when I arrived. Neither house had a telephone so I was taken straight back to Doris's in a taxi as she would have been worried to death wondering where I had disappeared to.

455 An English translation was published by Harrap, 1944, but I have not traced a French version. Habe was a Hungarian living in France at the outbreak of the War.

456 Pub. Harcourt, Brace and Company, New York, 1941.

I have plenty of chance to practise my French and German here, because we have scores of each working in the camp. The only difference is that the Italians live here, while the Jerries go back to the cages at night.[457]

Well, here's hoping I get the cable soon.

Love, Ron

As we have seen in Dad's letters, Norman Scarfe was a good friend in Egypt and Palestine. Norman returned to England in March and was to have visited Mum straight away, which he seems to have done. Mum must have written to thank him, as he wrote back straight away:

Capt. N Scarfe, R.A.
10, Harrington Gdns., SW 7
12 Apr 46

Dear Kath,

Thank you for a letter this morning – I had been unable to make up my mind to write, and became less able to as the time went on. Then three or four nights ago I rang you, and as there was no reply concluded that there must surely be news from you soon.

I do admire the philosophic calm with which you treat what we can only imagine to be an extremely uncomfortable state: it's very easy to say "Of course, one is reasonable about these things." One is also a human being.

Anyway Ron writes (I received his letter the day I tried to ring) that he fortifies himself with the thought that you are the most sensible girl in the world about such things etc, etc. I repeat this to you in order that you will fortify yourself with the thought that he fortifies himself with the thought and so on. If you are still keeping him waiting this time next week my clear duty is to report to him that he may fortify himself with the thought that you fortify yourself with the thought that he is fortifying himself with the thought. By then we shall all have

---

457 There seems to be some confusion of nationalities here. I presume he must mean "practise my *Italian* and German…".

forgotten what the thought is and I shall be confused and not know what to write about. So make haste and good luck.

Yrs ever, Norman.

On 13th April, things start happening at Southlands Hospital, Shoreham, just round the corner from Doris and Gordon's bungalow.

My sister Jean must have been born quite early in the morning as Mum receives a telegram from her parents before 9.30am on the same day. Her mother had sent it in Shoreham at 9.26am.

Soon after that there's another:

CONGRATULATIONS SO GLAD IT'S A GIRL = VERA AND JIMMY[458]

But Dad had not heard anything yet and is getting desperate for news. He sends a telegram which takes two days to arrive at Mum's parents' house.

---

458 This will be Jimmy A with whom Dad had worked in Taunton. (See page 113.)

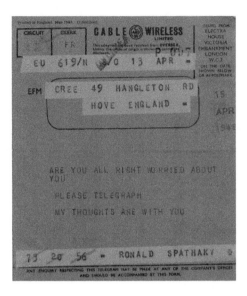

The following day, Dad still hadn't heard anything. He wrote:

Lt. Spathaky, A.E.C.,
HQ Edn 3 Br Inf. Div
M.E.F. 14.4.46.

Dearest K,

I'm afraid my epistles have been scrappy recently. As you guessed, it is because I have been waiting for the big news. Today I felt I had been in the dark too long, so I sent off a telegram to find out the latest news from your Ma.

You see I still don't know where to write to; I think I shall send this letter to No 49, as I have written several times to the hospital.

What makes the situation still more chancy is that I have moved back to Div HQ again and I suppose your Ma's cable will go to the school. Luckily the telephone line from Fanara is quite reasonably and they will phone me as soon as they get the wire.

I hope to goodness you're all right. Please pull through the thing in the approved manner, won't you?

I know I haven't appeared interested enough, as usual, but I am really, thus the colossal "flap" which I have on at the present time.

There seems to be a fair amount of work to do here, but it's a bit difficult picking up the threads of administration when one has been on courses followed by local leave and a period of travel.

Apparently our group leaves Div HQ some time around May 28th, if all goes well. There is still no proved threat of D.O.V., though they are going to be in a bad fix when we go, as far as I can see.

We spend about a week at the staging camp at Sidi Bish, somewhere near Port Said, and thenceforth the movement by sea is pretty swift, I am told. Personally I should like it to be even swifter.

Egypt is a grand country for the Egyptians but for Englishmen it's an ash-heap.

Lots of love

Ron

As a measure of his anxiety Dad writes another letter the same day, or perhaps there's another dating error somewhere:

Lt. Spathaky, A.E.C.,

HQ Edn 3 Br. Inf. Div.

M.E.F. 14.4.46.

Dearest Kath,

Here I am back in the Egyptian desert, with a fair amount of work to do but still too much time to think of things that might be going wrong with you. Since I received the last letter from you some four or five days ago I have had little else in mind.

There is one thing about being at Div HQ, however, I get the latest official news on the Middle East and since you have taken good care that I am supplied with the unofficial stuff I can bring myself completely up to date. Then there is the work with troops around Div HQ to do, so I should begin to make up for the isolation I endured during the last week or two at the Div school.

You will perhaps be a little surprised to know that I feel in a more militant mood than ever. I have seen the works of imperialism from close at hand and I think they confirm the Marxist view a hundred per cent.

It is plain that the coming to power of a Labour government affects but slightly the general structure of imperialism, though it provides the possibility of working-class advance in a way that a reactionary Tory government could not.

The economic forces within the old structure continually force the Labour right-wing to act in an imperialistic manner, while the incessant pressure from the world labour movement and the Soviet Union irritate them from the other side. They reveal themselves as completely opportunistic, delaying remedies until desperate pressure from either side forces them to make concessions.

Thus the Anglo-American Investigation Committee in Palestine, designed to delay the advance of real democracy and to work out a solution based on "divide and rule" and to appease the reactionary elements among both Jews and Arabs by giving in to their plans a little at the expense of the Jewish and Arab masses. In Egypt the present treaty negotiations will no doubt result in concessions made to the puppet King Farouk at the expense of the bourgeois-democratic Wafd party.

If one wanted a real test of Bevin's imperialist policy – Greece is the key.[459] Can anything be more blatant then the power-politics he has played here, forcing an election which gives the Greek people over to monarchist and fascist terror.

Though I must stabilise my own position when I get home I see that I have a duty to you and all like us to teach the lessons I have learned while I have been away.

You will be glad to know that I have kept my own subjects up to date while I have been out here. My French is obviously better than it ever was and we work in an army that has so many working POW's in it that my Italian and German are quite good as well.

I read quite a lot of other stuff as well, like "The History of the Common People" by G.D.H. Cole,[460] H.A.L. Fisher's "History of

---

459 Ernest Bevin, Foreign Secretary in the post-war Labour government 1945-51, right-wing, anti-Communist trade unionist.
460 *The Common People 1746-1946* by G D H Cole and Raymond Postgate, pub. Methuen, 1946.

Europe"[461] and various Left Book Club books I get hold of. I have started Stuart Gelder's "Chinese Communists" in that series recently.[462]

I know all this is a far cry from the thing that is really worrying me, but I have to write to you about the things that are affecting me at first-hand.

Otherwise I should only keep repeating to you that I love you and hope this is the last big problem you will have to face by yourself.

xxxxx Lots of love, Ron

Meanwhile, back in hospital in Shoreham, Mum continues to receive congratulatory messages, such as this one from friends Eileen and Percy Ireland:[463]

"Glen"
High View
Patcham
Brighton 6
15.4.46.

Dear Kath,

We were delighted to hear your daughter had arrived safely. I do hope you and she are making good progress. Percy saw your mother last Thursday I think it was, and heard you were having some injections and we were wondering how you were getting on. Then last night he called on the Reigates and Dennis, who'd seen Dick Pennifold,[464] [who] said you had a daughter! It's amazing how the news gets around! Your card arrived today and has made me eager to get some like it, to save writing to my various relatives. You are much better than we are, we cannot choose a name – Percy suggested Patrick, if it's a boy, but I think Paddy Ireland is unfair on a child.

I'm very envious of you for two reasons, one, for having achieved the baby, and two, for having managed one of each. My lump keeps

---

461 *A History of Europe* by H A L Fisher, pub. Methuen, 2 vols.: 1922 and 1935
462 *The Chinese Communists* by Gelder Stuart, pub. Victor Gollancz, 1946.
463 Percy and Eileen Ireland – see page 72.
464 See page 20.

growing, they tell me it's an elephant so I hope it won't be tardy in its arrival like Jean. This last stage is very boring, isn't it? At the moment I have no ambition for more than two! Hence my envy of your having one of each – you've nothing left to try for!

I'd love to come and see you, Kath, but I know you'll understand that I can't get around very gaily just at the moment. A little later I hope you'll come over like you did with Michael and spend the day with us. Then we can have a good jaw and compare notes!

All the best to you from Percy and myself,

Yours Eileen

The following day Dad at last receives the good news he's been waiting for and sends Mum a telegram, which takes two days to arrive. He followed it up with a letter

Lt. Spathaky, A.E.C.,
HQ 3 Br. Inf. Div.
M.E.F. 16.4.46.

Dearest K,

I got the telegram yesterday. Hope you received the reply fairly soon afterwards. I think it's a good change to have a girl. A boy grows up better if he knows something of female company and vice versa. Hope everything goes well during the first few weeks. No doubt you will let me know what it (sorry, she) weighs as soon as you are able to write.

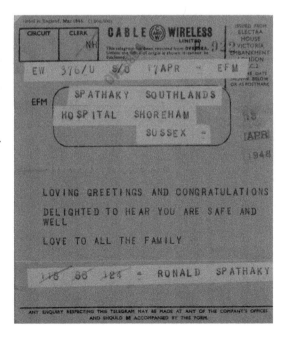

Was the delivery <u>very</u> painful or just painful?

I have got up very early to write this and only have a few minutes before I start work. Sent off a packet of Turkish delight and sweets yesterday.

I shall have to ask you to send me the measurement for the shoes again. They were not available in Palestine and unfortunately I lost them. So please send when you can, making Michael's measurements a little bigger then "life-size" to allow for growing.

Love,

Ron

Letters from friends and family continued to flow to Mum; this one, written on 15th April, is from Renée Shulman:

23 Upper North Street

Brighton, 1

Monday a.m.

My dear Kath,

I phoned your mother yesterday evening, having got a bit worried, and heard the news. Congratulations!! I <u>am</u> glad it's a girl – she will make a nice change – it's Jean, I suppose? I was glad to hear you didn't have too bad a time – you deserved a bit of relief after all the waiting and fuss.

I have heard from the University and the whole thing is off, I fear. It's a bit of a blow, as you will imagine

Looking forward to the first sight of Jean.

Look after yourself

All my love

Renée

<u>P.S.</u> Hope you can read this scrawl – I want to get it in the post early.

A couple of days later there was this card from Norman Scarfe:

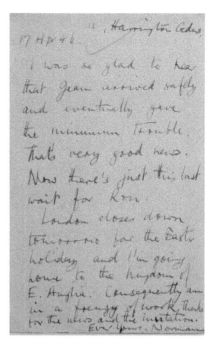

Further cards also arrived from Mum's aunts, Kitty and Gertie. Then there was a letter from a Sylvia, whom I cannot identify:

> 241, Coventry Rd
> Ilford
> Essex
> 18.4.46

My dear Kath,

I was quite delighted to hear that your daughter had arrived. I spoke to your mother on Sunday *[14th April]* when I went down to Brighton and she sounded very thrilled and said that Jean was lovely and you feeling very well.

Needless to say I am longing to see you both and will make my way to your house as soon after I get to Brighton as possible, some time after 25th May.

I am feeling rather tired after all our labours getting the house in order and I dislike Ilford anyway and miss all my friends in Brighton.

My sister came out of hospital on Tuesday and it is nice having somebody about the house to talk to.

Philip will be home today for four days Easter holidays.

I wish that my job was over and that my daughter? was born. I am weary of carrying this about and would like to put it down for a few hours just to have a rest; you lucky thing, feeling slim again.

Forgive this short note but miles of work is staring me in the face and I must start in.

The children are thrilled about Jean and send their love to her and to Michael and of course to you.

Get well quickly

Love Sylvia

P.S. Doris gave me your address and I tried to remember it, hope I've got it correctly.

A brief postcard arrived from someone called Mary in Chesterfield. I don't think this is a relative so it must a friend or neighbour of one of the Chesterfield aunts. Its slightly formal style suggests she is not family.

There is also a card from "all the Comrades at Southwick" – I suspect a branch of the Communist Party or the Co-operative Women's Guild. Southwick is a suburb between Shoreham and Hove:

The Homestead,
Southwick.

Congratulations and best wishes from all the Comrades at Southwick.

Then, on 20th April, Mum received a telegram from her brother Gordon, who was stationed in Austria:

CONGRATULATIONS KAY SEE YOU BOTH SOON – LOVE GORDON CREE

Dad wrote to Mum on 20th April:

Lt. R. Spathaky, A.E.C.,
HQ 3 Br. Inf. Div.
M.E.F. 20.4.46

Dearest K,

Received the telegram pronto. I had been posted back from the Div School to Div HQ, so the A.P.O. at Div HQ captured the wire at Div HQ as it went through, which saved time.

I wrote a letter to you yesterday, which I hope very much you received, because to tell you the truth I can't remember posting it. Such fits of absent-mindedness are very rare with me these days, but I can't find the blooming thing, so I suppose I must have posted it.

The latest news is a) that I am in what is called Python Group J4, so I leave this HQ for the last time on May 20th; as I may have told you, we spend about 10 days at Port Said waiting for the members of the same Release Group who are coming from the Far East and India, b) I have sent in applications for two jobs at Portsmouth, at North Grammar School and South Grammar School. If you can find my original references when you get home and send me written copies of a couple or three of the best ones it would help me very much in this job-hunting business. Also I need my registered number as a teacher, which is probably on my Certificate and Diploma of Teaching (issued by the Board of Education).

Don't bother about these requests, however, since I know you have many more important things to do at the moment.

I am thrilled to death by your description of the young Jean. Of course she had to be good-looking, with such a father and mother contributing (somewhat unequally!) to her make-up!?!

We are starting a new education scheme, for under 45s (age-groups, that is). It will probably be a much bigger thing than anything we have done before and I shall only see the preliminary stages, but they should give a useful insight into what the Army Education Scheme will be like when the Army has settled down to peace-time conditions.

It was very brave of you to write me a letter the very day after your production effort. I must admit I was getting a bit worried. It will be interesting to see Michael's first reaction to Jean's arrival. When I arrive we shall be able to tackle more easily the problem of dividing our attention between them.

I'm afraid that having returned to the camp where the man makes the suede half-boots, I have lost the patterns. Please send some more.

More later,

Love, Ron

On 21st April Mum received a pencilled note from a friend called Gren:

23 Edburton Ave.
Brighton
21/4/46

My dear Kath,

Congratulations on your second baby – imagine a girl! What wonderful luck. I like her name very much and I bet Michael is tickled to bits.

I hope you're feeling well and that you didn't have a too rough time. Perhaps I'll be able to get along some time soon and say Hello to Jean. So until then take care of yourself.

Cheerio – love
> Gren

On about the same day Mum received an Air Letter (addressed to "Mrs R Spathaky") from Len Hevey, a schoolteacher also serving in the Middle East:

[From] Capt. N J Hevey RA[465]
AG.5. GHQ.
MEF.

Tuesday 23rd April, 1946.

---

465 Royal Artillery.

Dear Kath,

Congratulations, you must be feeling very pleased with yourself, and to be capable of sending out cards immediately after the birth would indicate that you were feeling quite well, too.

I had a letter from Gordon last week. It was very welcome too, especially to hear someone expressing your own particular sentiments which in your own particular circle, are considered outrageous.

You should see some of the efforts out here, they are bad enough in England, but seem to put on a special act for the benefit of the natives, no doubt, "shewing the flag" and all that, you know. We are the master race.

I am now living on Gezira island, which is across the Nile from Cairo. I have a furnished room in a flat and eat in a Pension across the way. The tenants of the flat are of Italian extraction, but were born here. The husband is an engineer and is a very charming person. We have some very interesting talks, in French (mine is pretty deadly). He was interned here for 3½ years, and had a pretty rough time at the hands of the Egyptians. All the male Italians were interned willy-nilly, irrespective of their particular circs.

Bevin[466] seems to be doing better than Chamberlain in his policy towards Greece and Spain. It is disgustingly hypocritical that a socialist foreign secretary can carry out such a reactionary policy. Most of the officers, who have no sympathy with the Labour cause, are full of praise for Bevin – mainly for his anti-Soviet attitude. I see the Co-op Conference had something to say on the subject, and I am now looking forward to Whitsun.

I have been warned that I am likely to be deferred for three months, but intend to appeal against it.

Regards to your Mum and Dad. I hope Ron is keeping fit; he will soon be home, won't he, or are they deferring AEC too?

Yours sincerely,

Len

---

466 Ernest Bevin, Foreign Secretary in the post-war Labour government 1945-51 and right-wing, anti-Communist trade unionist.

Then there was another letter from Dad:

HQ 3 Br. Inf. Div.
M.E.F. 24.4.46.

Dearest K,

Yours of the 18th and 19th to hand, Madame, for which receive the thanks of the undersigned, your 'usband.

I'm sure Michael will take the arrival of Jean as naturally as millions of other children in dozens of other countries. I think your concern for these problems is very laudable. Most children have to adjust themselves by a hit-and-miss method. It is obviously more sensible to do something to help them.

There is still no suggestion of D.O.V.-ing here, though I fail to see how they can replace the Major and myself, who already do the jobs of four officers at this HQ. (I'm trying to get the money for one of the Staff-Captaincies though I shall not get the rank.)

Today it is hot beyond belief. It's almost up to the old Tunisian standards. During a couple of hours of the afternoon one can do little except sleep and I sleep from 9.30 p.m. to 7.15 a.m. It will take me some time to cut down this terrible amount of sleep, but I expect the freezing English climate, the children and you will help me to acquire English ideas again pretty quickly.

Unfortunately heat is a factor militating against long letter-writing but perhaps a little and often is better than much and rarely!

I manage to do a bit of reading during the afternoon, since that can be done in the horizontal. I've just finished "Le Grand Meaulnes" by Alain-Fournier, rather a curious novel for me to read.[467] It was written in 1913 and is one of the last novels of the French "Romantic" School, and a very fine one at that; betrothals of children at mock ceremonies in old village schools, perilous quests of boys for girls lost in pony-traps, the moon scudding across dark clouds seen from old country houses in the Cher district right in the middle of France, and the death of the beloved while her new bridegroom is away seeking

---

467 *Le Grand Meaulnes* by Henri Fournier (Alain-Fournier was a pseudonym), pub. Emile-Paul, 1913.

to reconcile his best friend and the girl the friend loves. All very old-fashioned, but beautifully written and adding to one's total knowledge of France.

I have never given up the idea that when you have organised (or we have organised) this family of ours to some extent, you will brush up the considerable knowledge of French you have. In which case I shall be able to recommend this and one or two other books I have really liked.

Lots of love

(24 days more before starting home)

Ron

It is five days before Dad writes again, and he seems to feel guilty:

HQ 3 Div,

29.4.46.

Dearest K,

There has obviously been some hold-up in the A.P.O. again, since I only got your letter dated the 21st today. However, I am hastening to make up for epistolary omissions during the last three or four days.

On Saturday night we had a dance in our Mess, the first while I have been at HQ. I was nominated Second-in-Command of the Shrubbery and Floral Decoration section. In other words I had to use the blisteringly hot afternoons of several days this last week to range far over the countryside in a truck and find odd bits of greenery to decorate the hall. Since we live inside quite a respectably-sized young desert (and most of Egypt is half-desert) the finding of an odd palm-tree with a few leaves on it was quite a triumph.

The local goats eat everything on the few trees growing at a low level and the Arabs cut most of the rest for thatch, fuel and all kinds of purposes. However, by paying exorbitant prices to "Bushir Mahmud" (the Gardener Mahmud) at the Officers Club at Ismailia, we managed to get a collection of palm-fronds.

The dance was not much of a success because there were not enough women, but the M.C. was pretty poor and that didn't help. He should have got people mixed up together much more. As it was the few blokes who managed to grab somebody at the beginning hung on to them during the whole of the evening.

I danced with a moderately interesting but rather young nurse for the first part of the evening, then the Deputy Assistant Provost-Marshall got hold of her during one of the only excuse-me's and I retired from the fight with Roman dignity.

Today I went out in the truck to Lake Timsah and instead of the usual swimming I hired a small yacht. As I have never been sailing before I found it quite good fun. I also drove the truck both ways (45 miles) under the careful supervision of my driver, who is also my batman.

You needn't be afraid of my repeating my Rouen escapade, however. That was just sheer bad luck and in any case beginners are always allowed one crash, which induces due caution in them. Or didn't I tell you how I crashed a truck in Rouen nine months or so ago? If not I will tell you when I bore you with the rest of my anecdotes and descriptions.

I am very glad to hear that the last few days in hospital were quite pleasant. By now I suppose you have had the remarkable experience of introducing the Spathakys to the Spathakys. I hope it was done fairly casually and without the dramatisation that Victorian parents always organised, which must have exasperated their children beyond measure. I'm sure they always got a superior thrill out of forcing children to make each other's acquaintance and then saying, "Ah look at the dear little things. They're shy. Now be good and kiss the little baby!" Grrrrrh!

If one child chooses to ignore another one for a time I'm sure he or she has the right to do so. Children are innately friendly in the long run and will overcome initial frostiness.

Well, it's a real scorcher tonight; it is 9.45 p.m. and still 80° inside the Mess.[468] I going to bed early and going to try getting up early in the morning.

How's the old tummy?

Love and kisses,

Ron

---

468 26° C.

The next letter we have is dated ten days later:

Lt. Spathaky, A.E.C.,
HQ 3 Inf. Div.
M.E.F. 9.5.46.

Dearest wife,

Don't worry about your letters, or even the lack of them. I know perfectly well that you have had to readjust your hours and habits very radically once again and I shall be glad of the shortest scribbled note. In any case you won't have the burden of correspondence for very long now. Two big boxes in which I have to pack my kit are in the tent as I write and I hope to start for Sidi Bishr a fortnight today.

There was a brief scare the day before yesterday. An order came out that officers of Group 30 in infantry, R.A.C. and "extra-regimentally" employed, were to be delayed until June 30th. We rang up GHQ immediately to enquire whether we were "extra-regimental" and were assured that we were not. So at the moment all goes well. However, the signal shows that even if there were a last minute deferment it would only be for a very brief time. These other unfortunates will only be delayed a matter of a fortnight or three weeks.

I go for my release medical exam tomorrow and my Release Book is due here.

So I hope you will bear your dual burden cheerfully until I can come and help you. After all, part of the burden is not still inside! I should think that must help.

I have just been reading the first part of Alex Tolstoy's "Road to Calvary"[469] which I bought in Cairo the day before yesterday. It is really excellent and has helped to spur me on to a last effort at this rather routine educational work which we are doing at present.

In Cairo the other day I met Mrs. Terni, an Italian who is a friend of Togliatti (Ercoli),[470] of whom I think you must have heard.

---

469 An English translation of the trilogy *Khozhdeniye po mukam* (1935), pub. Boni & Liveright, New York, 1923 (sic).

470 Palmiro Togliatti (*nom de guerre*, Ercole Ercoli) was a founding member of the Communist Party of Italy. From 1927 until his death in 1964 he was its Secretary and undisputed leader, having spent the war years in the Soviet Union.

She gave me some interesting facts about the Egyptian Wafdist party and the situation in general. If I get a chance to go into Cairo again I shall be able to get an interview with an Egyptian journalist who knows the movement well. Unfortunately I rather doubt if this is possible, but it would be interesting to have a talk with <u>one</u> English-speaking Arab on political matters. It must sound very strange to you that I have not done so before but the distances here are so great and communication so difficult that it has been impossible.

I have almost succeeded in getting promotion to Staff Captain for the period in Jan-Feb-March when I was at the Div School. It means Captain's pay and staff pay in addition and I think there is a chance of me drawing leave pay at that rate. If it comes off all right it will be a slight help to offset the increased cost of living.

I have just received two more belated copies of "Times Educational Supplement" from Percy Ireland. I will try and write to thank him, but if you are ever on the telephone to him you might remember to do so.

My colleague John posted a parcel of dates, Turkish delight, fruit and other stuff to you when he was in Cairo about a fortnight ago. It will probably arrive after I get back but that's better than trying to carry it, with all my kit.

I will look around for some stockings if I go into a town before leaving Egypt. The bother is that those measurements don't mean a thing out here but I suppose I could try measuring the feet of the stockings. Presumably you want silk ones, do you?

Lots of love,
Ron

xxxxxxxxxx

Two days later, Dad writes again:

HQ 3 Div
M.E.F.
11.5.46.

Dearest Kath,

I have been thinking over one or two of my post-war aims this evening. Here is a provisional list of them:-

1. A room in the House in which any member of our family can go, as long as he or she remains quiet so that others can work in it, i.e. prepare lessons, etc.
2. To give as much help with the children as possible, seeing my lack of knowledge of them.
3. That you and I should find some means of going out together occasionally, or when not possible together, alone.
4. To take up an effective amount of political work again, but not to the extent of becoming anyone's uncle.
5. Buy a wireless as soon as possible. I understand they can be found for £10 now.
6. To seek out again some of our old friends and make some new ones. In connection with the last one, when is Bernard Stone[471] due back? Now what is <u>your</u> list?

Love,
Ron

xxxxx

Dad now gets moved to Suez. The next letter is postmarked "Egypt 16 MA 46":

reply to Lt. Spathaky, A.E.C.,
HQ 3 Inf. Div.
M.E.F. 14.5.46.

Dear K,

Just a line to tell you I have been shifted down to Suez for a few days to do a job. Also they have put off our day of departure for a

---

471 Former teaching colleague at Brighton Intermediate School.

week, i.e. until the 1st June, due to congestion of release troops at the ports.

I am very browned-off with this extra week but I suppose I'll survive it. Time seems to stand still at present. I am within sight of the headwaters of the Indian Ocean from my tent but I am not thrilled.

This part of the world is just a burnt-up cinder-heap of land between two seas. There is only the bright sunshine to relieve its monotony, and the smoking stacks of the big oil-refineries near Suez.

Will write as soon as I have settled down.

Lots of love,

xxxxxxxx Ron

A couple of days later Dad has returned to Divisional HQ:

HEADQUARTERS
HQ 3 Infantry Div.
M.E.F. 18.5.46.

Dear K,

Just a note to let you know I have returned to Qassasain after four days down at Suez, the furthest east I have been so far.

Returning to HQ I was a little bit concerned to find no letter – this makes a week without any. However, I told you I would not worry you about writing, but I hope everything is going well.

I have still not been D.O.V.'d, and if I can get through the next six days it is just possible I may get away on the 24th instead of the 1st of June.

If they DOV me for even a few weeks, at the last minute, I shall feel very sore about it, but one cannot tell. My A.E.C. boss is fairly optimistic about it and he's 31 group himself and in the same boat.

It is pretty certain I shall be Captain (S.O. III Education) for the period 7 Jan to 29 March, which includes Staff-Pay. I gather I have another £5 to claim on Mediterranean kit allowance which I did not draw when I arrived here. So we ought to be fairly straight with our finances when I get home. I shall also have:-

1 camp-bed

1 valise

3 or 4 U.S. Army hospital blankets,

2 prs long trousers (light-drill).

2 light drill shirts

1 light drill "bush" coat.

3 pairs drill shorts

chair collapsible

wash-bowl & canvas bath

and several pairs of long stockings. All of these can be worn as they are not of a special military pattern.

I hope they get home by the Military Forwarding Office. This stuff is in addition to the normal odds and ends one retains.

Lots of love, Ron

This postscript was on the last page of the letter.

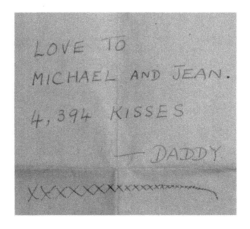

HQ 3 Div.

M.E.F. 22.5.46.

Dearest K,

I never suspected there was inefficiency in demob., but there is. I should have had my Release Book 12 days ago. It hasn't even arrived here from "O2E, GHQ, M.E.F.!"

We rang today. They said

a) They had no confirmation of my Release Gp.
   (Comment – It was confirmed in B.A.O.R.)
b) They had no "Record of Service."
   (Comment – I have filled in at least 30 at various times.)
c) In any case I must have signed on for a year, in order to have a commission. (!%?*!)
   But they conceded that I could ring tomorrow.

If I get the same balderdash tomorrow I shall send telegrams to both MPs (Brighton and N. Universities) and I shall write particulars to you for you to do the same.

It's unlawful detention.

Lots of love and wrath!

– Ron

P.S. I'll write tomorrow to let you know. They can't keep me long I think.

They kept him about another week:

'A' Block, 1 M.C.C.

Sidi Bishr, M.E.F.

28.5.46.

Dearest K,

I'm still waiting at the Collecting Camp, with the prospect of a boat on Thursday 30th. Yesterday I went into Alex with another officer and I bought a pair of silk stockings for you. I hope they are real silk and that I don't have to pay too much duty on them at Newhaven or Folkestone. For Michael I managed to get a football at the Naafi shop here. I believe they're unobtainable in the U.K. He can throw it about even if he doesn't feel like kicking it.

Alexandria is a large place, much more modern than Cairo; with large foreign communities, most of whom speak French. The upper-class Egyptians also speak it among themselves, especially the women. I think the reason for this is that many women were educated by French nuns.

It is an interesting place and it is a pity in a way that it is becoming more and more difficult to walk about in the streets without being set upon. The tide of Egyptian national revolt flows very close to the military camps. I have the impression that any breakdown in negotiations would be followed by large-scale attacks and I'm glad I'm just getting out in time.

The Collecting Camp is well-organised and the food is too much for me, I've cut down my breakfasts and dinners radically since the summer heat started. Unfortunately there are a lot of mosquitos in our tent and yesterday, as a result of continuous bites, I had a touch of fever. It passed off this morning and the M.O. said it couldn't have been malaria.

I rather dislike this waste of time, though it was a relief to get out of the clutches of the Division. There's not much chance of serious delay now, because we're outside normal Army command and in the hands of Demob Movements. But I should have liked to have moved around quickly during my last few weeks in the Forces, then I could have relaxed all the more on arrival home. Still, I have the boat voyage and the journey across France in front of me.

This afternoon I shall read for a bit, have my vaccinations checked and then go down to the Bathing Beach. It is far too hot to do anything more energetic. Every day and any day the sun streams down, turning the tents and buildings white. I expect you would like a little of it, but you would soon become weary of it.

I am looking forward to seeing the new babe. I hope she turns out as well as Michael has done. If she does we shall have reasonable cause to be satisfied.

Lots of love,
Ron

There follows a one-liner which, if written in May, he may have enclosed with the previous letter. The problem is that 29th May was a Wednesday. It cannot be 29th June, which was a Saturday, since the letter of 1st June was written on board the ship to France and his service record shows he disembarked in England on 8th June.

Sat 29th

Dear K.

How long, oh Lord, how long?
Best Wishes!

Love,
Ron

The frustration is palpable. Within a couple of days or so, however, Dad was at last on his way home:

S.S.Staffordshire,
Mediterranean,
1-6-46

Dearest wife,

We are now a couple of hundred miles east of Malta, where this mail will be dropped tomorrow morning. I believe we then stay for twelve hours in Malta harbour before ploughing on to Toulon.

It is very relaxing on board ship this weather. I feel like sleeping most of the day, though I force myself to read, talk and to walk the regulation eleven times around the boat deck which constitutes a mile.

There are one hundred officers and a thousand men on board the ship, with a sprinkling of civilians. When I came home from Italy half the Glider Pilots were on this boat. The other half got another boat and were forced in consequence to take the long train-journey from Bizerta to Algiers and to wait for three damp weeks in the transit-camp at Blidah. You may remember me writing some letters from there.[472]

I am not quite certain whether I shall go to the Dispersal unit at Guildford or that at Aldershot. The former would be better, obviously. It would be curious to end my glorious military career at the same place to which I turned up as an eager recruit – but I am not keen on the long journey in that slow train which you know as well.

---

472 See page 358.

I still can't imagine what it will feel like to get rid of this uniform. For the first month or two I am sure I shall always have a lurking feeling that I have to "report back" somewhere.

Hope Jean has stopped her restless bouts in the evening. It must have been very tiring for you. Still, I'm sure you must have acquired ever such a lot of maternal technique after four years with Michael.

By the way, if you do want to write to me you could send a letter to me:

c/o Officers' Mess

M.E.F. Release Draft A 308,

Transit Camp, Calais, B.A.O.R.

It would probably get to me safely. I shall reach Calais on about 7th or 8th. The train meanders around France a fair way, starting off westward through Toulouse and then up through Limoges and Orleans to Paris. It should be reasonably interesting since I have read so much about these districts of France but have never been there. A little while ago I read "Le Grand Meaulnes,"[473] which deals with the Vierzon and Bourges district, through which we shall go.

(I've just had a colossal spill with the ink, so cheerio, for now)

Love

Ron

Six days later Dad has at last reached the French naval base of Toulon. He writes in pencil, seemingly in haste (7th June was actually a Friday):

Toulon

Thursday 7th

Dear K,

Going through the transit machinery at Toulon. No sign of my release bottleneck yet. Hope to see you Tues or Wed next.

Lots of love,

Ron

---

473 See page 546.

Dad probably arrived home on 11th or 12th June 1946. I was just four years old, and I remember walking with Mum down Hangleton Road as he walked up to meet us. Many decades later I described the event in a poem I wrote for his seventieth birthday. This was the first verse:

We met when I was three or four
And you a tall stranger in khaki
And big black boots.
My Mum had put red lipstick on;
I'd not seen that before.

While transcribing these letters, I have worked out, since Jean was not in my mind-picture, that my memory must have been of an earlier occasion, when Dad came home on leave. I have also deduced that our family, Mum and Dad, Jean and I, had 49 Hangleton Road, Hove, to ourselves for a few weeks. I guess Grandpop had retired from the railway works and he and Nan (Sid and Annie Cree) had moved to Peacehaven, a few miles along the coast east of Brighton.

In July we went to visit them in their new home, which was a spacious first-floor flat above the Co-operative shop, with a large garden at the rear.

This photograph shows the extended family and friends relaxing on the lawn. I am standing with Dad on the left. My cousin Helen Cree is in the wheelbarrow with Michael Ward. Helen's father, my Uncle Gordon, is asleep on the right. Annie Cree with white hair is in the tent with Mrs Ward (wife of Bill Ward and mother of Jack Ward) and an unidentified person who appears to be a young man. The Ward family would have come down from Sheffield. Young Mrs Ward (widow of Eric and mother of Michael) is behind Gordon. The woman at the back to the left of the tent is probably Mrs Alan Ward.[474] The photograph is marked "July '46". Peacehaven was indeed aptly named that year.

The house holds many happy memories for me, as we spent most summer holidays there with Nan and Grandpop for the next ten years. It was named 'Domus'[475] and it always felt very homely. I loved the views of the Downs to the north and the chalk cliffs and sea to the south. I remember the lean-to conservatory that is shown in this photo and I loved playing on that lawn.

---

474 See Chapter 1 – Kath's origins – for more on the Ward family.
475 Latin for 'home'.

Chapter 24
A New Life

We might expect a story told through letters like this to have a sudden ending, leaving the reader in suspense. What happened next? It seems inevitable: he arrives home; there is no need to write letters any more – ever.

We are fortunate, however, to have a continuation, a rounding off, in the form of a small set of letters written by Dad as a civilian. They portray him laying the foundations of the new life as a family that he had yearned for throughout the wartime years.

Dad obtained a teaching post at Holly Lodge Grammar School for Boys in Smethwick, part of the sprawling conurbation that is Birmingham. In September he went there on his own to start teaching and to find a house for us all to live in. He wrote to Mum on a Sunday evening, the day before the start of the new school year:

44, Holly Lane,
Smethwick,
8.9.46 7.0 p.m.

Dearest Kath,

I am just starting the last lap as regards my preparation, and apart from the small amount of 6th Form work which still remains to be done I cannot think of anything to impair confidence in tomorrow's opening session. I even have a fair notion of the layout of the building.

Yesterday I took the liberty of calling on one of the staff, the chief history man by the name of Watson-Taylor, who also lives a cat's jump from the School. His wife invited me to tea this afternoon and before the meal he took me over the building. It was enough to take one's breath away and would not disgrace a leading Public School. In fact it makes a fine oasis of buildings in the middle of Smethwick and what with the playing-fields around it and West Park over the road it is a worthy centre for learning, or teaching.

I will describe the buildings more fully to you later, but in general it takes the form of a square built around a very fine cloister. The main Hall is simply magnificent. Though it was built as recently as 1931 it has a touch of medieval magnificence about it, with stately windows (traceried with the best Black Country iron), a large gallery, a magnificent floor and quite pleasant roof and lamp fittings. There is a smaller Hall, nicknamed "Crush Hall," a spacious library, comfortable staff-room, a gymnasium with showers and dressing-rooms, prefects' room and a whole side of building devoted to science laboratories. The manual workshops are in a building a little apart.

The total effect is magnificent and a relief to the eye. Nothing is ostentatious but all inspires. At least it did me as I looked at it.

Finally, I have even managed to borrow a gown from a local clergyman, who hadn't worn it for many years and was glad to have someone make use of it.

So tomorrow I make my ceremonial way to the beak's seat and start making little boys' lives an inferno of avoirs and êtres, concevoirs and recevoirs, grands siècles and séparations des pouvoirs.

My impression of Watson-Taylor leads me to think that the school is a bit of a forcing-machine for certificates, but perhaps not too inhuman about it.

I have not had time to think very much about the housing question, but I have reason not to be too pessimistic about it. The old lady who is putting me up has a little property, which her children inhabit, and she tells me there are quite a lot of largish houses near here, with few people in them, so I do not despair of influencing someone – if you will not!

– Lots of love,

Ron

He wrote again the next evening to report on how the day went:

44, Holly Lane,
Smethwick,
9.9.46 9.15 p.m.

Dearest K,

Just a line to thank you for your letter, which contained several little gleams of encouragement in the gloom of separation. One was the N.U.T. business; the other was your apparent stoicism in the face of the domestic problem.

You will be as glad as I am to hear that the first day went down very well. First days always have, however, and I reserve my judgement until I have been there a month or two. The boys seem to have a reasonable French accent, and my preparation of the last few weeks appears to have been on the right lines.

I am not writing much tonight because I must drop my Ma a line, but <u>please</u> try and talk to Michael a bit about me and how we shall all be together as soon as we can.

I know you will be courageous and I on my side promise with all my heart to peg away at the housing problem and get you up here as soon as ever I can.

My digs appear reasonable. They certainly give me good food and I don't think they will have the heart to overcharge me, being elderly retired folk.

Lots of love,
Ron,

PS. Would you please send me some D.W.s[476] and the whistle which is in the house somewhere?

Dad wrote again the following Sunday, addressing the envelope to "Mrs. & Master Spathaky" and posting it the following morning by 9.30 am on his way to school:

---

476 *Daily Worker* (newspaper of the CPGB).

44, Holly Lane,
Smethwick, Staffs
15.9.46 5.30 p.m.

Dearest K,

Your goodly supply of letters has done a lot to ward off the pangs of separation. If I don't reply at quite as much length for a time you'll know it's because I'm busy. It was useful to have won our minor action with the Education Committee. I'll pay the money in as soon as I can.

On Friday evening I went to see your aunt, who was quite pleasant and hospitable. Her daughter and husband who live next door were even more so, I thought. The old lady had evidently been looking out for a place or two, though she was rather gloomy about the prospect.

Saturday morning I followed this up with a visit to Jack Houghton, the nephew, who was quite genial. He seemed to think we <u>should</u> be able to buy a house, in the reasonable part of Smethwick, and though he hasn't got one in these parts he offered to keep his eyes open and to value for me anything I prospected. It seems that the "Smethwick Telephone" is the best source of information although he did mention the name of an estate agent in Smethwick. However, I was somewhat, though soberly, encouraged by his attitude.

I'm glad to hear you're doing a bit of reading. Baker's Molière, the New Statesman and so on. Prof. Baker died about two years after I left the University. He was a fine old character, thoroughly courteous, and a keen intellect, though I always thought he had buried himself somewhat in his Ancient French world. He was an authority on old French grammar. We have as a text-book at this School a good edition of Victor Hugo's *Lyrics* which he did.

Last night I went to a D.W.[477] Social in Brumm.[478] The first chap I saw on going in was Andy McCullough, a staff-sergeant of the G.P.R.,[479] who was in our group in the regiment with Fanny.[480] He had a bride of six months standing with him and we had a pleasant chat. I could only stay for an hour because of the distance but they invited

---

477 Daily Worker.
478 Normally 'Brum', the locals' nickname for Birmingham.
479 Glider Pilot Regiment.
480 Fanny Waldron – see Appendix 2.

me out. They live in Kingstanding, which is up north of Perry Barr, where we were to have gone to see the house.

Apparently he glided down into Yugoslavia with the Russian military mission to Tito when the former first entered the country.

My landlady charges me £2-2-0 a week; my dinners cost me 5/5 a week. Beyond that I haven't spent much.

Love to all,

Yours with much longing,

Ron

Then, on a separate page, with a sketch map on the reverse, Dad wrote this to me. By now I was four and able to read:

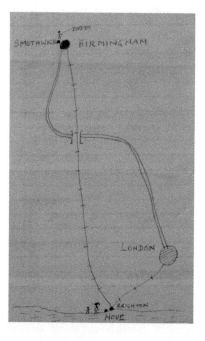

SMETHWICK,
15 SEPTEMBER 1946

DEAR MICHAEL,

THANK YOU FOR THE SWEETS.

I HOPE YOU COME HERE SOON.

LOVE,

DADDY

P.T.O.

Dad wrote again on the Wednesday:

44, Holly Lane,
Smethwick. 18.9.46 10.15 p.m.
(Somewhat flat out!)

Dearest wife,

I cannot at the moment lay my hands on the letter from you which I received this a.m., but just a note to let you know I am still buckling into the work and this next week-end will buckle in to the house-hunting.

Perhaps you would write to the Min. of Ed., since you know all about it. Sign it for me if you do.

I have written to put our name down on the Borough Council list for houses.

I have not been out, apart from a local parish whist-drive I was dragged into by a member of staff, on Monday evening.

Things go well, if somewhat arduously, at school.

I <u>do</u> want you to move up here <u>soon</u>.

Hope you are bearing up to the responsibilities of the formidable rear-party of our family.

Lots of love,

xxxxxxxx P.S. Thanks for the papers. Ron

On the Sunday he wrote:

44, Holly Lane,

Smethwick,

22.9.46.

Dearest K,

I have been over a house this morning. It is in South Smethwick, near Warley Park and partly overlooking Nettlefold's Recreation Ground. It is freehold and the bloke wants £1500. It has a covered-in garage with a glass roof, which he built himself and which would be quite useful.

The water-heating is by the universal Smethwick method of fire-heating. The internal decoration of some of the rooms has got into a bit of a mess through the children but structurally it seems quite a good place.

There is the same number of rooms as in the other one, but they are bigger (with the usual small 3rd bedroom, however).

It is practically on a main bus-route, with a lay-out something like this:-

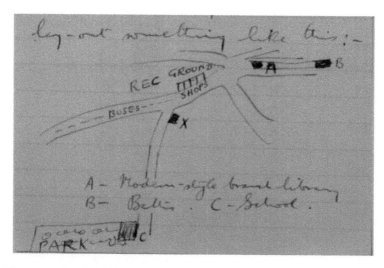

There are lots of shops (including a Co-op) because the X-roads are the centre of a big estate district.

It is certainly a Labour district. I think you would like it, partly because of the large number of trees.

Anyway I have clinched nothing, but have told Jack Houghton I would like his advice on it.

Will keep you posted.

Yours busily,

Love,

Ron

xxxxxxx

Dad wrote again on the following Monday, and the envelope was postmarked 1st October 6.45 pm (Tuesday evening):

44, Holly Lane,

Sm. 30.9.46.

Dearest K,

Very sorry letters have not appeared. You must know why.

About the house; Houghton advised me that it was a fair bargain (at present prices) at £1400 and that the position was so bad here with people flocking in to take new jobs that I ought to grab it.

I'll give what description of it I can.

1. <u>Downstairs</u>: Front room – fairly large. Good bay-window, electric plug. Quite pleasant outlook on small front garden. Decoration:- fair, but bad patch on one wall.

   Back room:- Large, French window to garden. Electric plug. Decoration bad. This is the one that he agreed to have done.

   Kitchen – Small, but looks on to garden. Sink, draining board.

   Garage – pent-house type communicating direct to kitchen, which I think is an advantage. Contains gas boiler – for quick heating of water.

   Coal-shed near kitchen door.

   Hall – red tile variety, small but reasonable & I think the tiles an asset.

   Larder – usual. Stone slabs (I think)

   Garden – large, planted with something or other, I forget what. Good view over trees of valley, which is very rare in Smethwick.

<u>Upstairs</u> – 2 large bed-rooms. Decoration fair. One small room, but big enough for double-bed. Plugs (I think).

   <u>Bath-room and lavatory</u> separate upstairs.

I'm afraid these are scattered notes but they're the best I can do at the moment.

This letter ends abruptly here with no signing off. The day after posting it Dad wrote again:

Wed, 10.45 p.m.

Dearest K,

   Sorry I haven't written. I've been very busy at school. Afraid there is no progress as regards the house in Rathbone Rd., but Jack Houghton is going to see it. He is apprehensive about the value from the point of view of a building society.

I am going to see Alderman Perry tomorrow. He is Chairman of the Governors and may be able to arrange a special mortgage if I can set about it the right way.

It's very late now, but I'll just write a few words for M and report progress to you later.

Courage!

Love,

xxxxxxx
Ron

It is Monday before Dad writes again. The envelope is noteworthy to me as it shows Nan and Grandpop's new address:

"Domus," Coast Road, Peacehaven, E. Sussex.

Mum, Jean and I must have gone over to Peacehaven to stay for a few days, or perhaps 49 Hangleton Road had been sold:

44, Holly Lane,

Smethwick. Mon. 7.10.46.

Dearest K,

1. The Haldanes are moving out this Friday (11th). She is leaving some curtains up at the front of the house. I'll go and see the electricity, gas, fuel and rating people tomorrow.
2. I suggest we leave the place empty over the weekend and I'll do what I can to clean up.
3. You can move when you feel up to it the following week. Probably the day before the furniture would be best, but let me know.
4. If the furniture moves in on Monday afternoon it will be best for me, as I can get the afternoon off.

<u>Or</u> you could come up on Wednesday and stay at my digs and let the moving take place on Thursday.

Monday and Thursday are the only afternoons I can get off.

<u>Please</u>, <u>please</u> don't do anything to strain yourself by lifting or worrying unduly about it. It would be better for us to lose any of our furniture than for you to do one thing that would hurt you.

Keep me informed by telegram or 'phone of dates.

The curtain roller-system is the one with little trollies, but unfortunately she has to take the gadgets with her.

Courage! Love

Ron

SMETHWICK

DEAR MICHAEL,

I WILL SEE YOU SOON.

LOVE,

DADDY

The next letter is dated 14th October, but in the second paragraph Dad refers to "Yesterday (Saturday) afternoon" and the envelope is postmarked "13 OCT 1946" so, since 13th October was a Sunday, the letter must have been written then. How appropriate that, in the last letter of this whole collection, Dad was, as ever, showing confusion about what date it was!

Dad had made a fair start at his new teaching post and the house purchase was complete. Kath and Ron were about to start the family life they have dreamt of with their two small children, Michael and Jean:

44, Holly Lane,

Smethwick.

14 October 46.

Dearest K,

I'm glad to find that you view the moving with your usual cheerful practical outlook. I thought it might seem a rather radical uprooting after your long stay in Brighton and district.

Yesterday (Saturday) afternoon I went into the house and swept all the floors and walls. They had left the place in a reasonable state, apart from those things that the dustmen will take away.

There are four bags of coal and as much wood as we shall want for some time, together with an old cabin trunk full of logs.

Work has gone pretty well during the last week, apart from one form of "C" boys who are a bit of a problem.

The gas is on in the house, water and light also. I have authorised payment of the £4-7-1 to the electric light company after all; the chap was good enough to waive the contract I had already signed for an electric cooker (£21 + £4-10-0 fitting) but said it would help if I allowed the cheque to be placed to our credit in respect of the next quarter.

Hardaker has left us the gas-stove for £12, which is better than £25-10-0, and he will wait for the money until the end of the month, if not a little longer.

I have written an article for the Modern Quarterly[481] and part of a short story which I will show you.

Will you be carrying much on Thursday? I suppose we'd better have a taxi in any case.

Love, Ron

XXXXXXX

109 Rathbone Road, Smethwick
(Jean in pram)

---

481 An academic journal dedicated to Marxism and associated with the CPGB.

Epilogue

And so it was that the four of us – Mum, Dad, Jean and I – started our family life in our own home in Smethwick on Thursday 17th October 1946.

Mum and Dad continued their political activities. I remember accompanying Dad as he sold Daily Workers. Mum stood as a Communist Party candidate for the local council in 1949. A local paper reported:

Without make-up, attractive, brown-haired, Mrs. Kathleen Spathaky of 107, Rathbone Road, Smethwick, is to conduct a soap-box campaign on Warley street corners.

Mrs, Spathaky, thirty years old and mother of Michael (7), and Jean (3), will tell electors why she is standing as a Communist for the Warley Woods ward by-election.

One reason is that young Michael is in a class of 50 pupils at Abbey Road schools; another that Jean will soon be eligible for nursery school. Mrs Spathaky wants smaller classes and a nursery school in Abbey Road.

In 1950 we moved to Northern Ireland, where we lived for six years, during which time my brother Dave was born.

Once the horrors of Stalinist Russia became known, Mum and Dad's adherence to a political party that was closely allied to the Soviet Union became, for them, untenable. By 1956 they had both left the Communist Party.

In 1956 we moved to Norfolk, where Dad continued to teach French until his retirement in the 1970s, also becoming Deputy Head Teacher of

Thorpe Grammar School. As Jean and David grew up, Mum was able to move from part-time to full-time work as a hospital pharmacist. Mum and Dad became members of the Society of Friends (Quakers) in the 1960s. Dad was also an early activist in the ecological movement and helped to set up the Norwich branch of the Ecology Party (the Green Party).

They spent many years of retirement in Cambridgeshire where Jean and her family had settled. They celebrated their seventy-fifth wedding anniversary on 21st December 2012, but Dad was not well and he died aged ninety-eight on 13th January 2013. Mum survived another four years and was also ninety-eight when she died on 2nd February 2017.

Appendix 1
John Jordan

During the last months of 2016, while I was in Sydney and making good progress in transcribing Dad's letters, I came across a number of mentions of a person called John.[482] It was clear from the letters that he was a close friend of Mum and Dad, at least from 1941 to 1943; that he lived in Brighton and that he was an active member of the local Communist Party. Dad eventually gave his surname, Jordan, in a letter. Because of the particular arrangements for the weekend of 23-24th August 1942, exactly forty weeks before I was born, I became convinced that I was named John (my first name) after this John. I had never heard Mum or Dad speak about John Jordan, or any other friend called John.

In December 2016 I asked my sister Jean to ask Mum about John Jordan. She recorded the conversations on video on her phone and sent them to me in Sydney. What follows is my transcription of those conversations. They may seem very confused, but that was Mum 'on a good day'. She had been diagnosed with Lewy bodies syndrome, an intermittent form of dementia. Her hearing was quite bad even when she wore her hearing aid; her memory was not good; she confused names, even of family members, and her speech was halting, with sentences frequently unfinished as she tried to find the right words to express herself and then gave up. Even so, she managed to make some sense of Jean's questions and to make a positive last contribution to this story.

Through all the difficulties, I found the conversations, together with Mum's facial expressions and her laughter, fascinating and revealing. And, of course, it was great just to see Mum still enjoying life, just before

---

482 See pages 59, 83–4, 86–7, 90, 105, 122, 133, 162 and 209.

she died and some four months since I had last been with her. I am very grateful to Jean for making these recordings.

Conversation 1

Jean: Who was John Jordan, Mum?

Mum: He was a Party member in Brighton, a senior... He was a lecturer at the Tech., in engineering. We thought a lot of John. But I never heard from him again all through the war.

Conversation 2

Jean: Mike said that he had found John Jordan's name in some letters.

Mum: Well, I mean, Jordan was a Welsh connection. He was known as coming from Wales. But that's all I know about him and I never met him again.

Jean: Was he a special friend? Of yours? Or Dad's?

Mum: No.

Conversation 3

(Clearly this recording only started when the conversation was in progress.)

Mum: ... activities at that time.

Jean: You kept them quiet? Why?

Mum: We weren't *[?]* ... We weren't legal. We weren't illegal either. We were likely to become illegal.

Jean: Oh. What? You mean the Communist Party?

Mum: Yes.

Jean: What role did John Jordan have? What did John Jordan do?

Mum: That's right. But he was a very quiet, strong... er... But... not much sense.

Jean: Really? *[pause]* Did you like him?

Mum: He was all right. *[smiles]* We didn't have many women in the Party... really.

Jean: And was John Jordan a family man?

Mum: Yes. They were young, very young, enthusiastic... teenagers.

Jean: Who was? Who was the teenager? John? Or his children? Who were the teenagers? John was a teenager? *[Recording ends here.]*

Conversation 4

To me, the fourth and last recording is a vital conversation. To clarify Mum's confusion over names, I should explain that I was named John Michael. I was the son conceived in 1941. Here she confuses me with my brother Dave, who was born in 1954 and named David Victor. (Dad was Ronald Victor.) It is a well-known family story that, almost as soon as I was born and registered, Mum realised that there was scope for confusion between Dad and me (Ron and John), so they started to call me by my middle name, Michael, straight away – and Michael or Mike I have been ever since.

It is important to realise that it was Mum who made the connection, unprompted, in this conversation in the last week or two of her life, between John Jordan, the event of my conception and the naming issue. Her statement that he was a teenager was also unprompted.

Jean: Where did John Jordan live? In Patcham, did you say?

Mum: Yes. *[smiles]*

Jean: Tell me about him.

Mum: He was... *[laughs]* There's a story attached to him.

Jean: Tell me. *[Mum laughs a lot.]*

Mum: We went to Brighton by train from... to visit a friend *[laughs]*, with the sole purpose of conceiving a child – to have David – to conceive a child – not David, Michael. His name... But we assumed that we would get pregnant immediately and so, as far as we knew, that's how it happened. We didn't take any precautions, so... we had a baby.

Jean: Where did John Jordan come into this?

Mum: He was going to be David Victor... Michael Victor, but then we... It was too much like Ron, so we moved it from John to Ron... I don't know why.

Jean: Do you mean that you called Mike 'John' instead of 'Victor' because of John Jordan? Did you call Mike after John Jordan?

I tried to find references to John Jordan on the Internet. He is unlikely to be alive now, of course. I am accustomed to doing searches like this, through many years of genealogy. It's unusual not to find any references at all to someone who lived in Britain in the twentieth century. This appeared to be the case with John Jordan, however. There seem to be no births or deaths that fit Mum and Dad's friend.

Eventually I located a web page[483] about a wartime British Flying Training School (BFTS) in Florida in the USA. It contained a photograph and the following biography:

John Jordan attended 5 BFTS (Course 13) from January-July 1943.

John was born in Guilin, China in 1923 where his Plymouth Brethren parents were missionaries with the China Inland Mission. Apart from visiting England in 1927/28, John was educated in China until he was fifteen. He then travelled back to England in 1939 on his own to complete his education.

In 1942, having completed his education, John signed up to join the RAF and was sent to Riddle Field, Clewiston [*Florida*] to train with No 5 British Flying Training School. He then became a flying instructor. When the war in Europe ended he transferred to the Fleet Air Arm in the hope that he would see action in the Pacific. However he remained in England and was demobbed in 1946.

John remained in the South of England and started a career in construction administration helping to build the "new" towns. In

---

483 http://www.americanairmuseum.com/person/241714.

1975 he and his family emigrated to Canada where he continued his work in construction administration…

A separate source contained this brief note:

John Jordan… Canada died 23/9/1996.

The above details would explain why I didn't find a birth or death record for John Jordan. Joining the RAF and later migrating to Canada would account for his disappearance from Dad's letters. The timing fits precisely – born 1923; completed his education in 1942 – with him being a teenager and a student at Brighton Tech. in 1941.

Through the organiser of the 5BFTS website I was able to contact Nick Jordan, who lives in Canada, who confirmed that he was the son of John Jordan of the RAF. However, he had no knowledge of any connection John might have had with Brighton and dismissed the idea that he had even dallied with communism, however briefly. I sent my transcriptions of a few relevant letters, and Nick replied:

I mentioned to my Mum yesterday about your message, at which point (and for the first time ever!) she commented that my Dad had indeed gone on to college after he finished school, which is where he met his best friend Harry. They were each other's best man. However she is almost certain that because Harry was a Suffolk man they went to college somewhere in East Anglia, and definitely not on the south coast.

I get a sense from the letters, and from your Mum's conversation, that their John Jordan was a maturer individual than my Dad would have been. Especially since this person was named as executor for your Dad. And to cap it all, unless Dad had a complete reversal in political outlook, he was always as conservative as can be. My maternal grandfather was a staunch unionist and Secretary of the Oxford TUC and he and Dad had many 'spirited' conversations about their different political ideologies.

So I have to conclude that the John Jordan you are looking for was not my Dad.

Well, I am not so sure. An uncanny coincidence links John Jordan of Guilin with Dad's other and later 'best friend' in the Army, namely Alec Waldron, the subject of Appendix 2 below. The coincidence is that both were brought up as Plymouth Brethren. Presumably John left this religious community, as Alec did, since the Brethren, a strictly pacifist sect, would not have countenanced him joining the armed services. Alec Waldron describes the trauma of this break in his book, Pacifist to Glider Pilot, where he wrote:

On reflection I have wondered whether the appeal of the highly disciplined Communist Party wasn't some kind of replacement to fill the void created by my leaving the Exclusives, an equally disciplined and doctrinaire organisation. [484]

Nick's father, John Jordan, was aged seventeen in the year Mum and Dad first mention their friend John.[485] As for 'our' John Jordan being a "maturer individual" than Nick's father would have been, the evidence is that he was the same age and, as Mum said, "But he was a very quiet, strong... er... But... not much sense... They were young, very young, enthusiastic... teenagers." This doesn't sound like 'mature'.

So, was Nick Jordan's father Mum and Dad's Brighton friend? The date, 1942, when he joined the RAF, matches the disappearance of his name from Dad's letters from June 1942 onwards. Dad implied in a letter of 1941 that John had a partner or girlfriend called Marie.[486] It is clear too that he was at Brighton Technical College. In June 1943, on leaving for North Africa, Dad nominated John Jordan as executor of his will.[487] But this was a very hurried action, insisted upon by the Army as the move of the Glider Pilot Regiment to North Africa was imminent and top secret, so it does not necessarily imply that he was still in touch with John.

Dad's 1943 letter about his will is the only place where he gives John's surname. It is Mum's recollections on video that confirm that the

---

484 See Appendix 2.
485 See page 59 and Appendix 1
486 See page 84.
487 See page 209.

John referred to throughout 1941 and 1942 was John Jordan. The birth year, 1923, of John Jordan of Guilin fits with Mum's description of John Jordan of Brighton as being a teenager in 1941-42. A marriage, listed in the General Register Office indexes, of a John L Jordan in Oxford in 1952, also fits. Children of this marriage were born in the 1950s, one named Nicholas – clearly the Nick whom I emailed.

In spite of Nick Jordan's view, I think the balance of probabilities is that his father was my parents' friend John Jordan.

Appendix 2
Alec Waldron

It was towards the end of 1942 that Dad was joined on Salisbury Plain by Staff Sergeant Alec Waldron, known at that time by the nickname 'Fanny'. They became friends; in fact, both Mum and Dad were friends with Fanny and his wife Hilda until the end of the war. Dad refers to him often in his letters[488] – there is one letter from Fanny too.[489] Over fifty years later, in a book about his wartime experiences, Fanny gave his view of their relationship and of Dad's work at Bulford:[490]

To describe a featureless Nissen hutted camp in the middle of nowhere as 'luxury' was some overstatement! From the southern end of the camp, Stonehenge could be seen on a damp and misty winter's morning, monumental and brooding in the near distance, an impression etched deep into my memory and destroying any interest in its unquestionably fascinating past. These two locations, Bulford and Fargo, were to be my 'home' for the six months prior to our departure to North Africa in April 1943…

In sharp contrast to the drabness of our living quarters were three outstanding and wonderful characters, two of whom were to become life-long friends…

The third member of the trio, WO2 Ron Spathaky, attached to us from the Army Education Corps, had a profound and lasting effect on my political thinking even though I lost touch with him shortly

---

488 See pages 181, 189, 192, 217, 221, 226, 233–4, 246, 248, 251, 256, 259, 276, 307, 375, 405, 460 and 563.
489 See page 196.
490 *Pacifist to Glider Pilot*, by Alec Waldron, pub. Woodfield, 2000, pp129-136.

after my demob in October 1946… An ex-schoolmaster, peering out from behind his steel rimmed spectacles, apparently bemused by his position as a Warrant Officer in His Majesty's Armed Forces, he was in many ways the epitome of the absent-minded professor. A dedicated Marxist and a member of the Communist Party, he enthused me with visions of a Classless Society as portrayed in the writings of Marx and Engels, introduced me to an analytical reading of history and persuaded me to join the Communist Party, a short-lived experience terminated early in 1944 when I was disillusioned over the 'Second Front Now' campaign then being propagated by 'The Party'. On reflection I have wondered whether the appeal of the highly disciplined CP wasn't some kind of replacement to fill the void created by my leaving the Exclusives, an equally disciplined and doctrinaire organisation. Despite my brief membership of 'The Party', Ron's clandestine educational activities in the field of Marxism and Dialectical Materialism have influenced me throughout all my post-war political activities within the Labour Party. Even now as I read Eric Hobsbawm's brilliant four volume history covering the period 1789 to 1991, I revel in the insights that his Marxist thinking brings to bear on the ebb and flow of human affairs. But I have digressed. I had but one brief post-war encounter with Ron Spathaky when he sought to persuade me to rejoin the Communist Party, but I firmly rejected his overtures and we were never again to meet. Sadly I realised that our 'friendship' was wholly dependent on political affiliation!

The way in which each of this 'trio' was to impinge on my new life as Intelligence NCO was unknown to me… I was 'chucked in at the deep end' in the planning phase of the Sicilian operation, a story yet to be told…

The tedium of HQ life at this time was not relieved by our move to Fargo. Ron Spathaky was in his element as ABCA (Army Bureau of Current Affairs) lectures were focussing on the Soviet Union our ally since June 1941 when Germany had invaded the country and a small group of us continued to have 'extra-mural' instruction from him into the esoterical world of Karl Marx. Far from having any adverse effect, it inculcated into us a more positive attitude to our involvement in World War 2. But for this would I have reacted as I did on receipt of a Top Secret letter in the Intelligence Section, signed by no less a dignitary than Bomber Command Harris, in which he proposed to limit post-training Glider flying hours to a derisory 7 hours per year! Needless to say had such a policy been adopted it would have been the death of the Glider Pilot Regiment in more ways than one! I broke confidentiality by discussing this Top Secret document with Ron Spathaky and, not without fear and trepidation, I agreed to arrangements for me to meet D.N. Pritt K.C, an ultra-left M.P.[491] The meeting duly took place in his Middle Temple Chambers. He was a formidable figure and a brilliant K.C. possessed of impressive forensic abilities which enabled him to study the brief and assess its significance in but a few minutes. His immediate reaction was that a matter of such importance warranted the placing of a Parliamentary Question to the Prime Minister but recent research has revealed that he in fact wrote to Churchill (I have a copy on file) who in turn called for a report from his Secretaries of State for War and Air. At the conclusion of the interview he thanked me for my intervention, commented on the risks I had run and then, fearing that his Chambers were under surveillance, instructed his Clerk to lead me through a labyrinth of back alleys to the anonymity of Fleet Street and the Strand. A chance meeting with a senior Air Force Officer many years later revealed that Churchill had in fact called Harris to a meeting at which, following much discussion, he was given an ultimatum – tow gliders or resign. The crisis was resolved, the necessary flying resources were allocated to the Regiment and in due course two Wings were trained, one of which served with the 1st Airborne Division and the other with the 6th. Whilst all of these to-ings and fro-ings were taking place behind the scenes, unknown to me at the time, I had departed with the advance party to North Africa to help plan and participate in the ill-fated Sicilian fiasco.

---

491 See also page 91.

Dad followed sometime later, and they spent time together in Tunisia before and after the Sicily landings. Bad planning, and grossly mismanaged communications about wind speeds in the landing areas, led to the fiasco in which a large proportion of airborne troops failed to reach their landing zones in Sicily and many died. Alec Waldron played a heroic role as a pilot, ditching his glider in the sea in such a way that all the troops he was carrying managed to make the shore. He being a non-swimmer hung on to the glider for some hours before being rescued and returned to Tunisia.

He describes his experiences with nonchalant good humour in his book, which also covers the Arnhem landings where, amid further mismanagement by top brass, he played an even more heroic role for which he was mentioned in despatches and received a commission.

Acknowledgements

I owe a debt of gratitude to Emma Gawlinski, Helen Mogford, Jean Reeves, the late Dr. Jane Sherwood, John Spathaky, Dave Spathaky and especially to my wife Marian Spathaky for their helpful comments on the draft and their advice and support during the preparation of this book.